DIC·TIO·NARY
of MARKETING
COMMUNICATIONS

Norman A. Govoni
Babson College

SAGE Publications
International Educational and Professional Publisher
Thousand Oaks ■ London ■ New Delhi

For information:

Sage Publications, Inc.
2455 Teller Road
Thousand Oaks, California 91320
E-mail: order@sagepub.com

Sage Publications Ltd.
6 Bonhill Street
London EC2A 4PU
United Kingdom

Sage Publications India Pvt. Ltd.
B-42, Panchsheel Enclave
Post Box 4109
New Delhi 110 017 India

Printed in the United States of America

Library of Congress Cataloging-in-Publication Data

Govoni, Norman A. P.
Dictionary of marketing communications / Norman A. Govoni.
    p. cm.
Includes bibliographical references.
ISBN 0-7619-2770-0 (cloth)—ISBN 0-7619-2771-9 (pbk.)
   1. Marketing—Dictionaries. 2. Communication in marketing—Dictionaries. I. Title.
HF5412.G68 2004
380.1′03—dc21
              2003007359

03   04   05   06   10 9 8 7 6 5 4 3 2 1

Acquisitions Editor:	Al Bruckner
Editorial Assistant:	MaryAnn Vail
Production Editor:	Melanie Birdsall
Copy Editor:	Teresa Herlinger
Typesetter:	C&M Digitals (P) Ltd.
Proofreader:	Cheryl Rivard
Cover Designer:	Janet Foulger

Contents

To my wife, Terry, the most beautiful person on Earth.

Preface

The *Dictionary of Marketing Communications* has been compiled to serve as a comprehensive list of the terms and concepts essential to an understanding of marketing communications. No attempt has been made to reinvent the wheel; instead, the pursuit has been to identify the vocabulary most relevant to marketing communications and present the jargon in easy-to-comprehend language.

More than 4,000 terms and concepts are identified and defined herein. Each has been selected for its pertinence and application to marketing communications; each has been reviewed for appropriateness and accuracy by people who know. The dictionary is the result of many years of teaching marketing communications, as well as consulting many sources on the subject. It is a glossary for students, practitioners, and anyone interested in the lexicon of this challenging and exciting field of endeavor. The authoritative sources consulted, as well as others that should prove valuable to anyone interested in marketing communications, are identified, 120-strong, in the Resources section at the back of the dictionary.

For some, the dictionary will advance the pursuit of new knowledge, while for others, it will be a needed refresher. For all, the *Dictionary of Marketing Communications* will be a handy reference to ensure they know how to talk the talk of the fascinating discipline of marketing communications.

AAAA see *American Association of Advertising Agencies.*

AAF see *American Advertising Federation.*

ABC see *Audit Bureau of Circulations.*

ABM see *American Business Media.*

ABP see *American Business Press.*

ACB see *Advertising Checking Bureau.*

ADI see *Area of Dominant Influence.*

AFTRA see *American Federation of Television and Radio Artists.*

AIGA see *American Institute of Graphic Arts.*

AIM see *Association for Interactive Media.*

AMA see *American Marketing Association.*

ANA see *Association of National Advertisers.*

ANPA see *American Newspaper Publishers Association.*

AOR see *agency of record.*

ARF see *Advertising Research Foundation.*

ASI see *ASI Recall Test* and *Ipsos-ASI Advertising Research.*

AQH see a*verage quarter-hour audience.*

A County see *ABCD Counties.*

a la carte agency an agency that offers only part of its services on a particular assignment for an advertiser, or even for another advertising agency; compensation is determined by a negotiated fee.

A/B split a copytesting method by which the advertiser places different advertisements for the same product in every other copy of the same issue of a publication, and then measures the response for each by recording the number of coupons returned, telephone calls made for further information, or by whatever action was requested; method also employed in direct mailings, using alternate envelopes. Often used to test and compare the effectiveness of alternate advertisements. See also *split run, split-run test, demographic split run, geographic split run,* and *subscription/ newsstand split run.*

ABCD Counties the classification of U.S. counties based on Census Bureau population statistics and metropolitan proximity; *"A" Counties* are all counties belonging to the 21 largest Metropolitan Statistical Areas (MSAs) (i.e., highly urban), *"B" Counties* are counties not in the "A" Counties category that have more than 85,000 households, *"C" Counties* are counties not defined as "A" or "B" Counties that have more than 20,000 households or are in Metropolitan Statistical Areas (MSAs) or Consolidated Metropolitan Statistical Areas (CMSAs) with more than 20,000 households, and *"D" Counties"* are all those not classified as "A," "B," or "C" (i.e., rural). Designations are those as defined by the *A.C. Nielsen Company.* See also *Metropolitan Statistical Area (MSA)* and *Consolidated Metropolitan Statistical Area (CMSA).*

abeyance order placing an advertising order for time or space at a time when none is available; the order is held in suspension until time or space becomes available, or indefinitely. More common in television than other media.

AUTHOR'S NOTE: Italicized terms within definitions indicate that these terms are other entries in the *Dictionary of Marketing Communications.*

A-board a ground sign formed by two boards that lean against each other and are joined by a cross-brace at the top, forming an "A"; often seen at the curb outside retail locations.

above-the-fold the top half of a *broadsheet* newspaper, as opposed to below-the-fold. On the Web, the term refers to the portion of a given page, such as the homepage, that can be viewed without scrolling down. An advertisement on the Internet is above-the-fold when it is viewable in its entirety as soon as the Web page opens, without having to scroll down to see any portion of it. See also *below-the-fold.*

above-the-line costs advertising costs incurred during the creative part of production, e.g., acting, music, photography, script writing. Often used in "higher profile" advertising media such as television and magazines, as well as the traditional major media. See also *below-the-line costs.*

A.C. Nielsen a major market research firm and leading provider of a wide range of marketing information to consumer goods manufacturers and retailers; information provided includes retail-level product movement, market share, distribution, pricing, merchandising and promotional activities, and other market-sensitive information; also manages test marketing programs for new and established products, and provides customized research services at all stages of product marketing, including identification of market opportunities, development of product concepts, product positioning, sales forecasting, advertising testing, and tracking. Operates consumer panel services that provide detailed data on actual purchases made by household members, as well their retail shopping patterns and demographic profiles, covering more than 126,000 households worldwide. Especially useful in helping to understand competitive performance. Part of *VNU*. See also *Nielsen Media Research.*

access see *prime time access.*

accordion fold a direct-mail piece or other promotional literature consisting of several panels that fold and unfold in the manner of an accordion.

account the advertiser or organization for whom the agency is doing work; also called the *client.*

account conflict occurs when an advertising agency handles two different marketers' brands of directly competing products; may occur as a result of two agencies merging or when an advertising agency decides to pitch and try to win a company's account that includes a brand that competes directly with a product already advertised by the agency (in which case, the agency, should it win the new account, would give up the existing account at the insistence of one of the competing accounts). Often, an agency is precluded from going after a new account if it already handles a directly competing product.

account executive the individual in the advertising agency who is the daily contact between the agency and the client, and who directs, coordinates, and manages the entire process and services involved in serving the client, constantly communicating and interacting with both the agency and client teams; liaison between the advertising agency and the client. Reports to the *account supervisor.* See also *account supervisor* and *director of account services.*

account management overseeing the design, implementation, maintenance, review, and follow-up of all activities and programs involved in an organization's relationship with its customers or clients; see also *key account management.*

account opener a premium offered to a customer for opening a new account, e.g., a bank's offer of a hand-held calculator for anyone opening a new account.

account planner the individual in an advertising agency who is responsible for ensuring that the agency's strategic and creative focus is on the consumer; the account planner makes extensive use of both qualitative and quantitative research. See also *account planning.*

account planning the discipline within an advertising agency that makes sure the consumer's perspective is fully considered when advertising is developed and that the marketer forges a strong connection with the consumer; includes the study of how consumers make use of marketing communications and the design of an action plan for communicating effectively with consumers. Research, both qualitative and quantitative, is the primary tool used in account planning. See also *account planner.*

account review a process by which advertising agencies, at the invitation of a client, compete for the client's account by presenting their credentials and advertising and promotional ideas for the client's marketing communications program; a full-scale evaluation of a current advertising agency by a prospective client, either against the agency's performance record alone or against competing proposals from prospective new agencies interested in serving that client. See also *agency search consultant.*

account services at an advertising agency, all the activities that go into the design and development of an advertising and marketing communications plan for a client; the *account executives* and *account supervisors* are the key account services individuals charged with making sure the agency teams get the right work done in the right way at the right time. See also *director of account services, account executive,* and *account supervisor.*

account-specific promotion sales promotion programs jointly developed by manufacturers and retailers, customized for individual retail accounts, and which serve to enhance the equity of both the brand and the store.

account supervisor the individual at the advertising agency who supervises the account executive; reports to the director of account services. See also *account executive* and *director of account services.*

accrual account in cooperative advertising, an advertising fund established for the retailer by the manufacturer, against which the cooperative advertising costs are charged; see also *fixed accrual, percentage accrual,* and *cooperative advertising.*

across-the-board in television and radio, a particular program that is aired at the same time each day, Monday through Friday; e.g., a television soap opera or a radio talk show. See also *strip advertising* and *strip programming.*

across-vehicle duplication a particular audience's exposure to the same advertisement or commercial in different media vehicles; e.g., exposure to the same ad in *Cosmopolitan* and *Redbook, Golf Digest* and *Sports Illustrated, NFL football* and *ABC news.* Also called *between-vehicle duplication.* See also *within-vehicle duplication.*

action the advertiser's major objective in using advertising and other forms of promotion; what the advertiser aims for with its communications to the target audience.

action advertising advertising that seeks a quick response and action from its target audience.

action card see *bingo card.*

Action for Children's Television (ACT) an activist group formed in 1968 to lobby the federal government for improved quality of television programming aimed at children and to press for stringent restrictions and measures related to the amount and the content of advertising directed to children; disbanded shortly after passage of the *Children's Television Act of 1990.* See also *Children's Television Act of 1990.*

action response device any of a number of tools used to make it easy for an individual to respond to the advertiser's call for action; e.g., a reply card in a direct-mail package, a coupon in an advertisement, or an 800 number for a person to call.

actives in direct mail, mailing list customers who have made a recent purchase, generally within the past year.

activity analysis a detailed breakdown, review, and evaluation of the nonselling work done by a salesperson; e.g., the time and work devoted to display setups or doing paperwork. Often involves a breakdown, analysis, and comparison between selling and nonselling functions.

activity quota see *quota.*

actual product the tangible, physical object with all its features; see also *augmented product* and *core product.*

ad avail see *availabilities.*

ad banner see *banner* and *banner ad.*

ad click see *click.*

ad clickthrough see *clickthrough.*

ad display in Internet advertising, the successful display of an advertisement on the browser screen.

ad download in Internet advertising, the successful delivery of an advertisement to a browser, as measured by the server that actually delivered the advertisement.

ad hoc network in television, a temporary group of stations formed for the showing of a special, one-time program or series.

ad hoc research in marketing or advertising, research specifically designed to address a particular problem or issue on a one-time basis, as opposed to an ongoing research program on that topic.

ad impression see *ad view.*

ad pod see *pod.*

ad pod ratings in television advertising, the audience rating during commercial breaks in television programs; by comparing the average rating during the program content of a show with the average rating during commercial breaks, a retention rate may be determined, showing the extent to which commercials are likely being watched. See also *pod* and *rating.*

ad request in Internet advertising, the initial request for an advertisement from the browser, as measured by the server that redirects the browser to the specific location of the advertisement; see also *hit* and *click.*

ad slicks camera-ready product advertisements provided by manufacturers to local advertisers, such as retailers, for use in print ads that feature the manufacturer's product.

ads on wheels see *mobile billboard, bus wrap, car wrap,* and *truckside advertising.*

ad stream in Internet advertising, the series of advertisements viewed by a user during a single visit to a particular Web site; also called an *impression stream.*

Ad Track index an advertising tracking service that appears as a weekly feature on www.usatoday.com, reporting consumer opinions about the effectiveness of selected current advertisements and campaigns; the feature includes survey results, detailed analysis of the advertising in question, and comparisons with other campaigns. A collaboration between *USA Today* and *Harris Interactive.*

ad tracking see *tracking study.*

ad transfer see *clickthrough.*

ad view in Internet advertising, a single advertisement that appears in full view, usually without scrolling, on a Web page when the page first loads; also referred to as an *ad impression* or *view.*

adcentives see *advertising promotional products.*

added value see *value added.*

address on the Internet, the e-mail address of a computer user or a Web site's URL.

ADDY awards recognition for excellence in advertising creativity; sponsored by the *American Advertising Federation (AAF).*

ad/edit ratio in print media, the number of advertising pages relative to editorial pages; e.g., 65/35 indicates that 65 percent of all pages in that particular vehicle are advertising.

adjacency television or radio broadcast commercial time immediately preceding or following a network program, or during a station break, when the network releases time to its local affiliates so they can place a spot television commercial; i.e., the availability of commercial time for local sales by local television stations before or after a network program. Also called a *break position.* See also *in-program placement* and *spot.*

administered VMS a vertical marketing system (VMS) in which the distribution channel members agree to informally cooperate with each other, as opposed to being bound together by corporate ownership or by contractual agreement; the leadership role is determined by the size and power of the various production and distribution members in the marketing system. See also *vertical marketing system (VMS), corporate VMS, contractual VMS, conventional marketing system, horizontal marketing system,* and *hybrid marketing system.*

administered price a deliberately set price, rather than one dictated solely by market forces, such as competition.

Adnorm statistics compiled by Starch to show average readership of advertisements broken down by publication, size, color, and type of product being advertised; see *Starch Readership Studies.*

adopter categories a classification of consumers based on how early or late an individual accepts a new product, service, or idea relative to other adopters; based on the time it takes an individual to make the initial purchase of a new product, the classification scheme includes *innovators, early adopter, early majority, late majority,* and *laggards.* See also *adoption process, adoption curve, diffusion process, innovators, early adopters, early majority, late majority,* and *laggards.*

adoption curve a graphic depiction of how consumers go about adopting a new product, service, or idea, showing when people accept a new entry; see also *adoption process, adopter categories, diffusion process, innovators, early adopters, early majority, late majority,* and *laggards.*

adoption process a series of stages through which an individual goes in deciding whether to accept a product idea and become a regular user of that product, or to reject it; see also *awareness stage, interest stage, evaluation stage, trial stage,* and *adoption stage.* Also see *diffusion process.*

adoption stage the fifth and final stage of the adoption process, in which the consumer decides whether to adopt or reject the new idea; see also *adoption process, awareness stage, interest stage, evaluation stage,* and *trial stage.*

AdRelevance a leading online advertising measurement service; part of *Nielsen/Net Ratings.*

advances in television, the ratings estimates for local audiences that are available to advertisers and agencies prior to distribution of ratings reports containing actual ratings numbers.

advertisement a sponsor-paid advertising message that appears in a print publication, such as a magazine or newspaper; the print equivalent of a broadcast commercial. See *commercial.*

advertiser any individual, organization, or other entity that uses advertising in an attempt to sell its product (broadly defined) or influence people in some way; see also *client.*

advertiser's copy see *checking copy, affidavit of performance,* and *tearsheet.*

advertiser-supported broadcasting television and radio networks and stations whose primary source of revenue comes from the broadcast of commercials sponsored by advertisers, making the programming free to viewers and listeners; noncommercial networks and stations and pay television seek funds from viewers, listeners, foundations, government, and other sources. See also *cable television (CATV), noncommercial broadcasting,* and *public broadcasting.*

advertising the use of paid media by an identified sponsor to communicate information about products (including objects, services, ideas, causes, and organizations) in order to influence people's thoughts and behavior or otherwise stimulate some action.

Advertising Age key weekly publication featuring complete, up-to-date marketing and advertising news and information for practitioners and nonpractitioners alike.

advertising agency an independent service organization that specializes in planning, creating, developing, preparing, and placing advertising and promotion programs for its clients, i.e., advertisers; also arranges for or contracts for purchase of media space and time, as well as appraisal of the advertising and promotion efforts. Also called a *shop.* See also *full-service advertising agency, limited-service advertising agency, creative boutique,* and *nontraditional advertising agency.*

advertising agency review see *agency review.*

advertising allowance money paid by a manufacturer to a retailer for advertising and other promotion the retailer does for the manufacturer's product at the local level; instead of an outright payment, the allowance may take the form of a price reduction on the goods the retailer buys from the manufacturer. See also *promotional allowance.*

advertising appeals see *appeals.*

advertising appropriation the amount of money allocated for advertising expenditures during a particular accounting period; see also *budgeting methods.*

advertising budget see *budgeting methods.*

advertising campaign a series of individual, but coordinated, advertisements and other promotional messages for a product or service placed in a variety of media under a single common theme that serves as the unifying force of the campaign, and running for a specified period of time; multiple messages under a single theme.

Advertising Checking Bureau (ACB) an organization devoted to managing trade allowance programs of all types for companies involved in cooperative advertising and other partnerships with retailers; services include verification, auditing, complete research services, and general efforts to foster better, more profitable relationships between parties.

advertising clutter see *clutter.*

advertising contract the formal and binding agreement between the advertiser and the media, specifying all details surrounding the placement of advertising, including the obligations of each party.

advertising copy see *copy.*

Advertising Council a not-for-profit organization that creates free public service advertising and campaigns in the general interest, promoting issues and causes, and stimulating awareness of and action against significant social problems in the United States; totally supported by advertisers, advertising agencies, and the media.

advertising creativity see *creativity.*

advertising design the particular arrangement, motif, pattern, and style of the visual elements in advertising; see also *balance, contrast, emphasis, flow, gaze motion, harmony,* and *unity.* Also see *art* and *graphics.*

advertising effectiveness the extent to which an advertising campaign or an individual advertisement or commercial achieves its objectives.

advertising elasticity the sensitivity of sales to advertising expenditures; i.e., the extent to which a change in the advertising budget affects a product's or service's sales.

advertising execution see *execution.*

advertising intensity the level of advertising during an advertising campaign or particular period within a campaign.

advertising layout see *layout.*

advertising manager the individual who runs the advertising department at the client organization.

advertising measurement see *advertising research.*

advertising media see *media.*

advertising medium see *medium.*

advertising message the primary idea contained in an advertiser's communication with its target audience; see also *message.*

advertising objectives results that the advertising efforts are expected to achieve; usually framed in terms of awareness, attitude, liking, or preference. A well-stated advertising objective identifies a specific communications *task* to be accomplished with a specific *target audience* during a specific *time period* to achieve a particular *degree of change* as evaluated by a specific *measurement.*

advertising plan the blueprint for the design and implementation of an advertising program; identifies all tasks and rationales for every stage of an advertising effort. An outgrowth of the *marketing plan.* See also *campaign plan* and *marketing plan.*

advertising platform see *copy platform.*

advertising production see *production stage.*

advertising promotional products promotional giveaway items used for goodwill and typically imprinted with the advertiser's name, address, telephone number, logo, or even a short message; e.g., caps, T-shirts, pens, coffee mugs, calendars, key tags. Also called *advertising specialties, giveaways, adcentives,* or *promotional products,* and often referred to as *specialty advertising.* See also *promotional products marketing.*

advertising productivity audit any of several techniques for measuring the return on the advertising investment; *return-on-investment* approach *(ROI).*

Advertising Red Books see *Standard Directory of Advertisers, Standard Directory of Advertising Agencies,* and *Standard Directory of International Advertisers & Agencies.*

advertising research the systematic gathering, analyzing, and evaluating of information relevant to an advertising program, such as that relating to advertising message and media strategies; see, for example, *message research, media research, readership studies, copytesting, pretesting, posttesting, aided recall, unaided recall, theater test, split-run test.*

Advertising Research Foundation (ARF) a professional association of advertisers, advertising agencies, research firms, media companies, and educators; dedicated to the pursuit of effective advertising and marketing communications through the practice of objective advertising, media, and marketing research; conducts research and stages conferences. Publisher of the *Journal of Advertising Research.*

Advertising Research System (ARS) see *ARS Group.*

advertising response curve the relationship between advertising expenditures and sales; sometimes used to help establish the advertising budget. See also *concave response curve, S-shaped response curve,* and *advertising-to-sales ratio.*

Advertising Response Modeling in advertising research, a copytesting technique that measures and analyzes the cognitive and image value of advertising. A product of *Gallup and Robinson (G&R).* See also *copytesting, Gallup and Robinson (G&R), InTeleTest, In-View Test,* and *Magazine Impact Research Service (MIRS).*

advertising scheduling see *media scheduling.*

advertising specialties see *advertising promotional products.*

advertising spiral the different stages through which a product's advertising passes; namely, pioneering (i.e., informative) advertising, competitive (i.e., persuasive) advertising, and retentive (i.e., reminder) advertising. See also *informative advertising, persuasive advertising,* and *reminder advertising.*

advertising strategy the direction the message will take to achieve the advertising objective; what and how the advertising is to communicate. See also *creative brief.*

advertising testing see *advertising research.*

advertising substantiation the requirement that an advertiser must provide adequate evidence and support for all claims about a product's features and benefits made in its advertising; documented proof of an advertiser's claim about its product. Under purview of the *Federal Trade Commission (FTC).*

advertising vehicle see *media vehicle.*

advertising wearout see *wearout.*

advertising weight the total amount of advertising used to support a specific campaign; may be expressed in several ways, such as media cost, gross impressions, gross rating points, or target rating points. Also referred to as *message weight.* See also *gross impressions, gross rating points,* and *target rating points.*

advertising-to-editorial ratio in print advertising, a measure of the relative amount of advertising vs. editorial content in a magazine or newspaper; i.e., the number of advertising pages compared with the number of pages with editorial content.

advertising-to-program content in broadcast advertising, a measure of the relative amount of advertising vs. program content in television or radio; i.e., the amount of time given to commercials compared with the amount of time devoted to the program, per thirty or sixty minutes.

advertising-to-sales ratio advertising expenditures expressed as percentage of sales revenue; see also *advertising response curve.*

advertorial print advertising that presents editorial matter in an attempt to influence public opinion on a particular issue, while at the same time, though not its primary purpose, promoting the advertiser's product(s); usually styled to resemble the editorial format and typeface of the publication in which it appears. Often done in a "special advertising section" format, consisting of two or more consecutive pages in a publication. For example, a drug company whose major purpose in the "advertising" is to focus on key issues in health care for senior citizens, but also includes promotional copy for its own drug product(s). The print counterpart to television's infomercial. See also *infomercial.*

advocacy advertising advertising that presents an organization's position or viewpoint on a public issue, often a controversial issue, even though it may not relate to the organization's line of business; used primarily to demonstrate that the organization takes its social responsibility seriously, and commenting on important public issues is part of that commitment. Public service advertising that attempts to influence public opinion on a particular social, political, or environmental issue the advertiser believes to be important. Also called *issue advertising.*

AdWeek a weekly trade publication serving the entire advertising industry, with news, insights, analysis, research, and editorial content covering all phases of advertising, and aimed at advertisers, agencies, and the media; the magazine is published in several regional editions. See also *BrandWeek* and *MediaWeek.*

AdWeek Directory an annual publication containing comprehensive reports on advertising agencies, public relations firms, media buying services, and specialty advertising shops; see also *BrandWeek Directory, MediaWeek Directory,* and *IQ Directory.*

aerial advertising a company name or message displayed on the side of a blimp, on a banner trailing a small airplane, or that is affixed to another airborne vehicle for the distinct purpose of advertising; also may refer to *skywriting* used for advertising messages.

affidavit of performance   a signed and notarized statement from a radio or television station to the advertising agency that confirms that the advertising ran as scheduled; a legal proof of performance. The broadcast equivalent of a *tearsheet*. See also *tearsheet*.

affiliate   see *network affiliate*.

affiliate marketing   in Internet marketing, a Web site that sells products of other Web sites; an agreement between two Web sites whereby one site features an advertisement aimed at driving traffic to the other site. For example, *www.usatoday.com* posting an advertisement selling Foot-Joy golf shoes with a direct link to *www.mammothgolf.com*, or *www.amazon.com* having an advertisement for office products with a direct link to another Web site selling such products or services. Generally, a revenue-sharing arrangement whereby two companies agree to link to one another on the Internet and, when a user clicks from Site A and then buys something at Site B, Site A receives a commission on the sale.

affinity marketing   where a group of customers has interest in a particular area (e.g., financial services or sports equipment), sellers of different products and services joining together to offer the customers an array of related products; marketing efforts directed to individuals having common interests that move them toward a particular product or service. Examples: To retain loyal customers, a merchant offers a credit card with incentives built in; an organization may issue a credit card with its name on it to allow the consumer to emphasize his or her identification or association with that organization, such as a Wal-Mart MasterCard or Harley-Davidson Visa card.

affirmative disclosure   when an advertiser, in its commercial message, makes known the limitations, consequences, or conditions associated with and surrounding the use of a product; e.g., when a pharmaceutical company reveals possible side effects of a drug or the conditions under which it was tested for effectiveness. A Federal Trade Commission requirement designed to make sure the consumer has enough information to make an informed decision. A legal concept of consumer protection. Also referred to as *full disclosure*. See also *Federal Trade Commission*.

affordable method   an advertising (or other promotion element) budgeting method in which the amount allocated to advertising is determined by what is left over after budgeting for everything else in marketing; a top-down approach to budgeting. See also *arbitrary method, competitive parity method, objective-and-task method, percentage-of-sales method,* and *unit-of-sales method*. Also see *build-up approach to budgeting* and *top-down approach to budgeting*.

afternoon-evening drive time   in the radio broadcast day, the time period of 3:00 P.M. to 7:00 P.M.; see also *dayparts (radio)*.

agate line   a unit of newspaper advertising space that measures one column wide by one-fourteenth of an inch deep; there are 14 agate lines to one column inch of depth; see also *column inch, lineage,* and *standard advertising unit (SAU)*.

agency   see *advertising agency*.

agency brand   an independent or merged advertising agency that does not own subsidiary agencies; e.g., Ogilvy & Mather, Arnold Communications, Hill Holliday, Young & Rubicam, BBDO Worldwide, Goodby, Silverstein & Partners, DDB Worldwide, or Leo Burnett. See also *megabrand, agency megabrand,* and *agency network*.

agency commission   payment to the advertising agency from the advertising media vehicle as compensation for the agency's placing its client's advertising with that vehicle; an agency compensation method based on the amount of media space or time purchased for the advertiser. Traditionally, 15 percent of the cost of the advertising space or time.

agency compensation method   the way in which an advertising agency is paid for its services by its client; several ways to determine compensation, but whatever specific method or combination is used, it essentially involves three elements: fee, commission, and results produced. See also *fee method, commission method, combination method,* and *performance-based method*. Also see *agency commission* and *sliding rate*.

agency evaluation   an organization's review and assessment of the performance of its advertising agency or other firm providing marketing or promotion services.

agency group   see *agency network*.

agency megabrand   the huge parent organization of a group of several individual advertising agencies, each a large entity in itself, under its ownership; e.g., WPP, with Ogilvy & Mather, Young & Rubicam, and J. Walter Thompson, Interpublic, with McCann-Erickson, FCB, and True North, or Omnicom, with BBDO Worldwide, DDB Worldwide, and Goodby, Silverstein & Partners. See also *megabrand, agency network,* and *agency brand.*

agency network   a group of advertising agencies that combine efforts and exchange ideas and services with one another, or the collection of advertising agencies under single ownership, i.e., an *agency megabrand.* Also called *agency group.* See also *megabrand, agency megabrand,* and *agency brand.*

agency of record (AOR)   in situations where an advertiser uses more than one advertising agency for the promotion of its products, the single agency whose responsibility it is to coordinate the efforts of all the agencies working for the advertiser; also refers to an independent media-buying company officially designated by an advertiser to purchase media time and space for all the agencies that serve that advertiser; commonly called *lead agency,* and also referred to as *captain agency* or *master agency.* See also *roster.*

agency reel   a videotape (typically about 10 minutes in length) of an advertising agency's recent television commercials for its clients; sent to prospective clients as a sample of the creative concepts and executions produced by the agency. Often used in the screening process when an advertiser is searching for a new agency.

agency review   the process of investigating and evaluating the performance of an advertising agency by the advertiser-client, typically for the purpose of selecting a new agency to handle the account; also called an *account review.* See also *account review* and *agency search consultant.*

agency review consultant   see *agency search consultant.*

agency roster   see *roster.*

agency search   the process by which an advertiser-client seeks a specialist firm to handle its advertising, sales promotion, public relations, or other activities associated with marketing communications; see also *account review* and *agency search consultant.*

agency search consultant   a firm that specializes in providing counsel for a company seeking an advertising agency (or any other specialist agency); consultant takes charge of the search process, offering advice and services relative to the evaluation, selection, compensation, and management of advertising agencies. Maintains a current library of work samples and detailed information on agencies to aid the search. See also *account review.*

agent middleman   in the distribution channel, a wholesaler who does not take title to the products it sells; see also *merchant wholesaler.*

agricultural advertising   advertising and promotion programs aimed at farmers and other members and organizations in the agricultural industry; also called *farm advertising.*

AIDA model   a way to view the major tasks assigned to advertising and promotion in the attempt to get consumers to respond; gain *attention,* spark *interest,* stimulate *desire,* and get *action.*

aided recall   in measuring and evaluating advertising or other promotional element, a research technique in which the respondent's memory is helped by the researcher who provides clues by showing or describing something; for example, the respondent may be shown an advertisement and asked whether he or she has seen it and can remember the ad's content. A research technique in which the interviewer provides a verbal or visual cue to help the respondent remember something prior to or during a response to a question. The researcher might ask, "What pickup truck commercial do you recall seeing on TV last night?" or even "What digital camera commercial that had a high school reunion as the setting do you recall seeing on TV last night?" See also *unaided recall.*

AIO   attitudes, interests, and opinions; the variables that form the psychographic or lifestyle characteristics of consumers. Often used by researchers to investigate and group consumers. See also *psychographic segmentation.*

air check   recording the broadcast of a television or radio program for the purpose of keeping the tape as a file copy as evidence of the airing of a commercial.

air date   in television and radio advertising, the broadcast date of the advertiser's message; also applies to the date of a program's broadcast.

airport display   in out-of-home advertising media, a display at an airport terminal, such as a diorama or a poster; see also *diorama* and *terminal poster.*

aisle spanner a promotional banner or sign suspended across an aisle in a supermarket, department store, drug store, or other retail store; typically hung from the ceiling by wires.

all night in the radio broadcast day, the time period from 12:00 A.M. to 6:00 A.M.; see also *dayparts (radio).*

alliance marketing generally, any marketing programs and activities in which two or more marketers join forces for a common effort.

allotment in outdoor advertising, the number and type of outdoor posters that constitute a showing; the number of units needed to have a desired gross rating point (GRP) level in a particular market. See also *gross rating point (GRP)* and *showing.*

allowances a general term for price reductions, payments, or other considerations given by a manufacturer to distribution channel members, such as retailers, to encourage them to do something on behalf of the manufacturer's product; e.g., see *advertising allowance, display allowance, trade allowance,* and *cooperative advertising.*

alpha testing in the new-product development process, testing a prototype product within the organization; concept may be applied to testing advertising or other promotion tools. See also *beta testing* and *new-product development process.*

alternate sponsorship a television or radio program that has two sponsors, with each advertiser sponsoring every other week's program; see also *cross-plug.*

alternative broadcast see *alternative media.*

alternative media media other than the so-called "traditional media" (broadcast and print media) typically used in advertising and promotion campaigns; usually used to complement the traditional media. Any of a variety of media vehicles aimed at audiences whose tastes and preferences are not fully satisfied by the traditional or existing media choices, e.g., radio stations whose format caters to a young, entertainment-oriented audience. See also *new media, nontraditional media, support media, unmeasured media,* and *traditional media.*

alternative press see *alternative media.*

ambassador an individual who is a spokesperson or representative for a company or a product, especially in the role of promoting goodwill; see also *goodwill, spokesperson, company ambassador,* and *product ambassador.*

ambush marketing in event marketing, when a non-official sponsor uses marketing and promotion tactics in an attempt to give the impression that it is an official sponsor; the tactic may involve tactics such as an official sponsor's competitor placing elaborate signage at the outskirts of the event venue or advertising during the broadcast of the event.

American Academy of Advertising a professional organization serving advertising teachers and practitioners, especially through its efforts of collecting and disseminating information for the betterment of the art; publisher of the *Journal of Advertising.*

American Advertising Federation (AAF) a professional association of advertisers, advertising agencies, media owners, local advertising clubs, suppliers, and academics that promotes truth and fairness in advertising, as well as supporting educational programs; annually presents the ADDY awards for excellence in national and local advertising, and also sponsors the Advertising Hall of Fame.

American Association of Advertising Agencies (AAAA) the premier national association of advertising agencies; dedicated to maintaining the highest standards of conduct of the advertising agency business and advertising practice. Particularly concerned with the responsibilities of advertising agencies to be a constructive force in business by adhering to the highest level of ethical practice and the idea that agencies must recognize the obligation to serve the best interests of their clients, the public, the media, and each other. See also *Standards of Practice, Creative Code,* and *Guidelines for Comparative Advertising.*

American Business Media (ABM) the major industry association for business-to-business information providers, including producers of magazines, CD-ROMS, Web sites, trade shows, and other ancillary products that build upon and enhance print communications.

American Business Press (ABP) an association of publishers of specialized business publications; a source of industry information, it encourages the exchange of ideas to make business publications better and more attractive as an advertising medium.

American Federation of Television and Radio Artists (AFTRA)   a broadcasting industry union for all workers; union membership is required of all *talent* who appear in television and radio commercials.

American Institute of Graphic Arts (AIGA)   a major industry organization whose mission includes promoting excellence in communication design as a strategic tool for business; the organization encourages design professionals to exchange ideas and information, participate in research and critical analysis, and to advance education and ethical practice of the discipline.

American Marketing Association (AMA)   a major professional association for marketing teachers, practitioners, and anyone interested in studying the marketing discipline; dedicated to advancing marketing thought and application, playing an active role in the development and exchange of information between and among those involved in practicing and teaching marketing, and promoting the highest standards of ethical conduct. Extremely active in organizing and staging many conferences and programs, as well as the publisher of several journals that help to advance marketing thought and practice.

American Newspaper Publishers Association (ANPA)   an organization serving the newspaper industry through its programs to advance the professionalism of the press and its efforts to strengthen public understanding of the press, all aimed at developing more and better informed newspaper readers.

ancillary market   see *secondary market.*

angled poster   an outdoor poster that is placed at an angle to the road, so the advertising message is visible to traffic in one direction only; see also *parallel location.*

animatic   in pretesting television commercials, a preliminary version (a series of still drawings) of a commercial, in which a videotape of the sequential frames of a storyboard are combined with a synchronized audio track; a rough of a television commercial to give the client an idea of what the advertising execution will look like without going to the expense of a finished commercial. See also *pretesting, liveamatic, photomatic, ripoamatic, storyboard,* and *rough.*

animation format   in advertising, a creative execution format that utilizes moving visual elements other than live action in a television commercial; involves a series of still drawings filmed one at a time to give the illusion they are moving. Most common form is the cartoon. For example: a lawnmower by itself mowing grass, a driverless automobile zooming off into the sunset, a single automobile tire rolling on a rain-slicked road, or a created character, such as the *Jolly Green Giant* or the *Energizer Bunny.* Also may refer to *billboard* or other *out-of-home media* and the use of moving components, flashing lights, or other special effects. See also *straightforward factual, news, demonstration, problem-solution, slice-of-life, dramatization, symbolic association, fantasy, still-life, humor, spokesperson, testimonial,* and *comparison formats.*

announcement   in broadcast media, an advertising message of any length that occurs within or between programs. Also called a *commercial.* Often referred to as a *spot.*

answer print   the final version of a television commercial presented to the advertiser for final approval prior to making duplicate copies and sending them to the networks and stations.

Anti-Drug Abuse Act   a law passed in 1988 requiring all producers of alcohol to place labels on their products warning that pregnant women should not consume alcoholic beverages, and that alcohol consumption impairs an individual's ability to operate an automobile or heavy machinery.

appeals   the basis of attraction or core message in advertising meant to stimulate the consumer's interest and influence his or her feelings and desire to buy a product, service, or other subject of the advertising; a means by which the advertiser hopes to forge a link between the product and the customer's needs, a link based on emotion and/or logic. See also *emotional appeals* and *rational appeals.*

application positioning   see *positioning by use.*

approach   the total distance along the line of travel that advertising copy on an outdoor structure is readable; measured from the point where the advertising structure and copy first become visible to the point where the copy is no longer readable. Typically 1,500, 1,000, or 500 feet. Also, a stage in the personal selling process in which the salesperson makes the first face-to-face contact with the prospect and attempts to get the relationship off to a good start. See also *prospecting,* *preapproach, presentation, handling objections, closing,* and *follow-up.*

arbitrary method a method for determining the advertising or promotion budget based on the discretion and judgment, usually unsupported, of the individuals involved in making the budget decisions; marked by the absence of systematic thinking. A *top-down approach to budgeting.* See also *affordable method, competitive parity method, objective-and-task method, percentage-of-sales method,* and *unit-of-sales method.* See also *build-up approach to budgeting* and *top-down approach to budgeting.*

Arbitron the leading supplier of radio audience information for radio stations, advertisers, advertising agencies, media buying services, radio networks, radio syndicators, and others involved in radio advertising; data on audience size and demographics are collected in about 260 U.S. markets by means of more than one million personal seven-day diaries throughout the year. Audience estimates and demographics for every radio station are published in a series of *Arbitron Radio Market Reports,* which are used to plan and execute radio advertising buys, to assist radio programming decision makers, and to help radio station account executives promote their stations as attractive advertising vehicles.

Area of Dominant Influence (ADI) a television market area, as defined by Arbitron, which no longer does TV ratings, but the term is still used; an exclusive geographic area made up of all counties in which the home-market stations get the majority of the viewing. See also *Designated Market Area.*

area sample see *cluster sample.*

arena signage see *stadium signage.*

ARS Group (Advertising Research System) a premier provider of a broad range of measurements and information on the persuasiveness of advertising and advertising's ability to have an impact on sales change; a complete copytesting service for evaluating advertising's impact on sales, projecting advertising's contribution to meeting marketing objectives, gathering consumer insight, and identifying improvement opportunities. See also *ARS Persuasion Measure* and *ARS Related Recall.*

ARS Persuasion Measure in advertising copy research, a pretesting measure of the ability of a brand's advertising to have a positive impact on sales; see also *ARS Group (Advertising Research System).*

ARS Related Recall in advertising research, a post-testing measure of the memorability of a brand's advertising and what was communicated; see also *ARS Group (Advertising Research System).*

art refers to the visual presentation of an advertisement or commercial, including design elements such as illustrations, photographs, color, size and style of type, symbols, and the logo; the arrangement or layout of the visual elements in advertising. See also *graphics.*

art direction the process of managing the entire visual presentation of an advertisement or commercial.

art director the individual in an advertising agency who has responsibility for the design and graphics elements, plus the creative positioning, of advertising produced by the agency; the person who determines the look and feel of a message. See also *art* and *graphics.*

arterial bulletin an outdoor billboard on a major secondary street of a city or town, where speeds are somewhat lower than on major highways or freeways; see also *outdoor bulletin.*

artist see *talent.*

arts marketing a promotion strategy or program that links a company or advertiser to the visual or performing arts, usually in the form of sponsorship; e.g., a local bank's sponsorship of a museum exhibit or a consumer products company such as Gillette sponsoring a Boston Pops tour. See also *sponsorship.*

ASI Recall Test in advertising research, a leader in the day-after-recall technique of measuring advertising effectiveness for television commercials; provides test scores for unaided recall and aided recall. Selects viewers by calling the day after a commercial appears, until they reach and get cooperation from a specified number of respondents, in contrast to the Gallup & Robinson day-after-recall approach that uses pre-recruited respondents. Formerly known as *Burke Day-After-Recall Test.* See also *day-after-recall test, unaided recall, aided recall,* and *Gallup & Robinson.*

as-it-falls method in advertising and media research when conducting a media test market, employing the exact same media weight in the test market as would be employed in a national plan, purchasing the media locally.

aspirational reference group a group whose norms, values, and behavior have such a positive attraction and influence on an individual that he or she uses the group as a guide or role model in the purchase of specific products and brands; also may refer to a group that a nonmember would like to join, but is unlikely to do so. See also *reference group.*

associate sponsor a sponsor of an event whose financial and other commitments are not as great as the primary or title sponsor(s); essentially a designation commensurate with the organization's financial commitment to the event and secondary to another sponsor(s). See also *primary sponsor* and *title sponsor.*

Associated score in magazine readership studies, the percentage of readers of a specific issue of a magazine who not only noted a particular advertisement but also saw or read some part of it that clearly indicated the brand or the advertiser; see also *Noted score, Read Most score,* and *Read Some score.* A measure of *The Starch Readership Report.*

Association of National Advertisers (ANA) an industry trade association representing national and regional advertisers; dedicated to maintaining the highest standards of advertising conduct and to serving the interests of companies and organizations that market and advertise their products and services.

Association for Interactive Media (AIM) an industry trade association dedicated to the advancement of the interactive media industries through research and programs focused on the business use of the Internet and interactive media to efficiently and effectively reach consumers and markets; an independent subsidiary of the Direct Marketing Association (DMA). See also *Direct Marketing Association (DMA).*

association test in advertising research, a type of projective technique in which consumers express their feelings and thoughts after hearing or seeing a brand name or after seeing a logo.

assorting in the distribution channel, the process whereby the intermediary (e.g., wholesaler or retailer) assembles and puts together the range and variety of products needed to satisfy the demand requirements of its customers and target markets.

assortment see *product assortment,* as well as *product line* and *product item.*

assortment depth see *product assortment depth.*

assortment width see *product assortment width.*

asymmetric balance see *informal balance.*

at-site order an order for goods placed at the booth or location of a trade show; also called an *on-site order.*

attack advertising see *comparison advertising.*

attitude an individual's learned and enduring predisposition or evaluative judgment toward an object, idea, or subject; based on previous experiences and affects how the individual receives and looks at something. For example, attitude influences how favorably or unfavorably a person may view advertising for a particular product.

attitude-change study a type of advertising research in which consumer attitudes toward a product are studied both before and after he or she is exposed to advertising for that product; a type of posttest to measure advertising effectiveness.

attribute positioning see *positioning by attribute.*

attrition rate the loss of a publication's subscribers, a mailing list's names, or a research panel's members for any of a variety of reasons; normally expressed as a percentage.

auction see *online reverse auction.*

audience the total number of different individuals or households who are exposed to an advertising medium, a media vehicle, or to a complete media plan; equivalent to *reach.* The object of a sender's message. Also referred to as *audience accumulation.* See also *reach* and *target audience.*

audience accumulation the total number of different individuals or households exposed to a single media vehicle or group of vehicles over a particular period of time; see also *audience.*

audience composition the demographic and other characteristics of the individuals in a medium's or media vehicle's audience; can be measured over time, e.g., at periodic intervals during the telecast of a football game. See also *audience profile.*

audience delivery data estimates of the number of individuals or households reached by a medium, media vehicle, or media schedule.

audience duplication   the number or percentage of individuals or households who are exposed two or more times to the same message in the same media vehicle or combination of vehicles; may also apply to audiences of different media classes or a particular medium. The extent to which the audience of one television station or one magazine is also exposed to, i.e., reached, by another station or magazine. See also *media vehicle, media classes,* and *medium.*

audience flow   in television or radio, refers to the programs immediately before and after a given program, and the extent to which the audience stays tuned to a particular station from one program to the next or changes stations; see also *audience turnover, holdover audience, lead-in,* and *lead-out.*

audience objectives   the specific types of people the advertiser attempts to reach; see also *target audience.*

audience profile   essentially the same as audience composition, i.e., a description of the audience's characteristics (e.g., size, age, sex, income, education, occupation, media habits, and the like), but particularly as it applies to the audience of a specific media vehicle, such as a particular magazine or television program; see also *audience composition* and *consumer profile.*

audience tune-out   in television and radio advertising, the extent to which viewers or listeners pay little or no attention to the commercials.

audience turnover   in broadcast media, similar to audience flow, but may also refer to just one program's audience, in which case it is the ratio of the program's cumulative audience to the average audience viewing or listening to that program; the part of an audience that changes over time. Also known as *churn.* See also *audience flow.*

Audilog   the name of a paper diary once used by Nielsen Media Research to gather demographic data from the households in its national sample television viewership; used as a complement to the electronic measurement of viewership. An electronic meter (called the Recordimeter) verified the accuracy of the diary entries.

Audimeter   the forerunner to the People Meter, it was an early electronic device used by Nielsen Media Research to measure television audiences; the device was hooked up to the television set to monitor when the set was turned on and to record the channel to

which the set was tuned at any given time. The device measured only the channel to which the set was tuned, with no provision for who was watching at any time or their demographic profile. Essentially the old-time name for the *set-tuning meter* in use today. See also *People Meter* and *set-tuning meter.*

audio   the sound portion of a television commercial or program; i.e., voices, music, sound effects. See also *video.*

Audit Bureau of Circulations (ABC)   a self-regulatory auditing organization for the independent verification and dissemination of circulation, readership, and audience information; in addition to auditing print media, services include auditing online traffic and advertising activity, exhibition attendance and demographics, and nontraditional media such as schoolbook covers and posters. Created by and responsible to advertisers, advertising agencies, and the media. See also *Business Publication Audit (BPA).*

audited circulation   common to many media, the independent accounting and verification of circulation and audience data; e.g., the work done by the *Audit Bureau of Circulations (ABC)* or the *Traffic Audit Bureau of Media Measurement (TAB).* Standards and procedures generally established and agreed to by the parties who have a stake in the examination of circulation data.

audited publication   a publication whose circulation is examined and certified by an independent organization; see also *Audit Bureau of Circulations (ABC).*

augmented product   the basic tangible product supplemented or enhanced by additional services and benefits that give it greater value to the consumer; e.g., installation, a warranty, a repair service contract, a free upgrade option. See also *actual product* and *core product.*

availabilities   television time slots as yet unsold and therefore available for purchase by an advertiser; commonly called *avails.* Can refer to the inventory of advertising time and space available for purchase in any media class, subclass, or media vehicle, such as an outdoor billboard.

avails   see *availabilities.*

average   see *mean.*

average audience (AA)   in television, the number of homes or individuals tuned to a particular television program for an average minute of that program; a Nielsen statistic. In print, the number of readers who looked into an average issue of a particular publication, as measured by readership studies.

average daily traffic (ADT)   in out-of-home advertising, a measurement of the total number of vehicles passing a specific location, based on complete 24-hour counts done for an entire year; see also *traffic count.*

average exposure   the mean number of times an individual has been exposed to an advertisement or commercial in a specified time period; see *average frequency.*

average frequency   the average number of times individuals or households in the target audience are *exposed* to a media vehicle over a specific period of time. To calculate: divide total exposures by audience *reach,* i.e., divide gross rating points (GRPs) by total non-duplicated audience (*reach* or *cume*). Term is often used interchangeably with *frequency.* See also *frequency, gross rating points, reach,* and *cume.*

average hours   in television or radio, the average number of hours viewed or listened to per TV or radio household, per day, per week, or any time period.

average issue audience   the number of individuals who have read an average issue of a publication; see also *average audience.*

average net paid circulation   in print vehicles, the mean number of copies distributed and bought per issue of the publication, over a weekly, monthly, or yearly period; as verified by the *Audit Bureau of Circulations (ABC).* Obtained by dividing the total of all paid copies by the total number of copies issued. Also called *average paid circulation.* See also *net paid circulation* and *Audit Bureau of Circulations (ABC).*

average order   in direct mail, a way to measure the effectiveness of a program by focusing on the average value of an order associated with the particular campaign; calculated as total revenue divided by the number of orders.

average paid circulation   see *average net paid circulation.*

average quarter-hour audience (AQH)   the average number of persons listening to a specific radio station for at least 5 minutes during a 15-minute period of a

particular daypart. An Arbitron measurement of radio-audience size. Sometimes referred to as *average quarter-hour persons (AQH persons).* See also *Arbitron, daypart, average quarter-hour share,* and *average quarter-hour rating.*

average quarter-hour rating   the average quarter-hour audience (AQH) estimate expressed as a percentage of the area population; i.e., a radio station's audience during a particular quarter-hour *daypart,* expressed as a percentage of the measurement area's total population. To calculate: divide the average quarter-hour audience by the area population (or by the target audience). A measure of *Arbitron* for the size of radio audiences. See also *Arbitron, daypart, average quarter-hour share,* and *average quarter-hour audience (AQH).*

average quarter-hour share   the percentage of people listening to the radio (any station) in a given area who are tuned to a specific station during a particular quarter-hour in a particular *daypart.* To calculate: divide the average quarter-hour audience listening to a specific station by the average quarter-hour audience listening to all stations. A measure of Arbitron for radio-audience size. See also *Arbitron, daypart, average quarter-hour audience (AQH),* and *average quarter-hour rating.*

average time per visit   in Internet advertising, the total elapsed time a particular Web site or advertisement is in view (all visits) divided by the number of unique visitors; see also *unique audience.*

awareness   see *brand awareness.*

awareness advertising   advertising that seeks to make people familiar with a brand name or a company.

awareness level   the percentage of individuals who know of the existence of an advertiser's product, service, or company.

awareness set   in a particular product category, all the brands known to the consumer; see also *evoked set.*

awareness stage   the first stage of the adoption process, in which the consumer becomes alert to a product but knows little about its features and what it will do for them; see also *adoption process, interest stage, evaluation stage, trial stage,* and *adoption stage.*

away-from-home listening   in radio advertising, an estimate of the number of people listening to the radio at locations outside the home; e.g., in the car, at work, or elsewhere.

axis   in print advertising, an imaginary line that runs through an advertisement from which the ad's elements branch off; an aid to aligning visual elements and relating them to make sure the advertisement's layout is logical and facilitates the reader's eye movement in the way intended by the ad's creator.

B

BAR   see *Broadcast Advertising Reports.*

BATF   see *Bureau of Alcohol, Tobacco, and Firearms.*

BBB   see *Better Business Bureau.*

BDI   see *Brand Development Index.*

BEP   see *break-even point.*

BMA   see *Business Marketing Association.*

BPA   see *Business Publication Audit.*

BPI   see *Buying Power Index.*

BTA   see *best-time-available.*

B County   see *ABCD Counties.*

B2B   see *business marketing.*

B2C   see *consumer marketing.*

baby billboard   see *car card.*

back cover   see *inside back cover* and *outside back cover.*

backgrounder   a document containing basic information about a company, its mission, place in the industry, products, and other information serving as a snapshot of that company.

back-end display   an advertising sign on the outside rear of a bus or rapid-transit vehicle, mounted below the window; also called a *taillight poster.* See also *front-end display* and *taillight poster.*

back-end load   in advertising scheduling, allocating the major part of advertising or promotion budget expenditures to the late segment of a campaign; see also *front-end load.*

back-end promotion   a sales promotion effort that begins after a particular event occurs; featuring a product at a special event such as a sports event or a concert and following up with a formal sales promotion program in the weeks or months ahead, or placing a product in a movie and then initiating a sales promotion program, such as point-of-purchase advertising and a special deal.

back-to-back   in radio and television, describes two commercials or programs broadcast in succession; in television, particularly those commercials aired for two products of the same company. Also called *piggyback commercial* and *double spotting.* See also *piggyback commercial,* *competitive separation,* and *commercial protection.*

backlighted unit   see *backlit.*

backlit   in outdoor advertising, a structure that is illuminated to throw light through the advertisement for higher visibility, especially at night; the ads must be printed on special translucent surfaces. Also called a *backlighted unit.*

backup order   the advertisers "in line" to take a spot on a sold-out program in case an already-committed advertiser backs out; for example, the Academy Awards show typically sells all advertising time well in advance of the television broadcast, with subsequent would-be advertisers falling in line in case an advertiser decides to back out.

bait advertising   the practice whereby a retail store advertises a product at an unusually low price, making it appear to be an extremely attractive bargain, for the sole purpose of getting traffic to the store, with few, if any, of the item actually in stock and available for sale; see also *bait-and-switch tactics.*

bait pricing   see *bait-and-switch tactics.*

bait-and-switch tactics   a marketing ploy that starts with a retail store's advertising a product offered at a very attractive price to lure customers into the store,

17

at which point a strong attempt is made to sell the consumer a higher-priced or a higher-profit product, to the extreme that sometimes the salesperson even refuses to sell the advertised item; an illegal practice. See also *bait advertising.*

balance in advertising design and layout, the principle that the elements of the advertisement should be arranged so as to have a degree of symmetry, proportionality, and compatibility, avoiding an appearance of the elements being unstable or disproportional to one another. Movement through an advertisement should be orderly and comfortable to the audience's eyes. See also *contrast, emphasis, flow, gaze motion, harmony,* and *unity,* as well as *informal balance* and *formal balance.*

balloon advertising copy set in a "balloon" so it seems to be coming from the mouth of one of the characters illustrated in the advertisement; also called a *blurb.*

banded premium see *on-pack premium.*

bandwidth transmission capacity of a telecommunications link, such as a television line or a computer line, i.e., capacity to carry information.

bangtail envelope in direct mail, an additional flap on an envelope that is used as a response form; the receiver can tear it off, fill it out, and mail it back to the marketer.

banner a headline in large letters running across the entire page, usually in bold print; see also *banner ad.*

banner ad in Internet advertising, an advertisement generally located at the top of a Web page and running across the page, with a link to the advertiser's site by use of a *clickthrough;* commonly measures 468 pixels wide × 60 pixels high (i.e., a 468 × 60 banner ad). Also referred to as simply a *banner.* See also *clickthrough, pixels, skyscraper ad, rectangle ad, square pop-up, pop-up advertising,* and *pop-under advertising.*

bargaining power the amount of influence a party has in negotiation with another; e.g., the strength of an advertiser in negotiating rates with the media, or sponsorship fees with the director of a special event.

barriers to entry factors and conditions that make it difficult for a new firm to enter a particular market or industry; e.g., large advertising and promotion budgets of existing companies that serve as a major obstacle for a new firm to enter the market. Some critics claim the result of large budgets is less competition because the large advertisers have competitive advantages such as economies of scale, particularly those associated with media costs. See also *competitive barriers.*

barter acquisition of broadcast time or print space by an advertiser or agency in exchange for merchandise, services, or other nonmonetary considerations; no cash is involved. Commonly negotiated through a barter agent or other intermediary. Bartering can involve any advertising medium. Essentially, trading one resource for another or exchanging one product or service for another product or service of like value. Can also involve the purchase of media time or space by a media company in exchange for similar time or space. Example: a dentist trading dental work on a baseball team's players for two season tickets, a rental car company providing automobiles for golf tournament guests in exchange for signage at the event, or a printing firm printing the souvenir program for a football team in exchange for signage at the stadium.

barter house an organization that acts as a wholesaler or broker of television time by maintaining an inventory of broadcast time accumulated through various barter deals, and then selling it to advertisers and agencies; see also *barter.*

barter syndication providing first-run or off-network syndication television programs to local stations at a reduced rate or free of charge, but with some of the advertising time already presold to national advertisers by the syndicator or by the owner of the program; the remaining commercial time then can be sold to local advertisers by the station. A syndicated television program offered by a syndicator to a station in exchange for some commercial time slots within the program. See also *cash syndication, cash-barter syndication, first-run syndication, off-network syndication, syndicator,* and *syndication.*

base rate in print advertising, the highest rate charged to an advertiser for a single insertion, without the agency commission or other media discounts of any kind, i.e., the full rate; also called *card rate, gross rate, one-time rate, open rate,* and *transient rate.* See also *agency commission, media discounts, card rate,* and *open rate.*

baseline measures see *benchmark.*

basic bus in transit advertising, when an advertiser purchases all the inside advertising space, or car cards, on a group of buses, enabling the advertiser to achieve complete domination of the space; also called a *total bus*. See also *car card*.

basic cable a cable television provider's basic offering of channels, available at no extra charge, i.e., basic service, excluding those channels for which there is a premium charge; carries the lowest monthly fee.

battle kit in personal selling, the collection of promotional items used by the sales force in selling its accounts.

battle of the brands refers to the competition between manufacturer brands and dealer brands; fighting for shelf space and consumer patronage. See also *manufacturer brands* and *dealer brands*.

beauty shot in print advertising, particularly magazines, an advertisement whose focus is almost entirely on the visual appeal of the product; the attractiveness of the product dominates the advertisement. For example, an especially eye-appealing photo of a box of chocolates in all its splendor, or an automobile pictured as luxurious and elegant.

behavioristic segmentation dividing the market (i.e., consumers) into segments or groups based on buyer behavior variables such as benefits sought, user status, usage rate, occasion of use, loyalty status, or buyer-readiness stage; see also *demographic segmentation, geographic segmentation, geodemographic segmentation,* and *psychographic segmentation*.

BehaviorScan a consumer purchasing behavior tracking service across multiple trade channels, including supermarkets, drugstores, mass merchandisers, supercenters, and others, providing comprehensive measurement and evaluation of new-product programs and advertising campaigns; the service can deliver different TV ads to selected homes within the same market, along with the ability to read the impact of the advertising on consumers' actual purchasing behavior and attitudes. The service's ad testing package includes exclusive testing rights in a given product category, consultation on test market selection and test design, selection of matched test and control groups of households, execution of test and control advertising plans via cable TV cut-ins, and analysis of results. A *single-source data* system. A product of *Information Resources, Inc. (IRI)*. See also *Information Resources, Inc. (IRI), InfoScan,* and *single-source data*.

belief an individual's viewpoint or assessment of something, such as a particular brand of product, based on the brand's features and benefits; stems from the consumer's knowledge and feelings about, say, a specific product or a specific issue, that have accumulated over time, resulting in a particular sentiment or conviction about that product or issue.

below-the-fold the bottom half of a broadsheet newspaper; as opposed to above-the-fold. On the Web, the term refers to the portion of a given page, such as the homepage, that can be viewed only by scrolling down. An advertisement on a Web site is below-the-fold when the entire advertisement can be viewed only by scrolling down for at least a portion of it. See also *above-the-fold* and *broadsheet*.

below-the-line costs advertising production costs incurred for everything other than creative work; e.g., props, equipment, stage sets. Also may refer to "lower profile" advertising media such as direct mail. See also *above-the-line costs*.

benchmark the criteria used to gauge the market (e.g., sales, market share, consumer attitudes, consumer perceptions) just prior to the beginning of a promotion campaign, to serve as a yardstick or reference point against which campaign results can be measured; where things stand immediately before a marketing communications campaign. A vital part of the tracking method of measuring and evaluating campaign progress and results. Can also refer to a firm's sales before an advertising or promotion campaign. Also called *baseline measure*. See also *benchmarking, benchmark study,* and *tracking*.

benchmarking a process by which a firm investigates other companies to learn how and why they achieve a particular level of performance, say, in advertising or sales promotion, with the intention of matching or improving the best practices, thereby improving the firm's performance; see also *benchmark, benchmark study,* and *tracking*.

benchmark study in marketing and advertising research, the initial study against which all subsequent data are compared; see also *benchmark, benchmarking,* and *tracking*.

benefit the reason why a consumer chooses a particular product; the gain or improved state that results from use of a product or service. What the user gets from a product or service beyond the physical features or characteristics.

benefit headline   a type of headline for an advertisement or commercial that directly promises the audience that use of the product will be rewarding; e.g., "Keeps you warm and dry. No matter what falls out of the sky." (Gore-Tex fabrics) or "Big Allergies, Big Relief." (Zyrtec tablets). See also *headline,* as well as *command headline, curiosity headline, news-information headline,* and *question headline.*

benefit positioning   see *positioning by benefit.*

benefit segmentation   dividing or breaking the total market into a series of smaller markets, or segments, based on the different benefits sought from the product by consumers.

best practice   a particular technique or approach considered to be an excellent example of effective performance; sometimes described in the form of a case study.

best-time-available (BTA)   on an insertion order, an instruction to the television or radio station to run the commercial in the most favorable or best time slot available; also referred to as *run-of-schedule (ROS).* See also *run-of-schedule.*

beta testing   in the new-product development process, testing a prototype product by letting a carefully selected group of consumers use the product and register their reactions; concept may be applied to testing advertising or other promotion tools. See also *alpha testing* and *new-product development process.*

Better Business Bureau (BBB)   a not-for-profit self-regulatory organization established and supported by the business community, with local bureaus located in cities throughout the United States; its mission is to control and promote fair and ethical advertising and selling practices. Local bureaus offer a variety of services such as providing reports on firms to consumers before they make purchases, helping to resolve disputes between consumers and firms, and investigating advertising and selling practices when a consumer files a complaint against a firm. Sometimes forwards complaints to the National Advertising Division (NAD) for evaluation. See also *Council of Better Business Bureaus (CBBB)* and *National Advertising Division (NAD).*

between-vehicle duplication   see *across-vehicle duplication.*

Big Idea   the single most compelling and powerful benefit that provides the central theme in an advertisement or a campaign; the major selling point.

bill   see *poster.*

bill enclosure   see *statement stuffer.*

bill-back allowance   an incentive, usually monetary, provided by the advertiser to a retailer in return for the retailer featuring the advertiser's product in the store's advertising or in a special store display; not to be confused with *cooperative advertising.*

billboard   a large flat upright structure with advertising affixed and which is intended for viewing from extended distances, i.e., more than 50 feet; usually erected on the sides of roads and highways and within easy notice of people in passing vehicles. Includes displays such as *30-sheet poster, 24-sheet poster, 8-sheet poster, bulletin, poster panel,* and *stadium* or *arena signage,* to mention a few. In television or radio advertising, the term also applies to the brief announcement (10 seconds or less) at the beginning, middle, or end of a broadcast program in the form of, "The following portion of this program is brought (has been brought) to you by (sponsor's name)." See also *open billboard, middle billboard,* and *close billboard.*

billboard bag   a flexible wrapping bag for home-delivery newspapers, containing on its surface a promotional message for a product and, often, a trial-size sample affixed to the bag; also called a *polybag.*

billings   the total revenue of an advertising agency; composed largely of the charges made to the advertiser based on media time and space purchased on its behalf, plus other charges and fees incurred by the agency and passed along to the advertiser; commonly used to indicate agency size.

bingo card   in a magazine, a reader-reply card containing numbers that can be circled by the reader to receive information about products and services from an advertiser in that periodical; generally located near the back of the publication. Also called *action card.*

blackout   in television, when a sports or special event in a local area is not carried by a television station by reason of a formal agreement with the league or owner of the event.

blanket contract an agreement by which a media vehicle extends a special rate or discount to an advertiser who advertises more than one of its products in that vehicle through more than one advertising agency; e.g., Procter & Gamble with advertisements in *Good Housekeeping* for Crest, Cheer, and Bounty, each handled by a different advertising agency. See also *corporate discounting.*

blanking in outdoor advertising, a white paper border surrounding the poster copy area; see also *bleed-face bulletin.*

blanking out in outdoor advertising, when white paper is used to cover a poster; usually used to cover an advertisement when the contract has expired and until a new advertisement is posted to the site.

bleed in print media advertising, copy that extends to the edge of the advertising surface on all sides, with no margin or border; e.g., as on a poster or a magazine page.

bleed charge an extra charge for producing a bleed advertisement; see also *bleed.*

bleed page a magazine advertisement that goes to the very edges of the page, with no margin or white space on the borders; bleed ads often carry a premium charge, called a *bleed charge.*

bleed poster see *bleed-face bulletin.*

bleed-face the outdoor equivalent of a *bleed page;* see also *bleed page.*

bleed-face bulletin in outdoor advertising, a poster that has *blanking* paper of the same color as the poster background running all the way to the edge of the billboard, and the copy usually goes to the very edge of the panel; the outdoor equivalent of a bleed page in a print advertisement. Also called a *bleed poster.* See also *blanking* and *bleed page.*

bleed-through in outdoor advertising, a production flaw that allows the previously posted sign to show through the current message; may result from the type and quality of paper used or from excessive rainwater. See also *coat-out.*

blind offer see *hidden offer.*

blind outer in direct-mail marketing, an outside envelope without a logo or any identity of the sender; an attempt to increase opening rate by masking the identity of the sender to prevent recipients from dismissing it as junk mail and throwing it away without opening. See also *opening rate.*

blinking a media scheduling pattern consisting of many short periods (flights) of advertising alternated with short periods of no advertising at all (hiatuses); e.g., one week on, one week off, alternating over a period of time. See also *flight, flighting,* and *hiatus.*

blister pack a small package that has a cardboard or other stiff material as backing, with a hard transparent plastic bubble attached to it (heat-sealed), with the product housed inside the bubble; also called a *bubble card.*

blitz a concentrated, intensive, and very noticeable burst of advertising and promotion activity over a relatively short time frame, for the purpose of creating maximum exposure and impact while reducing the perceived presence of competitors' messages; see also *bursting* and *heavy-up scheduling.*

block in radio and television, two or more consecutive hours or broadcast time periods.

block programming in television, scheduling programs back-to-back that are aimed at individuals with common demographics.

blocking chart see *flowchart.*

blurb a short, concise statement about a company, a product, an event, or other point of interest placed in the official program of an event; can also refer to a press release. See also *news release* and *press release.* Also see *balloon.*

board see *poster panel* and *painted bulletin.*

body copy in a print advertisement, the main text that tells the full story; does not include headlines, illustrations, or any matter other than the words used to tell the story. See also *copy.*

boiler plate standardized copy ready for use at any time it's needed; often used when an advertisement must include certain statements or copy, such as warnings, qualifiers, or disclaimers required by law on alcohol, tobacco, pharmaceutical, and other products. May also be used to eliminate the need for new writing or copy when a specific communication requirement is likely to arise frequently. Ready-to-go copy.

bonus goods a trade deal or type of allowance in which the manufacturer provides extra goods at no charge to the retailer; i.e., "Buy one, get one free."

bonus pack special packaging that gives the consumer an extra amount of product with no increase in the regular price; see also *twin pack.*

bonus spot in television advertising, when a station provides commercial time to an advertiser free of charge, as a promotional tool to encourage buying additional time; term is sometimes applied to a make-good, or "free" time given to an advertiser when the advertiser's program does not deliver the promised audience level. See also *make-good.*

book a common term for a *magazine.*

booking the act of making a firm commitment to schedule advertising in magazines or on radio or television.

booth an area consisting of one or more units of exhibit space; typically sold in 10 sq. ft. increments. See also *trade show.*

booth personnel the individuals working an exhibitor's booth at a trade show.

border in print advertising, the space surrounding an advertisement; purpose is to prevent the advertisement from running to the edge of another ad or to the edge of editorial matter.

borrowed interest in advertising creative strategy, the use of an inherently appealing subject or image to capture the interest of the audience and generate good feelings during exposure to the advertising; e.g., a baby, a puppy, or anything that sparks a warm, tender, and affectionate feeling that can be used for its carry-over value for the product being advertised. Principle also applies to the use of celebrity endorsers, who have instant attention-getting power.

bottom-up approach to budgeting see *build-up approach to budgeting.*

bounceback an additional offer made to consumers who respond to a previous offer by the same marketer; the new offer is sent with the product delivered in fulfillment of the first promotion. The new offer, or bounceback, may take the form of a *coupon* or other enclosure that promises a special deal on that product or other products sold by the same company.

boutique see *creative boutique.*

brainstorming a free-wheeling, sky's-the-limit method of generating ideas for a new product, advertising approach, sales promotion activity, or any other element of the marketing program; purpose is to get ideas on the table and not to judge their worth.

brand a name, word, group of words, symbol, design, or other element, or any combination of these, that identifies a company's product and sets it apart from that of competitors.

brand association extent to which a particular brand is thought of within the context of a specific product category; see also *share of mind* and *brand awareness.*

brand awareness the extent to which the consumer recognizes and knows the existence of a particular brand; see also *brand familiarity.*

brand building a marketing and promotion strategy aimed at polishing or sharpening a product's or organization's image; a strategy designed to push a name rather than simply sell more goods.

brand consciousness the level of awareness a consumer has about a particular brand and the extent to which a product's brand name influences the consumer's purchase decision.

Brand Development Index (BDI) a measure of the relative sales strength of a given brand in a specific market area of the United States. To calculate: divide the percentage of brand A's total U.S. sales in market X by the percentage of the total U.S. population in market X, then multiply the result by 100 to get the index number. Especially useful, along with the Category Development Index (CDI), in deciding media allocations and how much advertising or other promotion effort to put into different market areas. See also *Category Development Index (CDI).*

brand equity a measure of a brand's value or worth to the company that owns it and to the customers who purchase it; consists of intangible and tangible values.

brand extension a brand strategy in which the marketer introduces a product in a new category, using the same brand name from its current offering; e.g., Disney Cruise Lines, Starbucks ice cream, Motorola cellular phones, Coleman vacuum cleaners, Nike golf balls, Reebok sunglasses, exercise bikes and treadmills, and headwear, or Ralph Lauren clothing, fragrance, carpeting, upholstery, and paint. A form of *brand leveraging.* See also *brand strategy, line extension, multibranding,* and *new-brand strategy.*

brand familiarity the extent to which a consumer recognizes a particular brand, including its features, benefits, and its capacity for providing the degree of satisfaction the consumer is looking for; see also *brand rejection, brand nonrecognition, brand recognition, brand preference,* and *brand insistence.*

brand harvesting see *harvesting.*

brand identity all the cues that collectively provide a particular look or recognition of a brand; colors, distinctive typography, symbols, and other factors that make a brand identifiable as a distinct entity.

brand image the complete set of beliefs and perceptions held by consumers toward a particular brand; the particular impression consumers have about a brand.

brand image strategy in advertising, a creative approach that attempts to differentiate an advertiser's brand from others by focusing on psychological rather than physical differences in the product.

brand insistence a level of brand familiarity in which the consumer will not accept a substitute and, if necessary, is willing to make a special effort to obtain it; see also *brand rejection, brand nonrecognition, brand recognition, brand preference,* and *brand loyalty.*

brand integration see *product integration.*

brand interest the degree of consumer curiosity about a particular brand.

brand leveraging the marketing practice of using the power and strength of an existing brand name to help a company move into a new, usually related product category; e.g., Minute Maid orange juice with its Minute Maid soda, Reese's candy with its Reese's peanut butter, or Bic pens with its Bic razors. See also *brand extension.*

brand licensing see *licensing* and *licensed brand.*

brand loyalty a consumer's continuing, repeat purchase of the same brand in a particular product category; a strong, unyielding attachment, patronage, and commitment to a specific brand. See also *brand switching.*

brand management the supervision of and responsibility for all aspects of the marketing program for a particular brand, as opposed to an entire category or line of products; for example, the Doritos brand for Frito-Lay. See also *category management.*

brand manager the individual responsible for all aspects of the marketing program for a specific brand; also called a *product manager.* See also *brand management.*

brand mark a symbol, design, or distinctive lettering or coloring that cannot be spoken. Exclusive use by the owner is guaranteed only if it is registered as a *trademark.* See also *trademark.*

brand name a word, letter, number, or groups thereof, that can be spoken; i.e., the portion of a brand that can be spoken. Exclusive use by the owner is guaranteed only if it is registered as a *trademark.* See also *trademark.*

brand nonrecognition a level of brand familiarity in which the consumer simply does not know or recognize the brand name; for some products, such lack of familiarity may not deter a consumer from purchasing it, e.g., ice melting mix or paper plates. See also *brand rejection, brand recognition, brand preference,* and *brand insistence.*

brand personality see *brand image.*

brand placement see *product placement.*

brand position see *positioning* and *position.*

brand preference a level of brand familiarity in which the consumer is inclined, even strongly so, to choose the particular brand over others based on past experience, but is willing to accept a substitute for a given purchase occasion; see also *brand rejection, brand nonrecognition, brand recognition,* and *brand insistence.*

brand proliferation the increase in the number of new brands that have been introduced to the consumer market; the result of marketers attempting to develop products for specific market segments and specific needs of consumers.

brand recognition a level of brand familiarity in which the consumer knows the brand and has a general idea of its features and what it can do; see also *brand rejection, brand nonrecognition, brand preference,* and *brand insistence.*

brand reinvention remaking or repositioning a particular brand that has grown old in the minds of consumers and is in need of a rejuvenation that attempts to project a new mood, tone, or point of view, resulting in a stronger emotional connection with its market; a means to win back customers by revitalizing the brand. See also *repositioning.*

brand rejection a level of brand familiarity in which the consumer knows the brand, but will not purchase it for any reason, perhaps related to past experience, price, poor quality, word-of-mouth, or poor image; see also *brand nonrecognition, brand recognition, brand preference,* and *brand insistence.*

brand strategy in naming and marketing a product, the four options available to the marketer; see also *line extension, brand extension, multibranding,* and *new-brand strategy.*

brand switchers a market segment consisting of consumers who show no loyalty to a particular brand, instead choosing that which they believe offers the best deal; also called *variety seekers.* See also *brand switching.*

brand switching in a particular product category, a purchasing pattern characterized by consumers changing from one brand to another; often motivated by sales promotion deals (the "best" deal at the time), the quest for the "perfect" solution, or simply the idea of change or something different. Getting consumers to change brands may be an advertiser's goal in a particular campaign. Also known as *variety-seeking.* See also *brand loyalty.*

branding the all-inclusive process whereby a *brand* and a *brand image* are developed and differentiated from all other products.

BrandWeek a national weekly trade magazine featuring news, insights, opinions, and analysis of marketing and brand issues, with in-depth articles on relevant matters and case histories; see also *AdWeek* and *MediaWeek.* Also see *Superbrands.*

BrandWeek Directory an annual publication that provides profiles of U.S. brands and the companies that market them; see also *AdWeek Directory* and *MediaWeek Directory.*

breadth of assortment see *product line width.*

break in television and radio media scheduling, the time period between programs or between segments of a single program that is available for commercials, announcements, or news briefs.

breakdown in business advertising media, classifying circulation by type of business or industry, geographical location, functions and titles of readers, demographics of recipients, and other factors considered relevant.

break-even analysis an evaluation of the relationship between costs and revenues; helps determine whether the firm can cover all its costs with a particular product or service price. Allows the marketer to calculate the effects of several different prices. See also *break-even point (BEP).*

break-even point (BEP) the precise quantity at which total costs equal total revenues, telling the marketer exactly how many units must be sold at a particular price to just cover costs; in units, the point is calculated by dividing total fixed cost by fixed cost contribution per unit (selling price per unit minus variable cost per unit). See also *break-even analysis.*

breakthrough opportunity a marketer's strategy that gives it a true competitive advantage over all others, and which yields an attractive and profitable long-term return for the company.

bricks-and-mortar the actual physical-plant businesses, such as a retail store, as opposed to an online marketer; see also *clicks-and-mortar* and *online marketing.*

bridge buying see *forward buying.*

bridging in television programming, a ploy to keep an audience away from another program by scheduling a program so it is in progress at the time the other show begins.

brick-and-click see *clicks-and-mortar.*

brief see *creative brief.*

broadband high-speed cable transmission over the Internet.

broadcast coverage area in television or radio, the entire geographic area that receives the originating station's signal; see also *coverage, spill-in,* and *spill-out.*

broadcast media media that rely on electronic means to operate, i.e., broadcast television, cable television, and radio, and which sell commercial time to companies and organizations that have an advertising message to deliver to their target audiences; see also *print media.*

broadcast monitoring service   an organization that regularly checks the broadcast media for mention of a company's name; operates on a contract basis for an advertiser-client. See also *monitoring service.*

broadcast network   in television, as defined by Nielsen Media Research, an organization that distributes programming and announcements for simultaneous distribution to contractually affiliated local stations, has coverage of at least 70 percent of U.S. television households for the majority of its programs, and that telecasts at least 15 hours of programming per week; in situations where less than 15 but at least 10 hours of programming per week are telecast, the organization is considered a "limited network." See also *network.*

broadcast production   see *production.*

broadcast television   a television delivery system in which the signals are transmitted through the air, rather than via wires, as in the case of cable television (CATV).

Broadcasting Advertiser Reports (BAR)   in television and radio advertising, an organization that monitors network and spot television advertising and network radio advertising, and issues reports on its findings; a good source for competitive spending and scheduling patterns.

broadcasting   television or radio programming with appeal to large general-interest audiences; the broadcast equivalent of *general-interest* or *mass magazine.* See also *narrowcasting.*

broadsheet   a standard or full-size newspaper in which a page measures approximately 22″ deep × 13½″ wide and has six columns; as opposed to a tabloid, which measures about 14″ deep × 10½″ wide and has five columns. For advertising purposes, a full page measures 126 column inches (21 × 6). See also *tabloid.*

broadside   a direct-mail piece or other promotional literature that unfolds to a large sheet approximately the size of a regular (i.e., *broadsheet*) newspaper page.

brochure   a specially designed booklet used for promoting the advertiser's product, service, or the

organization as a whole; usually published on heavier paper stock and often features color photography, illustrations, and elaborate typography.

broker   in the distribution of goods, an agent middleman, i.e., does not take title to the goods, who brings buyers and sellers together for a transaction; represents either the buyer or the seller, but not both in the same transaction.

browser   a software program on a computer that can request, load, and display documents or Web sites residing on the Internet; employed by the Internet user to gain access to Web sites. Examples: Internet Explorer or Netscape Communicator.

Bruzzone Market Research   a leading provider of custom and syndicated research data covering a broad range of advertising, including tracking studies, pretesting, posttesting, copytesting, and other methods.

bubble card   see *blister pack.*

bubble test   see *cartoon method.*

buckslip   in direct mail, a small insert contained in the mail package, offering additional information or calling attention to a special deal or incentive for the consumer to respond; so called because the insert is about the size of a dollar bill.

budget determination   see *affordable method, arbitrary method, competitive parity method, objective-and-task method, percentage-of-sales method,* and *unit-of-sales method.* See also *build-up approach to budgeting* and *top-down approach to budgeting.*

build-up approach to budgeting   a procedure for establishing the marketing communications or individual promotion element budget, such as advertising; involves first setting marketing communications objectives, then identifying the tasks required to accomplish the objectives and estimating the costs of the tasks, at which time the costs are totaled to arrive at the budget number. See also *objective-and-task method* and *top-down approach to budgeting.*

bulk discount   in print advertising, especially newspaper, decreasing rates given to advertisers as they use more space; e.g., a lower rate per column inch (or page) as the advertiser uses more inches (or pages). See also *bulk plan.*

bulk mailing a way of sending multiple copies of a publication, direct-mail letter, or other items through the postal system under a permit or precanceled stamps; certain requirements and restrictions apply as to number of pieces, weight, and preparation for mailing.

bulk plan in radio advertising, when an advertiser, often a retailer, contractually commits to buying a certain number of spots over an extended period, usually one year; same concept applies to television advertising. See also *bulk discount.*

bulk sales in print publications, large-quantity, reduced-price purchases of magazines or newspapers for redistribution; e.g., those bought and distributed by hotels or airlines.

bulldog edition the earliest edition of a newspaper, generally a big-city, large-circulation newspaper; followed by later editions, sometimes up to four total.

bulletin the traditional and largest standardized outdoor advertising format available; measures 14′ high × 48′ wide. Copy is done by hand-painting directly on the surface, vinyl lettering, computer techniques, or printing on paper. There are two types of bulletins: see *permanent bulletin* and *rotary bulletin.*

bundling the practice of selling two or more products or services together, but at a single price; e.g., personal computers are typically sold containing several software packages, a home improvement service may combine several renovation services and offer a single price to the homeowner, or two media may join together as an advertising package, such as AOL Time Warner and CBS combining and offering advertising time as a package. See also *cross-media advertising* and *multimedia buy.*

Bureau of Alcohol, Tobacco, and Firearms (BATF) the federal agency that regulates and controls all aspects of alcoholic beverages advertising, including the information that can appear in the advertising and what constitutes false and misleading advertising.

buried offer see *hidden offer.*

buried position in magazine or newspaper advertising, an advertisement placed among several others, reducing the likelihood of it being noticed or read.

Burke Day-After-Recall Test (Burke Test) see *ASI Recall Test.*

Burke, Inc. a leading market research organization, providing a vast array of research and analysis services for marketers and advertisers; work covers virtually all aspects of marketing and promotion, including product testing, pricing research, market segmentation, positioning studies, and many others. Provides both custom and syndicated research.

Burrelle's Information Services primarily consists of a published directory that features a comprehensive database of media information, including national and local print and broadcast data, as well electronic newspapers and magazines; service includes same-day monitoring and delivery of data on daily and nondaily newspapers, consumer and trade magazines, network and local TV, network radio, and the World Wide Web.

bursting scheduling the same commercial to run several times in a short period of time on the same television station; e.g., two or even three times during the same program or every thirty minutes in prime time.

bus wrap a form of out-of-home advertising in which a bus is wrapped with a high-quality vinyl adhesive material on which is imprinted an advertising message; see also *rolling billboard* and *car wrap.*

business advertising advertising directed at individuals who buy, use, or influence the purchase of goods and services in other businesses or organizations (often referred to as *industrial* goods and services or *organizational* goods and services); also known as *business-to-business advertising.* See also *trade advertising.*

business book see *business publication.*

business customers see *organizational buyers.*

business journal see *business publication.*

business magazine see *business publication.*

business market composed of the institutional buyers who purchase products and services for making other products and services, or for resale to other businesses; also called *organizational market.* See also *business marketing.*

business marketing all activities involved in marketing goods and services to organizations, groups, or individuals who purchase for reasons other than personal consumption, such as business and organizational customers who require goods and services to produce other goods and services for resale or to support their operations; also known as *business-to-business marketing*. Commonly called *B2B*. See also *business market*.

Business Marketing Association (BMA) the primary information and resources organization serving the business-to-business marketing industry; promotes best practices, fosters communications, and serves the information and networking needs of business-to-business marketers.

business media the wide variety of publications and other media directed to the trade, production, professional, executive or managerial, and institutional audience, as opposed to consumers; aimed at specialized business audiences. See also *business publication*.

business paper see *business publication*.

business press see *business media*.

business products products and services bought for use in running a business or an organization, i.e., not for personal consumption.

business publication a specialized business publication aimed at manufacturers and intermediaries who buy products and services for use in producing a product and those who buy and sell for resale, and other individuals who in some way are involved with the movement of goods through distribution channels; editorial matter (and advertising) is directed toward a specific industry, profession, or occupation. Term sometimes is used to denote a general category of magazines that target business readers, including *trade publications, industrial magazines,* and *professional journals.* Also referred to as a *trade publication, business* or *trade book, business* or *trade journal, business* or *trade magazine, business* or *trade paper,* and *industrial magazine.* See also *horizontal publication* and *vertical publication*.

Business Publication Audit (BPA) an independent, self-regulated auditing organization that provides verification of circulation, audience, and other data for business magazines (and a limited number of consumer publications), business newspapers, trade shows, Web site traffic, and other advertising-supported information providers; see also *Audit Bureau of Circulations (ABC)*.

business-to-business advertising see *business advertising*.

business-to-business agency a firm that specializes in representing and acting on behalf of companies that market their products to other businesses; sometimes referred to as a *high-tech agency*. See also *business marketing*.

business-to-business marketing see *business marketing*.

bus-o-rama a large illuminated sign that sits atop a bus and stretches the entire length of the bus.

buy see *media buy*.

buy detail report see *media buy sheet*.

buy sheet see *media buy sheet*.

buyback allowance payment by a manufacturer to a retailer to take its existing product off the retail shelf and replace it with a new product in the same space.

buyer any individual or organization that purchases products or services for personal or organizational use or for use by other people or organizations; generally referred to as the customer.

buying center those individuals in an organization, usually in the form of a committee, who participate in that organization's purchasing decisions, evaluating products and services, and deciding on a course of action; the individuals have roles that include *initiators, users, influencers, deciders, approvers, buyers,* and *gatekeepers*.

buying criteria the factors and standards used by the prospective purchaser of a product or service in evaluating choices and making a decision; also called *purchase criteria*.

buying decision any of the several judgments and choices a prospective buyer has to make during the consumer decision process; which brand to purchase, what features to buy, how many stores to visit in deciding what to buy, what store to buy from, or any of the many choices that must be made once the individual has decided to enter the marketplace for a product or service. Also called *purchase decision*. See also *buying criteria* and *buying influences*.

buying function in business products and markets, the purchasing of goods and services to be used in the operations of the business unit; an important responsibility at each level of the distribution channel and other organizational entities.

buying influences all the individuals who have any effect on a person's decision-making process and selection of a product or service.

buying loader see *dealer loader.*

Buying Power Index (BPI) a measurement of the relative buying power of cities, counties, states, and metropolitan areas; based on population, effective buying income, and total retail sales. A statistic reported in the annual *Survey of Buying Power,* compiled by *Sales and Marketing Management* magazine.

buying service see *media buying service.*

buying signal any verbal or nonverbal communication from a prospective customer that indicates he or she is strongly considering or is ready to purchase.

buzz marketing marketing tactics designed to create a stir or get people talking about a product or brand; see also *word-of-mouth advertising.*

BWP a magazine advertising rate card designation for a black-and-white, full-page advertisement; can also be expressed in other ways, such as 1pBW or B/WPg.

by-the-book marketing a marketing approach that relies on conventional wisdom and traditional proven practices, with the emphasis on tried-and-true, proven-over-time strategies and tactics; see also *on-the-edge marketing.*

C

CAA see *Creative Artists Agency.*

CAB see *Cablevision Advertising Bureau.*

CARU see *Children's Advertising Review Unit.*

CASIE see *Coalition for Advertising Supported Information and Entertainment.*

CASRO see *Council of American Survey Research Organizations.*

CATV see *cable television.*

CBBB see *Council of Better Business Bureaus.*

CDI see *Category Development Index.*

CLTV see *customer lifetime value.*

CMR see *Competitive Media Reporting.*

CMSA see *Consolidated Metropolitan Statistical Area.*

CPC see *cost-per-click.*

CPM see *cost-per-thousand.*

CPM-TA see *cost-per-thousand—target audience.*

CPO see *cost-per-order.*

CPP see *cost-per-point.*

CPV see *customer-perceived value.*

CRM see *customer relationship management.*

CTA see *clickthrough.*

CTR see *clickthrough rate.*

CUME see *cumulative audience.*

C County see *ABCD Counties.*

cablecasting see *cable television (CATV).*

Cable Communications Policy Act a 1984 amendment to the Communications Act of 1934, which included provisions aimed at promoting competition in the cable television industry, establishing regulatory guidelines while minimizing regulation that would severely restrict cable systems in their activities, and assuring that cable systems are responsive to the needs of the local communities; the act also restricted the cable systems' collection, maintenance, and dissemination of cable subscriber data. See also *Communications Act* and *Cable Television Consumer Protection and Competition Act.*

cable interconnect see *interconnect.*

cable network a television network of interconnected stations capable of broadcasting programs simultaneously, which is available only to subscribers to a cable service; see also *cable penetration, cable provider,* and *cable television,* as well as *network.*

cable penetration the number or percentage of households that subscribe to a cable television service; generally refers to a specific area.

cable provider see *cable system operator.*

cable system operator the organization that owns and maintains the cable television system in a particular community; local cable operators who pick up via satellite the signals transmitted by the cable network and redistribute the signals to cable subscribers. Also called *cable provider.*

cable television (CATV) a television delivery system in which the signals are transmitted via wires (cable) to subscriber households, rather than sending the signal through the air, as in the case of broadcast television; subscribers pay for the cable programming. Transmission of video programming to subscribers. Cable networks and stations also generate funds from advertisers. See also *advertiser-supported broadcasting, noncommercial broadcasting,* and *public broadcasting.*

Cable Television Consumer Protection and Competition Act a 1992 law designed to promote competition in the cable TV industry, foster better service for subscribers, and control subscription rates for the various services; enforced by the *Federal Communications Commission (FCC)*.

Cablevision Advertising Bureau (CAB) an industry association of cable networks, cable systems, and cable providers; promotes the use of national, regional, and local cable television as an advertising medium.

camera-ready art a finished advertisement, ready for printing exactly as it appears; any drawing, illustration, lettering, or other element in advertising that is suitable for photographic reproduction as is. See also *mechanical*.

campaign see *advertising campaign* and *marketing communications campaign*.

campaign flowchart a grid format or bar chart that shows the entire range of promotion activities over the duration of the marketing communications campaign; i.e., the timing of each activity's use in the campaign. On the vertical axis is a list of the specific activities (e.g., television advertising, magazine advertising, bus wrap, coupon program, road race sponsorship, festival sponsorship, publicity release, direct-mail letter, point-of-purchase displays, and so on), and on the horizontal axis are the months of the campaign broken into weeks, with a bar running from left to right indicating which activities will be used in each week of the campaign. An at-a-glance picture or summary of the entire promotion campaign schedule of activities. See also *media flowchart* and *work flowchart*.

campaign launch the formal introduction of a new advertising or promotion campaign.

campaign plan the blueprint for the design and implementation of a full-scale marketing communications program; identifies all tasks and rationales for every stage of the promotion plan. Components include: situation analysis, company snapshot, product review, competitive review, buyer analysis, existing promotion program, strengths and weaknesses, threats and opportunities, marketing goals, target market, promotion objectives and strategies, positioning and campaign theme, creative recommendations, media plan, sales promotion recommendations (consumer and trade), direct-marketing recommendations,

public relations recommendations, personal selling recommendations, campaign flowchart, measurement and evaluation, budget, and timetable.

campaign theme the major selling idea that serves as the central premise or foundation of a marketing communications campaign.

campaign tracking see *tracking study*.

cancellation period specified period of time during which a media contract may be terminated.

cancellation rate in magazine and newspaper advertising, the proportion of individuals who do not renew subscriptions; may refer to the proportion of advertisers who do not renew their advertising contracts or agreements with a media vehicle. Also may refer to the proportion of consumers who, after trying a particular product, do not repurchase it.

canned presentation a standard, all-purpose sales message or pitch, memorized by the salesperson for delivery to each potential buyer; the basic selling message may be modified as prospective customers or conditions warrant.

Cannes Lions to recognize superlative creative achievement in advertising, annual awards given in a worldwide competition for the best advertising each year; competition is held at the International Advertising Festival, Cannes, France.

cannibalization in a company's product line, the loss of sales of one item to another item within the same line; introduction of a new product sometimes results in the new product simply taking away sales from an existing product in the company's line, adding little or no extra sales.

capitalized billings an accounting adjustment designed to make fee billings comparable to media commission billings. To express fees as the equivalent of a 15% commission, multiply the fee by 6.667. Example: assume a $3,000 fee paid to the advertising agency by the advertiser, and the agency (or client) wants to determine what billings would be needed to produce the same $3,000 earnings as the fee; multiplying $3,000 by the 6.667 factor yields $20,000, or the amount of billings the agency would need to earn $3,000 under the 15% commission method of compensation. (For a 12% commission, use a factor of 8.333; for a 10% commission, use a factor of 10.0; and for an

8% commission, use a factor of 12.50.) Using a capitalized billings approach provides a basis for media revenue comparisons for agencies who operate on a variety of fee and commission arrangements.

capabilities presentation   see *credentials presentation.*

captain agency   see *agency of record (AOR).*

caption text   copy accompanying a photograph or an illustration in an advertisement; sometimes referred to as a *cutline.*

car card   an advertisement on the inside or outside of a bus, train, subway, or other public transportation vehicle; sometimes referred to as a *baby billboard.*

car wrap   a form of out-of-home advertising in which an automobile is wrapped with a high-quality vinyl adhesive material on which is imprinted an advertising message; see also *rolling billboard* and *bus wrap.*

card deck   a stack of advertisements on postcard-size units, each promoting a different product or service; entire collection is distributed as a group. The postcard is usually preaddressed for the customer to mail it back to the advertiser to request more information, place an order, or ask that some other action be taken.

card rate   the cost of advertising time or space, as quoted on the media vehicle's rate card; the basic full rate without the agency commission or special media discounts of any kind. Also called *base rate, gross rate, open rate, one-time rate,* and *transient rate.* See also *base rate, open rate, rate card, agency commission,* and *media discount.*

car-end poster   in transit advertising, an advertisement on the back of the vehicle.

carryover audience   see *holdover audience.*

carryover effect   the impact of an advertising or other promotion campaign or activity that lasts after the completion of the campaign.

cartoon method   in qualitative advertising research, a projective technique in which the respondent is shown a cartoon and asked to describe what is happening, the dialogue among the characters, what is being portrayed, and what thoughts come to mind; typically, the respondent is asked to fill in the words or thoughts of the character(s) in the cartoon. Similar to the picture response test. See also *word association test, sentence completion test, story completion test, third-person method,* and *picture response test,* as well as *qualitative research* and *projective research techniques.*

car-topper   an advertising display attached to the top of an automobile or some transit vehicle.

cash discount   a discount, usually 2 percent, offered by the media for prompt payment of invoices; more generally, any price reduction offered to buyers who pay their bills promptly.

cash refund offer   a sales promotion practice in which cash is offered to the consumer for submission of a mail-in request form, along with proof of purchase of the product.

cash sponsorship deal   a sponsorship that includes the advertiser providing cash to help defray the costs of staging an event, in return for special consideration such as mention in the event's advertising, program, or publicity releases.

cash syndication   a situation in which the syndicator, or owner of the program, provides *first-run* or *off-network syndication* television programs to local stations, which pay the syndicator a cash license fee for the right to air the show over a period of time; the advertising time is owned and sold by the local station. See also *barter syndication, cash-barter syndication, first-run syndication, off-network syndication, syndicator,* and *syndication.*

cash-barter syndication   a combination of *cash syndication* and *barter syndication,* in which the television station gives up commercial time and also pays a license fee for the right to broadcast syndicated programs; see also *barter syndication, cash syndication, first-run syndication, off-network syndication,* and *syndication.*

catalog   a book that identifies and describes products for sale by a manufacturer, distributor, or retailer; see also *catalog marketing.*

catalog buyer   in direct marketing, an individual who has made a purchase from a catalog.

catalog house   the marketer, i.e., seller, using a catalog as its major means of communicating its offering to prospective consumers.

catalog marketing   a direct-marketing method that involves a book containing descriptions of products available for sale, which is mailed to prospective customers, who place orders by telephone or by mail; see also *catalog.*

Category Development Index (CDI)   a measure of the relative sales strength of a particular product category in a specific market area of the United States. To calculate: divide the percentage of product category A's total U.S. sales in market X by the percentage of total U.S. population in market X, then multiply the result by 100 to get the index number. Especially useful, along with Brand Development Index (BDI), in deciding media allocations and how much advertising and other promotion effort to put into different market areas. See also *Brand Development Index (BDI).*

category exclusivity   in sponsorship marketing, a contractual agreement giving a sponsor the right to be the only company in its product category associated with the sponsored property; term may also apply to a similar arrangement given to an advertiser by any media vehicle.

category management   the supervision of and responsibility for all aspects of the marketing program for a particular type of product or line of products, as opposed to a specific brand; e.g., the salty snacks category for Frito-Lay. See also *brand management.*

category manager   in the advertiser's organization, the individual who coordinates and is responsible for the marketing of an entire group of related products or an entire product category, as opposed to a specific brand within that product category.

causal relationship   in marketing and advertising research, when it can be inferred that two variables are related in some way; e.g., when a point-of-purchase display results in an increase in sales during the display period, even though the price remains the same.

causal research   a type of research, with specific hypotheses, designed to determine exactly how one variable influences another to change; i.e., seeks to identify the reasons for a particular marketing or advertising phenomenon. For example: how an advertiser's side-by-side comparison of its product vs. another brand affects consumer perception of the product; or the effect on sales produced by an increase in advertising expenditures; or how a particular advertising appeal, tone, or execution format affects the consumer's reaction to an advertisement. Seeks

cause-and-effect relationships. See also *descriptive research* and *exploratory research.*

cause-related marketing   a public relations sponsorship-type activity in which the advertiser, for purposes of goodwill, aligns itself with a not-for-profit organization or program, generally contributing money (and sometimes people) to the program in exchange for the advertiser's name being promoted in connection with the cause; often takes the form of a portion-of-the-revenues contribution to the cause from the advertiser each time the advertiser's product is purchased. Often aimed at socially responsible consumers to motivate them to buy the advertiser's product as a result of the advertiser's pledge to donate part of the sales price to a specific cause. May be done to influence consumers to change their attitudes toward the company or its product. Also called *cause marketing.*

caveat emptor   the idea that the customer should bear the responsibility of determining the capability of a product or service and its ability to meet the customer's needs, and if an error in judgment is made, the consumer is the one to bear the burden; the opposite of the marketing concept. A Latin term meaning "let the buyer beware." See also *marketing concept.*

cease-and-desist order   a Federal Trade Commission order to an advertiser prohibiting further use of an advertisement or promotion practice considered by the FTC to be misleading or deceptive; may be issued if the advertiser refuses to sign a *consent decree.* See also *consent decree.*

celebrity endorsement   see *endorsement.*

census   in marketing and advertising research, the collection of data from all units in a particular population of interest (as opposed to collecting data from only a portion of the population); e.g., a survey of all advertising agencies that have an automobile account among their lists of clients. A complete count of a research *universe.* See also *universe* and *sample.*

center of influence   an actual customer or opinion leader whose actions are respected by others and who may influence their marketplace behavior; see also *opinion leader.*

center spread   a single advertisement that occupies two facing pages at the exact middle of a publication; also called a *double-page spread* or *double truck.* See also *two-page spread.*

central location in marketing and advertising research, a single site at which the research is conducted; e.g., a shopping center or a venue at which respondents are assembled.

cents-off deal a consumer sales promotion in which the consumer pays a price lower than the regular price; the amount of savings (i.e., cents-off) is imprinted on or affixed to the package; see also *price pack.*

certification mark a sign or symbol that identifies and guarantees the origin or quality of a particular product; owner may permit another party to use the mark in commerce; e.g., Teflon II is a certification mark owned by DuPont for its Teflon-coated cookware, and the cookware producers have DuPont's permission to use the mark in advertising the fact that their particular brand of cookware is made with Teflon. See also *trademark, service mark,* and *Lanham Act.*

chain a group of newspapers or magazines under single ownership or control; also may refer to a broadcast *network.*

chain break in broadcast network programming, the time during which a network allows an affiliate station to give a *station identification (ID);* often a 30-second break, consisting of a 10-second spot and a 20-second ID.

challenger see *market challenger.*

champion an individual with a great interest in an activity, process, or particular cause and who acts as a group's prime leader and mover in getting action; a passionate, action-oriented spokesperson for a particular matter or issue.

change agent an individual who has such a degree of influence and credibility, often greater than the marketer's advertising and promotion efforts, that he or she is a major force in getting consumers to change their purchasing and consumption behavior.

channel any medium or means by which an advertiser's message is sent to the receiver or target audience; e.g., magazines, television.

channel captain in the distribution channel, the organization that takes the lead role in directing, managing, and coordinating the activities of the intermediaries throughout the entire channel; acts as the arbitrator and facilitator for channel conflicts. Typically, the organization with the best combination of size, power, influence, respect, and ability to act as a mediator.

channel conflict in the distribution channel, disagreement between or among intermediaries as to objectives, responsibilities, expectations, or any marketing or nonmarketing matters relating to the conduct of business in the channel; see also *channel captain.*

channel grazing in television advertising, looking in on other channels and programming via remote control during the time a commercial is airing on the channel being watched; also called *channel surfing.*

channel length see *distribution channel length.*

channel management the marketer's activities involved in organizing, directing, and controlling the marketing efforts of the intermediaries in its distribution channel, with the purpose of developing and maintaining an efficient, effective, and smoothly functioning team of intermediaries.

channel of communications see *media.*

channel of distribution see *distribution channel.*

channel surfing see *channel grazing.*

charting the showing in out-of-home advertising, the process of determining individual unit locations in a particular market to maximize objectives; circulation is based on traffic volume in a specific market.

checkerboard programming in television, the most common method of scheduling programs in prime time, whereby a different program is offered in the exact same time period every night; as opposed to strip programming, which is the common scheduling approach for programs in all other *dayparts.* Also called *checkerboarding.* See also *strip programming, prime time,* and *dayparts.*

checking the process of confirming the actual appearance or airing of an advertisement or commercial; applies to all media.

checking copy formal evidence and verification that an advertisement did appear as scheduled; sent to the advertising agency and advertiser as confirmation. Also known as *advertiser's copy.* See also *affidavit of performance, tearsheet,* and *unpaid distribution.*

Child Protection Act a law passed in 1966 to extend labeling requirements to include dangerous toys and children's products, as well as all hazardous household products (not just those that are packaged, per the

Federal Hazardous Substances Labeling Act); also established standards for child-resistant packaging. See also *Federal Hazardous Substances Labeling Act.*

Child Protection and Toy Safety Act   a 1969 law regulating all aspects of toy safety, including development, monitoring, and enforcement of safety standards.

Children's Advertising Review Unit (CARU)   an organization devoted to promoting responsible advertising directed to children and to responding to public concerns; a part of the *National Advertising Review Council (NARC)* along with the *National Advertising Division (NAD),* this body performs the same type of work as the *NAD,* but specializes in monitoring, reviewing, and evaluating advertising directed at children under 12 years of age. Major concern is that advertising to the children be fair, truthful, accurate, and socially responsible, and in keeping with the council's self-regulatory *Guidelines for Children's Advertising.* See also *National Advertising Review Council (NARC), National Advertising Division (NAD),* and *Guidelines for Children's Advertising.*

Children's Television Act   a 1990 law designed to improve the quality of children's programming on broadcast television; establishes standards pertaining to the number of hours of core educational and informational programming each week, as well as encourages commercial time limits on children's programming. See also *Action for Children's Television (ACT).*

choice set   the short list of brands from which the consumer makes his or her final purchase decision, following elimination of some brands from the larger, *evoked set* (or *consideration set*); see also *evoked set.*

churn   customer loss; see *audience turnover.*

Cigarette Labeling Act   see *Federal Cigarette Labeling and Advertising Act.*

cinema advertising   advertising in movie theaters.

cinemads   commercials on the big screen in movie theaters, generally appearing before the feature attraction; often are made-for-TV-like ads, created specifically for movie theaters.

circular   a single-page advertisement mailed or hand-delivered; also called a *flyer.* See also *handbill.*

circulation   most commonly refers to distribution of a publication, but can apply to other media as well. In print, the number of copies of the publication that are distributed, on average, in its normal distribution period; e.g., the average number of newspapers distributed daily, or the average number of magazines distributed weekly. *Nonpaid circulation* refers to the number of copies distributed free of charge, as distinguished from *paid circulation.* In broadcast media, the number of households tuned to a station within a period of time; e.g., the number of households tuned to a particular television station at least once a day. In transit venues, the number of riders who have an opportunity to see a *car card* in an average day, week, or month. In outdoor venues, the number of people, based on traffic volume, who have an opportunity to see a billboard during a specific period of time, such as daily or weekly. Not to be confused with the term *audience.* See also *controlled circulation, nonpaid circulation, paid circulation,* and *qualified circulation.*

circulation audit   in print media, a complete accounting and analysis of every aspect of a publication's distribution, including methods of distribution, paid and nonpaid circulation, distribution outlets, and geographical distribution; see also *Audit Bureau of Circulations (ABC).*

circulation rate base   the guaranteed minimum number of copies of a publication that are sold with each issue; the basis for determining the advertising rate.

circulation waste   the number of individuals in an advertiser's audience who, though they have been reached by the paid message of the advertiser, are not customers or genuine prospects of the advertiser; commonly called *waste circulation.*

circus layout   in print advertising, a layout style consisting of a variety of font sizes and typefaces, illustrations, slanted copy and graphics, and any other means to set the advertisement apart from others and to make it entertaining; also called an *omnibus layout.*

city magazine   a consumer publication whose editorial and subject matter, as well as its audience focus, is centered around a particular locality, generally a metropolitan area or perhaps a region of a state.

city-zone circulation   in newspaper advertising, the number of newspapers distributed within a city's limits by the paper, as opposed to outlying or suburban areas.

claimed-recall score in television advertising research, a finding reported by a *day-after-recall test,* identifying the percentage of respondents who remember seeing the commercial in question; see also *related-recall score, day-after-recall test,* and *ASI Recall Test.*

claims what the advertising promises the product or service will do for the buyer and user; product-centered statements describing the product and the benefits to be gained by the buyer. See also *substantiation of claims.*

Claritas, Inc. a leading provider of comprehensive databases for a broad range of marketing and advertising applications, including strategic planning, channel development, analysis of customer behavior for target marketing efforts aimed at customer acquisition and retention, and measurement of marketing program performance.

class magazine a publication that reaches a select, upscale audience; as opposed to a publication with a large, mass circulation. See also *special-interest magazine.*

classified advertising advertising, set in small type, in newspapers or magazines that is arranged by category, such as automotive, employment, or housing, and which typically appears in the "classified section" of the publication; a text-only format; i.e., the ad is entirely copy. See also *classified display advertising.*

classified display advertising similar to standard classified advertising, except that it also includes photos, artwork, or special borders; see also *classified advertising.*

Clayton Antitrust Act a 1914 act passed to amend, clarify, and supplement the *Sherman Antitrust Act;* prohibited exclusive sales contracts, forcing dealers to accept other products in a seller's line, as well as local price-cutting to freeze out competitors. See also *Sherman Antitrust Act* and *Robinson-Patman Act.*

clearance in television or radio, the permission given to stations to air a particular network or syndicated program; from the individual station's viewpoint, a promise made to the network to carry a particular program.

click on the Internet, when a Web site visitor interacts with an advertisement, actually clicking on it to be headed toward the advertiser's destination; does not mean the visitor actually waits to fully arrive at the destination, but simply that the visitor started to go there. Also called a *hit.* See also *ad request.*

click rate the number of clicks on a Web site relative to the number of ad requests made by users; ratio is computed as clicks divided by ad requests. See also *ad request.*

click stream on the Internet, the series of pages viewed by a user during a single visit to a particular Web site.

clicks-and-mortar a business that has merged an online presence with its physical plant; e.g., a retailer that gives customers the opportunity to buy products online or at the physical store location. Also called *brick-and-click.* See also *bricks-and-mortar* and *online marketing.*

clickthrough on the Internet, the successful arrival of a user at an advertiser's Web site; also called *ad transfer* and *clickthrough to advertiser (CTA).*

clickthrough rate (CTR) in Internet advertising, the percentage of times that users respond to an advertisement by clicking on it and actually arriving at the advertiser's Web site.

client the individual, organization, or other entity for which the advertising agency or other promotion services specialist does its work; the entity with the product or service to be marketed or advertised; also called the *account* or, in some cases, the *sponsor.*

Clio Awards prizes given to recognize advertising creativity and excellence worldwide; the organization, through its awards competition, is dedicated to the advancement of advertising professionals and the entire industry.

clip art professionally prepared, preprinted drawings, images, and other artwork that can be purchased or are otherwise available for use in creating advertisements, brochures, and other printed matter; as opposed to artwork specially commissioned for the assignment at hand. The images come on glossy paper, and are ready to use simply by cutting the image from the paper. Also available in computer software packages and on the Internet.

clipping bureau see *clipping service.*

clipping service an organization that monitors many periodicals for advertisers on a contract basis, securing and forwarding to the advertiser copies of its publicity releases, mention of the advertiser in conjunction with an event or a particular issue, competitors' advertisements, or any other matter of interest to the advertiser. Also called a *clipping bureau*. See also *monitoring service.*

close   see *closing.*

close billboard   a brief announcement at the end of a broadcast program during which the sponsors are acknowledged; often in the form of "The preceding portion of this program has been brought to you by (sponsor's name)." See also *open billboard* and *middle billboard.*

close date   see *closing date.*

closed-end questions   in survey research, questions in which the alternative answers are listed and from which the respondent must choose an answer; i.e., respondents are provided with a predetermined list of possible answers from which they select their answer. For example, multiple-choice, true-false, or rating-scale questions. Also called *structured questions.* See also *open-end questions.*

closing   the stage of the personal selling process in which the sales representative asks the potential customer for the order; the stage at which the sale is completed or the commitment is received from the prospect. See also *prospecting, preapproach, approach, presentation, handling objections,* and *follow-up.*

closing date   the deadline for submitting advertising material in production-ready form to a publication or station in order for the advertising to appear in a specific issue or on a particular broadcast.

closure   a sale or other final action desired or aimed for by a direct marketer.

cluster   in marketing and advertising research, a specific group that may be considered homogeneous in terms of demographic or lifestyle characteristics as determined by the researcher; in television and radio advertising, a group of commercials for broadcast during the same break (i.e., a pod).

cluster sample   in survey research for marketing and advertising, a type of probability sample that uses a method of choosing respondents in which the population is divided into mutually exclusive groups (e.g., counties, city blocks), and then a random sample

is drawn of the groups to include in the survey; also called an *area sample.* See also *probability sample, simple random sample, stratified random sample, nonprobability sample,* and *survey method.*

clustering   in marketing and advertising research, identifying and grouping similar characteristics and patterns within various sets of data; see also *cluster.*

ClusterPLUS   a *geodemographic segmentation* system that enables very specific targeting of consumers according to the lifestyle characteristics of individuals in a specific neighborhood; consumer profiles are developed on the basis of socioeconomic factors (e.g., education, occupation, income) and life cycle stage (e.g., age, family structure), permitting a sharp snapshot of individuals and their consumer behavior patterns. A product of Donnelly Marketing Information Services (part of Dun & Bradstreet Corporation). See *geodemographic segmentation.*

clutter   the total number of advertisements competing for attention of the audience, usually mentioned in the context of excessive amounts of advertising; can refer to the number of ads appearing in a media vehicle, a particular medium, or the totality of all media with advertising vying for reader and viewer attention. In television and radio, all non-program content. See also *nonprogram material.*

clutter reels   in advertising research, videotapes containing several television commercials, including the one(s) being tested; used to determine a particular commercial's ability to stand out from the rest of the commercials, draw attention, and measure awareness and comprehension, i.e., cut through the *clutter.*

Coalition for Advertising Supported Information and Entertainment (CASIE)   an organization formed by the *American Association of Advertising Agencies (AAAA)* and the *Association of National Advertisers (ANA)* to promote electronic commerce and advertising; its mission includes activities and programs designed to encourage new media services, such as the Internet, to rely on advertising as a major source of funding, research and tracking consumer use of the new media, and proactive efforts with legislative and regulatory agencies in dealing with the evolving new media. See also *American Association of Advertising Agencies (AAAA)* and *Association of National Advertisers (ANA).*

coat-out in outdoor advertising, covering an advertising message with paint to prevent old copy from showing through; see also *bleed-through*.

cobranding a promotional effort in which two or more established, well-known brands join together for a special offer to the consumer, are mentioned in the same advertising or on the same package, or unite for some other joint effort; e.g., American Airlines places its logo on MasterCard and then awards free air mileage points each time the credit card is used, an advertisement proclaiming that the Budweiser racing team uses Goodyear tires on all its cars, or a Pillsbury cake mix package or advertisement identifying Hershey chocolate as a key ingredient. Sometimes referred to as *dual branding*.

code of ethics standards and guidelines established by industry associations and other organizations, governing operating procedures and behavior in the conduct of marketing, advertising, and other businesses and endeavors.

cognition in marketing, the mental thought process of interpreting and integrating information, generally from a variety of sources, including advertising and direct experience; see also *cognitive learning*.

cognitive consistency the tendency for individuals to act in a way that supports their attitudes and beliefs, being drawn to and reacting positively to stimuli that conform to and agree with those attitudes and beliefs, while rejecting those that do not; see also *selective perception*.

cognitive dissonance in marketing, the mental discomfort, anxiety, or tension experienced by an individual in the postdecision stage of the consumer decision process; the doubt or uneasiness arises from the consumer not being sure a particular marketplace decision or choice was the right one, given the alternatives. Most likely to occur with difficult or high-involvement decisions where the perceived risks or consequences of an action such as product choice are greatest. Essentially, the consumer questions the wisdom of his or her decision. See also *postdecision evaluation stage*.

cognitive learning theory the acquisition of knowledge resulting from an internal mental process of problem solving by the consumer in the course of making marketplace decisions; the process by which consumers acquire new information as they seek to make appropriate purchase decisions. A view of learning that focuses on thinking, reasoning, and understanding.

cognitive processing see *cognitive learning theory, cognitive responses,* and *information processing.*

cognitive responses thoughts consumers form in response to advertising and other marketing communications activities based on thinking, reasoning, and understanding; such thoughts occur during *information processing*. An individual's change in opinion, attitude, or behavior as a result of his or her exposure to information. See also *information processing*.

coincidental interview in marketing and advertising research, an interviewing method in which the respondent is questioned during the particular activity of interest, such as a television program, watching an event, or participating in a promotion; interviewing may be done by telephone or in person. See also *telephone coincidental*.

coined word a word consisting of an original combination of consonants and vowels, and often used for brand names; e.g., Kodak, Cheerios, Advil, Tabasco, Kleenex, or Scrabble.

collaborative marketing in advertising, projects or campaigns that require the teamwork of many advertising agency offices, often in distant locales.

collateral materials supplementary, nonmedia material for concurrent use with advertising and other promotion campaign elements, especially materials designed for dealer use; e.g., brochures, catalogs, videotapes, exhibits, sales kits; noncommissionable media used in an advertising or promotion campaign. Typically called *collateral*.

collateral services the additional services needed to prepare the key elements in a marketing communications plan, such as marketing research, package design, event sponsorship planning, print and broadcast production, consultants, and other services required to make the plan ready for execution.

column in newspaper advertising, the standard vertical unit of space; see also *column inch*.

column inch in newspaper advertising, a unit of space measuring one column wide by one inch deep; one inch deep equals 14 agate lines. In a broadsheet, or standard-size newspaper, a full-page advertisement measures 126 column inches (six columns wide by

21 inches deep). See also *Standard Advertising Unit (SAU), inch rate,* and *agate line.*

comarketing   a general term for a wide variety of activities and programs in which two or more organizations combine resources and efforts to pursue a common marketing or promotion objective; a partnership effort between or among manufacturers and retailers to advance the branding message of each organization. Examples: Black & Decker and Home Depot joining forces to promote power tools for a given period of time, thereby leveraging the equity of both the brand and the store; Procter & Gamble and Wal-Mart developing a spring cleaning promotion that features P & G cleaning products at reduced prices in Wal-Mart stores; or Subaru automobiles and Head USA ski-maker joining together for sponsorship of nationwide skiing clinics for women. Usually initiated by the manufacturer when it involves a retailer. Sometimes referred to as *cross-marketing, dual marketing, joint marketing, partnership marketing,* or *promotional partnership.*

combination method of agency compensation   a method of compensating an advertising agency in which payment is based on some combination of fee, commission, and/or results; most often, a combination of fee and commission. See also *fee method, commission method,* and *performance-based method.* Also see *agency commission* and *sliding rate.*

combination offer   in sales promotion, when two related products are packaged together and offered at a lower price than if each were sold separately; e.g., toothpaste and toothbrush offered as part of the same package.

combination package   see *copack.*

combination program   in sales promotion, the use of two or more techniques in combination with one another.

combination rate   a special discounted advertising rate offered when the advertiser buys space or time in two or more publications or stations owned by the same company; e.g., the rate paid by an advertiser for space in two newspapers under common ownership, which is a lower rate than for space in the individual newspapers bought separately.

command headline   a type of headline for an advertisement or a commercial in which there is a strong statement or order telling the audience to do something, to take action; e.g., "Trust your swing. Trust your clubs. Attack the course." (Cobra golf clubs) or "Start the new year on the right foot." (Spenco insoles). See also *headline,* as well as *benefit headline, curiosity headline, news-information headline,* and *question headline.*

commercial   a sponsor-paid advertising message that is broadcast on a television or radio station; the broadcast equivalent of a print advertisement. Also called an *announcement.* See also *advertisement.*

commercial break   in television or radio, a pause in a program to air an advertising message, i.e., a *commercial,* for a company's product or service, or for some other message. See also *pod.*

commercial code number   a group of numbers and letters used to identify a particular broadcast commercial as that of a specific advertiser, product, and advertising agency; also includes the title of the commercial, such as "Sandlot Baseball."

commercial impressions   see *gross impressions.*

commercial lead-in   in television or radio, an announcer's introduction of an advertising message; e.g., "There's a break in the action, so we'll have a few words from our sponsors."

commercial life   the length of time an advertisement continues to be used; the length of time a particular execution is judged to be effective.

commercial load   the amount of time (i.e., minutes) consumed by advertising during a particular television or radio program, or some other time period such as one hour; also can refer to the advertising time available (i.e., before it is sold) in a certain time period.

commercial minute   in television or radio, 60 seconds of advertising time.

commercial pod   see *pod.*

commercial pool   an advertiser's ready-at-any-time reservoir of television or radio commercials available for use as the occasion presents itself.

commercial protection   a broadcast media vehicle's guarantee to an advertiser that there will be no commercial for a competing product within a specified time (e.g., 10 minutes) of the airing of the advertiser's commercial; see also *competitive separation* and *piggyback commercial.*

commercial retention rate in television and radio advertising, the extent to which a program's audience stays tuned to that station during commercial breaks and is therefore exposed to the advertising; see also *ad pod rating.*

commercial sign in outdoor advertising, structures on roofs or walls of buildings such as business establishments or factories to identify that particular business; privately owned by the business.

commercial speech speech that has as its goal some sort of transaction or action between a seller and a buyer, i.e., advertising; the First Amendment offers some protection to commercial speech as long as it is truthful. Examples of allowable commercial speech based on challenges in various states ultimately resolved by the Supreme Court: advertising by or for public utilities, gambling casinos, prescription drug prices, alcoholic beverage prices, or legal services.

commercialization the eighth and final stage of the new-product development process, in which the marketing plan is finalized based on the market test and the product is rolled out to select markets; see also *new-product development process, idea generation, idea screening, concept testing, market evaluation, product development, marketing plan,* and *market testing.* Also see *roll-out.*

commission method of agency compensation payment to the advertising agency from the advertising media vehicle as compensation for the agency placing its client's advertising with that vehicle; an agency compensation method based on the amount of media space or time purchased for the advertiser. Traditionally, 15 percent. See also *fee method, combination method,* and *performance-based method.* Also see *agency commission* and *sliding rate.*

commissionable media advertising media that pay a commission to an advertising agency for buying advertising space or time with them; e.g., television, radio, magazines, newspapers, outdoor, transit, and other traditional media. See also *agency commission* and *noncommissionable media.*

commodity a product perceived to be essentially the same regardless of brand, due to lack of significant differentiation among competing brands.

communicability the extent to which a product's or service's features benefits can be clearly and effectively described to the potential customer or target market.

communications oral, written, visual, or sensory information that travels between a sender and a receiver; the sending and receiving of messages.

Communications Act the 1934 federal act that established the *Federal Communications Commission (FCC).*

communications audit a comprehensive and systematic review and appraisal of a firm's or organization's entire marketing communications program, its organization, activities, strategies, and people; also referred to as a *promotion audit.*

communications channel the particular means or route by which a marketer or advertiser sends a message to its target audience; e.g., radio, magazine, billboard, direct mail, or personal selling. See also *media.*

communications effect of advertising the extent to which the consumer is influenced by an advertiser's message; see also *sales effect of advertising.*

communications-effect research measurement of the effectiveness of advertising on consumers; determination of whether the intended message got through to the consumer. See also *copytesting.*

communications mix the components of an organization's marketing communications program—advertising, sales promotion, public relations, direct marketing, and personal selling—and the way in which they are blended together to form an integrated plan; the particular combination of promotion elements and activities used by a company to pursue its communications and marketing objectives. See also *integrated marketing communications.*

communications objectives in advertising and promotion, an organization's campaign goals, such as to achieve a particular level of consumer awareness, influence attitudes and opinions, create or change an image, increase knowledge, or create or change preferences or purchase intentions.

communications plan a formal blueprint outlining an organization's situation analysis, budget, objectives, communications strategies, implementation guidelines, and measurement and control systems for the communications part of the marketing effort for a particular product or service; an action plan for all the components and activities needed to make a firm's *promotion plan* successful. Also referred to as a *promotion plan.*

communications platform   see *copy platform.*

communications satellite   a space vehicle deployed to receive television and radio signals and transmit those signals back to Earth.

communications task   the job of advertising, such as creating awareness, comprehension, conviction, or action; see also *DAGMAR.*

communications test   in advertising research, pretesting a message to determine if it is communicating the intended points.

communications vehicle   see *media vehicle.*

community marketing   see *municipal marketing.*

community newspaper   a newspaper published and circulated in a local area, such as a town or small group of contiguous towns; usually a weekly publication.

community-access television programming   see *public access* and *public-access channel.*

commuter clock   a rapid transit terminal poster or sign with a built-in clock; measures approximately 21″ high × 46″ wide. See also *terminal poster.*

comp   see *comprehensive layout.*

company ambassador   an individual appearing as a spokesperson or representative on behalf of a particular company or organization as part of the marketing and promotion program, particularly in the role of promotion goodwill; e.g., Tiger Woods for Buick or Michael Jordan for Nike. Title and role as a true ambassador often reserved for those individuals perceived by the audience as extraordinary in their field of endeavor, and who are believable, trustworthy, and of impeccable character. Same principle as *product ambassador.* See also *goodwill, spokesperson,* and *product ambassador.*

company magazine   see *house publication.*

comparison advertising   advertising in which the advertiser compares its product or service to a competitor's offering, either by direct comparison of attributes (naming the competitor) or indirect comparison (implying the identity of the rival); generally used by an advertiser to claim superiority over one or more competitors. Also referred to as *attack advertising* or *comparative advertising.*

comparison format   in advertising, a creative *execution format* featuring a side-by-side evaluation of one product against another; e.g., a Progresso chicken noodle soup commercial making a direct comparison with Campbell's chicken noodle soup, a Total cereal commercial showing how it delivers more vitamins per serving than does Kellogg's or Quaker products, a commercial comparing Advil's pain-relief effectiveness against Tylenol, or a Ford pickup truck advertisement showing its features in a side-by-side comparison with Chevrolet. See also *straightforward factual, news, demonstration, problem-solution, slice-of-life, dramatization, symbolic association, fantasy, animation, still-life, humor, spokesperson,* and *testimonial formats.* See also *comparison advertising.*

comparison advertising guidelines   see *Guidelines for Comparison Advertising.*

compensation plan   see *agency compensation method.*

compensatory decision rule   a decision rule in which the consumer, choosing between two or more alternatives, evaluates each brand on each relevant attribute and then chooses the brand that offers the best overall score; criteria are evaluated separately and then combined, so that a brand's favorable attributes or strengths can offset its shortcomings and unfavorable aspects or weaknesses when compared with competing brand alternatives. Also called *compensatory model.* See also *noncompensatory decision rule, lexicographic decision rule, consumer decision rules,* and *evoked set.*

competitive advantage   the enduring superiority a product or a company has over another; originates from a variety of factors, such as product features, company resources, dealer network, or advertising and promotion programs. The degree to which a firm's marketing mix or offering is perceived as better than that of a competitor. Also referred to as *differential advantage* or *relative advantage.*

competitive advertising   see *persuasive advertising.*

competitive barriers   the factors and conditions that make it difficult for an organization, once in operation, to effectively compete or even hold its own in an industry; include, among several others, pricing tactics of competitors, large expenditures for advertising, extensive sales promotion methods, and rapid innovation. See also *barriers to entry.*

competitive check   monitoring and analysis of the advertising levels and scheduling patterns of competitors; generally done using syndicated data, such as that provided by *Competitive Media Reporting (CMR), Broadcast Advertising Reports (BAR),* and other services. See also *Competitive Media Reporting (CMR), Broadcast Advertising Reports (BAR),* and *Leading National Advertisers (LNA).*

competitive environment   the number, types, and methods of competitors and the way they conduct their businesses.

competitive intelligence   the broad range of information an organization has that pertains to its market competitors.

Competitive Media Reporting (CMR)   the premier provider of advertising expenditure data and intelligence used by advertisers, advertising agencies, and the media; collects and disseminates advertising expenditures on network TV, network cable TV, spot TV, nationally syndicated TV, the Internet, consumer magazines, business magazines, international magazines, Sunday magazines, outdoor advertising, national newspapers, local newspapers, national radio, national spot radio, and local spot radio.

competitive parity method   a method of setting the advertising or promotion budget by matching the expenditures of competitors, either by dollar amount or rate of spending; a top-down approach to budgeting. See also *affordable method, arbitrary method, objective-and-task method, percentage-of-sales method,* and *unit-of-sales method.* See also *build-up approach to budgeting* and *top-down approach to budgeting.*

competitive positioning   the process of establishing a distinctive place in the minds of consumers, relative to the competition; see also *positioning.*

competitive report   a compilation of media spending and/or media usage statistics of a firm's competitors; generally broken down by individual brands.

competitive separation   the amount of space or time between advertisements or commercials for competing products; in a magazine, for example, the number of pages separating advertisements for Goodyear and Michelin automobile tires or, on television, the number of minutes elapsing between commercials for Bud Light and Coors Light beers. See also *commercial protection, piggyback commercial, product protection,* and *separation.*

competitor analysis   a complete examination and evaluation of all aspects of the important competitors, both current and potential, with an advertiser's product or service, their strengths and weaknesses, the threats they pose, and their vulnerabilities; an important part of the preliminary investigation that precedes development of a marketing communications plan. See also *situation analysis.*

competitor positioning   see *positioning by competitor.*

competitor repositioning   a marketer's strategy of getting consumers to change their attitudes and beliefs about a competitor's product; e.g., an attempt to alter consumers' strongly positive perceptions about the quality, value, or others claims of a competing brand. See also *positioning* and *repositioning.*

compiled list   a direct-mail list that has been assembled and organized by a source other than the advertiser or user; e.g., a readily available list of automobile owners, appliance stores, florists, recent home buyers, or marathon runners. See also *list compiler* and *list rental.*

complementary products   goods that are consumed or used together and that are normally demanded together; the price of one complement and the demand for the other have an inverse relationship; e.g., an increase in the price of one results in the decrease of demand for the other. Examples: cameras and film, VCRs and videotape cassettes, fountain pens and ink, hot dogs and hot dog buns. Often bundled for sales promotion programs. See also *substitute products, independent products,* and *bundling.*

completion technique   see *sentence completion test.*

complex message   an advertising or promotional message that is decidedly difficult for an individual to absorb and comprehend; often cannot be fully understood in just one exposure.

complex problem solving   see *extensive problem solving.*

complimentary copy   in print publications, a copy of a magazine or newspaper sent as a courtesy to advertisers, agencies, prospects, or anyone else deemed worthy by the publisher; see also *exchange copy.*

component in direct mail, any one of the elements in the package; e.g., sales letter, reply card, order form. See also *component test.*

component test in direct mail, a test of the effectiveness of an element in the package; e.g., measuring the results obtained with one sales letter vs. another, one incentive vs. another, or the addition or removal of an element such as a reply card or an incentive. See also *component.*

composite of sales force opinion a sales forecasting method that is based on information provided by members of the sales force; each salesperson estimates future product sales in his or her territory, with the individual estimates then combined to arrive at an overall *sales forecast.* See also *sales forecast, expert opinion, jury of executive opinion, test marketing, market potential,* and *sales potential.*

composition the demographic makeup of an audience.

comprehension a cognitive process of interpreting and understanding an advertiser's message.

comprehension test in advertising research, an effectiveness test to determine whether or not the advertisement or commercial communicated the intended message, i.e., whether or not the message "got through."

comprehensive see *comprehensive layout.*

comprehensive layout in the layout development process, a complete layout of a print advertisement, with all elements in their final places to show exactly what the finished ad will look like; usually computer-generated, it is intended as a true representation of the ad for the advertiser to evaluate just prior to producing the *mechanical* that will be sent to the printer. Commonly called a *comp.* See also *layout development process, thumbnail, rough layout,* and *mechanical.*

compressed advertising message in broadcast advertising; a commercial that is a shorter version of another commercial; e.g., a :60 reduced to a :30 spot. See also *resizing.*

compression a questionable practice by which a local television station, using what is called a "time machine," takes a live program and shrinks its content

by about 30 seconds every half hour (through a process of micro-editing done by the time machine), to permit extra commercial time and, therefore, additional advertising revenue for the station; since it occurs in real time and the time machine edits and eliminates meaningless video frames, the viewer cannot detect any loss of program content. A highly complex process, and very questionable from an ethical viewpoint.

computer clip art see *clip art.*

concave response curve a model of the relationship between advertising expenditures and sales, in which the effects of advertising expenditures follow the law of diminishing returns; as advertising outlays increase, incremental sales decrease; i.e., the initial outlays are most effective, but are followed by diminishing returns. When plotted on a graph, advertising expenditures are on the "x" axis, with sales on the "y" axis. See also *S-shaped response curve.*

concentrated marketing a marketing strategy whereby the firm's efforts focus on providing one or more products to a single market segment; see *differentiated marketing* and *mass marketing.*

concentrated media mix a media strategy of allocating an advertiser's entire media budget to one particular medium, such as radio; may also apply to placing all media dollars in one specific media vehicle, such as a particular magazine. See also *varied media mix.*

concept the underlying idea of a product or service, as well as the idea upon which the advertising is based; see also *concept statement* and *concept testing.*

concept reel in television advertising planning, an extra-long (e.g., 5-minute) commercial from which selected parts are taken, culminating in a :30 spot; used to get the feel of the commercial and have the opportunity to piece together the most appropriate parts, resulting in a "best" approach.

concept statement a written statement, sometimes including a visual element, of an idea underlying a product or service and describing its features and benefits; used for presentation to consumers to obtain their reaction prior to development of the product or service. Statement that describes and explains in consumer terms a product or advertising that does not yet exist in physical form. Same principle applies to getting reaction from consumers about advertising and other promotion activities. See also *concept testing*.

concept testing   a research method that calls for asking a representative sample of target customers to indicate their interest in a new product idea or "concept," even though the product does not exist in physical form; developmental research often done to determine the best appeals to use in advertising messages, using *focus groups*. In advertising usage, a commercial or advertisement may exist in rough form and the respondent is asked for an opinion or reaction to the idea underlying the execution, i.e., testing to measure the effectiveness of rough ideas prior to finalizing them (the concept may be presented verbally or in the form of a rough ad). The third stage of the new-product development process. See also *concept statement, new-product development process, idea generation, idea screening, market evaluation, product development, marketing plan, market testing,* and *commercialization.*

conceptualization   see *visualization.*

conclusive research   in marketing and advertising research, an approach aimed at evaluating different courses of action to find the best one.

conditioned response   automatic response to a given stimulus or situation as a result of repeated exposure.

conditioning theory   a theory of consumer behavior maintaining that learning is achieved through a process of trial and error; also called *stimulus-response theory.* See also *cognitive learning theory.*

confirmation   a formal statement given to an advertising agency and/or an advertiser by a media vehicle marking the vehicle's receipt and acceptance of an order for a commercial, advertisement, or media schedule.

conflicting accounts   see *account conflict.*

consent decree (order)   in situations where the Federal Trade Commission (FTC) believes a company is engaging in an unfair or deceptive practice, such as in their advertising, a legally binding document initiated by the FTC and signed by the advertiser, who voluntarily agrees to stop the advertising in question, with no admission of guilt, wrongdoing, or violation of any law, and who agrees to take steps to remedy the situation. See also *cease-and-desist order.*

consideration set   see *evoked set.*

Consolidated Metropolitan Statistical Area (CMSA)   in metropolitan areas where Primary Metropolitan Statistical Areas (PMSAs) are defined, the larger area of which the PMSAs are components; a definition of the U.S. Office of Management and Budget (OMB). See also *Metropolitan Area (MA), Metropolitan Statistical Area (MSA),* and *Primary Metropolitan Statistical Area (PMSA).*

consumer   the individuals and families who use the advertiser's products and services; also those individuals who influence other people's buying and consumption behavior.

consumer activists   groups or individuals who are champions of consumer rights and who take active and vigorous measures to get their message heard on any given issue; the people who believe so strongly about a particular consumer issue or cause that they organize formal movements and actions such as visits to legislative bodies, appearances on television, press releases, interviews, and letter-writing campaigns to get their message heard. See also *consumer advocates* and *consumerism.*

consumer advertising   advertising aimed at people who are the ultimate consumers of a product or service or who buy for someone else or in some way influence the purchase of consumer products and services.

consumer advocates   groups or individuals who are champions of consumer rights, doing their own research into questionable practices by marketers and actively investigating complaints received from consumers, to the point of requesting the marketer or advertiser to discontinue a practice if it is deemed objectionable; in the event of a marketer's noncompliance, the efforts often include a formal and methodical application of public criticism and pressure on the offending marketer. See also *consumer activists* and *consumerism.*

Consumer Affairs   see *Office of Consumer Affairs.*

consumer behavior   generally encompassing all the activities involved in and related to an individual's quest for need-satisfying products and services for personal or household use; see also *consumer decision process.*

Consumer Credit Protection Act   a law passed in 1968 to require full and complete disclosure of all terms and rates pertaining to credit and loans; see also *Fair Credit Reporting Act.*

consumer deal   a general term referring to any of a number of sales promotion activities that involve an incentive or a special offer beyond the usual terms of sale to encourage the consumer to purchase the product; e.g., see *bonus pack* and *cash refund offer.*

consumer decision process   a series of stages through which the consumer proceeds in making marketplace decisions, considering products and services for purchase; stages include *problem recognition, search for information, evaluation of information, the decision to purchase or not purchase,* and *post-decision evaluation.* See also *complex decision making, limited decision making,* and *routine decision making.* Also see *high-involvement decision making* and *low-involvement decision making.*

consumer decision rules   guidelines and procedures followed by consumers as they make marketplace decisions; usually established to reduce risks associated with purchasing behavior. Different decision rules for different purchasing decisions. See also *compensatory decision rule, noncompensatory decision rule, lexicographic decision rule,* and *evoked set.*

Consumer Goods Pricing Act   a federal law, passed in 1975, that repealed the Miller-Tydings Act (1937), which had allowed resale price maintenance contracts and agreements between manufacturers and resellers (i.e., *fair trade*); rendered resale price maintenance arrangements illegal. See also *fair trade* and *Miller-Tydings Act.*

consumer information networks   systems and organizations that exist for the dissemination and exchange of a wide range of marketing information relevant to consumers; most are formal entities and require membership.

consumer jury   a group of consumers from whom an advertiser seeks opinions and thoughts about advertising and other promotional elements, especially in pretesting; usually used on a special-purpose or single-case basis (i.e., *ad hoc* basis), as opposed to a permanent basis. See also *pretesting* and *consumer panel.*

consumer magazine   a publication aimed at people who buy products and services for personal or family use; sometimes referred to as a general-circulation or general-interest magazine, though such reference is inaccurate, since the publication can certainly be a special-interest magazine. See also *trade publication, general-circulation, magazine, special-interest magazine,* and *general-interest magazine.*

consumer market   the totality of individuals and households who buy or are genuine prospects to buy products and services for their own use or someone else's personal use; the people who go into the marketplace to satisfy their own specific needs or to help others do the same.

consumer marketing   marketing programs and activities directed at consumers who are making marketplace decision about products and services for personal consumption; often referred to as *B2C.* See also *business marketing, industrial marketing,* or *organizational marketing.*

consumer panel   a group of individuals, families, or households carefully recruited, retained, and monitored to provide an advertiser with continuous data, information, and opinions on marketing matters such as those relating to purchase behavior, consumption patterns, and advertising and promotion programs; typically kept intact over an extended period of time, sometimes for as long as three years. A type of *longitudinal research.* Often referred to as a *panel.* See also *longitudinal research.*

consumer problem solving   see *consumer decision process.*

consumer products   products or services purchased by individual consumers for personal or family use or consumption; see also *consumer products classification system.*

consumer products classification system   an arrangement of consumer products in groups based on how people buy the products; see also *convenience products, shopping products, specialty products,* and *unsought products.*

Consumer Products Safety Act   a 1972 law stating that the public should be protected against unreasonable risk of injury associated with consumer products, that consumers should be assisted in their evaluation of the comparative safety of products, and that there should be uniform safety standards for consumer goods; established the *Consumer Products Safety Commission.* See also *Consumer Products Safety Commission.*

Consumer Products Safety Commission the independent federal regulatory agency responsible for monitoring all aspects of consumer product safety and enforcing the provisions of the *Consumer Products Safety Act;* has the power to recall products suspected to be unsafe. See also *Consumer Products Safety Act.*

consumer profile a description of the buying habits and the demographic, geographic, psychographic, and behavioral characteristics of the individuals or households who are users or prospective users of a product; also called *user profile.* See also *audience profile, demographic segmentation, geographic segmentation, psychographic segmentation,* and *behavioristic segmentation.*

consumer protection the concept of safeguarding consumers' interests as they make marketplace decisions; includes initiatives and measures to assure that products are safe, advertising and selling messages are truthful and free from deception, prices do not contain hidden costs, relevant information is not withheld, products deliver the promised performance, and other assurances to enable the consumer to make informed choices, and where there is a wrong, to make certain a procedure exists to address and resolve the problem.

consumer research a wide variety of designs, methodologies, and techniques used to investigate and analyze buyer behavior; see also *consumer research process.*

consumer research process the several stages of the organized study of buyer behavior; generally consists of setting objectives, collecting secondary data, preparing the research design and methodology, collecting primary data, analyzing the data, and producing a formal report that focuses on the findings and recommendations for action.

consumer risk-taking see *risk-taking.*

consumer sales promotion short-term incentives directed at people who purchase products and services for personal consumption; e.g., coupons, sampling, premiums, deals. See also *trade sales promotion* and *sales promotion.*

consumer satisfaction the extent of an individual's fulfillment arising from the purchase and use of a product; the consumer's goal in purchase behavior. Based on his or her evaluation of the usage experience.

consumer socialization process the manner in which an individual becomes a skillful consumer, capable of making intelligent and informed marketplace decisions.

consumer survey survey research done on consumers; see also *dealer survey.*

consumerism refers to consumers' attempts, often acting as a group, to make known their position, exert power, and strongly influence an organization's marketing activities; actions aimed at preserving the rights of the buying and consuming public. See also *consumer advocates.*

container premium in promotional marketing, a special container (other than the product's standard package) that is reusable for another purpose or in a different form after its contents are consumed; e.g., a grape jelly container or package designed to be used as a drinking glass after the contents are depleted. See also *premium.*

content tie-in see *convergence.*

contest a sales promotion activity in which participants compete for prizes or money, with entries judged on the basis of skill; audience may be consumers or trade members. See also *game* and *sweepstakes.*

contiguity in broadcasting, the practice of showing two back-to-back programs without a break for commercials; more common in radio; see also *contiguity rate.*

contiguity rate in television or radio advertising, a reduced rate for an advertiser who sponsors two or more successive programs on the same station.

continuity in advertising media scheduling, the particular pattern or manner in which the advertising appears, i.e., the timing of the media insertions; see also *continuous scheduling, flighting,* and *pulsing.*

continuity discount see *frequency discount.*

continuity program a sales promotion activity used by the marketer to encourage consumers to make repeat purchases of a product by offering additional savings, premiums, or other values with the continuing purchases; see also *frequency program.*

continuous scheduling a pattern of media scheduling in which advertising runs at a steady, uninterrupted level over the duration of the campaign, and with little or no variation in pressure. See also *media scheduling, flighting,* and *pulsing.*

contract rate   a special rate offered by print media for advertisers who sign a contract to place a certain number of ads or use a certain amount of space during a given period of time; commonly offered by newspapers to local advertisers. See also *earned rate* and *short rate.*

contractual VMS   a vertical marketing system (VMS) in which independent distribution channel members at all stages work together by formal contractual commitment; channel members benefit from more efficient and effective marketing programs than could be achieved acting alone. See also *vertical marketing system (VMS), corporate VMS, administered VMS, conventional marketing system, horizontal marketing system,* and *hybrid marketing system.*

contrast   in advertising design and layout, the principle of presenting the advertisement's elements in different styles, sizes, shapes, and colors to help the ad stand out among other ads and to make it eye-catching and out-of-the-ordinary; usually, an attempt to cut through the *clutter.* See also *clutter, balance, emphasis, flow, gaze motion, harmony,* and *unity.*

contribution margin   the difference between a product's selling price to the consumer and the variable cost of the product; i.e., difference between a product's total revenue and its total variable cost, or what the product contributes to fixed cost. See also *fixed costs* and *variable costs.* Also see *break-even point (BEP).*

controllables   those elements and aspects of the *marketing mix* over which the marketing manager has full command and control; i.e., product, price, distribution, promotion. See also *uncontrollables* and *marketing mix.*

controlled circulation   free copies of publications, usually business magazines or newspapers, that go to a select list of qualified recipients the publisher believes are important, especially those in a position to influence buying decisions about the advertised products; see also *circulation, nonpaid circulation, paid circulation,* and *qualified circulation.*

convenience products   consumer products that the customer generally purchases frequently, with a minimum of time and effort, and that are usually relatively inexpensive; see also *consumer products*

classification system, shopping products, specialty products,* and *unsought products.*

convenience sample   in survey research for marketing and advertising, a type of nonprobability sample in which respondents are chosen by virtue of their accessibility and the ease with which they can be contacted; see also *nonprobability sample, judgment sample, quota sample, probability sample,* and *survey method.*

convenience store   a small retail store that carries a limited line of convenience-type goods, and is open seven days per week.

conventional marketing system   a distribution channel setup in which the various channel members, manufacturers, wholesalers, and retailers make little or no effort to cooperate with each other or to coordinate efforts; typically results in each channel member doing what it considers best for itself without regard to the other members or the system as a whole. See also *vertical marketing system (VMS), corporate VMS, contractual VMS, administered VMS, horizontal marketing system,* and *hybrid marketing system.*

convergence   in television, the practice of blending marketing messages into media content via product placement, reference to a company or brand, or any other method that makes the marketer's message an integral part of the program; essentially, an ultra form of product placement, one carried beyond the simple placement of the product in a scene. Also called *content tie-in* and *product immersion.* See also *product placement.*

cookie   a data file downloaded to a person's computer when he or she visits a particular Web site; the data file allows the Web site to track information on the user, such as the sites or pages he or she visits and the date of the most recent visit to a given site or page.

co-op   see *cooperative advertising.*

cooperative advertising   a joint advertising effort in which the cost is shared, typically on an equal basis, by the parties involved, such as a manufacturer, distributor, dealer, retailer, vendor, or supplier. For example, a manufacturer and retailer (*vertical cooperative advertising*) or a group of businesses related by the products they sell or by common interests (*horizontal cooperative advertising*). Manufacturer or industry association (in the case of *horizontal cooperative advertising*) usually provides the advertisements or commercials. Common to all media. Often called *co-op advertising* or just *co-op.* See also *horizontal cooperative advertising, vertical cooperative advertising,* and *cooperative advertising kit.* Also see *vendor support program.*

cooperative advertising kit a package of materials provided by a manufacturer or industry association to its partners in a cooperative advertising program; includes ready-to-use newspaper and magazine advertisements, television commercials, radio scripts, direct-mail pieces, brochures, sales promotion materials, participation guidelines, procedures for ordering materials, reimbursement guidelines and procedures, and other information relevant to making the joint advertising and promotion effort work smoothly and successfully. See also *cooperative advertising, horizontal cooperative advertising,* and *vertical cooperative advertising.*

cooperative mailing a promotional mailing in which several noncompeting advertisers targeting the same audience enclose materials in the same envelope on a shared-cost basis; e.g., several companies targeting the "do-it-yourself" home repairs market, each with a different product. Also called *direct-mail co-op, group mailing,* or *shared mailing.*

cooperative program a television or radio network broadcast that is sold on a local basis and is sponsored by both national and local advertisers; e.g., *The Tonight Show.* See also *network cooperative program.*

copack a sales promotion technique in which two complementary products are physically packaged together and priced as one unit; e.g., shampoo with conditioner or saline solution with daily cleaner for contact lenses.

copromotion see *tie-in promotion.*

copy the words, including headline and message, that comprise an advertisement or a commercial; see also *body copy.*

copy approach the manner in which the advertising copy delivers the message to the target audience; e.g., emphasis on facts or heavy use of emotion. Also called *copy style.* See also *copy slant, copy platform,* and *tone.*

copy area in out-of-home advertising, the viewing area or space available on an outdoor unit for placement of copy, illustration, or other display element.

copy platform a written statement, based on research and insight, that guides the creative team in developing an advertisement, providing direction and focus for what the ad will say and how the message will be executed, with a description of the target audience, key benefit, product features that are promised to the user, support, reassurance, and tone; an outline of the basic ideas that guide the creation of an advertisement. Also called the *creative brief* or *creative strategy statement.*

copy points the specific selling points or themes in a product's advertising.

copy research in advertising research, the review, analysis, and evaluation of an advertising message; see also *copytesting.*

copy slant the particular approach or perspective used in presenting the benefits, support, claims, and promises in an advertising message; see also *copy platform, copy approach,* and *tone.*

copy style see *copy approach.*

copy thrust see *copy platform.*

copycat marketer a marketer whose marketing activities, techniques, and programs essentially are carbon copies of others in the industry, showing very little originality or inventiveness.

copyfitting in print advertising, the process of estimating the amount of space the copy will take once it is set in type.

copy-heavy ad an advertisement dominated by the amount of copy; also called a *heavy-copy ad.*

copyright legal protection available to the author or owner of an original work, such as a literary, artistic, dramatic, or musical work, preventing others from using it without permission; per the *Library of Congress,* the owner has exclusive rights to print or reproduce the material for his or her lifetime, and the rights do not revert to the public domain until 50 years following the person's death. Only advertising that contains original copy or artwork can be copyrighted, but slogans and common symbols and designs cannot be protected. The vast majority of advertising is not copyrighted. See also *Library of Congress.*

copytesting in advertising research, a variety of procedures and measures used to determine the effectiveness of advertisements; measurement of the extent to which an advertisement performs well, i.e., the extent to which it is received, understood, and responded to in the way desired by the advertiser. Also referred to as *communications-effect research.* See also *message research, PACT, pretesting,* and *posttesting.*

copywriter the individual at the advertising agency who helps formulate the ideas for the advertising message and then writes the words (copy) for an advertisement or a commercial.

copywriter's rough an initial version of the text that will eventually appear in an advertisement or commercial that provides a basic idea of the style and manner of presentation; submitted to account management to get approval that the text is "on strategy" and will meet expectations.

copywriting the process of developing an action-inducing message about a product, service, idea, or whatever is being sold.

core product the advantages and benefits offered by a product; e.g., a stationary exercise bicycle provides the user with fitness, resulting in higher self-esteem, or lawn fertilizer produces a thicker, healthier lawn and pride of ownership to the user. See also *actual product* and *augmented product.*

corporate advertising public relations type of non-product advertising by a company for the primary purpose of promoting the firm overall by instilling favorable attitudes, enhancing its image and reputation, gaining name recognition, increasing public awareness of the firm, or building support, goodwill, and confidence among its publics, as opposed to directly promoting its products; generally geared toward long-term effects, rather than the relatively short-term effects sought in product advertising. Also called *image advertising, institutional advertising,* and *public relations advertising.* See also *advocacy advertising* and *cause-related marketing.*

corporate barter see *barter.*

corporate discounting a practice by which a media vehicle allows advertisers with multiple brands to combine the advertising schedules for their brands to earn a larger discount on time or space; an incentive to advertise with the particular vehicle; e.g., *Good Housekeeping* magazine allowing Procter & Gamble to buy space for a specific brand of product at a discounted rate based on the total space used by the company in that publication for its several brands. See also *blanket contract.*

corporate identity all the elements that combine to give a company its individuality or personality; e.g., the firm's name, logo, colors, slogan, and so on.

corporate image the public's perception of the company or organization as a whole; consists of many factors such as size of the company, its people, financial transactions, marketing practices, advertising, prices, sponsorship of events or causes, stance on important issues, local charitable efforts, and other elements that affect the company's appearance in the public mind.

corporate VMS a *vertical marketing system (VMS)* in which there is one channel member that has ownership of all stages along the distribution channel; leadership, cooperation, and coordination are achieved through the common ownership at each distribution channel stage. See also *vertical marketing system (VMS), contractual VMS, administered VMS, conventional marketing system, horizontal marketing system,* and *hybrid marketing system.*

corrective advertising advertising that is mandated by the Federal Trade Commission, in which the advertiser is to rectify false impressions or beliefs created by previous advertising that contained an error or that was deceptive or misleading in some way; an attempt to eliminate any residual effects of previous advertising deemed misleading or deceptive regarding the advertiser's claims about its product.

cosponsorship in event marketing, several advertisers sponsoring a particular event or property, with each assigned to a particular segment or location; e.g., multiple sponsors of a golf tournament. In the case of television advertising, the term refers to one advertiser joining with another to share the program's production costs and to share the commercial time as well. See also *sponsorship.*

cost efficiency the balance between media cost and audience size, reflected in the cost of reaching the target audience using a particular medium or vehicle, relative to the cost of reaching the total audience of the medium or vehicle; i.e., the effectiveness of an advertising medium or vehicle as measured by its delivery of the advertiser's target audience relative to the medium's or vehicle's total audience or circulation.

Also can refer to the cost of reaching the target audience using a particular medium compared with another medium, or a similar comparison of one media vehicle with another vehicle. The notion that media selection should take into consideration the medium's or media vehicle's ability to reach the largest target audience at the lowest unit cost. For commonly used measures of efficiency, see *cost-per-point (CPP), cost-per-thousand (CPM), cost-per-thousand—target audience (CPM-TA), cost-per-sale,* and the several other *"cost-per"* measures.

cost of goods sold the net cost to the company of the goods sold; i.e., the value at cost of the raw materials and the manufacturing of the finished products. See also *gross sales, gross profit, gross margin, net sales,* and *net profit.*

cost-benefit analysis an investigation into the relationship between what a product or service costs and the expected benefits of having it; where the comparison shows expected benefits exceed the costs of obtaining the product or service, there is justification to purchase it, while a reverse relationship makes the purchase difficult to justify.

cost-of-sales see *cost-of-goods-sold.*

cost-per-action (CPA) in Internet advertising, the amount an advertiser pays for each visitor who takes some specific action in response to an advertisement beyond simply clicking on it; e.g., a visitor to the Google Web site may click on an advertiser's site such as Betty Crocker or Sunglass Hut and take advantage of an offer by making a request to subscribe to the advertiser's periodic catalogs or newsletters.

cost-per-click (CPC) in Internet advertising, what an advertiser pays for each visitor to a Web site who "interacts with an advertisement," i.e., clicks on it to get headed toward the advertiser's Web site or destination (though the visitor may not actually wait to fully arrive at the destination); see also *click.*

cost-per-clickthrough (CPCT) in Internet advertising, what an advertiser pays for each visitor who actually arrives at the advertiser's Web site.

cost-per-impression media cost relative to the total number of target audience exposures, including duplication, to the vehicles in a *media schedule.* See also *gross impressions.*

cost-per-inquiry (CPI) in direct marketing or public relations, a measure of the number of inquiries (e.g., requests for information) produced relative to the cost of the activity.

cost-per-lead (CPL) in Internet advertising, what an advertiser pays for each visitor who provides enough information at the advertiser's site to be used as a genuine sales lead; i.e., a more specific form of cost-per-action. Also applies to the cost of generating prospects for direct marketing and personal selling efforts. See also *cost-per-action (CPA).*

cost-per-order (CPO) in direct marketing, the number of orders received relative to the cost of the direct-marketing effort; e.g., the number of sales generated by a direct-response advertisement or commercial. To calculate: divide the cost of the direct-marketing effort by the number of sales made. Also called *cost-per-sale* and can apply to personal selling efforts.

cost-per-point (CPP) the cost of reaching one percent of a television or radio audience in your target audience; i.e., cost of achieving one rating point. Used as a measure of cost efficiency by comparing different broadcast vehicle alternatives. To calculate: divide the cost of the commercial by the program's audience rating. Generally done by specific demographic group; e.g., females 25 to 44. Also called *cost-per-rating-point* (CPRP). See also *cost efficiency* and *rating.*

cost-per-rating-point (CPRP) see *cost-per-point.*

cost-per-sale (CPS) in Internet advertising, the amount of sales made relative to the cost of the advertising; sales figure is that of the product sold directly from the Web site or otherwise traceable to a sales lead resulting from the Web advertising. In personal selling, the dollar value of a sale divided by the total cost of getting the sale. Often used synonymously with *cost-per-order (CPO).*

cost-per-thousand (CPM) the cost of reaching 1,000 households or individuals in a media vehicle's audience; universally used as a measure of cost efficiency for intermedia comparisons (e.g., television vs. magazines, radio vs. newspapers) or intramedia comparisons (e.g., one magazine vs. another). To calculate: divide media cost by circulation and multiply by 1,000. Common to all media for use in relative cost comparisons. See also *cost-per-thousand—target audience (CPM-TA), cost efficiency,* and *circulation.*

cost-per-thousand—target audience (CPM-TA) the cost of reaching 1,000 households or individuals in a medium's or vehicle's audience who are members of the target audience sought by the advertiser. Used as a measure of cost efficiency in the same way as *CPM* and calculated using basic *CPM* formula with appropriate adjustment of circulation figure. See also *cost-per-thousand (CPM).* Also called *target cost-per-thousand* and *weighted cost-per-thousand.*

cost-plus method of agency compensation a way of compensating an advertising agency in which the agency is paid a fee for the work it performs plus an agreed-upon dollar sum for profit. See also *fee method, commission method, combination method,* and *performance-based method.* Also see *agency commission* and *sliding rate.*

cost-value ratio in sponsorship marketing, the cost of a particular sponsorship divided by the estimated value of the sponsorship.

Council of American Survey Research Organizations (CASRO) the trade association of survey research firms dedicated to developing guidelines aimed at promoting the highest standards of practice and conduct in the survey research process, including data collection, data processing, and reporting; its commitment to ethics and professionalism in the survey research industry is represented by its Code of Standards and Ethics for Survey Research, which must be followed by all member firms.

Council of Better Business Bureaus (CBBB) the parent organization of the locally oriented *Better Business Bureau (BBB),* but works at the national level; assists industries and companies in developing advertising codes and standards, as well as providing regulatory information to advertisers, advertising agencies, and the media. Plays a major role in the advertising industry's self-regulatory efforts, through two of its divisions—the *National Advertising Division (NAD)* and the *Children's Advertising Review Unit (CARU).* See also *Better Business Bureau (BBB), National Advertising Division (NAD),* and *Children's Advertising Review Unit (CARU).* Also see *self-regulation.*

counteradvertising advertising undertaken to challenge or oppose another advertiser or organization on a particular matter, such as its claims in a previous advertisement or its position on a given issue; e.g., an advertiser's response to a competitor's product claims, or a labor union presenting its case via media advertising against an employer in a labor dispute, or the company's response to the labor union's message.

counter card see *counter display.*

counter display an advertising card (called a *counter card* or *counter stand*) or a point-of-purchase display featuring merchandise or promotional material situated on a store counter, often at the checkout area.

counter programming in television or radio, purposely placing a program that is aimed at the exact same audience as that of a particular competing program that airs on another station at the same time on the same day.

counter stand see *counter display.*

counterattack see *counteradvertising.*

counting station in out-of-home advertising, the specific point on a street or other location where the number of vehicles or passersby is recorded to determine circulation statistics to be used in setting advertising rates; see also *traffic count, hand count,* and *official count.*

county size see *ABCD Counties.*

coupon a certificate for a stated value as a price reduction on a particular product, applied when the certificate is presented at the point of purchase.

coupon drop in sales promotion, the distribution of *coupons,* typically specified by geographical area.

coverage (area) the geographic area or the total number or percentage of individuals or households within a specific geographic area blanketed by a *media vehicle;* can also be expressed in terms of a *media class, subclass,* or a complete media plan; also a measure of the potential audience that is in a position to be reached by a media vehicle. Not to be confused with *reach,* which refers to a specific target audience. See also *reach.*

cover date the date of publication, located on a magazine's cover.

cover position advertisement placement on the inside front, inside back, or outside back cover of a magazine (called the second, third, and fourth cover); generally, a cover position carries a premium price.

cowcatcher a short commercial for a product at the very beginning of a television or radio program, the only time the product will be advertised during the program.

crawler see *promotional crawl*.

creative a catch-all term referring to the copy and artwork that comprise an advertising execution; also refers to the advertising agency department responsible for producing the copy and the artwork for a client.

Creative Artists Agency (CAA) a premier production and talent firm whose services include providing marketers, advertisers, and advertising agencies with creative artists and talent for advertising production and executions, particularly television commercials; provides an entertainment emphasis for brand marketing efforts. Typically works as an adjunct to an advertising agency, handling much of the creative effort, though the agency does independently create advertising concepts and television commercials.

creative auction see *online reverse auction*.

creative boutique an organization or advertising shop that specializes in providing creative work to advertisers and, sometimes, other advertising agencies; the focus is on developing advertising concepts, creating messages, copywriting, creating artwork, and designing advertising layouts.

creative brief see *copy platform*.

Creative Code a set of guidelines governing the standards of truthfulness, claim substantiation, and tastefulness of the written, spoken, and visual content and presentation of advertising; established by the *American Association of Advertising Agencies (AAAA)* as a standard for the highest level of moral and ethical conduct for its members. See also *American Association of Advertising Agencies (AAAA), Standards of Practice,* and *Guidelines for Comparative Advertising*.

creative concept the distinctive central idea or creative point-of-difference that sets a particular campaign apart from those of competitors; see also *unique selling proposition (USP)*.

creative director the individual in an advertising agency who is responsible for the copy and design elements of advertising produced by the agency; see also *copy* and *art*.

creative development research in advertising research, any of several specific types of qualitative research used during the creative stage of advertising development.

creative execution style see *execution format*.

creative plan the blueprint of the sequence that takes the creative strategy to final execution in the form of an advertisement or commercial; the copy platform, or a set of guidelines for the activities that must be coordinated during the copywriting and artwork phases of preparing advertising messages. Sometimes may refer to the *creative brief* itself. See also *creative brief*.

creative selling type of personal selling in which the salesperson's focus is on getting new business; order-getting vs. order-taking.

creative strategy statement see *copy platform*.

creative team the specific individuals—copywriters and art people—in the advertising agency's creative department who are responsible for the advertising executions in a campaign; they take the *copy platform* and bring it to life by creating advertisements and commercials that reflect the agreed-upon advertising strategy.

creativity the skill to produce and initiate compelling, distinctive, and suitable ideas to be used in all phases of the marketing communications plan.

credentials presentation that stage in a company's search for an advertising agency in which a personal visit is made to the agency by a prospective client to give the agency the opportunity to sell its capabilities, introduce their executives, management team, and key personnel, as well as to expound on their marketing and advertising philosophy; an opportunity for the agency to show a prospective client what it is all about and, for the company, to help determine if the agency is capable of handling its account. Sometimes referred to as a *credentials visit*. Also called a *capabilities presentation*.

credibility the believability and trust of the communication source, as perceived by the receiver; based on several factors such as the source's knowledge, experience, and objectivity. See also *source credibility*.

credit a monetary deduction given by the media vehicle to an advertiser when a commercial or advertisement fails to run or does not run according to the agreed-upon scheduling. See also *make-good* and *preemption.*

crisis management the actions and practices undertaken by an organization following an occurrence that has had or is likely to have a profound and significant negative impact on the organization, and that will get worse in the absence of remedial action; examples: the actions taken by Johnson & Johnson with the Tylenol tragedy or Firestone with the automobile tire disaster. Includes actions taken to dispel a rumor about a company or product if the rumor is having or is likely to have a negative impact.

cross-couponing use of a coupon that features a cents-off or other special offer for more than one product; providing a coupon with one product (usually inside the package) that is good for a price reduction on a product other than the one with which it came. See also *cross-ruff.*

cross-elasticity of demand the sensitivity or extent to which demand or consumption for one product is affected by a change in the price of a related product; e.g., the impact on demand for a golf pro shop's merchandise when the golf course greens fees are increased.

cross-media advertising occurs when a company places its advertising message in several different types of media that are available from a single company or organization; e.g., scheduling advertising in the *San Francisco Chronicle, Seattle Post-Intelligencer,* and *Houston Chronicle* newspapers, any combination of the Hearst Corporation's many broadcast television stations and cable TV networks, its radio stations, *Redbook, Town & Country, Cosmopolitan, House Beautiful,* and *Good Housekeeping* magazines, to mention just a few of the properties under the Hearst Corporation banner. See also *multimedia buy.*

cross-magazine advertising when two or more magazine publishers agree to make their magazines available to advertisers as one package deal or *buy;* see also *multimagazine deal.*

cross-marketing see *comarketing.*

cross-media bundling see *bundling, cross-media advertising,* and *multimedia buy.*

cross-media buy see *cross-media advertising* and *multimedia buy.*

cross-merchandising a sales promotion technique in which a point-of-purchase display for a particular product features savings on other brands, usually complementary or related in some way; can refer to when the products are placed in separate but adjacent or nearby displays. Sometimes referred to as *cross-selling.*

cross-ownership when one person or organization owns more than one communications medium in a particular market; e.g., single ownership of both a television station and a newspaper.

cross-plug in television or radio programs that are alternately sponsored by different advertisers, each advertiser places one commercial in the program sponsored by the other advertiser, thereby maintaining weekly exposure; see also *alternate sponsorship.*

cross-platform in media, an advertiser's use of two or more media types in a marketing communications program, i.e., use of several channels to carry a marketer's advertising message; e.g., newspapers, television, and radio.

cross-promotion a sales promotion technique whereby the advertising or promotion for one product includes a promotional message for another product, and the other product reciprocates in its advertising or promotion; e.g., a movie and a video game based on the movie. Term may also apply to a joint, integrated marketing effort by two sponsors of a particular event or property, in which the property itself provides the central theme for the promotion efforts.

cross-read in outdoor advertising, a poster or bulletin that is visible and readable from the opposite side of the road from where the automobile occupants who will view the board are traveling.

cross-ruff a coupon or other special offer contained in or placed on a particular brand's package that is good for another product or brand, which is usually a product of the same company, but could be for another company's product in a joint marketing effort or *tie-in;* e.g., a coupon for Bausch & Lomb daily cleaner for contact lenses placed inside the Bausch & Lomb saline solution package. Essentially synonymous with *cross-couponing,* but encompasses a slightly broader concept. See also *cross-couponing.*

cross-selling in direct marketing, offering existing customers a new or related product or even one that is unrelated; e.g., *Time* magazine offering its subscribers the opportunity to receive *Sports Illustrated, People,* or other magazine it publishes. Or, an online bookseller offering its customers the opportunity to purchase certain music selections. May apply to any promotion program directed at purchasers of other products in which the marketer uses the sale of one product to push for the sale of another product, usually related. See also *cross-merchandising.*

C-store display a *point-of-purchase display* located at the entrance to convenience stores.

cue a stimulus or impetus for action by the consumer; e.g., a catchword, slogan, advertisement, sign, brand name, distinctive color, or other stimuli that prompts a reaction from the consumer.

culture the complete set of learned beliefs, ideas, norms, values, morals, ethics, traditions, and behavior shared by members of a particular society; the basic and distinctive character of a society that governs much of its members' behavior, including consumer behavior. See also *subculture.*

cume see *cumulative audience.*

cume duplication the percentage of estimated cumulative audience (i.e., *cume persons*) for one station who also listen to another station; see also *cumulative audience.*

cume persons see *cumulative audience.*

cume rating the percentage of different people in a market area's population or target audience who were tuned to a particular radio station for at least 5 minutes during a given *daypart;* measures the *cumulative audience (cume)* during that *daypart.* To calculate: divide the *cume* by the population or target audience number. See also *daypart* and *cumulative audience.*

cumulative audience the number of different people *(unduplicated audience)* who listen to a particular radio station for at least 5 minutes during a given *daypart;* commonly called *cume* or *cume persons.* Sometimes called *cumulative reach.* Also refers to the total number of different individuals exposed to an advertisement, commercial, or campaign through multiple insertions in more than one medium, media vehicle, or in the entire campaign media schedule. See also *daypart, horizontal cume, vertical cume,* and *unduplicated audience.*

cumulative quantity discount a reduction in price offered to a customer based on the amount purchased over a specified period of time, e.g., one month or one year; see also *noncumulative quantity discount.*

curiosity headline a type of headline for an advertisement or commercial in which the advertiser attempts to raise the inquisitiveness of the audience and stimulate them to explore further, perhaps by making a provocative statement; e.g., "78 degrees and not a cloud in the sky. What a hazardous day for a drive." (Ray Ban sunglasses for driving) or "Instead of hiding our future technology, we sell tickets to it." (Ford Motorsports). Also called a *provocative headline.* See also *headline,* as well as *benefit headline, command headline, news-information headline,* and *question headline.*

custom exhibit in trade show marketing, a display designed and constructed to meet the specific requirements of an exhibitor.

custom marketing tailoring a product or service to the specific needs and requirements of an individual customer; more common in the industrial market than the consumer market.

customer acquisition cost the cost of acquiring a new customer or, in some cases, winning back a former customer.

customer database see *database.*

customer lifetime value (CLTV) the total profit generated for a marketer by a single customer during his or her lifetime; the extent to which the revenues derived from that customer are greater than the total costs of marketing to him or her.

customer perceived value (CPV) the extent to which the satisfaction of a product is greater than the cost of obtaining it, as measured by consumer perception; the consumer's view of the difference between the cost incurred to purchase a product or service and the satisfaction derived from its ownership and use. The consumer will favor the company or brand that he or she perceives to offer the highest delivered value.

customer profile a description of the buying habits and the demographic, geographic, psychographic, and behavioral characteristics of the individuals or households who are users or prospective users of a product; also called *user profile.* Term also applies to the description of business or trade customers, i.e., *organizational buyers.* See also *audience profile, demographic segmentation, geographic segmentation,* *psychographic segmentation,* and *behavioristic segmentation.*

customer relationship management (CRM) all activities designed to launch, preserve, and enhance a long-term bond and mutually beneficial connection between a company and its customers; see also *partner relationship management (PRM).*

customer satisfaction the consumer's ultimate goal in entering the marketplace and the marketer's ultimate goal in serving the needs, wants, and expectations of the consumer; the pleasure, happiness, and comfort emanating from a positive marketplace experience. In the final analysis, the degree to which the marketer meets the needs, expectations, and requirements of the customer.

customer service all the presale and, especially, postsale activities in dealing with the customer, designed to increase the product's value and the consumer's satisfaction with the product and the company behind it; the before-and-after activities surrounding the actual selling transaction and treatment accorded the customer. A key criterion in the consumer's final selection of a product or service.

customer value the difference between the cost incurred to purchase a product or service and the satisfaction derived from its ownership and use; the extent to which the satisfaction of a product is greater than the cost of obtaining it, as measured by consumer perception. The consumer will favor the company or brand that they perceive offers the highest delivered value.

customer-oriented marketing an approach to marketing whereby the organization views its major mission as focused on developing and executing a marketing program that results in unequaled delivery of value and satisfaction to the customer.

customized rotation see *rotary bulletin.*

custom magazine a magazine with editorial content directed at an audience with a very specific interest; often referred to as a special-interest magazine, although it is for a subset of a special-interest group. For example, the National Football League's publication *NFL Insider,* published for an audience with an intense interest in the latest inside information on the NFL and its teams. Also called an *enthusiast publication* or *niche magazine.* See also *special-interest magazine.*

cut-in a local commercial announcement inserted into a network program; a commercial that replaces a network commercial at the local level, i.e., in a specific local area. Often done to either test a new commercial in a representative market area or to give better or more customized support for the advertiser's product locally.

cutline see *caption text.*

cut-out in outdoor advertising, a display of letters, figures, mechanical devices, or lighting attached to the face of a bulletin to give a three-dimensional or special effect; used to draw attention to the advertising message. Also called an *embellishment.* See also *bulletin* and *extension.*

cybermarketing marketing, advertising, and promotion over the Internet.

D

DAR   see *day-after-recall test.*

DBS   see *direct broadcast satellite.*

DMA   see *Designated Market Area;* also see *Direct Marketing Association.*

DTC   see *direct-to-consumer marketing.*

DVR   see *digital video recorder.*

D county   see *ABCD Counties.*

DAGMAR   *Defining Advertising Goals for Measured Advertising Results;* a model designed to help establish advertising objectives and to measure the impact of an advertising campaign. Central premise is that communications goals, not sales goals, represent the most equitable test of advertising effectiveness. Proposed in 1961 by Russell Colley, in work done for the *Association of National Advertisers (ANA).*

dailies   in television advertising production, the first print or videotape of a day's work making a commercial, with no corrections yet made; used to determine if all the pieces of the commercial are in place. Often called *rushes.* Also refers to newspapers published on weekdays.

Daily Effective Circulation (DEC)   in out-of-home advertising, the number of potential viewers who are exposed to, i.e., have the opportunity to see, an advertising message during a typical 24-hour period; the estimated number of individuals who pass an outdoor location on an average day.

daily inch rate   see *inch rate.*

data collection   the process of using research to gather information relevant to the specific purpose at hand; includes the gathering of both *primary data* and *secondary data.*

data collection instrument   in marketing and advertising research, the specific device used to gather data from respondents; e.g., a questionnaire.

data collection method   the particular means used to gather information from respondents or about a specific matter of interest to the researcher; e.g., *observation, experiment, survey,* or "library" research.

data mining   extracting meaning and drawing implications from databases; going through a large amount of data to gain insight and knowledge for ultimate use in developing marketing programs.

database   a comprehensive, organized file of up-to-date and specific information about individuals in the advertiser's target audience; e.g., data pertaining to geographic, demographic, psychographic, and behavioral characteristics, as well as purchase patterns and history, mail-order buying, and other information relevant to the advertiser. Organized and stored for easy access. See also *database marketing.*

database marketing   using the information in a *database* to plan, design, and implement targeted direct-marketing efforts and to develop targeted advertising and marketing communications programs, with the intent of facilitating an ongoing relationship between those consumers and the marketer. See also *database.*

day-after-recall test (DAR)   in television advertising research, a method of measuring an audience's recall of specific commercials to determine their impact; respondents are telephoned the day after a commercial appeared on a particular program, and once it is established that the respondent watched that show, he or she is questioned about the program's advertising and, in particular, about the commercial being researched, to determine if the respondent remembered it and can recall something specific about it. See also *ASI Recall Test.*

daypart mix in television and radio advertising, the particular combination of time segments used by an advertiser for its commercials.

dayparts (radio) the time segments of the broadcast day for radio; advertising rates vary by daypart. Typical *dayparts* for radio are: *morning drive time* (6:00 A.M.–10:00 A.M.), *daytime* (10:00 A.M.–3:00 P.M.), *afternoon-evening drive time* (3:00 P.M.–7:00 P.M.), *nighttime* (7:00 P.M.–12:00 A.M.), and *all night* (12:00 A.M.–6:00 A.M.). The times of the dayparts may vary slightly at individual stations, and all times are EST.

dayparts (television) the time segments of the broadcast day for television; advertising rates vary by daypart. Typical *dayparts* for television are: *early morning* (6:00 A.M.–9:00 A.M.), *daytime* (9:00 A.M.–3:30 P.M.), *early fringe* (3:30 P.M.–5:30 P.M.), *early news* (5:30 P.M.–7:00 P.M.), *prime access* (7:00 P.M.–8:00 P.M.), *prime* (8:00 P.M.–11:00 P.M., except Sunday when it is 7:00 P.M.–11:00 P.M.), *late news* (11:00 P.M.–11:30 P.M.), *late fringe* (11:30 P.M.–1:00 A.M.), and *late night* (1:00 A.M.–6:00 A.M.). The times of the dayparts may vary slightly by markets and by individual stations, and all times are EST.

daytime in the radio broadcast day, the time period of 10:00 A.M.–3:00 P.M.; in the television broadcast day, the time period of 9:00 A.M.–3:30 P.M. See also *dayparts (radio)* and *dayparts (television).*

daytime station a radio station whose broadcast day is restricted to just before sunrise to just after sunset per the *Federal Communications Commission (FCC)* license.

deadline the day or hour that advertising material or work is due in order for the publication or broadcast schedule to be met, and after which the material or work will not be accepted; applies to any material or work associated with any stage of a marketing communications campaign. See also *closing date.*

deal see *consumer deal, trade deal,* and *dealer allowance.*

deal fulfillment see *fulfillment.*

deal pack a specially packaged product that promotes a *consumer deal* (a premium, price reduction, two-for-the-price-of-one, extra contents, or some other offer) with a preprinted message on the outside of the package.

deal sheet a formal description of the important details and conditions of an advertiser's promotional or merchandising offer, given to the participating retailer.

dealer a *middleman* who buys for resale to the ultimate consumer; i.e., a *retailer.*

dealer allowance a general term for a sales promotion activity that involves some form of price reduction offered by the advertiser for a limited time to retailers and other members of the trade as incentives to buy the product, buy more of it, make the product an in-store feature, advertise it, or otherwise give some sort of preference to the advertiser's product; see also *advertising allowance, display allowance,* and *trade sales promotion.*

dealer brand a brand owned by a retailer, wholesaler, or other distributor, as opposed to a manufacturer; also called a *distributor brand, private brand,* or *private label.*

dealer display see *point-of-purchase advertising.*

dealer imprint a local retailer's identification (name, address, telephone number) added to an advertisement or commercial, most often a national advertiser- or manufacturer-prepared execution as might be used in a cooperative advertising program; see also *dealer listing* and *dealer tie-in.* Also see *snipe.*

dealer incentive see *dealer allowance.*

dealer listing that part of a manufacturer's advertisement or commercial (typically, the bottom portion) that lists the local retailers who carry the advertised product; also called a *dealer tie-in.* See also *dealer imprint.*

dealer loader in trade sales promotion, a premium or other offer given by an advertiser to a retailer as an inducement to buy and stock a particular quantity of the advertiser's goods, usually in an amount that represents an increase in normal buying; see also *display loader* and *premium.*

dealer survey survey research done on retailers; see also *consumer survey.*

dealer tie-in a manufacturer-sponsored sales promotion activity, such as a contest, sweepstakes, or sampling, in which retailers actively participate in some way and are mentioned in the manufacturer's advertising (which may take the form of cooperative advertising) of the sales promotion; can also refer to any listing or mention of retailers in a manufacturer's advertising; sometimes referred to as a *dealer imprint* or *dealer listing.* See also *tie-in advertising.*

deal-prone consumers individuals who are heavily influenced by price reductions, deals, or other sales promotion activity; tend not to be brand loyal, switching brands often, with buying behavior focusing on the brand that at the moment offers the best and most attractive bargain; see also *non-deal-prone consumers.*

deceptive advertising by *Federal Trade Commission* guidelines, advertising that involves a misrepresentation, omission, or practice likely to mislead a reasonable consumer and that results in a purchase decision that would be different were it not for the deception, because of consequences unfavorable to the consumer; also referred to as *misleading advertising* or *misrepresentation.*

decider in a business or organizational *buying center,* the individual who has authority to make the buying decision.

decision a choice between two or more alternative actions.

decision rules see *consumer decision rules.*

decision stage the fourth stage in the consumer decision process, in which the judgment is made to either purchase, not purchase, or postpone the decision subject to further search and evaluation; see *consumer decision process.*

decision-making process see *consumer decision process.*

deck panels see *stacked panels.*

decline stage the fourth and final stage of the product life cycle, in which sales and profits drop to the point that the product is taken off the market, although some marketers take this action faster than others. See also *product life cycle, introduction stage, growth stage,* and *maturity stage.*

decoding the process by which the receiver (consumer) interprets or assigns meaning to an advertising message; see also *encoding.*

decoy use of a phony name or entry on a direct-mail list so the list owner can track the list buyer's use of it and ensure it is used in accordance with the list rental agreement; see also *salting.*

defensive marketing marketing programs, strategies, and tactics used by an organization to protect and maintain its market position and prevent competitors from making inroads into its market share; sometimes called *maintenance marketing* or *status-quo marketing.* See also *offensive marketing.*

defensive spending advertising and promotion expenditures in response to competitive expenditures; related to the competitive parity method of budgeting, but more of a short-term tactic to combat increased expenditures by competitors. See also *offensive spending* and *competitive parity method.*

delayed broadcast in television or radio broadcasting, when an individual station airs a network program after its scheduled broadcast time.

delayed effect in advertising or other promotion activity, the sale of a product or other desired response that occurs after the advertising or promoting activity stops.

delivery the number of individuals or households reached by a medium, media vehicle, or media schedule.

demand a consumer's need or want for a product or service coupled with the ability and willingness to pay for it; the various amounts of a product or service a consumer is willing and able to buy at different prices. See also *supply.*

demand curve a graph that shows the relationship between price and quantity demanded.

demand elasticity see *price elasticity of demand.*

demand-backward pricing an approach to pricing in which the producer first determines an acceptable final price to offer the consumer and then works backward to determine what price it can charge for the product as it goes into the distribution channel.

demorating in television and radio, a program's rating for a specific demographic group, such as women 25–44; see also *rating.*

demographic edition an edition of a magazine targeted toward readers with particular demographic characteristics; e.g., *Time Magazine's Time Women Select,* an edition delivered to affluent, professional women, or the magazine's *Time Top Zips,* an edition circulated to the highest-income postal zip codes in the United States, or the *Newsweek 50 Plus* edition that goes to subscribers who are 50 years old or older. A type of *partial-run edition*. See also *metro edition, regional edition,* and *state edition.*

demographic segmentation dividing consumers into groups based on variables such as age, gender, income, occupation, education, family size, home ownership, stage in the family life cycle, generation, nationality, race or ethnicity, religion, and social class; see also *behavioristic segmentation, geographic segmentation, geodemographic segmentation,* and *psychographic segmentation.*

demographic split run placement of one advertisement in a particular demographic edition of a given publication and a different advertisement in another demographic edition of the same publication; the split may be between professionals and nonprofessionals, homeowners and nonhomeowners, or other demographic targets of a publication. Often used to test and compare the effectiveness of alternate advertisements. See also *split run, split-run test, geographic split run, subscription/newsstand sales split run,* and *A/B split.*

demographics data relating to the basic human characteristics of a market or population; see also *demographic segmentation.*

demonstration format in advertising, a creative *execution format* featuring the product in use; e.g., a television commercial showing an Echo brand leaf blower in action, a commercial showing the Black & Decker Workmate workbench being folded into different shapes for different jobs, or a Wagner power sprayer being used by a house painter. See also *straightforward factual, news, problem-solution, slice-of-life, dramatization, symbolic association, fantasy, animation, still-life, humor, spokesperson, testimonial,* and *comparison formats.*

department system of agency organization a system of organizing an advertising agency in which each agency function, such as account management, planning, creative, media, or research, is a separate department; each department works with all the agency's clients, being called upon when the need arises for its expertise. See also *advertising agency* and *group system of agency organization.*

dependent variable in research to determine a cause-and-effect relationship, the variable that is thought to be affected by some other variable; e.g., sales volume (dependent variable) is thought to be affected by the level of advertising expenditures (*independent variable*), or a brand's image (dependent variable) is thought to be affected by a particular message execution format (*independent variable*). See also *independent variable* and *experimental method.*

depth interview in marketing and advertising research, a method involving quite lengthy and unstructured personal interview sessions, marked by probing to determine consumers' perceptions, attitudes, beliefs, feelings, and motivations; see also *nondirective interview.*

depth of assortment see *product assortment depth.*

derived demand a condition in which the demand for a particular product is the result of the demand for another product; e.g., the demand for leather stems from the demand for furniture and the demand for sugar emanates from the consumption of jelly beans. Describes the idea that demand for business goods is dependent on the demand for consumer goods.

descriptive research a type of research designed to clearly define a problem; not concerned with the reasons or causes underlying the problem. Example: research into consumers' attitudes toward an advertiser's product, or consumer's opinions about the advertising messages for a particular product, or consumer opinion about different sales promotion activities. See also *causal research* and *exploratory research.*

design see *advertising design, art,* and *graphics.*

Designated Market Area (DMA) a group of U.S. counties in which the commercial television stations in the metro or central area achieve their largest audience share; exclusive or nonoverlapping geographic areas in which television stations attract most of their viewers; used for purposes of planning, buying, and evaluating television audiences. The major basis for reporting television audience size. There are 210 DMAs in the United States. Every U.S. county is assigned to a DMA. The term was created by and is owned by *Nielsen Media Research.*

developmental copy research in advertising research, copytesting done in the early stages of the advertising copy development process; designed to help copywriters fine-tune their work by providing audience reaction and interpretation of proposed copy. See also *evaluative copy research* and *pretesting.*

diagnostics in marketing and advertising research, a broad range of techniques involving data collection and analysis to acquire feedback from consumers on a variety of marketing, advertising, and promotion issues, for the purpose of gaining insight to aid the development and implementation of future marketing communications programs.

dialogue copy advertising copy that presents a product's or service's selling points by means of two or more individuals engaged in conversation; see also *narrative copy.*

diary the book or log in which an individual's television viewing or radio listening habits are recorded to determine audience estimates for individual programs; used by *Arbitron* (radio) and *Nielsen* (television). See also *diary method.*

diary method a way of tracking television viewing or radio listening habits, in which panel members record their experiences over a given period of time; used by research services such as *Nielsen* (television) and *Arbitron* (radio) to report program ratings. In television and radio advertising research, a basic method for gathering data on people's viewing and listening habits and, therefore, measuring audiences. Representative viewers and listeners in each of the television and radio markets throughout the United States maintain a formal record of their viewing and listening choices and submit the diaries to the research organizations. The resulting audience estimates for each market serve as a basis for setting advertising rates. For television, *Nielsen* diaries cover 210 markets, while for radio, *Arbitron* diaries cover 260 markets. In the case of the *Nielsen* diary method, the diaries are sent to participating households during the *sweeps* months of November, February, May, and July. Individuals in the households provide a wide range of demographic data on a questionnaire. Each member of the household, as well as guests, writes down the programs he or she watches, indicating who is watching, for how long, the name of the program, and other information considered key to determining viewing habits. See also *Arbitron, metered markets, Nielsen, overnight ratings, People Meter, set-tuning meter, telephone coincidental,* and *sweeps.*

diarykeeper the individual who is declared eligible to receive a *Nielsen* or *Arbitron* diary, and the person to whom all survey materials are sent; see also *diary* and *diary method.*

dichotomous questions research questions framed so that the respondent has only two choices from which to select an answer; a "yes-no" question or an "agree-disagree" question.

differential advantage see *competitive advantage.*

differentiated marketing occurs when the marketer or advertiser targets two or more distinct market segments or customer groups, and then designs separate tailor-made marketing mixes, offers, strategies, or programs for each segment; sometimes referred to as *selective marketing* or a *multiple target market approach.* See also *concentrated marketing, undifferentiated marketing,* and *single target market approach.*

differentiation for a marketer, the process of achieving an array of distinct, meaningful, and superior differences between its offering and competitors' offerings by means of elements such as the product, services provided, company personnel, channel members' efficiency, or through the marketing communications program; e.g., creating a position of distinctiveness vis-à-vis competitors by means of an image or perception that is the result of superior advertising executions, media strategy, cause marketing efforts, or event sponsorships.

diffusion of innovation see *diffusion process.*

diffusion process the process by which a new product, service, or idea is communicated, accepted, and spread over time through a population; marketing communications strategy changes as the brand moves through the various stages of diffusion. See also *adoption process, adopter categories, adoption curve, innovators, early adopters, early majority, late majority,* and *laggards.*

digest unit see *junior unit.*

digital insertion system see *virtual placement process;* also called *live-video insertion system.*

digital media any channel or vehicle capable of digital transmission; e.g., a personal computer for Internet advertising or television. See also *digital transmission.*

digital transmission sending audio or video messages from one point to another through the use of computer-generated codes.

digital video recorder (DVR) an interactive television recording device that records and plays back TV programs, thereby allowing the consumer to use a PC to access and view a television program anytime, anywhere; the device records a television program and replays it almost simultaneously—what appears to be a live telecast can then be manipulated as if it were a recorded program (which it actually is), because it is in digital form (vs. analog). The device makes it possible to skip through the program's commercials by using the 30-second "auto-skip" function of the device. Also known by other names, such as *personal video recorder (PVR), personal TV receiver, personal video station,* and *hard disk recorder.*

diminishing demand see *law of diminishing demand.*

diminishing marginal utility see *law of diminishing marginal utility.*

diminishing returns see *law of diminishing returns.*

diorama a three-dimensional advertising display, often having special-effects lighting and movement; standard size is approximately 42″ high × 62″ wide. Commonly seen in airports, bus terminals, shopping malls, and sports arenas. See also *terminal poster.*

direct account see *house account.*

direct broadcast satellite (DBS) video programming transmitted via satellite directly to the user's television set; the satellite signal goes directly to a receiver dish (usually on the roof of the house), which immediately transmits the signal to a set-top box or decoder on the TV set, allowing the consumer to get the satellite broadcast.

direct channel see *direct distribution.*

direct distribution a marketing system in which the manufacturer sells to the consumer without using wholesalers, distributors, or retailers; see also *indirect distribution.*

direct mail a major method of direct marketing that uses the U.S. postal system to deliver marketing literature and materials; see also *direct marketing.*

direct-mail co-op see *cooperative mailing.*

direct-mail package in direct marketing, the complete set of enclosures and elements in a mailing; also called simply a *package.* See also *direct marketing.*

direct marketing communicating directly with the target audience to obtain a particular response

(anywhere from creating awareness to gaining a transaction), rather than using intermediaries, such as retailers and wholesalers; i.e., an interactive marketing approach to the target audience using one or more advertising media to get a measurable response at any location. May employ a wide range of media, such as direct mail, television, radio, magazines, newspapers, or personal computers. Often seeks immediate response via mail, telephone, or personal computer.

Direct Marketing Association (DMA) the industry association representing direct-marketing firms using print, broadcast, telephone, mail, and other media in their direct-marketing programs; also the parent of the *Association for Interactive Media (AIM),* which is dedicated to the advancement of the Internet and interactive media as effective marketing and advertising tools. See also *Association for Interactive Media (AIM).*

direct observation see *observation method.*

direct questioning see *nondisguised research.*

direct selling a means of marketing goods or services to customers face-to-face rather than through a retail location or other nonpersonal means.

direct-action advertising see *direct-response advertising.*

directional medium an advertising medium employed by an advertiser simply to inform potential customers that they can purchase a product or service once they have made the decision to buy; as opposed to media used to create awareness or demand for the product or service. For example, the *Yellow Pages.*

direct-mail advertising advertising messages delivered to the target audience through the mail system (including private services).

direct-marketing agency a company specializing in the development of direct-marketing campaigns for clients; typically has large databases from which mailing lists are derived. Generally provides several services in addition to database management and mailing lists, such as creation and production of direct-mail efforts and research. Also called a *direct-response agency.*

direct-marketing media the message channels used by direct-marketing communications programs; e.g., direct mail, telemarketing, television, magazines. See also *direct marketing, direct mail,* and *telemarketing.*

director of account services the individual at the advertising agency, usually at the rank of vice president, who oversees the entire relationship and functioning between the agency and the client; the person who has the main responsibility for seeing to it that the agency produces an advertising plan that meets the client's satisfaction. Heavily involved with knowing the client's business, its marketing goals, advertising objectives, and all other factors that affect the formulation of advertising strategy. See also *account executive* and *account supervisor.*

directory advertising advertising that appears in a directory or buying guide; advertisements in *Marketer's Guide to Media, PROMO Magazine's Sourcebook,* the *Thomas Register, Standard Rate and Data Service* volumes, or the *Yellow Pages.*

direct-response advertising advertising that seeks to stimulate immediate action or response by individuals in the target audience; often used by, though not limited to, direct marketers. Major media are television, radio, and newspapers. Often involves 800/900 numbers or business reply cards. Also called *direct-action advertising.*

direct-response agency see *direct-marketing agency.*

direct-to-consumer (DTC) marketing marketing efforts, especially advertising, in which the manufacturer communicates directly with the consumer in an industry where a professional normally is the link between the product and the user; e.g., pharmaceutical companies advertising directly to the consumer, such as Lipitor using advertising to persuade people to ask their doctor about the cholesterol-fighting drug.

disclaimer copy in an advertisement or a commercial, the language that erases or limits the advertiser's liability stemming from promotional claims.

discount describes any of several types of price reductions offered by a seller to a buyer; e.g., see *cash discount* and *trade discount.*

discounted rate card a reduction in a media vehicle's published rate card gained by negotiation, especially where the advertiser has special power.

discrepancy of assortment the difference between the variety of products a producer makes and what is wanted by customers; the typical producer makes a relatively limited variety of products (e.g., pencils), while the customer requires many different products to satisfy multiple needs and wants (pencils, paper, notebook, ruler). A job of the distribution channel is to adjust the discrepancies so all parties are satisfied. See also *discrepancy of quantity.*

discrepancy of quantity the difference between the number of products a producer needs to make to achieve economies of scale and the number of products the customer usually wants; e.g., the producer makes thousands of refrigerators and the individual consumer wants one. See also *discrepancy of assortment.*

discretionary income what remains from an individual's disposable income after buying necessities; money a person can use in any way or for any purpose he or she elects.

disguised research in marketing and advertising research, any form of questioning in which the respondents are unaware of the true purpose of the research; also called *indirect questioning.* See also *nondisguised research.*

display see *point-of-purchase advertising.*

display advertising newspaper and magazine advertising that makes use of illustrations, photos, and other visual elements in addition to headlines and copy, i.e., advertising containing the standard elements of a print advertisement; advertising other than *classified advertising.* See also *classified advertising.*

display allowance a fee paid by the manufacturer to the retailer for making space available for an *end-of-aisle* or other *point-of-purchase display.*

display classified see *classified display advertising.*

display loader in trade sales promotion, a premium or other offer given by an advertiser to a retailer as an inducement to use a *point-of-purchase display* featuring the advertiser' product; see also *dealer loader* and *premium.*

display period the time period during which an outdoor advertising message is on display on an out-of-home structure such as a billboard, i.e., its exposure time; e.g., a poster or billboard whose contract runs for one month.

disposable income an individual's personal income less personal taxes; see also *discretionary income.*

dissatisfaction a purchase decision outcome in which the consumer perceives his or her choice as falling short of expectations.

dissolve in television advertising, when one picture fades out just as another picture simultaneously emerges on the screen.

dissonance see *cognitive dissonance.*

distribution one of the major marketing functions, involving all the activities associated with making products and services available to customers in the right quantities, at the right locations, at the right time; often referred to as *place,* which, along with *product, price,* and *promotion,* comprise the 4Ps of the marketing mix. Also, in *outdoor advertising,* the location of the specific advertising structures within a market, or the way they are deployed throughout the market.

distribution channel the path traveled by a product from manufacturer to final user, both consumer and industrial; a channel includes all the institutions, individuals, processes, and relationships involved in the flow of goods through the distribution network. Also called a *marketing channel.*

distribution channel length in the distribution channel, the number of levels of intermediaries; e.g., manufacturer-wholesaler-retailer-consumer = two levels, while manufacturer-retailer-consumer = one level, and manufacturer-direct-to-consumer = zero levels.

distribution intensity see *intensive distribution, selective distribution,* and *exclusive distribution.*

distribution management see *channel management.*

distributor see *middleman.*

distributor brand see *dealer brand.*

diversification an organization's growth strategy in which the firm tries to increase its sales and profits by entering new markets with new products; e.g., Honda automobile company getting into the business of lawnmowers and generators. See also *growth strategies, market penetration, market development,* and *product development.*

diversity marketing marketing activities and programs aimed at subcultures such as racial groups, national-origin groups, specific geographic regions, and other groups with particular needs that make them distinct from the general population as consumers of goods and services; also referred to as *ethnic marketing, minority marketing,* or *special-interest marketing.*

dog-and-pony show an elaborate, sometimes dazzling and flamboyant, pitch for an advertising campaign orchestrated by the advertising agency to the client; see also *pitch.*

domain name on the Internet, the unique name that identifies a particular site; e.g., *cnn.com.* Essentially the same as the URL, although the URL is the full address, as in *http://www.cnn.com.* See also *URL.*

donut see *doughnut.*

door-opener an article, such as an advertising specialty, given to a prospective buyer by a salesperson as an incentive to listen to a sales presentation.

door-to-door personal selling or other promotion activity such as sampling that involves going directly to the homes of the individuals in the target market in a specific geographic area.

dot.com refers to the Web site address of a company or organization that has a ".com" suffix on it; generally, the Internet presence of a firm or organization.

DoubleClick a leading company specializing in designing research-based Internet advertising campaigns for advertisers and Web publishers; involved with the planning, execution, and analysis of online, e-mail, and database marketing programs.

double coupons in sales promotion, when a retailer offers the consumer twice the face value of a manufacturer's coupon.

double spotting in television advertising, when the same advertiser runs two spot announcements, one right after the other, for different products; also known as a *piggyback commercial.*

double spread see *two-page spread.*

double truck see *two-page spread.*

double-face display a display with an advertising message on both the front and back.

double-page spread see *two-page spread.*

doughnut in radio or television advertising, a blank space within a prerecorded commercial; purpose is to allow the insertion of live advertising copy at the local station. The beginning and the end are prerecorded or the same from one execution to another, with the middle portion of the commercial customized or changed from execution to another.

downscale a descriptive term for an individual or group located at the lower end of the socioeconomic ranking; see also *upscale.*

dramatization format in advertising, a creative *execution format* that essentially tells a short story, attempting to attract the audience through the suspense or excitement of the "mini-drama" setting; e.g., a television commercial that features a short story involving the Lo-Jack auto theft detection system, whereby an automobile equipped with the device is recovered. See also *straightforward factual, news, demonstration, problem-solution, slice-of-life, symbolic association, fantasy, animation, still-life, humor, spokesperson, testimonial,* and *comparison formats.*

drive time in the radio broadcast day, the Monday–Friday time periods of 6:00 A.M.–10:00 A.M. and 3:00 P.M.–7:00 P.M., *morning drive time* and *afternoon-evening drive time,* respectively; see also *dayparts.*

drop-in ad in television advertising, a local commercial that is inserted during the airing of a nationally sponsored network telecast; also called a *hitchhiker.*

dubs copies of the master copy of a finished radio commercial that are sent to the individual radio stations for broadcast; see also *dupes.*

dual branding see *cobranding.*

dual distribution a situation in which a manufacturer uses two or more competing channels of distribution to reach the same target market; e.g., a power tool producer that uses a company sales force to sell to select key-account retailers, wholesalers to sell to all the other retailers, and an online store from which consumers can purchase the power tools. See also *hybrid marketing system.*

dual marketing see *comarketing.*

dummy preliminary layout or mock-up of all the elements in a brochure or other promotion material, to give an idea of what the finished product will look like; a replica of the final product just prior to printing. The equivalent of the *comprehensive* for print ads.

dummy magazine in advertising research, a magazine, complete with editorial content and advertisements, invented solely for the purpose of pretesting advertising messages; given to a test audience, whose responses to the advertisements are evaluated.

dupes copies of the master copy of a finished television commercial that are sent to the networks or TV stations for broadcasting; see also *dubs.*

duplicated reach see *audience duplication.*

duplication see *audience duplication.*

durable goods consumer goods that have a relatively long useful life and are purchased infrequently; e.g., a refrigerator, microwave oven, or personal computer. Sometimes referred to as *hard goods.* See also *nondurable goods.*

dyadic communications personal and direct communications between two parties; e.g., a sales representative and a customer. See also *monadic communications.*

dynamic ad placement in Internet advertising, the real-time insertion of a specific advertisement into a Web page's advertising space; the real-time ad insertion is based on the individual user's demographics, demonstrated interest in a particular product or service category, or time of day. Essentially, a "customization" of the ad space based on the Web site visitor's characteristics. See also *static ad placement.*

E

EDLP   see *everyday low pricing.*

EPA   see *Environmental Protection Agency.*

early adopters   the second group of adopter categories in the diffusion process of new products, services, or ideas, i.e., those individuals who adopt a new product after the innovators; are very often opinion leaders and generally motivated by social acceptance and a desire to be trendy. See also *adoption process, adopter categories, adoption curve, diffusion process, innovators, early majority, late majority,* and *laggards.*

early fringe   in the television broadcast day, the time period of 3:30 P.M.–7:00 P.M.; see also *dayparts (television).*

early majority   the third group of adopter categories in the diffusion process of new products, services, or ideas, i.e., those individuals who adopt a new product after the innovators and early adopters; tend to be somewhat cautious in accepting a new product, preferring to wait until it has proven successful with other people. See also *adoption process, adopter categories, adoption curve, diffusion process, innovators, early adopters, late majority,* and *laggards.*

early morning   in the television broadcast day, the time period of 6:00 A.M.–9:00 A.M.; see also *dayparts (television).*

early news   in the television broadcast day, the time period of 5:30 P.M.–7:00 P.M.; see also *dayparts (television).*

earned rate   the actual rate paid by an advertiser for time and space used during a contract period, including all discounts for volume and frequency; see also *card rate, contract rate,* and *short rate.*

e-business   see *electronic commerce.*

e-commerce   see *electronic commerce.*

economic cost   see *opportunity cost.*

economic indicators   various measures, statistics, and indices used to indicate the level and trend of economic activity and the state of business conditions; e.g., Consumer Price Index, employment rate, Dow-Jones Industrial Average, housing starts, gross national product.

economies of scale   the principle that describes lower average costs resulting from "mass" production of a product; as the quantity produced increases, the cost of each unit decreases. Principle can be applied to nonproduction situations, e.g., marketing economies that result when the cost of advertising is distributed over a high level of sales that occur from the advertising. A reason why market share is said to drive profitability.

editing   most commonly refers to television advertising production and the process of assembling the final version of the commercial from several different camera shots and scenes; may refer to any type of advertising and the modification of the ad's components to arrive at the final version.

edition   a copy of a publication that is printed from a single typesetting, although minor changes may be made during the printing run, such as may happen for late-breaking news as a newspaper goes to press; an edition becomes a *new* edition when major changes are made in the typesetting. See also *typesetting.*

editorial compatibility   the match, suitability, or fit between a company and its product and the editorial content offered by a particular publication or media vehicle; see also *program compatibility.*

editorial environment   the overall character of a publication, including elements such as content, appearance, style, philosophy, and anything else that affects its basic spirit.

editorial matter   the nonadvertising part of a publication; e.g., the text of a magazine, such as news articles.

effective circulation   see *reach* and *effective reach;* also see *circulation.*

effective frequency   the number (or range) of exposures or repetitions needed for advertising to be effective or have impact on the individuals in a target audience, such as to increase awareness, to change attitude, to generate action, or to stimulate a particular response; i.e., how many exposures are required for the message to achieve the advertiser's objectives, register with, or "get through" to the audience, or to have a minimum level of impact. See also *frequency.*

effective reach   the number or percentage of the target audience who have been exposed to the message enough times to be aware of it; may be viewed as the quality of exposure. See also *reach.*

effects   in television advertising, a variety of schemes electronically inserted within the commercial to increase visual attractiveness and impact; see also *wipe.*

efficiency   refers to the relative costs of media delivery to a specific audience; the balance between audience size and media cost. See also *cost efficiency.*

efficiency measures   in media planning, the specific tools used to evaluate the relationship between audience size and media cost; allow the media planner to make intermedia and intramedia comparisons. For commonly used tools and methods, see *cost-per-point (CPP), cost-per-thousand (CPM),* and *cost-per-thousand—target audience (CPM-TA).* See also *cost efficiency.*

Effie Awards   annual recognition of the most effective advertising campaigns based on achievement of the campaigns' stated objectives; organized and presented by the New York chapter of the American Marketing Association.

8-sheet poster   an outdoor advertising panel approximately one-fourth the size of the *30-sheet poster* (the standard poster and the most commonly used out-of-home format), with a 6′ high × 12′ wide surface and a 5′ high × 11′ wide live copy area; most frequently used in densely populated urban areas and neighborhoods, plus suburban shopping areas and point-of-purchase locales. Also called a *junior panel* or *junior poster.* See also *outdoor bulletin, out-of-home media, outdoor poster, 24-sheet poster, 30-sheet poster, permanent bulletin,* and *poster panel.*

80–20 rule   the concept that a relatively small portion of customers may account for a larger portion of a product's sales; e.g., in industrial marketing, the idea that 80 percent of a product's sales comes from 20 percent of the customers. Extended to marketing and advertising: the large majority of market share in a product category is held by a small number of companies or the large majority of advertising is done by a minority of the advertisers. Also called the *Pareto rule.*

elastic demand   a situation in which a specific percentage change in price leads to a larger percentage change in the quantity demanded; i.e., consumer demand for the product or service is price-sensitive. Example: a 3 percent reduction in price results in a 5 percent jump in the quantity demanded. See also *inelastic demand, skimming price policy,* and *penetration price policy.*

electronic advertising   an advertising message delivered via television, radio, or the Internet.

electronic billboard   an electronic sign that displays information and messages, including advertising messages, in public places such as sports stadiums, airline terminals, shopping centers, or at some highway locations; essentially a giant TV screen located in a public place.

electronic commerce   using the Internet to communicate with target audiences to arrange for buying and selling transactions; i.e., conducting business online.

electronic couponing   computer-generated in-store coupons issued by a machine at the point of purchase, most commonly at the checkout counter; also includes coupons downloaded off the Internet.

electronic mail   on the Internet, a means of individuals communicating with one another; messages are composed on a computer and sent electronically to one or more recipients.

electronic media   general term for television and radio as advertising media; also refers to the Internet; see also *broadcast media.*

electronic promotion   any promotion communicated to the target audience by means of a personal computer, and to which the consumer responds online.

electronic retail promotions   see *electronic couponing;* term also applies to instant price reductions taken at the time of checkout.

electronic retailing   see *e-tailing.*

electronic shopping   online shopping for products and service by means of a personal computer.

e-mail   see *electronic mail.*

e-mail advertising   the use of the Internet's electronic mail function for sending advertising messages.

embellishment   see *cut-out.*

emergency products   goods that are purchased immediately to satisfy an urgent need that if not filled right away, will cause major problems; beyond health- or safety-related needs and products, lost or stolen luggage may require an unplanned and immediate purchase of a new suit for a business meeting.

emotional appeals   in designing and executing advertising messages, a basis used to attract and engage the consumer through feelings and sentiments related to elements such as pleasure, pride, ambition, fear, humor, romance, status, protection of others, love, security, personal comfort, appearance, social approval, achievement, and a host of other links to the sensitivity of the individual's psychological and social need; see also *appeals* and *rational appeals.*

emotional motives   in consumer behavior, the personal or subjective reasons for choosing a particular alternative or course of action; as contrasted with *rational motives,* which focus on economic or objective bases in making marketplace decisions. See also *motive* and *rational motives.*

emphasis   in advertising design and layout, the principle related to making one element of the advertisement, such as the headline or an illustration, more prominent than the other elements as a means to get the reader's attention to focus on that element. See also *balance, contrast, flow, gaze motion, harmony,* and *unity.*

empirical research method   a research method based on the collection of new data from the marketplace; see also *primary data* and *secondary data.*

encoding   the manner and process by which an advertiser selects words and visuals to convey a particular message; the stage of the communications model in which the sender (advertiser) puts the message into language (words, symbols, illustrations) that will stimulate the receiver (prospective buyer) to the action desired by the advertiser. Putting the message into language, via words, symbols, tone, and other elements that make up language the advertiser believes will be understood and will influence the prospective buyer to take the particular action desired by the advertiser. Translating an idea into a message that will convey the intended meaning. See also *decoding.*

Encyclopedia of Associations   a comprehensive compilation of detailed information on not-for-profit associations; contains a huge database of descriptions, addresses, contact personnel, research activities, publications, and other key information on industry trade associations, professional societies, and organizations of all types.

end-of-aisle display   a point-of-purchase display located at the end of a shopping aisle; considered a prime location, commanding the highest fees. Often used for high-margin, impulse items. Also known as an *end, end cap,* or *end display.*

endorsement   a statement indicating approval of the product, service, idea, or other subject of the advertising, made by an individual or by an organization speaking on behalf of the advertiser; the individual, or spokesperson, may be a celebrity, an expert, an authority figure, or a typical consumer. As opposed to a testimonial, whose statement is based on actual experience, an endorsement may or may not be based on actual use of the product. *Federal Trade Commission* rules require substantiation or proof of the endorser's claims. See also *spokesperson* and *testimonial.*

endorser   the individual who appears in a commercial or advertisement in support of the advertiser or its product; see also *endorsement.*

end-user   the individual or company that actually uses the advertiser's product or service.

Engel's Law   the proposition that people shift their spending patterns as income rises; spending on food, housing, transportation, and other goods and services changes as income rises. Put forth by economist Ernst Engel.

engineering of consent   a term used to describe the overriding mission of public relations efforts, which most often involve an attempt to gain agreement or support for an issue or idea; coined by Edward L. Bernays, considered by many to be the "father of public relations."

entertainment   one of the major categories of sponsorship; includes festivals, fair, concert tours, theme parks, and other attractions.

enthusiast publication   see *special-interest magazine.*

envelope stuffer   promotional material or an item inserted into a direct-mail envelope along with what is being sent to fulfill an order or request for information.

environment analysis   an integral part of the situation analysis or preliminary investigation conducted prior to a promotion campaign; focus is on the social, cultural, economic, technological, and political factors as they affect consumers toward whom the advertising and promotion will be aimed.

environmental marketing   marketing programs and efforts designed with their environmental impact in mind and resulting in strategies and actions that have a beneficial effect on human health and on the natural world in which we reside.

Environmental Protection Agency (EPA)   the federal agency established in 1970 to protect human health and the natural environment (air, water, and land) by overseeing the repair to environmental damage, establishing standards and programs for a cleaner environment, and enforcing regulations pertaining to the environment. Provides leadership and works closely with other federal agencies, as well as with state and local governments, on all matters relating to the quality of the environment.

environmentalism   individuals' and organizations' concern, often via coalition or crusade-type drive, for the protection and improvement of the environment in which we live; a movement involving citizens who care about the environment, businesses of all types, and government at all levels.

equal opportunity rule   in television, the requirement that if a station permits the use of its broadcast facilities for one public office candidate, it must offer the same facilities to other candidates vying for the same public office; a *Federal Communications Commission (FCC)* rule as part of the *Communications Act.*

equal time   in television, the requirement that when a station sells (or gives) time to a candidate for public office, it must offer equivalent time to other candidates for the same public office; a *Federal Communications Commission (FCC)* rule as part of the *Communications Act.*

equivalency   see *media equivalency.*

e-tailing   conducting retailing activities via the Internet; see also *electronic commerce.*

ethics   in marketing and marketing communications, the moral standards, principles, and values underlying and surrounding the marketer's efforts toward the target audience; the realm of right and wrong.

ethnic advertising   see *ethnic marketing.*

ethnic advertising agency   an advertising agency that specializes in planning, creating, executing, and measuring advertising and promotion activities aimed at an ethnic target market(s).

ethnic marketing   marketing programs, advertising, and other efforts directed specifically toward ethnic consumers and groups among the larger consumer market; also referred to as *diversity marketing* or *minority marketing.*

ethnic media advertising   media such as magazines, newspapers, television, or radio that target specific ethnic groups, such as African Americans or Hispanics.

evaluation stage   the third stage of the adoption process, in which the consumer gives the product idea a mental trial, using the information assembled in the interest stage; see also *adoption process, awareness stage, interest stage, trial stage,* and *adoption stage.*

evaluative copy research   in advertising research, copytesting done after the advertising has been executed and run; audience reaction is examined and measured to determine approval or disapproval of the advertising. See also *developmental copy research* and *posttesting.*

evaluative criteria   the yardsticks or points of comparison used by consumers in making choices among alternatives; e.g., the product attributes a consumer uses to compare products and in deciding what specific brand to purchase. See also *consumer decision rules.*

even scheduling   see *continuous scheduling.*

event marketing   the advertising, promotion, and other marketing activities aimed at consumers who attend or are exposed in some way to a particular event, such as a sports event or festival; often used synonymously with *sponsorship,* although a sponsorship may be for any of a wide range of activities and may not involve an event. See also *event sponsorship* and *sponsorship.*

event sponsorship   an advertising and promotion strategy (often a part of a firm's public relations efforts) in which the advertiser forges a relationship by paying a sponsorship fee to have its company or product name associated with a particular sports, cultural, festival, or other public event; the event may be an existing one or one created specifically for purposes of public relations, and the event usually is owned and operated by an organization other than the advertiser-sponsor. See also *event marketing* and *sponsorship.*

event survey   audience research conducted at the location of a particular event, for any of a wide range of purposes; also called *visitor survey* or *venue survey.* See also *event sponsorship.*

evergreen   a timeless public relations piece that can be used to good advantage at any time; e.g., an article or advertisement on a particular environmental issue, the need for education, providing opportunities for children, or addressing the health and safety concerns of senior citizens.

everyday low pricing (EDLP)   a sales promotion tool whereby a company, such as Procter & Gamble, offers its product at a regularly low price in lieu of periodic and ever-changing promotional discounts and allowances to the trade and consumers; with the consistently lower price, the promotional allowances may be reduced or even eliminated.

evocative power   the ability of a particular message, medium, or media vehicle to communicate emotion.

evoked set   those brands that a consumer has in his or her memory that are considered acceptable and, therefore, will be seriously considered when that consumer chooses among alternatives in a particular product category; the brands a consumer draws from memory and that he or she will actively consider and evaluate when contemplating a purchase in a particular product category. Also called *consideration set.* See also *consumer decision rules.*

exchange   trading something of value for another thing of value, such as the consumer's payment of money for a product or service; a core concept of marketing, since it is the marketing function that facilitates buyers and sellers coming together to exchange things of value.

exchange copy   a complimentary or free copy of a publication sent by the publisher in exchange for a copy of another publisher's publication; see also *complimentary copy.*

exclusionary zones   in outdoor advertising, a voluntary agreement by outdoor advertising companies prohibiting billboards, posters, or outdoor signs advertising products illegal for sale to minors and that are near places of worship, schools, and hospitals; a provision of the voluntary Code of Advertising Practice established by the *Outdoor Advertising Association of America (OAAA).* See also *Outdoor Advertising Association of America (OAAA).*

exclusive cume   the audience in radio advertising; the number of different people listening to only one radio station during a particular *daypart;* see also *cumulative audience* and *daypart.*

exclusive distribution   a marketing strategy of severely limiting the number of wholesalers and/or retailers (usually to just one) in a given territory who are allowed to sell a manufacturer's product; done for reasons such as to protect a product's lofty image, maintain a premium price, or to protect dealers in a particular region. See also *intensive distribution* and *selective distribution.*

exclusivity   an agreement in which a media vehicle or sponsor of an event agrees to accept no advertising directly competitive with the advertiser purchasing time or space in the media vehicle or program.

execution   the process of taking the appeal and fashioning it into a finished advertisement or commercial; often referred to as the finished advertisement or commercial itself.

execution format   how the advertising appears or is presented; the specific technique or, more often, the combination of techniques used to present an advertising message and the setting in which the advertising is carried out. Examples: *straightforward factual, news, demonstration, problem-solution, slice-of-life, dramatization, symbolic association, fantasy, animation,* *still-life, humor, spokesperson, testimonial,* and *comparison formats.*

exhibit in sales promotion, a display set up by a marketer to show off its product or service; e.g., a display at a trade show. See also *trade show.*

exhibit producer a firm specializing in the design or manufacture of exhibits for trade shows.

exit fee a charge to the manufacturer to cover the handling costs for the distributor or retailer to remove a product from distribution; may be likened to a "de-slotting" fee. See also *failure fee.*

expectation the customer's anticipated outcome of a marketplace decision.

expected response rate an estimate of the likely number of responses from a promotion tool or a particular research project; e.g., the number of replies to a direct-mail piece, the number of entrants in a consumer contest or a sweepstakes, or the number of questionnaires returned in a mail survey. Generally, an estimate of the consumer reaction to a marketing, advertising, or other type of activity or program in which some specific action is requested.

experimental method in marketing and advertising research, a technique that utilizes a controlled situation in which one or more factors are manipulated by the marketer or advertiser, e.g., allowing subjects' behavior to be monitored to determine cause and effect; can be useful in helping to determine the impact of an increase in the advertising budget or the use of specific media vehicles. Essentially, the manipulation of an *independent variable* (e.g., advertising dollars) to observe the effect on a *dependent variable* of interest (e.g., sales) to the advertiser or researcher. Often used to compare the responses of two or more groups that are alike in all ways except for the variable being tested. Typically involves comparing a "test group" with a "control group," or the group not receiving the test treatment. See also *independent variable* and *dependent variable.*

expertise one of the characteristics that lends credibility to the source or sender of communications.

expert opinion a sales forecasting method that utilizes the judgments of dealers, distributors, suppliers, industry trade association, marketing consultants, or any other person or organization outside the firm with an in-depth knowledge of the product's market. See also *sales forecast, composite of sales force opinion, jury of executive opinion, test marketing, market potential,* and *sales potential.*

exploratory research a type of research designed to accumulate background information to help define a problem; a prelude to conclusive research that aims to help decision makers choose a course of action in a particular problem or situation. Characterized by the lack of a formal research design. Examples: research to gather information on how consumers make decisions on computer purchases, including specific uses of the computer, the criteria used in evaluating alternatives, the number of brands and models considered, the number of stores visited, the importance of advertising in the brand selection process, and the importance of sales help at the retail level. Sometimes called *informal research.* See also *causal research* and *descriptive research.*

exposure an individual's actual physical contact with an advertising medium or advertising message; placement of an advertisement or commercial in a media vehicle that the target audience is known to or is reasonably expected to see, hear, or read. An expression of the extent to which an advertiser's message can be seen or read. Common to all media. See also *opportunity-to-see.*

expressway bulletin in outdoor advertising, a *billboard* located on a limited-access highway, i.e., a highway or freeway that normally has a 55-mph speed limit.

extensive problem solving consumer decision making characterized by significant time and effort spent in the search for information and evaluation of alternatives in the brand selection process; lengthy deliberation throughout the buying process to minimize the risk of a poor product decision, since the consumer perceives major consequences resulting from a wrong choice. Usually the case in making important or high-involvement purchase decisions, and when the consumer has very little or no experience in that particular product category. Often called *complex problem solving.* See also *limited problem solving* and *routine problem solving.* Also see *high-involvement decision making* and *low-involvement decision making.*

extension in outdoor advertising, an area of design or copy that extends beyond the basic rectangular space of an advertising structure such as a bulletin; done for its attention-getting value; see also *cut-out.*

exterior bus advertising   poster space on the outside of a bus or rapid-transit vehicle; also called *outside poster.* See also *headlight poster, taillight poster, queen-size poster,* and *king-size poster.*

external agency   any organization outside the firm that provides services needed for it to conduct its business.

external analysis   part of the situation analysis, or preliminary investigation of factors relevant to the development of a promotion plan; those elements relating to the firm's customers, competitors, and environment in which it operates; e.g., who buys the product, how the purchase decision is made, customer attitudes toward the product, the direct and indirect competitors, competitors' promotion budgets, positioning, message strategies, media strategies, plus the political, economic, social, and technological environment in which the firm finds itself. See also *internal analysis* and *situation analysis.*

external audience   in public relations, the individuals and groups, i.e., publics, who are outside the organization; e.g., the general public. See also *internal audience* and *stakeholders.*

external data source   information that comes from a source other than the company or organization doing the research; see also *primary data* and *secondary data.*

external list   in direct marketing, a mailing list purchased from a source outside the company, such as one bought from a list broker or list compiler; see also *internal list, list broker,* and *list compiler.*

external publication   a company's own house publication aimed at its customers, dealers, investors, or other important publics; also called *external house organ.* See also *house publication.*

external search   in the consumer decision-making process, the acquisition of information from marketplace sources; seeking information from sources other than one's memory. Examples: visiting retail stores, consulting friends, checking product rating services or other authoritative sources. See also *internal search.*

external secondary data   existing data that have been collected by a source other than the company or organization doing research; see also *secondary data.*

extrapolation   in marketing and advertising research, taking existing data and projecting it into the future as a guide for planning marketing, advertising, and other promotional programs; predicting expected or probable future conditions to aid long-term marketing planning.

eyeballs   in Internet advertising, the viewing audience for a Web site.

eye camera   a physiological measurement of an advertisement's effectiveness, in which a mechanical device traces and records movement of the eye in response to a visual stimulus; e.g., following an individual's eye movement as he or she reads a magazine advertisement.

eye-tracking system   see *eye camera.*

e-zine   on the Internet, an online magazine or newsletter.

F

FCC   see *Federal Communications Commission.*

FDA   see *Food and Drug Administration.*

FPLA   see *Fair Packaging and Labeling Act.*

FSI   see *free-standing insert.*

FTC   see *Federal Trade Commission.*

FWMTS   the marketing danger of an organization "forgetting what made them successful"; i.e., when something is working effectively, it is unwise to change simply for the sake of change. If an organization has successfully used an aggressive marketing approach and conditions have not changed, it's best to stay with it. No different than a football team successfully employing a particular strategy for three quarters and then changing its strategy to try to protect its lead, failing to remember what it was that got them the lead in the first place. Coined by Jack Trout and Al Ries in *Positioning: The Battle for the Mind.*

face   in out-of-home advertising, the surface area on which advertising copy appears.

face value   the redeemable value of a *coupon,* printed on the coupon itself.

facing   in outdoor advertising, a single billboard; also may refer to the direction of the billboard *face* relative to traffic flow; e.g., a billboard panel facing west can be read by traffic heading east. Term also refers to exposure of a product package in the front row of a retail shelf, with total exposure of a specific item measured by the number of facings it has along the front row on a horizontal plane (vertical stacks count as one facing).

facing editorial page   in print advertising, a position request or instruction from an advertiser to a publication to place an advertisement opposite editorial (text) matter; i.e., adjacent to a nonadvertising page. Also called *facing text.*

facing text   see *facing editorial page.*

factory pack   multiple units of a product, usually three, six, or twelve, wrapped or boxed together as one package by the manufacturer. The term can also refer to a premium attached to or inside a package, called an *on-pack premium* or an *in-pack premium,* respectively; see also *premium.*

fact sheet   a listing or description of a product's features and selling points given to the copywriter for use in creating an advertisement; supplements the *creative brief.* Also refers to a page that usually is part of a company's press kit, on which is printed a description of the business, its address, telephone number, key contacts, and other basic information. See also *creative brief.*

fact-sheet radio commercial   a live (vs. taped) radio commercial in which the announcer ad libs the commercial using a sheet containing only the key selling points of a product or service; as opposed to a formal and complete script used to read the commercial word-for-word. See also *live copy* and *live-script radio commercial.*

fad   a product or idea that is considered fashionable or "in" for a very short time before it is gone just as quickly as it came on the scene; see also *fashion* and *style.*

fade   in television advertising, the slow continuous evolution of an image on the screen, from black, or from another image, to a full clear picture (*fade-in*) or, in reverse, from a fully visible picture, a gradual disappearance to black, or to another image (*fade-out*).

failure fee   a trade promotion agreement whereby the manufacturer makes a payment as a penalty fee to the retailer when a product does not achieve an expected or mutually agreed-upon sales level in the retailer's store, usually resulting in the product being dropped from the retailer's inventory; see also *exit fee.*

Fair Credit Reporting Act a law passed in 1970 regulating all aspects of credit reporting. See also *Consumer Credit Protection Act.*

Fair Packaging and Labeling Act a 1966 federal law establishing mandatory labeling requirements and promoting voluntary industry adoption of packaging standards, including a limit on the number of sizes offered for sale; enacted to combat false, misleading, and deceptive packaging.

fair trade as provided by federal law (*Miller-Tydings Act* of 1937) and the individual states that adopted it, a formal agreement between a manufacturer and retailer in which the retailer agreed to a retail price for a product below which it would not be sold; law was ruled unconstitutional in 1975. Intent was to protect small retailers from the price competition of large retailers that, by virtue of high-volume buying, could offer unmatched low prices to the consumer. Also called *resale price maintenance.* See also *Miller-Tydings Act* and *Consumer Goods Pricing Act.*

Fairness Doctrine in television, a now-defunct requirement that a network or station was required to offer equal time to both sides of especially significant matters or issues; an order of the *Federal Communications Commission (FTC).*

familiarity see *brand familiarity.*

family see *type family.*

family brand when a manufacturer's several products are all marketed under the same brand name; e.g., Kellogg's cereals, Campbell's soups and tomato juice, Pastene pasta, tomato paste, vinegar, and olive oil. See also *individual brand.*

family decision making as opposed to consumer decision making, the process of decision making exhibited by the family as a unit, including the roles played by individual family members.

family life cycle a classification scheme based on changes in families over time; the family goes through various stages, affected by factors such as marriages, births, aging, and changes in income. Examples: *Full Nest 1*—youngest child under six; *Full Nest 2*—youngest child over six; *Empty Nest 1*—older marrieds, household head in workforce, no children at home; *Empty Nest 2*—older marrieds, household head retired, no children at home. Particularly noteworthy for marketers are the changes in buying behavior and consumption patterns that occur with changes in family size, ages, income, needs, wants, and other such factors.

fantasy format in advertising, a creative *execution format* that puts the consumer in another realm or lifestyle, i.e., a "dreamworld"; e.g., a Royal Caribbean Cruise Lines magazine advertisement showing the luxurious accommodations and pampering on a cruise, a commercial fast-forwards a young girl to being an Olympic champion on her Rossignol skis, or a commercial showing a weekend duffer outplaying Tiger Woods down the stretch to win the U.S. Open with his new Callaway golf clubs. See *straightforward factual, news, demonstration, problem-solution, slice-of-life, dramatization, symbolic association, animation, still-life, humor, spokesperson, testimonial,* and *comparison formats.*

farm advertising see *agricultural advertising.*

farm publication a print publication directed to those in the farming industry.

farmer a sales representative who "grows" sales on existing accounts.

fashion a currently popular fashion; see also *fad* and *style.*

fast-close advertising in magazine advertising, the opportunity for an advertiser to submit advertising materials after the closing date specified in the publication's media kit for publication in a particular issue; typically, there is a premium charge, and not all magazines provide the opportunity. See also *closing date.*

fear appeals an advertiser's attempt to draw consumers to its product by playing on the consumer's anxiety or uneasiness and the negative consequences that would result by not buying and using that particular brand; using a person's worries as a basis for connecting him or her to a product. Example: a financial services advertiser who shows a family in dire circumstances because the breadwinner did not have an adequate financial plan before his untimely end; or a computer maker's advertisement showing a young student far behind his or her classmates because there is no PC at home, implying there is no chance to catch up unless the advertiser's computer is bought.

feature analysis in the situation analysis stage of the marketing communications planning process, an advertiser's side-by-side, point-by-point comparison of the features and attributes of its product against the competitive products. See also *situation analysis.*

features   see *product features.*

Federal Cigarette Labeling and Advertising Act   a law passed in 1965 requiring all cigarette cartons and packages to include health warnings; periodic amendments strengthened the wording of the warning statement, prohibited cigarette advertising on any medium of electronic communication (e.g., television and radio), extended the warning statement requirement to all advertising, and required smokeless tobacco to adhere to the warning requirements and the prohibition of advertising on television and radio.

Federal Communications Act   a 1934 law to regulate all phases of broadcast communications; created the *Federal Communications Commission (FCC).*

Federal Communications Commission (FCC)   the federal government agency that regulates broadcast communications by radio, television, wire, satellite, and cable; its authority extends to all aspects of licensing broadcast stations and encouraging competition, as well as to control over advertising content and what products and services are acceptable to be advertised on radio or television, ensuring that broadcast programs and advertising are in the public interest. Established by the *Communications Act of 1934.* On matters of advertising regulation, the FCC works closely with the *Federal Trade Commission (FTC).* See also *Federal Trade Commission (FTC).*

Federal Food, Drug, and Cosmetic Act   a law passed in 1938 to prohibit harmful practices in the production of foods, drugs, and cosmetics. Several later amendments allowed for removal of any drug from the market if it became a public health hazard or if it was shown to be ineffective, established uniform standards for over-the-counter (OTC) drugs, and required manufacturers to provide more information on drug labels (including the common drug name, ingredients, and side effects). Other amendments included a provision relating to medical devices and nutrition labeling and education. The act established the Food and Drug Administration (FDA) as the enforcer of these regulations. See also *Food and Drug Administration (FDA), Medical Device Regulation Act,* and *Nutrition Labeling and Education Act (NLEA).* Also see *Food and Drugs Act.*

Federal Hazardous Substances Labeling Act   a 1960 law governing labeling requirements for all packaged household products that contain hazardous substances.

federal regulation   the entire set of acts, laws, and other measures sponsored, directed, and enforced by the federal government to control the conduct of marketers and marketing activities in the public interest; see also *state regulation, local regulation, in-house regulation,* and *self-regulation.*

Federal Trade Commission (FTC)   the principal federal government agency exercising regulatory authority and control over advertising practices and actions; protects both consumers and businesses from anticompetitive behavior and unfair, fraudulent, misleading, and deceptive practices. Has been empowered to enforce other consumer protection laws and to regulate advertising's effect on both consumers and businesses since enactment of the *Wheeler-Lea Amendment* in 1938. See also *Wheeler-Lea Amendment* and *Federal Trade Commission Act.*

Federal Trade Commission Act   the 1914 federal law that created the *Federal Trade Commission (FTC);* the act was designed to enforce antitrust laws (e.g., Sherman and Clayton Acts) by helping to restrain unfair practices and methods of competition including, in later interpretations, false advertising that resulted in injury to a competitor. Since an "injury-to-a-competitor" ruling does little to protect consumers from the advertising malpractices, the *Wheeler-Lea Amendment* was passed in 1938 to include protection of consumers. See also *Federal Trade Commission (FTC)* and *Wheeler-Lea Amendment.*

Federal Trade Commission Improvement Act   see *Magnusson-Moss Warranty Act.*

Federal Trademark Dilution Act   a 1995 federal statute that expanded the Lanham Act's provisions, with a purpose to "protect famous trademarks from subsequent uses that blur the distinctiveness of the mark or tarnish or disparage it, even in the absence of a likelihood of confusion"; proving infringement on its "famous" trademark does not require the trademark owner to show proof of economic harm. (Determination of what constitutes a "famous" trademark is done on a case-by-case approach, with a series of determining factors to be used in the judgment, as set forth by the act.) See also *Lanham Act, trademark,* and *Trademark Law Revision Act.*

fee method advertising agency compensation, in which the advertiser and the agency agree on a fixed sum (usually on an hourly basis, but sometimes on a monthly basis) for services provided by the agency on behalf of the client (as an alternative to the commission form of compensation); amount of compensation is determined by a cost-plus-fixed-fee formula. When the commission method is used, a fee may be in place, but only for those situations in which a commission is not given by the agency's supplier. The advertising agency's total compensation often is a fee-commission combination plan. Sometimes called *fixed-fee method, cost-plus method,* or *retainer method.* See also *commission method, combination method,* and *performance-based method.* Also see *agency commission* and *sliding rate.*

feedback the reaction of the receiver of an advertiser's or marketer's message, which travels back and is made known to the sender or source of the message.

fighter brand a brand used by a company that has another brand entry in the same product category to combat competing brands in hopes of protecting its other brand; firm uses this brand to respond to competitive tactics such as deals, price reductions, or other sales promotion activities and, in the process, insulates its other brand in that category.

field marketing the practice of a manufacturer deploying its sales representatives or other personnel to retail stores to generate greater interest and sales of its products; e.g., provide help with in-store promotions or assist the retailer in better store layout or use of displays. See also *missionary selling.*

field of experience the totality of what a consumer brings to the marketplace that influences the decision-making process; e.g., past experience, perceptions, attitudes, values, and other factors that affect his or her behavior in the marketplace.

field test in marketing and advertising research, any of a variety of attempts to measure consumers' reactions to advertising or other promotion techniques under actual conditions, as opposed to laboratory or artificial settings; see also *laboratory test.*

field work in marketing and advertising research, research activities such as surveys conducted at a location other than that of the firm, e.g., in the home or at a shopping mall.

:15 designation for a 15-second television or radio commercial.

15 percent see *agency commission.*

50 showing in outdoor advertising, an expression indicating that 50 percent of a given market's population will be reached by (i.e., will have the opportunity to see) a particular advertising message by virtue of the number and placement of an advertiser's billboard panels in the market, in a 30-day period; see also *outdoor advertising, showing, 25 showing, 75 showing,* and *100 showing.*

file copy generally, a second copy of an advertising execution, document, or any other matter relating to a marketing communications campaign, kept as a record by the client, agency, and media; e.g., see *air check.*

file proof proof copy of an advertisement filed away for record purposes and safekeeping.

fill-in in direct mail, copy that is inserted into a form letter to give it a personal touch; e.g., the recipient's name, comment about the recipient's attendance at a recent event or purchase of a particular product or service, or some other copy that has specific meaning to that individual recipient of the direct-mail piece.

financial risk in consumer decision making, the chance the buyer will pay too much or have to forgo other purchases; see also *risk-taking, performance risk, physical risk, social risk,* and *time-loss risk.*

finder's fee payment to a party who serves as an intermediary in bringing together two organizations for business dealing; e.g., an individual's compensation for connecting an advertiser with an advertising agency or for bringing a client into the fold for a sales promotion firm.

finished art *artwork* that is complete in all respects and is ready for reproduction; usually referred to as *camera-ready artwork.*

firewall a specially designed system that serves as a "wall" between a user's personal computer and the Internet system; a security measure to monitor Internet traffic and protect the user from unauthorized invasion or tampering.

First Amendment Rights see *commercial speech.*

first cover (1C) the front outside cover of a magazine; also called the *front cover.*

first right of refusal in sponsorship marketing, a formal agreement between a sponsor and a property in which the sponsor has the right to match another company's bid to take over the sponsorship at renewal time.

first-run syndication television programs produced specifically for the syndication market and sale to individual stations; e.g., *Jeopardy, Wheel of Fortune, Oprah Winfrey Show.* See also *off-network syndication* and *syndication.*

fixed accrual an approach to establishing a cooperative advertising fund in which, for the specified length of the cooperative advertising program, the advertising fund grows by a fixed amount with each product purchased by the retailer from the particular manufacturer; e.g., if the amount per digital camera is set at $8 for a particular model and $10 for another model, the fund accumulates the appropriate sum for each product the retailer purchases from the manufacturer. See also *accrual account, percentage accrual,* and *cooperative advertising.*

fixed costs costs that do not vary with the quantity produced or sold; see also *variable costs.*

fixed location the same, guaranteed location of an ad in a print vehicle taken by an advertiser for several consecutive issues; sold at a premium rate.

fixed position the guaranteed location of an advertiser's television or radio commercial at a specific time on a specific day; sold at a premium rate.

fixed rate a broadcast advertising rate that is guaranteed and cannot be taken away or preempted by another advertiser, even though that advertiser is willing to pay a higher rate; generally, the highest advertising rate charged or, at the least, a premium price is paid by the advertiser. See also *preemptible rate.*

fixed-cost contribution per unit selling price per unit minus variable cost per unit; see also *contribution margin.*

fixed-fee method a method of advertising agency compensation in which the advertiser and the agency, prior to the services being performed, agree on a set amount of money that will be paid to the agency for work done on behalf of the advertiser. See also *fee method, commission method, combination method,* and

performance-based method. Also see *agency commission* and *sliding rate.*

fixed-position messages primarily in sponsorship marketing, the banners, billboards, electronic messages, and other stationary signage often displayed on the site of the sponsored property.

flagging in outdoor advertising, a tear in the poster paper that causes it to hang loose from the billboard.

Flammable Fabrics Act a 1953 federal law that established flammability safety standards for fabrics.

flanker brand a new brand introduced to the market by a company that already has a brand in the same product category; purpose is to attract new customers from different market segments than those already served by the company with its other brand. For example, General Mills, already with its premium-quality Gold Medal flour, introducing lower-priced Robin Hood flour. Also called *multibranding.* See also *multibranding, brand extension,* and *line extension.*

flat rate the standard advertising rate in a print vehicle, with no discounts of any kind, including for volume or frequency, offered to the advertiser.

Flesch Reading Ease Score a technique for assessing the level of difficulty in reading the words in an advertisement, i.e., the ease with which advertising text or body copy matter may be read; computation involves determining the average number of words per sentence and the average number of syllables per word in the advertisement. Scores range from 0 to 100, with standard writing averaging a 60 to 70 score. The higher the score, the more people who can easily read and understand the advertising. Devised by Rudolf Flesch. See also *Gunning Fog Index.*

flight the period of advertising activity scheduled between periods of inactivity; i.e., each period during which there is advertising in a campaign media schedule that also calls for periods of no advertising. See also *flighting.*

flighting an intermittent advertising media scheduling pattern in which there are periods of advertising activity (flights) separated by periods of no advertising at all (hiatuses); for example, heavy advertising for two weeks, followed by a period of no advertising, and then another two weeks of heavy advertising. Sometimes referred to as *wave scheduling.* See also *blinking, bursting, continuous scheduling, flight, hiatus,* and *pulsing.*

floating time   see *run-of-schedule (ROS).*

floor planning help   assistance provided by the manufacturer to a retailer on the store's floor plan and layout to help the retailer do the best job of presenting the goods for sale; assistance is provided by a combination of a sales representative's efforts and formal blueprints and guidelines for the retailer to follow.

floorstand   a point-of-purchase display that is placed on the store's selling floor.

flow   in advertising design and layout, the concept that each element of an advertisement should be arranged in an orderly manner to allow the reader to move easily and effortlessly through the entire ad; the ad's elements should be arranged to capture the reader's attention and, once having done that, guide the reader from one element to the next in the order the advertiser wants it to happen. See also *balance, contrast, emphasis, gaze motion, harmony,* and *unity.*

flowchart   a diagram charting the arrangement and schedule sequence over time of the key elements of an advertising or promotion campaign; see also *campaign flowchart, media flowchart,* and *work flowchart.*

flush   in print advertising, printed matter (i.e., *copy*) that is perfectly aligned on the left side (*flush left*), the right side (*flush right*), or on both sides (*flush left and right,* or *justified*); see also *ragged.*

flyer   see *handbill.*

focus group   a qualitative research technique in which eight to twelve people participate in an unstructured group session akin to brainstorming, with the dialogue guided by a moderator; commonly used to identify and explore consumer attitudes and viewpoints on issues related to products, advertising, and promotion programs. Participants are encouraged to express their opinions and to react to those of the other participants. See also *moderator.*

focus group moderator   the individual who leads and facilitates a focus group research session; see also *focus group.*

focus of sale   the basic claim made in the advertising, around which the creative strategy and the message

itself are built; see also *Big Idea, key benefit,* and *unique selling proposition (USP).*

Fog Index   see *Gunning Fox Index.*

foldout   see *gatefold.*

follower   see *market follower.*

following reading matter   see *full position.*

follow-up   the stage in the personal selling process that follows the *close,* and in which the salesperson must attend to all details relating to the order and influencing customer satisfaction. Especially important to maintain contact and to do account maintenance, as after-sale efforts are critical to the development of long-term customer relationships. See also *prospecting, preapproach, approach, presentation, handling objections,* and *closing.* Also see *relationship marketing.*

font   see *type font.*

Food and Drug Administration (FDA)   the U.S. agency that oversees and has authority over all aspects of labeling, packaging, branding, ingredient listing, and advertising of packaged foods, drug products (both prescription and over-the-counter), cosmetics, medical devices, and hearing aids; created in 1938 by the *Federal Food, Drug, and Cosmetic Act,* although its real beginnings can be traced to the 1906 *Food and Drugs Act.*

Food and Drugs Act   the predecessor to the *Federal Food, Drug, and Cosmetic Act (1938),* this original legislation, passed into law in 1906, created the *Food and Drug Administration (FDA);* gave the FDA the responsibility of testing all food and drugs destined for human consumption, and charged the FDA with the task of overseeing label warnings for certain classes of products, such as habit-forming drugs. See *Food and Drug Administration (FDA)* and *Federal Food, Drug, and Cosmetic Act.*

Food, Drug, and Cosmetic Act   see *Federal Food, Drug, and Cosmetic Act.*

forecast   see *sales forecast.*

forced exposure   in advertising research, a research setting in which respondents are shown an advertisement or commercial in a testing facility (such as a theater or mall storefront facility), as opposed to a "personal-interview" or "on-air" type of exposure.

forced-ranking question   a type of research question in which respondents are asked to rank a series of factors or items in top-to-bottom, first-to-last order to reflect their opinion or belief on some matter; also called a *rank-order scale.*

forced-rating scale   in marketing and advertising research, a particular question's answer scale that does not allow for a neutral or "no opinion" choice.

forgetting rate   a measure of the extent to which individuals remember an advertisement, especially during the time between exposures.

formal balance   in print advertising, a very symmetrical layout in which the ad's elements, including white space, are presented with equal weight distribution from top to bottom and side to side; as if there were two imaginary lines through the advertisement, one vertical and one horizontal, splitting the page from top to bottom and side to side, the components in each quadrant are approximately equal in size and shape, i.e., weight. Also called *symmetric balance.* See also *informal balance.*

formal group   a well-defined, structured, and organized collection of individuals whose association with one another is governed by a charter, a code, or a set of rules; e.g., a community service organization. See also *informal group, primary group, secondary group,* and *reference group.*

formal research   the collection and subsequent analysis of primary data for marketing, advertising, and promotion program purposes; see also *primary data.*

format   see *execution format.*

former buyer   a customer who has not made a purchase from a company for a certain period of time, or one who has discontinued the use of a particular product; same as *former user.*

form utility   the benefits a consumer receives by virtue of an organization converting raw materials into a finished product or service that has value for the consumer; see also *utility, possession utility, place utility,* and *time utility.*

Forrester Research   the premier independent Internet research organization, with enormous data collection, analysis, and interpretation capabilities, providing great insight into the impact of technological change on marketers, consumers, and society at large.

forward buying   related to sales promotion activities, the retailer's practice of buying larger-than-usual quantities to take advantage of a manufacturer's trade deal; sometimes a retailer will buy enough inventory to carry it to the next anticipated trade deal. Sometimes called *bridge buying.*

four-color   in print advertising, an advertisement that uses a full range of colors; i.e., black, as well as red, yellow, and blue, which, when combined, yield a full-color advertisement. Also called *full-color.*

4CP   a magazine advertising rate card designation for a four-color, full-page advertisement; can also be expressed in other ways, such as 1p4c or 4C1Pg.

4Ps   the *product, price, place* (distribution), and *promotion* components of the marketing mix and the marketing program; see also *marketing mix.*

fourth cover (4C)   the back outside cover of a magazine; generally carries the highest advertising rate in the magazine.

fractional ad   see *fractional page.*

fractional page   in print advertising, any advertisement of less-than-full-page size.

fractional showing   in outdoor advertising, a number of billboards, or a showing that is less than one-fourth the number needed for a full or 100 showing; i.e., something less than a 25 showing. See also *full showing* and *showing.*

fragmentation   refers to the increased number of choices people have regarding media, with their viewing, listening, and readership spread over a greater array of media types and, in particular, special-interest broadcast and print vehicles.

frame   see *sample frame.*

franchise position   a specific position in a periodical (e.g., back cover of a magazine) reserved for use by an advertiser through agreement with the publisher, as long as the advertiser continues to use the position; a position may be negotiated for a particular issue or for a minimum frequency level (e.g., 26 of 52 issues).

franchise-building promotions   sales promotion activities used in an attempt to enhance a brand's image and to foster long-term relationships with consumers, as opposed to promotions designed for immediate action with little attention to contributing to the brand's identity; e.g., an annual contest in conjunction with a charity or cause. See also *nonfranchise-building promotions*.

franchising   a type of vertical marketing system in which there is a formal contract between an organization (manufacturer or service organization) and an independent party; i.e., franchiser and franchisee, whereby the latter buys ownership and operating rights to a unit(s) in the system. Under terms of agreement, the franchiser grants the franchisee a license to be part of the system, with certain stipulations. The franchiser provides the marketing strategy and the franchisee implements the strategy in its own unit(s). Examples: Ford automobile dealerships, Coca-Cola bottlers, Hertz auto rental, McDonald's fast food, or Holiday Inn motels.

free circulation   see *nonpaid circulation*.

free circulation publication   a controlled circulation publication distributed to a select audience without charge; also called a *free publication*. See also *controlled circulation*.

free goods   a sales promotion activity in which a manufacturer distributes merchandise to retailers or dealers free of charge and without obligation.

free offer   see *giveaway*.

free premium   see *premium*.

free publication   see *free circulation publication*.

freelance   independent per-job copywriting, artwork, photography, design, layout, or production of advertising, typically done by an individual ("freelancer") on a specific assignment from an advertiser or an advertising agency; see also *Rolodex agency*.

free-standing insert (FSI)   a preprinted advertisement or, most often, a coupon sheet(s) placed loosely in a newspaper (especially the Sunday edition); can be one page or, more commonly, several pages in a stand-alone "booklet" inserted in the Sunday newspaper.

freeze frame   in television advertising, when a specific frame, or individual picture, is held still for several seconds on the screen; often-used technique at the close of a commercial.

frequency   the number of times individuals in the target audience are exposed to (reached by) a media vehicle during a given period of time, say, one week or one month; see also *average frequency, effective frequency, reach,* and *effective reach*.

frequency discount   a price reduction offered to the advertiser by a media vehicle, based on the total amount of advertising space or time bought by the advertiser in a specified period of time, such as one year; the more often the advertiser advertises in the media vehicle in a given time period, the greater the discount. Occasionally referred to as *continuity discount*. See also *per-issue rate*.

frequency marketing   see *frequency program*.

frequency program   a consumer sales promotion activity in which there is a continuous offer of free merchandise, services, or discounted prices on future purchases, based on volume or frequency of purchases by the consumer; designed for customer retention, getting customers to make repeat purchases. Also called *frequent-shopper/reward program, frequent-user program, loyalty program, continuity program, frequency marketing,* or *patronage reward*.

frequent-shopper program   see *frequency program*.

fringe   in the television broadcast day, refers to *early fringe* (4:00 P.M.–7:00 P.M.) or *late fringe* (11:30 P.M.–1:00 A.M.); i.e., the periods immediately before *prime time* and immediately after *late news*. See also *dayparts*.

fringe area   the outermost area touched by a television or radio station's signal or a publication's distribution; the fringe area for one vehicle normally is overlapped by or just inside another vehicle's primary coverage area.

fringe publication   a periodical of secondary importance to the advertiser in that it does not reach the target audience as efficiently or as effectively as others.

fringe time   see *fringe*.

front cover   the outside cover page of a magazine, i.e., the title page; also called the *first cover (1C)*.

front-end display   an advertising sign on the outside front of a bus or rapid-transit vehicle, mounted between the headlights; also called a *headlight poster*. See also *back-end display* and *headlight poster*.

front-end load   in advertising scheduling, allocating the major part of advertising or promotion budget expenditures to the early segment of a campaign; see also *back-end load*.

front-of-store display a promotional display at the front section of a retail store, in view immediately upon entering the store; a prime location for a store display.

fulfillment the process of carrying out all details relative to a marketer's sales promotion program to make sure qualified consumers receive the offer in full; see also *fulfillment house.*

fulfillment house (center) a firm that provides the services needed to make good on or fulfill offers to consumers made by marketers; e.g., verifying, picking, packing, and mailing samples, prizes, coupons, premiums, or rebates to consumers who have met all requirements set by the marketer for the promotion. Also called a *handling house.*

full disclosure see *affirmative disclosure.*

full position in newspaper advertising, a preferred position in which the advertisement follows and is adjacent to text, or is placed near the top of the page and on top of text; usually sold at a premium price. Also called *following reading matter.* See also *preferred position, run-of-the-press (ROP) position,* and *island position.*

full run insertion of an advertisement in every edition of a publication; also refers to when an advertiser has a *car card* in every bus or car in a transit system. See also *full showing.*

full showing in outdoor advertising, the number of billboards needed to obtain complete coverage of the traffic population (i.e., reach everyone at least once) in a particular market, generally as measured over a 30-day period; in transit advertising, an advertiser's *car card* in every vehicle in a transit line's system. Also called a *100 showing.* See also *outdoor advertising, transit advertising, full run,* and *showing.*

full-color see *four-color.*

full-function wholesaler see *service wholesaler.*

full-program sponsorship a broadcast program sponsored in its entirety by a single advertiser.

full-service advertising agency an agency that offers its advertisers/clients a complete range of advertising services, such as management, planning, creative, media, research, production, and accounting, plus the capabilities to direct or handle the client's sales promotion, public relations, and direct-marketing efforts; an agency capable of handling all the promotional needs of its clients. See also *limited-service advertising agency.*

full-service wholesaler see *service wholesaler.*

functional audit an in-depth review and appraisal of all aspects of one part of an organization's marketing program, such as marketing communications, or advertising, sales promotion, or public relations.

functional discount see *trade discount.*

functional risk see *performance risk.*

functions of intermediaries see *middleman functions.*

fusion marketing in Internet marketing, mixing banners with electronic mail advertising and other types of promotion.

G

GRPs   see *gross rating points.*

Gallup and Robinson (G & R)   a leading marketing and advertising research organization with a wide range of research capabilities providing marketers, advertisers, and agencies with data and tools to assess the efficiency and effectiveness of advertising; specializes in copytesting, tracking studies, concept testing, media research, claims substantiation, spokesperson testing, and event sponsorship evaluation, plus custom-research projects covering all aspects of marketing communications (television, magazine, newspapers, radio, and the Internet) in both the consumer and business-to-business markets. See also *InTeleTest, In-View Test, Magazine Impact Research Service (MIRS),* and *Advertising Response Modeling (ARM).*

galvanic skin response   a person's reaction to a stimulus, as measured by electrical monitoring of minute amounts of skin perspiration upon exposure to the stimulus; a physiological testing technique that aims to determine the level of arousal caused by an advertisement. See also *galvanometer.*

galvanometer   in advertising research, an instrument that detects galvanic (electrical) skin response to a stimulus such as an advertisement; used to obtain a physiological measurement of extremely small changes in perspiration that suggest emotional response or arousal related to some stimulus, such as an advertisement. Used to help measure advertising effectiveness. Also called *psychogalvanometer.* See also *galvanic skin response* and *physiological testing measures.*

game   a sales promotion activity that features the offering of prizes based on chance and that requires little skill to play; generally, play continues for a period of time, often involving repeated trips to the store to continue playing for the prizes. See also *contest* and *sweepstakes.*

gap analysis   in marketing research, evaluation of data to uncover a market, large or small, that is currently not being served well or, perhaps, not being served at all, thereby representing an opportunity for the marketer.

gatefold   a magazine page that is larger than the other pages when fully displayed, but that is folded inward so that it fits into the magazine as the same size as the other pages (although when folded into the magazine, it can appear as less than a page or as two or more pages); when the page is opened and unfolded outward, it swings out like a gate to reveal the full advertisement. In effect, it is a four-page sheet when unfolded, or an extra-wide ad. The space is sold at a premium. Also called a *foldout.*

gatekeeper   the individual in an organization or the family member who controls the flow of information to the people who are part of the decision-making unit or are affected by its actions; monitors and evaluates information such as the potential value of a product or service in a way that determines what does and does not get through to the decision makers and users. Also called a *screener.*

gaze motion   the movement of an individual's eyes in reading an advertisement or viewing a commercial; eye movement can be tracked by an *eye camera.* See also *balance, contrast, emphasis, flow,* and *unity.*

general advertising   advertising other than *local advertising;* e.g., national or regional.

general magazine   see *general-interest magazine.*

general rate   in newspaper advertising, the space rate charged to a national or nonlocal advertiser; a higher rate than the local rate. Also called *national rate.* See also *local advertising, local rate,* and *national rate.*

general-circulation magazine   see *general-interest magazine.*

general-interest magazine a consumer magazine that has popular appeal and is directed to a broad rather than a specific or special-interest audience; also called a *general-circulation magazine, general magazine, mass magazine,* or *mass publication.*

generic advertising see *primary demand advertising.*

generic demand see *primary demand.*

geodemographic segmentation the demographics of people living in a particular geographic area; dividing the market into geographic clusters by combining demographic and geographic segmentation variables; the concept is based on the premise that people residing in similar areas (e.g., the same zip code or the same neighborhood) are likely to share common demographic and lifestyle characteristics, so the marketer can get a general profile of the people in each area. See also *behavioristic segmentation, demographic segmentation, geographic segmentation,* and *psychographic segmentation.* Also see *PRIZM.*

geographic edition an edition of a magazine targeted toward a particular geographic region or area, and for which a different set of advertising rates applies; e.g., the eastern edition of *Sports Illustrated,* which has a different set of rates than the southeastern and other *SI* editions. A type of *partial-run edition.* See also *demographic edition, metro edition, regional edition,* and *state edition.*

geographic segmentation dividing the total market into different geographical units or segments, such as states, regions, counties, cities, or *Designated Market Areas (DMAs);* see also *behavioristic segmentation, demographic segmentation, geodemographic segmentation,* and *psychographic segmentation.*

geographic split run placement of one advertisement in a particular geographic area served by a given publication, and a different advertisement in another geographic area covered by the same publication; the split may be between regional editions of a publication or between a particular region and the rest of the country for the same publication. Often used to test and compare the effectiveness of alternate advertisements. See also *split run, split-run test, demographic split run, subscription/newsstand split run,* and *A/B split.*

geographical weighting a media scheduling strategy in which particular geographical areas or regions are allocated a higher or lower level of advertising intensity, usually depending on sales potential; see also *Brand Development Index (BDI)* and *Category Development Index (CDI).*

geo-targeting the placement of advertising and marketing force or emphasis in geographic areas or regions that offer the best opportunities for a product or brand to achieve success; concentrating advertising or marketing efforts in selected geographic areas where there is likely to be greater incidence of purchase of a particular brand.

gimmick an unusual or novel tool, idea, or technique designed to capture an audience's attention in advertising or promotion.

giveaway a sales promotion activity in which one of a variety of promotional items is distributed at no cost or obligation to customers or prospective customers; also known as a *free offer.*

global advertising an advertising approach in which a firm uses a single plan or pattern, with a common theme and presentation, in all the countries in which it operates; see also *international advertising.*

global agency an advertising agency with worldwide capabilities, including agency offices and operations around the world.

global campaign see *global advertising* and *global marketing.*

global marketer an organization that markets its products or services worldwide; see also *global marketing.*

global marketing an approach in which a product is marketed essentially the same way everywhere in the world, with the marketer using the same marketing plan and marketing strategy across all countries in which it operates, including the same message and execution.

global markets see *international markets.*

global media the aggregate means, carriers, or channels of communications through which global advertisers get their messages to their intended audiences in international markets; there is considerable variation from country to country when it comes to media availability and effectiveness of advertising, so advertisers must adapt their message to these different markets and communication channels.

globalization in international advertising, when the advertiser uses a single campaign for all the countries in which it does business; see also *localization* and *regionalization.*

going dark a situation in which an advertiser temporarily discontinues its advertising due to special circumstances; e.g., an airline halting its advertising for a period after a mishap.

goods tangible, physical products.

goodwill the positive attitudes, opinions, and feelings toward a marketer or advertiser, its products, and programs generated by the organization's efforts and deeds that promote good relations among its several publics; e.g., a firm's advocacy or interest in supporting charitable causes or community initiatives, resulting in favorable attitudes toward the company.

government market the federal, state, county, and local agencies that purchase goods and services needed to perform their public service operations.

government regulation see *federal regulation, state regulation,* and *local regulation.*

graphic design arranging and fitting the visual devices and presentation of an advertising or promotion message; all the efforts devoted to giving the message the right look and feel. See also *graphics.*

graphics visual devices employed to enhance the impact of the other elements of an advertisement and to make the total design and effect more eye-catching, interesting, and stimulating; graphic elements involve shape, dimension, and placement of the various parts of an advertisement, including illustrations, color, typefaces, and other elements; see also *art.*

gravure see *rotogravure.*

grazing see *channel grazing.*

green consumers individuals who are very much concerned about the natural environment and are willing to modify their purchasing and consumption behavior to help protect the environment, e.g., by buying environmentally safe products.

green marketing marketing strategies and practices that are designed with their environmental impact in mind, emphasizing protection of the natural environment; marketing and promotion activities directed to individual and groups who are environmentally conscious.

grid a series of horizontal and vertical lines used to assist the copy, art, and layout people in the design of an advertisement; an advertising design planning tool.

grid card a system of presenting television and radio station spot advertising rates in which the *rate card,* usually set in a matrix format, shows the different rates for the various commercial positions, with individual spot charges set according to audience ratings and the demand for the spots by advertisers; see also *spot advertising rates* and *rate card.*

gridlocking a media scheduling strategy that calls for scheduling a television commercial on one network while the same commercial is scheduled immediately before it or after it on the other networks.

gross amount the grand total or sum, prior to any reductions or adjustments; see also *net amount.*

gross audience see *gross impressions.*

gross billings the total monetary worth of an advertising agency's purchase of media time and space on behalf of its advertisers/clients, valued at the highest rate, without regard to agency commissions or discounts of any kind. See also *gross rate.*

gross impressions an expression of the weight of a media plan; the sum of all target audience exposures to the media vehicles in a media plan, including duplications (each exposure = one impression). Also called *gross audience.* See also *advertising weight, message weight, net audience, net impressions, gross rating points, target rating points,* and *unduplicated audience.*

gross margin net sales minus cost of goods sold; the money available to pay for marketing and other expenses needed to operate the business. See also *gross sales, gross profit, net sales, net profit,* and *cost of goods sold.*

gross message weight see *gross impressions* and *gross rating points.*

gross profit sales revenue minus sales costs; see also *gross margin, gross sales, net sales, net profit,* and *cost of goods sold.*

gross rate see *open rate.*

gross rating points (GRPs) a measure of audience size, in which *reach × average frequency = gross rating* *points;* the total duplicated audience that is exposed to all the vehicles in a particular media schedule, typically expressed for a given time period within the schedule, such as a four-week period. One rating point equals one percent of the audience. An expression of the total advertising weight in an advertising schedule. The sum of ratings delivered by all media vehicles in an advertising schedule. Example: 20 commercials each with a 12 rating yield a total of 240 GRPs. See also *reach, average frequency, advertising weight, gross impressions, message weight,* and *target rating points (TRPs).*

gross rating point buy the basic method of buying outdoor advertising; for example, a *100-GRP buy* is the number of posters needed to deliver exposure to 100 percent of the market's population, as quoted on a daily, weekly, or monthly basis; a *75-GRP buy, 50-GRP buy,* or *25-GRP buy* would deliver exposures accordingly. See also *gross rating points (GRPs)* and *showing.*

gross sales the invoice value of sales before deducting customer discounts, returns, and allowances; i.e., the total amount paid by customers before deductions. See also *gross profit, gross margin, net sales, net profit,* and *cost of goods sold.*

gross-up see *markup charge* and *production add-on.*

group two or more individuals sharing a set of beliefs, values, and behavioral patterns; see *reference group.*

group advertising advertising undertaken by a number of independent retailers, acting together in a common interest; see also *horizontal cooperative advertising.*

group discount in media, a lower advertising rate given to an advertiser that agrees to place advertisements in a particular set of publications owned by a single publisher or that have joined in an effort to attract advertising revenue; e.g., Conde Nast publications that include, among others, *Gourmet, Bon Appetit, Vogue, Self, Allure, Bride's, Glamour, Modern Bride, Vanity Fair,* and *Conde Nast Traveler,* or, in business media, Fairchild publications, such as *Home Furnishings News* and *InFurniture* magazine, both serving members of the home furnishings industry.

group mailing see *cooperative mailing.*

group promotion a sales promotion event that features several brands of the same company joined together under a common theme; as opposed to a *tie-in* or joint promotion, which involves different companies' brands under a unified theme. See *tie-in promotion.*

group system of agency organization a system of organizing a team or group in an advertising agency to work together on a specific account; each group is managed by an account executive or account supervisor and consists of individuals with account management, planning, creative, media, research, production, sales promotion, direct marketing, and/or interactive marketing expertise—whatever is needed for the group to work together as a unit to effectively serve the clients being handled by the particular group. Each agency team or group may be viewed as a "little agency" unto itself. See also *advertising agency* and *department system of agency organization.*

growth stage the second stage of the product life cycle, in which the product's sales begin to climb quickly, at an increasing rate through much of the stage; industry profits peak toward the end of the stage. Often characterized by new models and product versions for different market segments, and heightened competition, especially from less expensive substitutes. Building *selective demand* is key. See also *product life cycle, introduction stage, maturity stage,* and *decline stage.*

growth strategies the approaches and methods a firm might pursue to take advantage of opportunities for increasing and strengthening its sales and profits; see also *market penetration, market development, product development,* and *diversification.*

guaranteed circulation the minimum number of copies of a particular issue of a publication stated and guaranteed by the publisher to be delivered; publisher refunds advertiser if this number is not reached. See also *Audit Bureau of Circulations (ABC).*

guaranteed rate base in print media, the circulation number that is the basis for a periodical's advertising, and which is officially verified by an audit, such as that done by the *Audit Bureau of Circulations (ABC);* see also *rate base* and *Audit Bureau of Circulations (ABC).*

guerrilla marketing strategically competing for market share by using creative, unconventional, nontraditional marketing tactics that often go to the edge.

Guidelines for Children's Advertising   a set of principles governing advertising directed to children under 12 and applying to all media, including print, broadcast television, cable television, radio, video, point-of-sale, online advertising, and packaging; major purpose is to prevent deception and to take into account the level of knowledge, impressionability, and vulnerability of the child audience. A self-regulatory set of guidelines advanced by the *Children's Advertising Review Unit (CARU)*. See also *Children's Advertising Review Unit (CARU)*.

Guidelines for Comparative Advertising   a set of standards for the ethical use of comparative advertising, governing the truthfulness, claim substantiation, and tastefulness of advertising that seeks to make comparisons between and among different products or services; established by the *American Association of Advertising Agencies (AAAA)* for the use and benefit of its members. See also *American Association of Advertising Agencies (AAAA), Standards of Practice,* and *Creative Code.*

Gunning Fog Index   a readability index that assesses the ease with which advertising writing, i.e., copy, can be read; result is the minimum grade level at which the writing can be easily read. Computation of this index involves determining the average number of words per sentence, determining the percentage of "hard" words (e.g., abstract words or long words), adding the two factors, and then multiplying by 0.4. Example: advertising copy consisting of 80 words in 8 sentences, with 16 hard words, yields an average sentence length of 10 words, with 20% deemed hard words; therefore, $10 + 20 = 30 \times 0.4 = 12.0$, or a 12th-grade level of reading difficulty. Devised by Robert Gunning. See also *Flesch Reading Ease Score.*

gutter   in a magazine, the margin where two facing pages come together at the binding on the inside of the page; the inner margin of a magazine page, next to the binding.

gutter bleed   a magazine advertisement that goes all the way to the inside edge of the page, through the *gutter* into the binding of the magazine.

gutter position   an advertising position beside the *gutter* on a magazine page. See also *gutter.*

H

HDTV see *High Definition Television.*

HUR see *households using radio.*

HUT see *households using television.*

habitual buying behavior consumer decision making characterized by an individual repeating his or her previous purchases of a specific brand in a particular product category, with little or no thought given to the purchase; most often involves a *low-involvement* purchase.

half run in *car card* advertising, placing a card in every other vehicle in the transit system; see also *car card, full run,* and *full showing.*

half showing in outdoor and transit advertising, one-half of a full showing; i.e., a 50 showing. See also *full run, full showing, half run,* and *25 showing.*

half-page double spread see *half-page spread.*

half-page island position in magazine advertising, a preferred position in which the half-page advertisement has no other ad on the other half of the page; not all publications make this option available.

half-page spread in magazine or other print advertising, an advertisement that is spread horizontally across the two facing pages, occupying the entire upper half or lower half of the two pages; sometimes called *half-page double spread.* See also *double-page spread, double spread,* and *double truck.*

halo effect a phenomenon in which an individual transfers an impression about, say, one product to other products of the same marketer, by association; attributing qualities of one entity to another, based on knowledge and opinions about the former. For example, positive thoughts about an organization's previous civic or charitable efforts are transferred, by association, to the current effort.

hand count in out-of-home advertising, a *traffic count* for a particular advertising structure's location done when there is no official source available or when the existing data are obsolete; usually performed by the plant operator. See also *traffic count, official count,* and *counting station.*

handbill an advertising piece distributed by hand to homes, public places, people in the street, and other locations; generally, a single-page advertising message. Also called a *flyer.* See also *circular.*

handling allowance payment by a manufacturer to a retailer for functions performed as part of a given promotion activity or program; e.g., coupon redemption, stocking greater quantities of a product being featured in a promotion, or other promotion activities requiring special handling by a manufacturer's distributor.

handling house see *fulfillment house.*

handling objections the stage in the personal selling process in which the salesperson deals with a prospective customer's resistance to buying; focus is on identifying the precise nature of the objections, discussing them, and overcoming the prospect's resistance in a convincing way. See also *prospecting, preapproach, approach, presentation, closing,* and *follow-up.*

hard goods see *durable goods.*

hard-sell advertising an advertising style that is very direct, aggressive, and forceful in its attempt to influence the audience; see also *soft-sell advertising.*

harmony in advertising design and layout, the principle relating to the compatibility of all the elements comprising an advertisement; e.g., the typeface and type size of the copy should be compatible or "fit" with the typeface and type size used in the headline. See also *balance, contrast, emphasis, flow, gaze motion,* and *unity.*

Harris Interactive a leading marketing and advertising research firm offering advertisers, agencies, media buyers, and the media a broad range of syndicated and custom data, including copytesting, communications testing, concept testing, brand tracking, brand image studies, segmentation studies, product positioning studies, Web site evaluation, Internet advertising assessment, and several other types of research; partners with *USA Today* with the *Ad Track index,* an advertising effectiveness tracking service reported weekly at *www.usatoday.com.*

harvesting at the point in a product's or service's sales or profit level where further decline is inevitable and the *opportunity costs* of trying to rejuvenate it are too high, the practice of significantly reducing, even eliminating, the marketing and advertising expenditures on the product or service and letting it ride as long as the most loyal customers sustain it.

Hazardous Substances Act see *Federal Hazardous Substances Labeling Act.*

head see *headline.*

head of household for marketing purposes, the individual in a family who is responsible for major buying decisions.

headlight poster an advertising sign mounted between the headlights of a bus or rapid-transit vehicle; measures approximately 21″ high × 44″ wide. See also *exterior bus, taillight poster, queen-size poster,* and *king-size poster.*

headline the most prominent copy in an advertisement, usually at or near the top of the ad (though sometimes at the bottom) and set in bigger, bolder type than the body copy; intended as an attention-getting device, since its words are the first that are seen and read in the ad. See also *benefit headline, command headline, curiosity headline, news-information headline,* and *question headline.* Also see *subhead.*

head-on position in outdoor advertising, placement of a poster or advertising structure so that it directly faces oncoming traffic.

health and safety risk see *physical risk.*

heavy users consumers who purchase and use a product or service in much larger quantities and/or much more frequently than others, in contrast to *moderate users, light users,* or *nonusers.*

heavy-copy ad see *copy-heavy ad.*

heavy-up scheduling in media scheduling, to increase advertising intensity; increasing expenditures at any time within a media schedule, i.e., a *burst,* or *blitz,* of advertising activity. Can involve higher total expenditures across the entire range of an advertiser's media schedule or added use of a particular medium or media vehicle. See also *blitz, bursting,* and *pulsing.*

hedonism in consumer behavior, placing disproportionate weight on pleasure-seeking in making marketplace decisions; i.e., the pursuit of products that provide the greatest self-gratification or pleasure without regard to more prudent or realistic choices.

hello money in sales promotion, a fee paid by a manufacturer for making a sales presentation to a retailer; also called a *presentation fee.*

heterogeneous shopping products shopping products that the consumer regards as different from one another in some meaningful way, and therefore searches the alternatives for quality, style, and overall suitability prior to purchasing; price is a secondary factor. See also *homogeneous shopping products, consumer products classification system, convenience products, shopping products, specialty products,* and *unsought products.*

heuristics rules of thumb or very simple guidelines used by consumers to simplify and expedite their decisions in choosing among alternatives; e.g., buy the least expensive brand or buy the product that sponsors a favorite baseball team's telecasts.

hiatus in media scheduling, the period of complete advertising inactivity within a *flighting* schedule that alternates periods of advertising with periods of no advertising; a period of nonactivity between advertising flights. See *flighting.*

hidden offer a free offer of some kind "buried" near the end of an advertisement that is mostly text, with no attention called to it beforehand; often used as a test to determine the extent to which the ad was read. Also called a *buried offer* or *blind offer.*

hierarchy of effects a model of advertising's effects on consumers; the idea that consumer response to advertising progresses in stages, going along the following path: awareness-knowledge-liking-preference-conviction-purchase; can help in setting advertising objectives. Can be used by the advertiser to define advertising and promotion program goals. Proposed by researchers Robert Lavidge and Gary Steiner. See also *communications objectives* and *promotion objectives.*

hierarchy of needs   a theory of motivation that suggests a person will satisfy lower-level needs before attempting to satisfy higher-level needs; in sequential stages, a person will satisfy his or her physiological needs first, and then, in order, his or her safety needs, love and belongingness needs, esteem needs, and, finally, self-actualization (self-fulfillment) needs. A theory of psychologist Abraham Maslow.

High Definition Television (HDTV)   a technological system that provides the highest quality television picture and sound.

high-involvement decision making   marketplace decisions on products and services that have high personal relevance for the consumer and for which the perceived risks and consequences of the decision are significant in the mind of the consumer; consumer engages in extensive information search and evaluation. See also *consumer decision process* and *low-involvement decision making.*

high-spot bulletin   in outdoor advertising, placement of an advertising structure at a strategic spot to give it greater exposure and visibility; sometimes larger than other bulletins in the same market.

Highway Beautification Act of 1965 (HBA)   Federal legislation that mandates state controls related to outdoor media on interstate highways, placing strong controls over the placement of billboards and other outdoor signs.

hit   a visit to a Web site or to an advertisement; also called a *click, page view,* or *ad request.*

hitchhiker   a television or radio commercial, placed at the end of a program, that features a product not advertised earlier in the program, by an advertiser who previously promoted another of its products in the program; also may be used to denote any local commercial that is inserted in a national program. Often referred to as a *drop-in ad.* Sometimes refers to promotional material added to a direct mailing sent to consumers for another purpose. See also *ride-along* and *statement stuffer.*

holding power   the degree to which a television or radio program keeps its audience throughout the entire program. To calculate: divide average audience by total audience and multiply by 100, to express it as a percentage.

holdover audience   that portion of a television or radio program's audience that carries over from the program immediately preceding it on the same station; also known as *carryover audience* or *inherited audience.*

Hollywood-model advertising agency   organization and staffing that features low overhead and a reliance on freelancers and contract workers.

home shopping networks   see *shoppers network/ programs.*

homepage   on the Internet, the first page that appears on the computer screen after entering a particular organization's address or Web site; also can refer to the Web site itself. See also *Web site.*

homes passed   the number of households in which CATV is either in service or has the potential to be because the cable provider's lines are in place for a hookup on request.

homes using TV (HUT)   see *households using television (HUT).*

homogeneous shopping products   shopping products that the consumer regards as quite similar and, therefore, searches for the best available price among them; see also *heterogeneous shopping products, consumer products classification system, convenience products, shopping products, specialty products,* and *unsought products.*

hook   a particular feature of a commercial or an advertisement (e.g., a product attribute, a benefit, an emotion, a clever phrase, a jingle, a person) that sparks immediate attention, interest, and desire for action by the consumer; what the consumer grabs onto in the advertising. The specific feature that makes the advertising memorable.

horizontal buy   buying advertising time or space in several different media classes (e.g., television, magazines, and outdoor) to achieve maximum *reach* or exposure; in contrast to a *vertical buy,* in which the advertiser buys time or space in several different vehicles in the same medium, such as magazines. See also *vertical buy.*

horizontal cooperative advertising a joint advertising effort by a group of businesses or organizations related by the products or services they sell (e.g., auto dealers, milk producers, apple growers, fast-food franchises, realtors) or by the sharing of common interests (e.g., retail stores in a shopping mall or town, local merchants in support of public education); advertising costs are shared and resources are pooled to run advertising that generates interest and traffic for the benefit of all involved. See also *cooperative advertising* and *vertical cooperative advertising*. Also see *cooperative advertising kit*.

horizontal cume in television or radio, the total number of people or households tuned to a particular station or network at the same time on different days of the week; can also refer to the audience of two programs in the same time slot on successive days; see also *vertical cume* and *cumulative audience*.

horizontal discount a discount offered by a media vehicle to an advertiser who buys advertising time or space over an extended period of time, generally one year.

horizontal half-page an advertisement that occupies the upper half or the lower half of a page in a periodical; see also *vertical half-page*.

horizontal marketing system a distribution channel arrangement whereby two or more organizations at the same level join together for marketing purposes to capitalize on a new opportunity; e.g., a bank and a supermarket agree to have the bank's ATMs located at the supermarket's sites, two manufacturers combining to achieve economies of scale that wouldn't be possible with each acting alone, in meeting the needs and demands of a very large retailer, or two wholesalers joining together to serve a particular region at a certain time of year. See also *vertical marketing system (VMS), corporate VMS, contractual VMS, administered VMS, conventional marketing system,* and *hybrid marketing system.*

horizontal publication a trade magazine or paper editorially designed for individuals holding similar positions or job functions in different industries or types of businesses; e.g., publications aimed at purchasing agents, computer programmers, sales managers, or public relations directors regardless of industry or business. Examples: *Purchasing, Auditing, Sales & Marketing Management, Public Relations Quarterly, Advertising Age.* See also *vertical publication.*

horizontal saturation (rotation) in television or radio advertising scheduling, buying advertising time on the same program or in the same time period on several days each week; see also *vertical saturation.*

hot button the major point or element in an advertisement that strikes a sensitive chord and motivates the prospective buyer to a response or action desired by the advertiser; what "turns on" the buyer. See also *Big Idea, hook,* and *unique selling proposition (USP).*

house account an advertising or other promotion client that is handled by the advertising agency's owner or top management, rather than assigned to an account executive; when done, it is typically for a client who is special by way of size, prestige, or other factor. In addition, refers to a particularly important customer handled by a firm's home office executives rather than the field sales force or regional office. Also called a *direct account.*

house ad advertising by a media vehicle for itself in its own vehicle; e.g., an advertisement for a particular newspaper that appears in its own newspaper, or a commercial for a radio station that airs on its own station. Sometimes refers to a company's advertising itself, as opposed to it products or services, i.e., *institutional* or *corporate advertising.*

house agency see *in-house agency.*

house list an organization's exclusively owned list generated from its internal records, and which contains names, addresses, and other information on individuals considered important to the advertiser, such as present customers, past customers, or good prospects; usually for direct-marketing purposes. See also *internal list* and *external list.*

house organ see *house publication.*

house publication a controlled-circulation periodical published by an organization, generally for public relations purposes, to keep key people informed of matters of central importance to the organization; i.e., a company's own publication. An *internal house publication,* or simply *internal publication,* is published primarily for company personnel, including the sales force, while an *external house publication,* or *external publication,* is aimed at the company's customers, dealers, investors, and other important publics. Also known as a *company magazine* or *house organ.*

household   all individuals who occupy a single housing unit, i.e., a house, apartment, or even a single room, or those quarters having direct access from the outside or through a common hall and whose occupants do not live and eat with others persons in the building; according to the U.S. Department of Commerce, Bureau of the Census.

household consumers   consumers who are part of a *household;* see also *household.*

household ratings   the standard for measuring program tuning, i.e., what a household watches; see also *diary method, people meter, set-tuning meter,* and *sweeps.*

household tracking report   a report that shows, over an extended period of time, the individual program ratings for the different television networks; a *Nielsen Media Research* service.

households using radio (HUR)   the number of households in a given local market or nationally that were listening to a particular radio program or were listening to any station during a certain time period.

households using television (HUT)   the number of households in a given local market or nationally that were watching a particular television program or were watching any station during a given time period; used as a base for ratings. Also called *sets in use.* A *Nielsen Media Research* term. See also *ratings, persons using television (PUT),* and *sets-in-use.*

HTML (Hyper Text Transfer Protocol)   the computer language used to create pages and content on the Web.

humor format   in advertising, a creative *execution format* showing people and situations marked by comedy, silliness, or frivolity; e.g., a commercial showing a house literally falling apart shortly after a do-it-yourself homeowner did some repairs using, of course, the "wrong" products. See also *straightforward factual, news, demonstration, problem-solution, slice-of-life, dramatization, symbolic association, fantasy, animation, still-life, spokesperson, testimonial,* and *comparison formats.*

hunter   a sales representative who finds and brings in new business.

hybrid marketing   the use of a broad range of marketing activities, approaches, and channels in an attempt to make sure the target audience is exposed to the marketer's message and appeals at some point in the decision-making process.

hybrid marketing system   a distribution system in which one firm establishes two or more separate marketing channels to serve its customers; e.g., a computer company with a sales force selling directly to institutional accounts, while also selling its products to retailers as well as through its own online store. See also *vertical marketing system (VMS), corporate VMS, contractual VMS, administered VMS, conventional marketing system,* and *horizontal marketing system.* Also see *dual distribution.*

hypermarket   see *superstore.*

hyping   in television, a station's or network's attempt to increase audiences and ratings by means of special programming, such as that involving investigative reporting on a major issue, contests, blockbuster movies, and the like; especially common during *sweeps* periods. See also *sweeps.*

I

IAA   see *International Advertising Association.*

IAB   see *Interactive Advertising Bureau.*

IBC   see *inside back cover.*

ID   see *station identification.*

IFC   see *inside front cover.*

IMC   see *integrated marketing communications.*

IRI   see *Information Resources, Inc.*

ISP   see *Internet Service Provider.*

iceberg principle   the idea that the greater part of the problem is often hidden from view, i.e., the more valuable information is that which is not immediately apparent; the major part of a problem or situation is not readily seen, but rather is below the surface.

idea advertising   nonproduct advertising, such as that for environmental issues, anti-substance abuse, gun control, or nutrition awareness; see also *product advertising, nonproduct advertising,* and *services advertising.*

idea generation   the first stage of the new-product development process, in which ideas are elicited from a variety of sources, such as marketing research, customers, competitors, intermediaries, suppliers, research and development, and the sales force; see also *new-product development process, idea screening, concept testing, market evaluation, product development, marketing plan, market testing,* and *commercialization.*

idea screening   the second stage of the new-product development process, in which each product idea that has been generated is judged on criteria such as its potential strengths and weaknesses, how well it would fit with the company's objectives and mission, its compatibility with market trends, and a rough estimate of its potential for an acceptable return-on-investment (ROI); see also *new-product development process, idea generation, concept testing, market evaluation, product development, marketing plan, market testing,* and *commercialization.*

ideal self   a person's idea of what he or she would like to be; see also *self-image.*

ideation   the process of forming and conceptualizing new and improved ideas and approaches to marketing issues and problems.

identification commercial (ID)   a short (:10) television or radio commercial aired during a station break, often with the station's call letters tagged on at the end; the commercial is actually 8 seconds in length, with the other 2 seconds for the station identification.

identity media   a variety of visual means, other than those associated with the common methods and activities of marketing communications, through which a company calls attention to itself by providing instant recognition of the company or organization name; e.g., company logo, stationery, business cards, uniforms, rolling stock (trucks, delivery vans).

illuminated panel   an outdoor poster or billboard that is lighted during the evening hours to permit easy visibility of an advertising message; lighting usually operates from dusk to midnight. See also *billboard.*

illustration   in print advertising, any of a number of different drawings, sketches, diagrams, figures, photographs, or other representations that are a visual component of an advertisement.

illustrator   the person who creates the pictures used in print advertising.

image   what the consumer thinks, as a result of seeing, hearing about, or otherwise coming into contact with an organization, product, or service; the entire collection of thoughts summed up in a single mental picture from the consumer's viewpoint. See also *brand image, perceived value,* and *perception.*

image advertising   see *corporate advertising.*

image analysis   an appraisal of the various beliefs and impressions held by individuals toward a company, product, service, or any activity.

I-marketing   see *online marketing.*

IMC audit   research that completely investigates and appraises all aspects of a marketing communications program.

immediate-response advertising   see *direct-response advertising.*

impact   the effect an advertising message or program has on the target audience; see also *penetration.*

impact advertising   advertising designed to deliver a particularly forceful message and register with the audience in an especially powerful way so that consumers immediately take notice; a message that packs a wallop by virtue of what is said and how it is said.

impact plan   see *total audience plan (TAP).*

impact scheduling   in television or radio advertising, running the same commercial (or very similar commercials) within a short period of time on a given program, often within the same *pod,* or group of commercials between segments of a program; see also *pod.*

impersonal communications   see *nonpersonal communications.*

implementation   see *marketing implementation.*

impression   one exposure of the advertising message, i.e., any time an individual is exposed to a commercial message.

impression stream   see *ad stream.*

impressions   the total number of audience exposures, including duplication, to all media vehicles in a complete media schedule, with one exposure equaling one impression; in Internet advertising, refers to the number of times an ad banner or other ad is viewed, including duplication (also referred to as an *ad view*). See also *gross impressions.*

imprint   see *dealer imprint;* also, in outdoor advertising, refers to the small sign at the bottom (or top) of an outdoor poster identifying the owner of the billboard.

impulse purchase   an unplanned purchase, with the consumer making a spur-of-the-moment, spontaneous, in-store decision to buy.

in period   in a *flighting* pattern of *media scheduling,* the time period in which there is advertising activity; see also *flighting* and *out period.*

in-and-out promotion   a retail promotion that lasts for a very short time, often one or two days; intended as a store traffic-builder or as a merchandise sellout.

in-ad coupon   a manufacturer's coupon included as part of a retailer's advertisement and redeemable only at that store or, sometimes, at a select group of stores identified in the advertisement.

in-aisle display   at the retail level, a *point-of-purchase display* located in an aisle between shelves.

inbound telemarketing   in telemarketing, handling the details associated with order-taking; e.g., a consumer makes a selection from a catalog and telephones the order to customer service. See also *outbound telemarketing* and *telemarketing.*

incentive   any of a wide variety of sales promotion tools designed to motivate the trade, dealers, or the sales force to an activity, cooperation, or other response desired by the advertiser; used to increase the likelihood of positive action. Can also refer to consumer sales promotion efforts. Also called an *inducement.*

incentive-based method of agency compensation   see *performance-based method of agency compensation.*

incoming posters   the outdoor advertising posters seen by the traffic entering a central business district, as opposed to *outgoing posters.*

inch rate   in newspaper advertising, the cost of an advertisement based on space that measures one inch deep and one column wide; sometimes called *daily inch rate.* See also *column inch* and *Standard Advertising Unit (SAU).*

inducement   see *incentive.*

incremental cost   see *incremental effect.*

incremental effect   the additional sales or other response such as contributions to a cause, volunteer sign-ups, or membership registrations achieved by virtue of a particular activity, such as a *burst* of advertising, an additional sales representative, a point-of-purchase display, a sampling program, or other promotion effort, in which the sales jump can be attributed directly to that tactic and which would not have occurred without it. Applies in the same way to costs incurred as a result of a particular activity or program.

incremental sales   see *incremental effect*.

identification   see *station identification (ID)* and *network identification*.

independent agency   a stand-alone advertising or other promotion services firm, not owned by another firm.

independent products   goods that are not related to each other; a price change for one has no impact on demand for the other. Examples: peanut butter and paint, fountain pens and tomatoes, lawn fertilizer and bicycles. Also called *unrelated products*. See also *substitute products* and *complementary products*.

independent station   a television or radio station not affiliated with a network; also called an *indie*. See also *network*.

independent variable   in research, when determining a cause-and-effect relationship, the variable that is considered to affect some other variable; e.g., the level of advertising dollars spent (*independent variable*) and the effect on sales (*dependent variable*) or a particular message execution format (*independent variable*) and its effect on a brand's image (*dependent variable*). See also *dependent variable* and *experimental method*.

in-depth interview   see *depth interview*.

index number   a ratio or number that indicates the potential of a particular market; generally, a percentage above or below the national average. The measure of difference, usually expressed as a percentage, between one variable of a specific kind and another variable of the same kind, i.e., a number indicating the relationship between a particular factor and a base (which has a value of 100). For marketing use, the ratio helps to show a market's potential. Example: using data for "favorite brand" of domestic beer, broken down by age groups, we see an index number of 143 under Budweiser for individuals 25–34; the interpretation is that individuals 25–34 are 43 percent more likely than the rest of the adult population to have Budweiser as their favorite beer (an index number of 85 would mean they are 15 percent less likely).

indies   independent advertising agencies, or agencies that have not merged or consolidated with others, retaining independent ownership; may also refer to an independent television or radio station, i.e., one not affiliated with a *network*.

indirect advertising   sometimes used to refer to promotion of a product in an indirect way such as putting the Caterpillar brand name on clothing.

indirect channel   see *indirect distribution*.

indirect distribution   the use of intermediaries such as wholesalers, distributors, or retailers to get a manufacturer's product to the target customer; see also *direct distribution*.

indirect questioning   see *disguised research*.

individual brand   a separate brand name a manufacturer uses to market specific products; e.g., General Mills' Cheerios and Total cereals, Procter & Gamble's Crest toothpaste, Bold and Cheer detergents, Ivory soap, and Jif peanut butter.

individual location   in outdoor advertising, a site at which there is only a single *billboard* or poster structure in the immediate area.

individual product   see *product item*.

indoor panel   an advertising poster or sign on the inside of a stadium, arena, racetrack, terminal, or other building.

industrial advertising   an organization's advertising for its products and services directed to industrial firms, mostly manufacturers, i.e., to companies that need the advertiser's products and services to produce other products for eventual distribution.

industrial goods   products used in the production of other products.

industrial magazine   a magazine for those people involved in manufacturing and services; see also *business publication*.

industrial market   the market for goods and services that consists of manufacturers, businesses, and other organizations, rather than individual consumers; the totality of individuals and companies that buy or are genuine prospects to buy products for use in the production of other goods, in contrast to the consumer market. See also *business market* and *consumer market*.

industrial marketing   marketing programs and activities aimed at individuals and organizations who purchase products and services for use in the production of other products for purposes of resale. Commonly called *business marketing* or *B2B*. See also *business marketing* and *consumer marketing*.

industrial product   a product bought for use in running a business or an organization, i.e., not for personal consumption.

industry analysis   an investigation and evaluation of the characteristics, practices, and trends in a particular industry that are likely to impact an advertiser's advertising and promotion plan; an important section of a marketing communications plan. See also *integrated marketing communications plan*.

Industry Guides and Trade Regulation Rules   a publication of the *Federal Trade Commission (FTC)* that provides up-to-date information about FTC rules and regulations; important source of information for advertisers, agencies, and the media.

industry self-regulation   see *self-regulation*.

inelastic demand   a situation in which a specific percentage change in price results in a smaller percentage change in quantity demanded; i.e., consumer demand for the product or service is not price-sensitive. Example: a 3 percent increase in price leads to a 1 percent decrease in the quantity demanded or a situation where a 5 percent decrease in price leads to a 2 percent increase in the quantity demanded. Differentiation driven by advertising is thought to make demand more inelastic. See also *elastic demand, skimming price policy,* and *penetration price policy*.

inflatables   three-dimensional gas-filled displays, usually at *point-of-sale* or special-event locations; often in the form of a product or trademarked character.

in-flight advertising   advertising activities directed at airline passengers during the time they are in the air.

in-flight magazine   see *in-flight media*.

in-flight media   advertising media that aim at airline travelers during flight, the most common of which is the airline's own magazine published for its passengers; also includes movies and promotional specialties

such as playing cards or other items with the airline's logo (i.e., *identity media*). See also *in-transit media*.

in-focus exposure time   the amount of time a company or product name is clearly visible on the television screen during the broadcast of an event such as a golf tournament, an auto race, a tennis match, or a baseball game; e.g., a golf equipment manufacturer's name or logo on a golfer's hat or bag, or a sponsor's name painted on a race car. Amount of time the name is clearly visible to the viewer is then converted to its advertising value had the advertiser-sponsor purchased an equivalent amount of actual advertising time on that telecast. Comparable value is ultimately derived from combining the exact visual time and sponsor mentions and comparing it to the broadcaster's nondiscounted rate per :30 commercial, i.e., what the combined in-focus exposure time and sponsor mentions would have cost the sponsor to purchase commercial time on the telecast. A service of *Joyce Julius & Associates*. See also *media equivalencies, Sponsors Report, NTIV Analysis,* and *Joyce Julius & Associates*.

infomercial   a promotion for a product set in an entertaining television program format, usually on cable television, featuring information about a product, demonstrations, testimonials, and a sales pitch aimed at direct response from the audience; typically 30 minutes in length or, in some cases, one hour. Essentially, an unconventional form of television commercial for a product. Also called *paid programming* and *program-length commercial*. See also *advertorial*.

informal balance   in print advertising, an advertisement with components of unequally weighted size, shape, design, and color placed at varying distances from the optical center of the advertisement, i.e., arranged in an asymmetrical manner; as opposed to *formal balance*, in which all elements are equally distributed in weight throughout the entire ad, in perfect symmetry. Also called *asymmetric balance*. See also *formal balance*.

informal group   a loosely organized collection of individuals whose association with one another is based on friendship and involves considerable face-to-face interaction; e.g., a bowling group or a bridge-playing group. See also *formal group, primary group, secondary group,* and *reference group*.

informal research   see *exploratory research*.

information evaluation stage the third stage in the consumer decision process, often done simultaneously with the second stage, or information search; alternatives and information are weighed and evaluated according to criteria established by the consumer, such as how brands compare as to suitability, features, price, image, degree of need satisfaction, and other factors. See also *consumer decision process.*

information highway the entire collection of channels and means by which marketers communicate with their audiences; the complete set of routes the marketer uses to carry its message to its target audience. Truly a superhighway linked by interconnected paths.

information processing the activity by which consumers receive, organize, and interpret information from various sources, such as advertising, sales promotion, or friends, in the process of making marketplace decisions and choices; heavily influenced by the importance of the particular decision being made by the consumer, i.e., whether it is a high-involvement or low-involvement purchase decision or whether it involves complex or limited problem solving. Also referred to as *cognitive processing.* See also *cognitive learning theory* and *cognitive responses.*

Information Resources, Inc. (IRI) a major provider of marketing research information through its store tracking service involving a huge range of consumer packaged goods, with analysis and insights relevant to sales, market share, distribution, and pricing, as well as advertising and promotion; also maintains a huge database on individual consumer purchase behavior, because it collects, analyzes, and interprets a wide array of data on all aspects of consumer behavior through tracking the more than 55,000 household consumers who make up a panel. Company brands include *InfoScan* (store tracking) and *BehaviorScan* (consumer behavior tracking).

information search stage the second stage of the consumer decision process, when the consumer investigates information to aid in making the right decision in satisfying a need or want; information is sought on products, brands, stores, prices, and other factors the consumer believes relevant to a good decision. See also *consumer decision process.*

informational appeals see *rational appeals.*

informative advertising advertising whose basic purpose is to familiarize or educate the target audience about a new or existing product, as opposed to an attempt to persuade or exhort the audience to action; often involves an attempt to build primary demand. Also called *pioneering advertising.* See also *persuasive advertising* and *reminder advertising.*

informative power generally, the ability of a commercial or advertisement to deliver a cogent message.

informed decision making the state in which the consumer makes marketplace decisions based on information collected about a product.

InfoScan a store tracking service, using scanner-based marketing and sales information, that provides marketers and advertisers with detailed information on sales, market share, distribution, pricing, and promotion for hundreds of product categories; the service also includes consumer behavior tracking through a 55,000-member household panel. A single-source data system. A product of *Information Resources, Inc. (IRI).* See also *Information Resources, Inc. (IRI), BehaviorScan,* and *single-source data.*

ingredient branding when advertising or other promotion identifies a brand name of a product that is a component of another branded product; a variant of *cobranding* where branded materials are contained within other branded products. Examples: Briggs & Stratton engines in a Toro lawnmower, Beech-Nut baby foods with Chiquita bananas, Aunt Jemima waffles with Quaker oatmeal, Yoplait yogurt with Trix cereal, Post Raisin Bran cereal with Sun-Maid raisins.

ingredient labeling information appearing on a consumer product's package identifying the contents.

ingredient-sponsored cooperative advertising advertising jointly sponsored by a raw materials or component manufacturer and the end-product producer whose final product contains said material or component; designed to help promote the fact that the end product uses the company's materials or components. For example, "Intel Inside" and Compaq computers, "Teflon Non-Stick" and Revere cookware, or "Gore-Tex" and Nike running suits.

inherited audience see *holdover audience.*

in-home audience exposure to advertising and media in the home, rather than out-of-home;

e.g., radio listeners in the home vs. cars or offices, or magazine readers (subscribers and newsstand buyers) in the home vs. waiting rooms or libraries.

in-house agency an advertising agency owned or controlled by the advertiser; the agency is organized and staffed to operate in the manner of an independent, full-service agency, equipped to plan and execute all or some of the company's advertising and promotion program. Sometimes called a *house agency.*

in-house regulation a form of self-regulation involving internal efforts by an individual organization to establish standards of acceptability for operating in the best interests of consumers and in a competitively responsible way and, within that framework, to review all advertising and marketing practices prior to launch; see also *federal regulation, state regulation, local regulation,* and *self-regulation.*

ink refers to the press coverage given to an event, advertising campaign, product, individual, or any other marketing-related element; usually called *PR* or *publicity.*

in-kind sponsorship deal a company's payment of the sponsorship fee in goods or services instead of cash; e.g., an automobile company that provides transportation for participants and volunteers in a golf tournament in lieu of a cash payment, a power tool company that provides the power tools and one of its expert personnel to assist the host for a television station's "do-it-yourself" carpentry program, a wireless communications products company providing the communications equipment for an event, or an airline that provides transportation for the announcers and technicians for a football contest, all in lieu of a cash payment. See also *sponsorship.*

inline ad in Internet advertising, an advertiser's online *advertorial* positioned within a Web site.

in-magazine test in magazine advertising testing, a technique in which respondents are asked to go through a particular magazine and point out those advertisements he or she remembers seeing; see also *recognition method.*

in-market assessment in advertising research, studying and measuring ongoing advertising plans and strategies; see also *tracking study.*

innovation new product, service, or idea; see also *adoption process, adopter categories,* and *diffusion process.*

innovators the first group of the adopter categories in the diffusion process of new products, services, or ideas, i.e., the earliest purchasers of a new product; those individuals most willing to accept the risks associated with trying a new product. See also *adoption process, adopter categories, adoption curve, diffusion process, early adopters, early majority, late majority,* and *laggards.*

in-out display see *temporary display.*

in-pack coupon a coupon inserted into a product's package and available only when the buyer opens the package; see also *coupon.*

in-pack premium an item or other offer inserted into a product's package and available only when the buyer opens the package; see also *premium.*

in-program placement in television advertising, commercial time that is scheduled within the particular program, as opposed to immediately preceding or following the program during the break; see also *adjacency.*

inquiry a response sent directly from the message recipient to the advertiser, normally in answer to an advertisement, a commercial or a public relations piece; response may be by telephone, by mail, or in person, and usually involves a request for more information about a promotional offer or other subject of the message.

inquiry test a method of testing the effectiveness of a promotional program, especially advertising and public relations efforts, by tabulating the number of responses made by the audience, such as a request for information.

insert an ad, card, brochure, or other promotional piece, usually on heavier paper stock, placed inside a magazine, newspaper, or direct-mail envelope.

insertion an advertisement in a newspaper or magazine.

insertion order formal written instructions, specifications, and authorization from the advertiser or its agency to the print media vehicle to run an advertisement of a certain size on a particular date at an agreed-upon price and, if applicable, in a preferred position; the advertising copy may accompany the insertion order or follow soon thereafter. See also *media schedule* and *media scheduling.*

insertion schedule see *media schedule.*

inset a graphics or artwork element, including a photo, placed inside another graphics or art element (often in a little box) or which is surrounded by type, giving it a boxy appearance.

inside back cover (IBC) the inside of a magazine's back cover, an advertising position that commands a premium rate; also called the *third cover.* See also *inside front cover* and *outside back cover.*

inside card advertising placed on the interior of a bus, train, or any transit car; see *car card.*

inside front cover (IFC) the inside of the front cover of a magazine, an advertising position that commands a premium rate; also known as the *second cover.* See also *inside back cover* and *outside back cover.*

inside panel in a multiposter *showing* at a given location, any *billboard* in the group except the one closest to traffic; see also *outside panel.*

instant coupon a coupon attached to the outside of a product's package and easily removable and redeemable at the checkout counter for the current purchase; can also refer to coupons distributed to the consumer by other means inside the store. See also *in-store couponing.*

Instantaneous Audimeter see *Audimeter.*

Institute of Outdoor Advertising see *Outdoor Advertising Association of America (OAAA).*

institutional advertising an advertising message that promotes the image, reputation, and ideas of the company or organization, as opposed to the firm's products and services; typically is the focus of the entire advertisement or commercial, although such copy may be woven into the firm's product advertising to provide reassurance and to gain the confidence and trust of the target audience. See also *corporate advertising.*

institutional copy a form of body copy that focuses on the advertiser's organization rather than the merits of its product; may be used in combination with selling copy for the product or as the entire focus of the message in institutional advertising. See also *body copy* and *institutional advertising.*

institutional market consists of organizations such as schools and hospitals, or organizations whose mission is to care for and to serve people on its premises.

in-store couponing the distribution of coupons to customers inside the store, by means of shelf dispensers, electronic dispensers at checkout, handouts, and other ways.

in-store media the range of advertising and promotion vehicles that are deployed inside a store to reach the consumer while shopping; e.g., *point-of-purchase displays;* shopping carts; window, wall, and ceiling banners; loudspeakers; coupon dispensers; shelf signs; and in-store radio advertising.

in-store promotions a catch-all term for the wide variety of sales promotion and advertising efforts that occur at the *point-of-purchase;* includes activities such as in-store *sampling, displays,* features, and *electronic promotions.* See also *out-of-store promotions.*

in-store sampling a sales promotion activity that involves distributing free trial portions or sizes of a product to customers inside the store; e.g., food products or cosmetics.

in-tab sample in radio audience research, the number of usable *diaries* actually tabulated to produce an *Arbitron Radio Market Report.* See also *Arbitron.*

integrated marketing communications a cohesive combination of marketing communications activities, techniques, and media designed to deliver a coordinated message to a target market with a powerful and synergistic effect, while achieving a common objective or set of objectives; see also *integrated marketing communications plan* and *marketing communications campaign.*

integrated marketing communications plan a comprehensive blueprint that coordinates the activities and tools of marketing communications—advertising, sales promotion, public relations, direct marketing, and personal selling—to deliver a consistent and persuasive message to the target audience; i.e., coordination of the promotion mix elements, within the context of the marketing mix, to convey a consistent and unified message, with all elements designed to achieve a common objective(s).

InTeleTest in advertising research, a television commercial copytesting service that yields validated, evaluative, and full-sample diagnostic information in one system; television commercials are presented using an at-home, in-program context via VCR cassettes among widely dispersed samples. A product of *Gallup and Robinson (G&R)*. See also *copytesting, Gallup and Robinson (G&R), In-View Test, Magazine Impact Research Service (MIRS),* and *Advertising Response Modeling (ARM).*

intelligence see *marketing intelligence.*

IntelliQuest a leading research company providing data for the high-tech, Internet, and wireless communications industries; uses consumer panels and tracking to serve a broad range of research and information needs.

intensity in outdoor advertising, the extent to which the poster locations provide coverage of a particular market; a 100 *showing* = 100 intensity. Also refers to the amount of advertising effort in a given period of time.

intensive distribution a marketing strategy whereby a manufacturer sells its product in most every possible location to virtually any retailer who is willing to carry it, with quite minimum standards that must be met by the available retailers; also called *mass distribution.* See also *exclusive distribution* and *selective distribution.*

intention to purchase the consumer's expected future action regarding a particular product or service.

interactive advertising advertising that allows two-way communications between the advertiser and the consumer via a computer connection.

Interactive Advertising Bureau (IAB) an association dedicated to serving as the primary advocate for the interactive marketing and advertising industry, serving the needs and interests of interactive marketers and advertisers by establishing guidelines and standards to help make interactive a more attractive advertising choice, and to promote the qualities and effectiveness of interactive advertising to marketers, advertisers, agencies, and the press; see also *interactive advertising.*

interactive agency advertising and marketing firms specializing in the design and implementation of marketing communications programs that utilize the Internet, interactive kiosks, CD-ROMs, interactive television, and other such media; see also *interactive marketing* and *new media.*

interactive display see *interactive media.*

interactive kiosk see *interactive media* and *kiosk.*

interactive marketing a method of promotion or marketing in which the firm or organization customizes its marketing communications to stimulate a traceable and measurable response from individual receivers of a particular message.

interactive media a variety of media, including free-standing units such as special displays and kiosks, plus the Internet, through which the consumer can connect with and have a dialogue with the advertiser through a computer hookup, receiving product or other information, asking questions, and even ordering products and services, all on a path and at a pace controlled by the consumer.

interactive television describes the interaction of a TV viewer with the television set beyond channel selection and videotaping; basically combines traditional TV viewing with communicating via a network (e.g., the Internet). Includes playing games, banking and shopping from home, video-on-demand, e-mail, distance learning, videoconferencing, participating in polls and surveys, interactive wagering, instant ordering of pizza from a commercial, and many other applications.

intercept survey in marketing or advertising research, a procedure in which respondents are stopped at a given venue such as a shopping mall or an event, and asked to respond to a questionnaire or other research method.

interconnect a group of cable systems and cable providers that have joined forces for advertising purposes, selling advertising time on any combination of the linked systems; advertiser gets more economical rates than buying time from the individual cable system or provider. Also called *cable interconnect* or *regional interconnect.*

interest stage the second stage of the adoption process, in which the consumer gathers information about the product, its features, and attributes; see also *adoption process, awareness stage, evaluation stage, trial stage,* and *adoption stage.*

intermedia comparison comparison across media types or one medium against another (e.g., magazines vs. television or newspapers vs. radio), or even a comparison of a media vehicle in one medium against another vehicle in another medium (e.g., *Sports Illustrated* magazine vs. *Law & Order* television show). See also *intramedia comparison.*

intermediary   see *middleman.*

intermediary functions   see *middleman functions.*

internal agency   see *in-house agency.*

internal analysis   as part of the situation analysis, or preliminary investigation of factors relevant to the development of a promotion plan, analysis of those elements that involve the company itself and its product and services; e.g., organizational capabilities and resources, previous promotion programs, and the relative strengths and weaknesses of the product. See also *external analysis* and *situation analysis.*

internal audience   in public relations, the individuals or groups who are inside or have very close relationships with the organization; e.g., in-house employees or the company's distributors. See also *external audience.*

internal secondary data   information that comes from inside the company or organization doing the research; see also *secondary data.*

internal list   in direct marketing, a mailing list compiled from company records, such as those relating to customers, subscribers, donors, or inquirers; see also *external list.*

internal marketing   programs designed to gain support for an organization through activities and communications directed to the organization's employees; a marketing program whose intended audience is the firm's employees.

internal publication   a company's *house publication* published primarily for its own personnel, such as an employee newsletter; also called *internal house organ.* See also *house publication.*

internal search   in the consumer decision-making process, the retrieval of information from one's memory; see also *external search.*

International Advertising Association (IAA)   a global industry association consisting of advertisers, agencies, the media, and related services; major purpose is to promote the critical role and benefits of advertising as an important force behind all healthy economies, and to advance the notion of the significance of diverse, independent, and affordable media.

international advertising   advertising directed to individuals in foreign countries or markets; preparing and placing advertising in different markets throughout the world. See also *global advertising.*

international agency   an advertising agency with offices in foreign countries, capable of delivering the full range of advertising services needed by clients operating in a particular country or foreign market. Also referred to as a *global agency.*

international marketing   the marketing of goods and services in markets outside a company's home country; see also *global marketing.*

international markets   the different markets, or customers and potential customers, located in foreign countries; e.g., consumer market or business market. Also called *global markets.*

international media   media capable of delivering large or relevant audiences in various foreign countries; e.g., a television network or a magazine that goes into several foreign countries. Also called *global media.*

Internet   a vast, worldwide system of interconnected government, education, business, and other computer networks that permits a computer user (with a modem) to have instantaneous communications with other people, organizations, or information sources, as well as to engage in a wide variety of applications; a worldwide network of computers linked together so they can communicate with each other. See also *World Wide Web.*

Internet advertising   commercial messages that appear on Web sites.

Internet marketing   see *online marketing.*

Internet promotions   promotions on the Internet that appear on manufacturer-, retailer-, or other marketer-sponsored Web sites.

Internet Service Provider (ISP)   provider of a service that includes access· to and use of the Internet; e.g., *AmericaOnline (AOL).*

interpersonal communications   the two-way, face-to-face exchange of information between individuals; may be formal or informal.

interpersonal influences any of a variety of social influences on consumers in their marketplace decision making; e.g., the family or social groups.

Interstate Commerce Commission (ICC) now-defunct (1995) independent federal agency, created in 1887, that regulated the economics and services of companies and carriers that engaged in transportation between states, such as railroads, truckers, bus lines, pipelines, freight forwarders, water carriers, and others; with deregulation and the transfer of its functions to other agencies such as the Department of Transportation, the commission was folded. First regulatory agency in U.S. history.

interstitial in Internet advertising, flashes of an advertiser's brand information or imagery that appears between pages of a Web site while the new page is loading; a preliminary page that precedes the regular *homepage* of a Web site, usually promoting a particular site feature or providing advertising. Also referred to as a *splash page.*

interstitial programming in television, placing short programs between regular full-length programs; e.g., a cable television movie station having a short program between movies.

interviewer bias in marketing research, the researcher's influence on the respondent that affects the response and, therefore, the results of the survey; e.g., the tone of voice or facial expression used in asking a question, helping the respondent answer a question and coaxing a particular slant to an answer. May be intentional or unintentional.

intramedia comparison comparison of media vehicles within one particular medium or type of media; e.g., in print, *Time* vs. *Newsweek.* See also *intermedia comparison.*

intranet within a particular organization, a private network that permits shared applications and that is intended solely for internal company use; essentially, a company-specific *Internet.*

in-transit media a variety of publications, videotapes, and audiocassettes for the use of passengers on airlines, trains, buses, and other transportation modes; e.g., *in-flight magazines.* See also *in-flight media.*

introduction stage the first stage of the *product life cycle,* in which the product is first made available to the market; characterized by slowly rising sales and negative profit in the early period due to the high costs associated with distribution and promotion. Generally, only one or a very limited number of models. Building *primary demand* is key. See also *product life cycle, growth stage, maturity stage, decline stage,* and *primary demand.*

introductory offer a sales promotion tool aimed at consumers to stimulate interest in and encourage trial of new products or established products entering a new market; also refers to offers designed to encourage initial orders from dealers.

introductory price a temporary low initial price offered by a manufacturer to a dealer when introducing a new product, as an incentive for the dealer to accept the product and to speed its move to the market; after the agreed-upon price-deal period, the product's price is raised to its normal level. Unlike the *penetration price policy,* it is a low price for only a relatively short time. See also *skimming price policy* and *penetration price policy.*

intrusiveness the extent to which a commercial, advertisement, or campaign annoys the consumer to the point of a negative reaction toward the advertiser, extreme irritability, or, perhaps, avoidance of the advertiser's products; may result from the advertising content, its frequency of appearance, or any other factor that unsettles the consumer.

inventory the total number of advertisements (or amount of space) or commercials (or amount of time) a medium has available for sale over a given period of time.

In-View Test in advertising research, a copytesting technique that utilizes invited viewing for obtaining on-air performance (recall and persuasion); respondents are invited to view the show in which the commercial is airing or in which it has been placed for testing. A product of *Gallup and Robinson (G&R).* See also *copytesting, Gallup and Robinson (G&R), InTeleTest, Magazine Impact Research Service (MIRS),* and *Advertising Response Modeling (ARM).*

involvement the importance or degree of personal relevance of a particular product and the related decision process for that product, as perceived by the consumer; see also *high-involvement decision making* and *low-involvement decision making.*

Ipsos-ASI Advertising Research   one of the largest providers of advertising research data; performs wide range of research activities relating to *creative* development, *pretesting, posttesting, in-market assessment,* ad *tracking,* and *brand equity* evaluation.

IQ Directory   an annual directory that contains detailed data on companies involved in Internet marketing.

island ad   see *island position.*

island display   a *point-of-purchase display* or a display at another location that stands alone and can be approached from all sides.

island half   in print advertising, a half-page advertisement, at least two sides of which are next to editorial matter; usually sold at a premium rate. See also *island position.*

island position   a print advertisement that is surrounded on all sides by nonadvertising or editorial matter on the same page; usually sold at an extra charge. For example, an advertisement placed in the middle of a magazine page, with the words of a feature article surrounding the ad on all four sides. Can refer to any print advertisement that is not adjacent to any other advertising, or to a broadcast commercial aired away from any other commercial, with program content immediately before and after. See also *junior unit.*

isolated commercial   a television or radio commercial that runs alone with no other commercial just before it or just after it; typically referred to as an *isolated :30* or an *isolated :60.*

isolated :30   see *isolated commercial.*

isolated :60   see *isolated commercial.*

issue   all copies of a particular publication that are published on the same date.

issue advertising   see *advocacy advertising.*

issue life   the period during which a specific issue of a magazine is kept and read at least occasionally by the average reader of that magazine; normally considered to be five weeks for a weekly publication and three months for a monthly.

J

J.D. Power   see *Power, J.D.*

jingle   captivating music that is an integral part of the message in a television or radio commercial, generally including the advertising theme or slogan; can be an original song or an adaptation of popular music. Sometimes referred to as a *musical commercial.*

job description   a formal written statement detailing the duties, responsibilities, expectations, and conditions associated with a particular position in an organization.

joint marketing   see *comarketing.*

joint promotion   see *tie-in promotion.*

joint venturing   in international marketing, when a domestic firm forms a partnership with a foreign company to conduct production and/or marketing operations in the foreign country.

Joyce Julius & Associates   the premier company engaged in sponsorship evaluation research serving corporate sponsors, advertising agencies, and television networks; collects and distributes data that help to determine return-on-investment in sponsorships of televised sports and special events. See also *Sponsors Report* and *NTIV Analysis.*

jpg   on the Internet, a still-image file for saving and sending images from one computer to another.

judgment sample   in survey research for marketing and advertising, a type of nonprobability sample in which respondents are chosen based on the researcher's intuition that they would be truthful and representative of the population; see also *nonprobability sample, convenience sample, quota sample, probability sample,* and *survey method.*

junior page   see *junior unit.*

junior panel   in outdoor advertising, an 8-sheet poster, as opposed to the larger standard size, i.e., 30-sheet poster; see also *8-sheet poster* and *30-sheet poster.*

junior poster   see *junior panel.*

junior spread   in print advertising, an advertisement that appears on two facing pages, occupying only a portion of each page; see also *half-page spread.* Also called a *pony spread.*

junior unit   a magazine advertisement produced in a single size with dimensions that make it a full-page ad in some publications, but a partial page—a junior unit or page—in other publications, with editorial matter on at least two of its borders, but often surrounded entirely by editorial matter; e.g., the exact same ad both in content and size that occupies a full page in *Reader's Digest* is a less-than-full-page ad, or junior unit, in *Newsweek.* If the junior unit happens to be the same dimensions as a *Reader's Digest* page, it is sometimes referred to as a "d*igest unit*" or "*digest size*" in a larger magazine. Also called a *junior page.* See also *island position.*

Jupiter Media Metrix   a leading provider of Web site ratings; data are based on a national sample of Web users, whose Web activity is measured by special monitors attached to the computer.

jury of executive opinion   a sales forecasting method in which several of a firm's executives use their market knowledge to make judgments about the likely future sales picture for a product; individual executives' opinions are then discussed and combined to arrive at a consensus of predicted sales level. Typically involves seasoned veterans from several areas within the firm. See also *sales forecast, composite of sales force opinion, expert opinion, test marketing, market potential,* and *sales potential.*

jury test   in advertising research, presenting advertisements to a panel of consumers to get their reactions, opinions, and ratings of the ads; see also *portfolio test*.

just noticeable difference   the smallest amount of difference between two things that registers with and tells the consumer that there is a difference; may pertain to the difference between a regular price and a price reduction or increase in the same brand, a change in a product's features, or the difference between one brand and another. See also *Weber's Law*.

justified type   in print advertising, printed matter (i.e., *copy*) that is perfectly aligned on both sides, left and right; all lines are of the same length. See also *flush* and *ragged*.

K

key   see *key number.*

key account   a major client of an advertising agency, by virtue of its large advertising budget, the profitability to the agency, the portion of the agency's total billings it represents, or the prestige or presence it brings to the agency for having that particular client on the roster; may also refer to an especially important customer of a company, such as a major retail chain or a major department store, often handled by a key accounts sales force. See also *key account management* and *account management.*

key account management   overseeing the design, implementation, maintenance, review, and follow-up of all activities and programs involved in an organization's relationship with its most important customers or clients, by virtue of their profit, sales volume, or prestige value; see also *account management* and *key account.*

key number   a code placed within an advertisement or *coupon* so that an *inquiry,* coupon return, order, or other response can be traced to a specific ad or publication; the code may be a variation in address, a number, a letter, or some other such identification. Useful in testing to determine which headline, appeal, layout, or publication, for example, generated the most responses.

keyword   on the Internet, a word or group of words entered into the query window of a *search engine* (e.g., Google or Yahoo!) by the user to find documents or pages that contain the key word(s).

kicker   in print advertising, very brief copy in small type placed above the headline to introduce the advertisement.

kidvid   an informal term for television programming directly exclusively to children.

kill copy   a copy of a periodical that has been marked to indicate which advertising will not appear in the next issue.

kill order   an advertiser's instruction to cancel an *insertion* order, or any scheduled advertising or promotion.

killer copy   an advertising message that ignites in the individual an exceptionally strong desire to do just what the advertiser is asking.

kinetic board   in outdoor advertising, a *billboard* equipped with motorized special effects for a changing message or for an animated feature such as a waving hand, an emerging smile, moving legs, or a bouncing ball; see also *trivision board.*

king-size poster   in transit advertising, an advertising sign placed on the sides of a bus or transit vehicle, below the windows; poster measures 30″ high × 144″ wide. A *super king-size poster* measures 30″ high × 240″ wide. See also *exterior bus, headlight poster, taillight poster,* and *queen-size poster.*

kiosk   a stand-alone display unit or area that serves as an interactive information center whereby the consumer and advertiser can engage in two-way communications by computer hookup, even to the point of closing a sale; also refers to a stand at which personal sales transactions can be made.

knock-off   a look-alike product that plays off the acceptance of a famous-name brand and whose appeal is on the basis of price; e.g., replicas of Oakley sunglasses that sell for 20 percent of the price of the real thing. May also refer to the sound-alike name of a brand or a store, such as Victor's Secret playing off Victoria's Secret.

L

LMA see *local management agreement.*

LNA see *Leading National Advertisers.*

LTCV see *lifetime customer value.*

label copy the text that appears on the label of a product's package.

laboratory test in marketing and advertising research, a method whereby consumer behavior and reactions are measured under controlled conditions, as opposed to actual normal conditions the consumer would face in the marketplace; also referred to as a *simulated test market.* See also *field test* and *experimental method.*

laggards the fifth and last group of the adopter categories and the diffusion process of new products, services, or ideas; i.e., those individuals who are extremely slow to adopt a new product and do so only after the *innovators, early adopters, early majority,* and *late majority,* since they are individuals steeped in tradition and intent on shunning a new product because "what was good enough in the past is good enough now." Acceptance of a new product by this category of adopters is often the result of the unavailability of its predecessor. See also *adoption process, adopter categories, adoption curve, diffusion process, innovators, early adopters, early majority,* and *late majority.*

landscape format a layout of an advertisement in which the width is greater than the height, as opposed to the more common *portrait format* in which the height is greater than the width; see also *portrait format.*

Lanham Act a federal law, passed in 1946, dealing with trademark definition, registration, and protection, and that also regulates advertising by prohibiting false claims made by an advertiser about its own product or service; also permitted the registration of *service marks.* Unlike the *Federal Trade Commission Act,* this act permits an advertiser to file a civil suit against a competitor for false and deceptive claims the competitor makes about its own product or service in its advertising. Scope of civil action possibilities was broadened by the *Trademark Law Revision Act.* See also *trademark, service mark, certification mark,* and *Trademark Law Revision Act.*

large rectangle ad see *rectangle ad.*

last-chance method a selling technique in which the target audience is told that a particular deal or offer will no longer be available if they do not act promptly or immediately; e.g., often used in advertising messages near the end of a sales promotion program such as a rebate offer.

late fringe in the television broadcast day, the time period from 11:30 P.M.–1:00 A.M.; see also *dayparts (television).*

late majority the fourth group in the adopter categories and the diffusion process of new products, services, or ideas; i.e., those individuals who adopt a new product long after the *innovators, early adopters,* and *early majority,* and who are generally quite skeptical, uncertain, and cautious about new products, essentially satisfied with the product they are using, and when they do respond, it is because "the time has come to get in step with others." See also *adoption process, adopter categories, adoption curve, diffusion process, innovators, early adopters, early majority,* and *laggards.*

late news in the television broadcast day, the time period from 11:00 P.M.–11:30 P.M.; see also *dayparts (television).*

late night in the television broadcast day, the time period from 1:00 A.M.–6:00 A.M.; see also *dayparts (television).*

launch the formal introduction of a new product, service, advertising campaign, sales promotion activity, or an entire marketing communications campaign.

law of diminishing demand in the relationship between price and quantity demanded, the principle that suggests that if the price of a product is raised, a smaller quantity will be demanded; conversely, if the price of a product is lowered, a greater quantity will be demanded.

law of diminishing marginal utility the principle that suggests the consumer derives less benefit or satisfaction from each additional unit of a product or service consumed or used; e.g., the consumer gets less extra benefit (i.e., marginal utility) from buying and eating each additional Snickers candy bar, or from each additional hot dog, pair of sunglasses, or radio. See also *marginal utility* and *law of diminishing returns*. Note: popular usage in marketing is for the *law of diminishing marginal utility* and the *law of diminishing returns* to be used interchangeably.

law of diminishing returns the principle that suggests the gain from each additional unit of product, activity, or resource becomes smaller as more units are used; e.g., for the marketer, the benefit of each added dollar of advertising becomes smaller as more advertising is done. See also *marginal utility* and *law of diminishing marginal utility*. Note: popular usage in marketing is for the *law of diminishing returns* and the *law of diminishing marginal utility* to be used interchangeably.

layout the specific physical arrangement or exact placement of all the elements of a print advertisement, including headline, subheads, illustrations, body copy, logo, symbols, and whatever else appears in the advertisement; the total design and appearance of an ad. Often refers to a working drawing that shows how a print advertisement is to look and where all the elements are positioned in the ad. See also *balance, contrast, emphasis, flow, gaze motion, harmony,* and *unity*. Also see *thumbnail, rough layout, comprehensive,* and *mechanical*.

layout development process the various stages in creating the final design of a print advertisement; see also *thumbnail, rough layout, comprehensive,* and *mechanical*.

layout person the individual responsible for the physical arrangement of the elements in a print advertisement; see also *layout* and *layout development process*.

lead an individual or organization that has shown buying interest in a particular product or service.

lead agency see *agency of record (AOR)*.

lead generation refers to the several methods by which sales prospects are identified for future contact.

lead time the time period between the *closing date* (when all materials in final form must be in the hands of the media vehicle) and the running of the advertisement or commercial; see also *closing date*.

lead tracking in trade show marketing, the means by which an exhibitor follows up on a prospect whose interest was developed at the trade show.

leader see *market leader*.

leader pricing setting very low prices in an attempt to generate retail store traffic.

lead-in in television or radio, the program immediately preceding an advertiser's program on the same station; also can refer to the first few words in a television commercial or in the *body copy* of a print advertisement. See also *audience flow, holdover audience,* and *lead-out*.

leading in print advertising, the amount of space between lines of copy.

Leading National Advertisers (LNA) a research service of *Competitive Media Reporting (CMR)* that collects and reports advertising expenditures on a wide range of media; sharpest focus is on the top 100 advertisers by expenditure level. See also *Competitive Media Reporting (CMR)*.

lead-out in television or radio, the program immediately following an advertiser's program on the same station; see also *audience flow, holdover audience,* and *lead-in*.

lean-over marketing the practice whereby a marketer hires someone to talk about a product or service when there are people gathered within hearing distance, in hopes of generating a buzz about it; e.g., two company "agents," riding an elevator, discussing the merits of a particular tennis racket, restaurant, movie, sports medicine clinic, museum exhibit, or bank. Average people planted in a crowd, touting a product or service, with the audience unaware the agents are being paid for pitching the product. A questionable practice from an ethical viewpoint. See also *under-the-radar marketing, viral marketing,* and *word-of-mouth advertising.*

leap of faith when a marketer or advertiser engages in a move without the customary deliberation or testing, instead relying on instinct and judgment; creating and running an advertisement or commercial, based on the strong belief that it is the right thing to do and will work. Often employed when time is crucial to take advantage of an opportunity or to respond to a marketplace development.

learning changes in an individual's knowledge or behavior as a result of previous experience or exposure to new information; see also *reinforcement.*

leave-behind a promotional brochure or an advertising specialty item that is left with a prospect following a sales presentation; also called a *leave-piece.*

leave-piece see *leave-behind.*

legend the description or explanation accompanying an illustration such as a chart or graph in an advertisement.

length of assortment see *product line length.*

letterbox ads television commercials characterized by black borders across the top and bottom of the television screen; the rectangular format typically found in cinemas is converted to the more "boxy" format of the television screen, giving a wider field of view that is achieved by reducing the size of the image.

letterpress in print production, a process in which the printing surface or area to be printed is raised, rather than flat (as in *offset lithography* printing) or etched into a printing plate (as in *rotogravure* printing); virtually identical in concept to the use of a rubber ink stamp. See also *offset lithography* and *rotogravure.*

lettershop a company that serves a direct marketer by specializing in the production and mailing of sales letters, as well as other direct-mail pieces used by the marketer or advertiser.

lexicographic decision rule a decision rule whereby the consumer ranks in order all criteria considered important in a particular product being contemplated for purchase (e.g., brand image, warranty, durability, number of features, price, color, in order of importance), and then selects the brand that is judged best on the most important criterion; if more than one brand is rated "best" on this most important attribute, the choice depends on how those brands are rated on the next most important attribute. See also *compensatory decision rule, noncompensatory decision rule, consumer decision rules,* and *evoked set.*

library art see *stock art.*

Library of Congress the U.S. government agency that regulates and controls copyright materials; e.g., an advertisement can legally be copyrighted if it contains entirely original copy or artwork, but neither a slogan nor a common design or symbol can legally be copyrighted. See also *copyright.*

library research see *literature search.*

licensed brand a brand name that another company buys the right to for use in its marketing and advertising program; e.g., Russell Athletic purchases the right to use the National Football League (NFL) brand and logo on a line of sweatshirts, David sunflower seeds purchases the right to use the Major League Baseball (MLB) brand and logo in its advertising and sales promotion activities, and Reebok markets its NBA Collection series of apparel.

licensing the process by which an advertiser obtains permission to use in its advertising and promotional efforts a character, *trademark,* or other promotional entity owned by another person or organization; such rights are obtained by payment of a *licensing fee.* See also *licensing fee.*

licensing fee payment by an advertiser to obtain rights to use a person's or organization's logo, character, and other identifiable entity or terminology; see *licensing.*

life see *commercial life* and *publication life.*

lifestyle the general manner and behavior exhibited by individuals that characterize them and set them apart from other individuals who display another manner of behavior or pattern of living; basically, the way a person lives his or her life in terms of behavioral patterns, attitudes, opinions, interests, and activities. See also *AIO.*

lifestyle advertising generally upbeat advertising that features individuals and families engaging in the activities of everyday life, interacting with each other and with the world around them, expressing their attitudes, interests, opinions, and values in a "this is what we're all about" context.

Lifestyle Market Analyst a widely used and comprehensive reference source that breaks down the U.S. population geographically and demographically, and provides extensive lifestyle information on interests, hobbies, and activities; market profiles, lifestyle profiles, and consumer segment profiles data are presented for all 210 *Designated Market Areas (DMAs),* and includes regional- and national-level summary data and profiles. Includes a comprehensive list of consumer magazines and direct-mail lists targeted to each lifestyle profile. A publication of *Standard Rate and Data Service (SRDS).* See also *Standard Rate and Data Service (SRDS),* and the individual listing under *SRDS.*

lifestyle segmentation see *psychographic segmentation.*

lifetime customer value see *customer lifetime value.*

lift letter an additional letter or note included in a direct-mail package to increase the response; e.g., a "personal" note from the marketer, perhaps the CEO or marketing director.

light users consumers who purchase and use a product or service in much smaller quantities and/or much less frequently than others, in contrast to *heavy users, moderate users,* or *nonusers.*

likability the extent to which a commercial or advertisement is pleasant or engaging to the consumer; often used in pretesting to help predict the advertising's ability to meet its objectives. A measure of advertising effectiveness.

Likert scale a research technique that involves a scale on which there is a series of statements and respondents are asked to indicate the degree to which they agree or disagree with each statement; most often uses a five-point scale that includes strongly agree, agree, neither agree nor disagree, disagree, and strongly disagree. Some scales, though, are four-point scales, eliminating the midpoint to force the respondent to a choice on either side of neutral. Composite scores can be calculated by summing up responses to all the statements.

limited problem solving consumer decision making characterized by a moderate level of information seeking and evaluation of alternatives in the brand selection process; the consumer generally has previous experience with the particular need or problem, but is uncertain as to which course of action is best at the time. The consumer's perception of the risk of making a wrong choice is such that there is little motivation to engage in extensive information search or rigorous evaluation of alternatives. See also *extensive problem solving* and *routine problem solving.* Also see *high-involvement decision making* and *low-involvement decision making.*

limited-function wholesaler a merchant wholesaler (one who takes title to the goods) that provides some but not all of the functions normally associated with wholesaling; also called *limited-service wholesaler.* See also *middleman functions* and *service wholesaler.*

limited-service advertising agency an agency that offers less than a complete range of advertising services, instead confining its efforts to creative, copywriting, or media; see *creative boutique, full-service advertising agency,* and *media buying service.*

limited-time station a television or radio station that broadcasts only during certain hours of the normal broadcast day; i.e., a part-time station.

line in newspaper advertising, a unit for measuring space; see also *agate line* and *column inch.*

line drawings advertising drawings or images in black and white (no tones) that give excellent detail; referred to as *pen-and-ink drawings* and *line art.*

line extension a brand strategy whereby the marketer introduces a new product using the existing brand name; e.g., Post-It notes coming out with new colors in a variety of sizes, Advil adding a medication with special arthritis-fighting ingredients, Salada introducing green tea to its line of teas, Snickers with a new bite-size candy bar, or Turtle Wax using its brand name to extend its line of car-care products from the original car wax to car polish, car wash, leather cleaner/conditioner products, even lubricating oil. See also *brand strategy, brand extension, multibranding,* and *new-brand strategy.*

line of sight in out-of-home advertising, when an individual stands at or views one billboard location, all other billboards or units that can be seen simultaneously from that position.

line rate in newspaper advertising, the charge per line of space; see also *agate line, column inch,* and *Standard Advertising Unit (SAU).*

lineage in newspaper advertising, the total number of agate lines taken up by a single advertisement, several advertisements, or the total volume over time; may be viewed from the advertiser's side, the medium's or media vehicle's side, or as it relates to a particular product category. See also *agate line.*

line-up a listing of the television or radio stations carrying a particular program.

link on the Internet, a connection between one page and another on a Web site, allowing the user to click on it and be transferred to another page or Web site.

list a list of prospective buyers' names and addresses, or those of other individuals or organizations, used by direct marketing or other firms for a wide range of promotional purposes; see also *list catalog.*

list broker an individual or organization, working as an intermediary, that arranges for a list user to rent a mailing list from the owner of the list; represents the list user and is paid a commission by the list owner. Also called a *list house.*

list buyer in direct marketing, the individual or organization that purchases (actually, rents) and uses a mailing list from a *list compiler,* typically on a *one-time use* basis; term may also refer to the person or firm that actually buys a list for future rental. See also *list, list broker, list catalog, list compiler, list rental,* and *one-time use.*

list catalog a directory containing the collection of categories for which the list seller has names of individuals and organizations meeting the specifications of the marketer that seeks to use the list for direct-marketing purposes; e.g., a list of sports events, specific magazine readers, golfers, do-it-yourself home repair enthusiasts, ski resorts, individuals who attend art museums, individuals who regularly donate to charitable causes—a virtually endless set of lists.

list compiler an individual or organization that assembles and organizes mailing lists for rental and, sometimes, for sale to direct-marketing firms, advertisers, mail-order houses, or other organizations that use direct mail.

list exchange an arrangement between two marketers who agree to swap mailing lists for use in a direct-marketing program; applies to lists that are compiled by the firms involved in the exchange (i.e., not rented lists).

list house see *list broker.*

list maintenance in direct marketing, the activities involved in keeping a mailing list up-to-date.

list manager in direct-mail marketing, an individual or organization in charge of supervising and directing the efforts involved in marketing a list to buyers.

list marketing all the activities involved in locating potential buyers and selling them a direct-mail list that meets their needs; typically includes preparation and distribution of a *list catalog.* See also *list* and *list catalog.*

list owner in direct marketing, the individual or organization who holds title to a particular mailing list.

list rental payment for the use of a mailing list owned by someone else; generally, the rental fee is for a one-time use of the list.

list source the origin of a mailing list; e.g., an auto maker's list of new car buyers, a state golf association's list of public golf course owner-operators, a state bar association's list of attorneys, a subscription list of a magazine.

list user see *list buyer.*

listener an individual who is listening to a radio program.

listener diary see *diary method.*

listening area in radio broadcasting, the geographical area in which the station's signal can be heard clearly; the area in which the signal is totally static- or interference-free is known as the *primary listening area.*

listing allowance in trade promotion, money that a manufacturer or wholesaler gives to a retailer to advertise a product.

listservs on the Internet, electronic mailing lists allowing list members to participate in a dialogue on matters of mutual interest; e.g., an e-mail list of individuals who are interested in sponsorship marketing.

literature rack a display stand that holds promotional literature available for the taking by consumers.

literature search as part of the marketing communications planning process, the investigation of relevant book collections, journals, reports, Internet listings, and other available literature; also called *library research.*

lithography see *offset lithography.*

little America plan in marketing and advertising research, the idea of testing a campaign, in whole or in part, prior to national launch by putting it on trial in a selected market(s) that is representative of the entire country, in order to get a good look at how it might work on the national scale; see also *test market* and *test marketing.*

live action in television advertising, the use of real people, objects, and scenes in a commercial, as opposed to *animation.*

live copy in radio and television advertising, copy that is read on-the-spot by an announcer, as opposed to a taped commercial.

live copy area in out-of-home advertising, the space on a *billboard* within which all print should be placed; keeping all copy within this dimension enhances readability and prevents the copy from being too close to the structure's frame or edges.

live production in television or radio advertising, a live commercial; done to add realism and spontaneity, but it is a high-risk practice due to the lack of control over the commercial, with the potential that it will not achieve its goal.

live tag in a television or radio commercial, a short live message tacked on at the end, usually indicating dealer locations or an accompanying promotional offer.

liveamatic a technique of pretesting a television commercial in preliminary form, which involves filming live talent doing the commercial, but the commercial is a *rough,* i.e., is not in a completely finished form; see also *pretesting, animatic, liveamatic, photomatic, ripomatic, storyboard,* and *rough.*

live-script radio commercial a live (vs. taped) radio commercial in which the announcer reads from a formal, detailed script; see also *fact-sheet radio commercial* and *live copy.*

live-video insertion system see *virtual placement process.* Also called *digital insertion system.*

load factor in out-of-home advertising, the average number of people riding in each vehicle going past a particular advertising display unit; see also *traffic count.*

loader see *dealer loader* and *display loader.*

loading deal see *dealer loader* and *display loader.*

local advertiser a retailer that advertises in the same market where its place of business is located.

local advertising spot advertising undertaken by a local retailer; also can refer to advertising that focuses on a small area (e.g., county, city, town, or small trading area) in proximity to the retail store, or any advertising placed at the local rate (e.g., manufacturer-retailer *cooperative advertising* placed at the local rate available to the retailer). In contrast to *national advertising.* Also called *retail advertising.* See also *national advertising, retail advertising, local rate, cooperative advertising,* and *spot advertising.*

local agency in international advertising and marketing, an independent advertising agency in a foreign market, or one located in a foreign market and part of a global agency's network of shops, hired because of its knowledge of and capabilities with the specific local market conditions and culture; can also refer to any advertising agency located in any particular market area or region, in the United States or elsewhere, that handles an advertiser's program in that market because of its local knowledge and capabilities, often an agency whose scope of operations is limited primarily to that relatively small area or region.

local magazine see *city magazine.*

local management agreement (LMA) in television, an agreement through which a local station owner in a particular market manages some part of the business of another station, owned by another party, in the same market; also called a *local marketing agreement.*

local media advertising media whose circulation or coverage is limited geographically to a particular city, town, county, or other small region, usually the same area in which the media vehicle originates.

local metered-market ratings see *overnight ratings* and *set-tuning meters.*

local program   a television or radio program directed exclusively to a local audience, e.g., a town, city, or county.

local programming   in television or radio, programming created by and originating from local stations, rather than broadcast networks.

local radio   see *spot.*

local rate   the advertising rate charged by a local media vehicle, such as a newspaper, to a local advertiser; lower than the *national rate.* See also *general rate.*

local ratings   see *metered-market, diary method,* and *sweeps.*

local regulation   the local-level programs and efforts to control the activities of marketers and marketing in the best interests of the public; largely concerned with protecting local consumers against unfair or deceptive practices by local merchants, e.g., those involving advertising. See also *Better Business Bureau (BBB),* as well as *federal regulation, state regulation, in-house regulation,* and *self-regulation.*

local retail advertising   see *local advertising.*

local spot advertising   advertising bought by a local advertiser from a local television or radio station, and which is aimed only at the audience in the particular market; see also *spot* and *national spot advertising.*

local station   a low-powered television or radio station that broadcasts only to a small viewing or listening area.

local supplement   see *Sunday supplement.*

local tag   in a television or radio commercial, identification of local dealers at the end of the commercial, either prerecorded as part of the commercial (including as a graphic on a television commercial) or voiced live; see also *live tag.*

local television   television programming offered by network affiliates and independent stations that is not the programming of the broadcast networks; see also *spot.*

local time   in radio advertising, *spots* purchased by a local advertiser; see also *spot.*

local-channel station   a television or radio station restricted to broadcasting to its own locality; e.g., a college radio station whose license allows it to broadcast to its campus only or, perhaps, to the town in which it operates.

localization   see *localized marketing strategy.*

localized advertising strategy   in international advertising, an advertising strategy designed for a specific country or foreign market, as opposed to a single advertising strategy for several countries as might be used in a global approach; campaigns involving different messages and creative executions for each foreign market served by the company.

localized campaigns   advertising and promotion campaigns that feature different messages and executions for each foreign market a company is in; same principle can be applied to a domestic marketer targeting several regions of the country, i.e., *regional advertising.*

localized marketing strategy   in international marketing, an approach whereby marketing mix strategies are tailored and adapted for individual markets in which a marketer operates, as opposed to a more general approach; also referred to as *localization.* See also *globalization* and *regionalization.*

location   in television or radio advertising, a setting other than a production studio.

location list   in out-of-home advertising, a listing of all sites used in a particular promotion program; e.g., in *billboard* advertising, the exact location of all panels in a *showing.*

location map   see *spotted map.*

location media   see *outdoor advertising, transit advertising,* and *out-of-home media.*

location shoot   in television commercial production, filming the commercial at the actual site, e.g., a stadium, a tennis court, a mountaintop, or a retail store. See also *set shoot* and *production stage.*

log   the official minute-by-minute record of a television or radio station's programming; a licensing requirement of the *Federal Communications Commission (FCC).*

logical appeals   see *rational appeals.*

logistics   see *physical distribution.*

logo   the distinctive design of a company's or a product's name that provides individuality and immediate recognition in advertising, packaging, *point-of-purchase,* and other promotional efforts; short for *logotype.* Also called a *signature cut.* See also *identity media.*

logo merchandise a product on which is displayed a company, product, team, or event *logo* or other promotional image or message; e.g., a t-shirt, golf cap, notepad, or other object. Also called *advertising specialties.* See also *advertising promotional products* and *logo.*

logotype see *logo.*

longitudinal research in marketing and advertising research, a research design in which there is a fixed, i.e., continuing, sample of respondents whose marketplace behavior is repeatedly measured over time; see also *consumer panel.*

loyalty program see *frequency program.*

lottery a promotional activity or "game" in which an individual makes a payment in exchange for a chance to win a prize—the winner is determined by a random drawing among entries received; illegal as a promotional tool for advertisers. See also *contest* and *sweepstakes.*

low-involvement decision making marketplace decisions on products and services that have little personal relevance for the consumer and for which the perceived risks and consequences of the decision are not significant in the mind of the consumer; the consumer engages in a limited information search. See also *consumer decision process* and *high-involvement decision making.*

loyalty see *brand loyalty.*

M

MA see *Metropolitan Area.*

MIS see *marketing information system.*

MPA see *Magazine Publishers Association.*

MPR see *marketing public relations.*

MRI see *Mediamark Research, Inc.*

MSA see *Metropolitan Statistical Area.*

macroenvironment the extensive and all-embracing societal forces that affect an organization and its marketing efforts; includes forces such as demographics, economic, technological, political, legal, social, cultural, and environmental. See also *microenvironment.*

Madison Avenue a reference to the advertising industry collectively; historically, the street in New York City where many of the world's best-known advertising agencies and where the industry itself had its beginnings.

magalog in direct marketing, a catalog that closely resembles a magazine in appearance, if not content; often published several times a year featuring seasonal merchandise and even some editorial matter.

magazine a periodical, usually of coated paper and excellent production quality, that focuses on complete, in-depth treatment of its subjects and that has regular features issue-to-issue; usually published weekly or monthly. See also *consumer magazine* and *trade publication.*

magazine concept a television or radio program format in which there are several different stand-alone, usually unrelated segments run back-to-back; e.g., *60 Minutes.*

magazine group a collection of magazines comprising the offering of publications from the same publisher, typically appealing to different interest segments. For example: Primedia Publishing's *Soap Opera Digest, Skateboarder, Horticulture, Pro Football Weekly, American Baby, Crafts, Hot Rodding, Four-Wheeler, SUV,* and many more; or Hearst Corp.'s *Cosmopolitan, Good Housekeeping, Popular Mechanics, SmartMoney, Redbook,* and *House Beautiful,* to mention just a few. See also *magazine network.*

Magazine Impact Research Service (MIRS) in advertising research, a copytesting technique for magazines, in which advertisements are tested using an at-home, in-magazine context among widely dispersed samples; the test advertisements may naturally appear in the magazine or inserted for testing. A product of *Gallup and Robinson (G&R).* See also *copytesting, InTeleTest, In-View Test, Magazine Impact Research Service (MIRS),* and *Advertising Response Modeling (ARM).*

magazine insert see *insert.*

magazine network a group of magazines that sells advertising space to advertisers, who can buy space in several of the group's magazines at the same time with just one insertion order, i.e., buy space as a single purchase transaction or buy space in a package deal; Conde Nast publications include *Gourmet, Bon Appetit, Vogue, Self, Allure, Bride's, Glamour, Modern Bride, Vanity Fair, Conde Nast Traveler, The New Yorker, House & Garden, Lucky, GQ, Wired,* and *Architectural Digest.*

Magazine Publishers Association (MPA) the industry association for publishers of consumer magazines.

magazine supplement the preprinted magazine section of the Sunday edition of a metropolitan newspaper; e.g., *The New York Times Magazine,* which is included as a separate publication inserted into the Sunday *Times.* Also refers to a supplement that is distributed nationally in several different Sunday newspapers such as *Parade Magazine*. See also *Sunday supplement*.

Magnusson-Moss Warranty Act a federal law, passed in 1975, that governs consumer product warranties, requiring manufacturers and sellers of consumer products to provide consumers with detailed information about coverage; also called the *Federal Trade Commission Improvement Act*.

mail order a method of consummating a sales transaction that requires the buyer to submit to the seller a formal statement of intent to purchase the advertised product by filling out an order form, following which the product is shipped to the buyer.

mail response list a direct-mail list composed of names and addresses of individuals who have responded to an advertiser's previous mailing or, especially, those who have responded to mailings of other organizations whose products or services complement the advertiser's offering.

mail sampling a method of sampling in which the trial-size samples are distributed through the postal system; see also *sampling*.

mail survey a survey method of data collection by means of a questionnaire sent by mail to a respondent who completes the questionnaire and mails it back to the researcher.

mail-in offer any consumer sales promotion program in which the consumer is required to respond by mail in order to receive the promotional item or other *incentive;* usually requires some *proof-of-purchase* to be submitted.

mail-in premium a sales promotion tool in which the consumer mails some sort of offer sheet or other type of response to the firm and, in return, receives a *premium;* see also *premium*.

mailing list a list of prospective buyers' names and addresses, or those of other individuals or organizations, used by direct marketing or other firms for a wide range of promotional purposes.

mailing list profile a description of the common characteristics of the individuals or organizations that comprise a particular mailing list.

mail-order advertising advertising whose intent is to have the entire sales transaction completed using the advertising and a mail response.

mail-order house a retail organization that typically advertises via mail (including catalogs), accepts orders from consumers by mail or telephone (or the Internet), and delivers the goods by mail or carrier service.

mail-order selling the sales process when it is conducted entirely by mail rather than on a personal, face-to-face basis.

main head the most prominent headline in an advertisement; see also *subhead* and *headline*.

maintenance marketing see *defensive marketing*.

majority fallacy the questionable notion that a company should always pursue the market segment with the highest number of consumers and highest usage rates, ignoring the smaller markets; in fact, the smaller market may be less competitive, allow the marketer to gain a real differential advantage and firm foothold, and be more profitable in the long run.

major selling idea see *theme*.

make-good advertising time or space provided free by the medium or media vehicle to the advertiser to compensate for less-than-promised ratings or some error by the medium or media vehicle in running or failing to run a scheduled commercial or advertisement; also applies to a sponsorship property's failure to deliver a promised level of attendance. Arrangements other than free advertising may be employed.

makeup the arrangement or layout of all elements in an advertisement, brochure, or other promotional piece; see also *layout*.

makeup restriction guidelines issued to an advertiser by a publication to be sure an advertisement does not have unusual dimensions or features that would make it difficult for the publication to use the space efficiently.

mall display in out-of-home advertising, a display located at strategic points in shopping malls; usually a *backlit* advertising structure. See also *backlit*.

mall intercept see *intercept survey*.

mandatories elements of a message that, by order of account management and/or the client, must be included in the finished advertising, and often in a specific location of the advertisement or commercial; advertiser's Web address, telephone number, address, logo, "a family-owned company," or any other copy or element deemed essential.

mandatory copy   copy that is required by law to appear in an advertisement or commercial, on a package, or as an integral part of another promotion vehicle; e.g., the *Nutrition Facts* statement on food packages or the *Warning* statement on tobacco products.

manufacturer's brand   a brand owned by the maker of the product; also referred to as a *national brand,* although it may not be distributed nationally.

manufacturer's coupon   a coupon distributed to the consumer by a manufacturer; see also *coupon.*

manufacturers' representative   an agent middleman (does not take title to the goods) engaged in wholesaling who sells similar products for several noncompeting manufacturers; generally has limited authority regarding price and terms or conditions of sale and is paid by commission. See also *selling agent.*

marcom   short for *marketing communications.*

margin   in a publication, the area between the boundary of the printed matter and the edge of the page.

marginal analysis   a thorough examination of how costs affect sales and profits; e.g., the relationship between advertising costs and sales figures.

marginal utility   the extra benefits or extra satisfaction a consumer derives from having each additional unit of a product or service; e.g., the benefit a golfer gets from having two golf balls rather than only one. See also *utility* and *law of diminishing marginal utility.*

markdown   a reduction in a product's original selling price to encourage consumer purchasing of a slow-moving item, or simply as a sales promotion deal to generate more sales; usually promoted as a percentage reduction or savings.

market   all the customers or potential customers who have the following: a need or want for a product or service, the resources to offer as exchange, the willingness to make the purchase, and the authority to buy.

market analysis   that part of the advertising and promotion planning process that examines and evaluates the factors that shape the market for an organization's product or service; a major part of the situation analysis that precedes development of a marketing communications plan. See also *market, market profile,* and *situation analysis.*

market challenger   a company or organization whose marketing efforts are aimed at achieving a position of market leadership or supremacy; may apply to the company or organization as a whole or to a particular product or service. See also *market leader* and *market follower.*

market demand   total amount of purchases of a particular product or brand over a specified period of time; typically refers to actual purchases, but may relate to an estimate of likely demand in a specified future period; see also *market forecast* and *sales forecast.*

market development   an organization's growth strategy in which the firm attempts to increase sales by tapping new markets with its current products; involves moves such as promoting new uses for a product, expanding to a new geographic region, or adding new distribution outlets. See also *growth strategies, market penetration, product development,* and *diversification.*

Market Development Index   see *Category Development Index (CDI).*

market evaluation   the fourth stage of the new-product development process, in which the product idea is subjected to an extensive investigation and evaluation of its potential for sales, market share, costs, profitability, return-on-investment, and meeting customer needs; see also *new-product development process, idea generation, idea screening, concept testing, product development, marketing plan, market testing,* and *commercialization.*

Market Facts, Inc.   a leading market research company providing a wide array of data collection and analysis services, including brand tracking, concept testing, product testing, and sales forecasting for consumer packaged-goods firms, as well as companies in the financial and telecommunications industries.

market follower   a company or organization whose marketing efforts are aimed at simply following the lead of others, often imitating their tactics, and in no way acting as a challenger or aspiring to a leadership spot in the market; may apply to the company or organization as a whole or to a particular product or service. See also *market leader* and *market challenger.*

market forecast   in marketing planning, the estimated total demand for a product or service over a specified period of time, made prior to the full-scale development of a marketing program; demand projection is for all brands of the product. See also *sales forecast.*

market intelligence   key real-time information for use in developing marketing strategies and tactics aimed at gaining a competitive advantage; up-to-the-minute data collected from a variety of sources through the use of established procedures designed to assure a steady flow of relevant information.

market leader   a company or organization whose marketing efforts have propelled it to the number one position in the market, with the largest market share in the industry; may apply to the company or organization as a whole or to a particular product or service. See also *market challenger* and *market follower.*

market niche   see *niche marketing.*

market penetration   an organization's growth strategy that attempts to increase sales to its current markets with existing products; usually done with changes in the firm's *marketing mix,* such as a price reduction, increased advertising, using a different media mix, added sales promotion activities, more aggressive trade promotion, and other practices. See also *growth strategies, market development, product development,* and *diversification.*

market potential   an estimate of the total demand for a product or service in a particular industry or market segment, or what sales level a product or service can be expected to achieve; see also *sales potential* and *sales forecast.*

market profile   the specific features or characteristics of the customers and potential customers in a *market* for a particular product or service; see also *market.*

market response   the reaction of the target audience to an organization's advertising or promotional efforts.

market segment   a customer group in which the individuals share common characteristics, making them likely to respond in a similar way to a particular marketing program; consumers are homogeneous within a particular segment, but different from consumers in other segments or groups, i.e., homogeneity within and heterogeneity between. See also *market segmentation.*

market segmentation   dividing a large population into separate groups or markets based on a set of common characteristics, each group (segment) representing a distinct target market with its own requirements for a marketing program; breaking a large heterogeneous market into a series of smaller homogenous markets. See also *behavioristic segmentation, demographic segmentation, geographic segmentation, geodemographic segmentation,* and *psychographic segmentation.*

market share   a brand's percentage of total sales in a product category.

market share price objective   the goal of setting price at a level to achieve a particular market share goal; see also *target return, profit maximization, sales growth,* and *meeting competition price objectives.*

market structure   the character of an industry, based on the number of firms, barriers to entry, extent of product differentiation, control over price, and importance of nonprice competition; see also *pure competition, pure monopoly, monopolistic competition,* and *oligopolistic competition.*

market target   see *target market.*

market targeting   see *target marketing.*

market test   see *test market.*

market testing   see *test marketing.*

market-by-market   a method of allocating the advertising or promotion budget or intensity of effort; each local area is evaluated and receives a share of the budget or total effort on the basis of its past and potential sales picture, competitive situation, or other factor. See also *Brand Development Index (BDI)* and *Category Development Index (CDI).*

market-by-market buy   in the purchase of media, buying commercial time or advertising space a single market at a time, as opposed to buying time on the entire network of stations or the national edition of a publication; see also *network buy* and *national buy.*

market-driven   taking the cue from the marketplace in designing marketing activities and programs.

marketer an individual or an organization that engages in marketing, i.e., has something to sell such as a product, service, or idea; see also *marketing.*

Marketer's Guide to Media an *AdWeek* publication containing a wealth of advertising media data and information; an annual edition includes audience size, circulation figures, demographics, costs, and other data for broadcast television, cable television, syndicated television, radio, out-of-home, magazines, newspapers, online services, promotion media, the teen market, the Hispanic market, and others.

marketing the process of planning and executing the conception, pricing, promotion, and distribution of goods services, and ideas to create exchanges that satisfy individual and organizational objectives— the *American Marketing Association* definition.

marketing audit a comprehensive, systematic, and objective review and appraisal of every aspect of a firm's or organization's marketing program, its organization, activities, strategies, and people.

marketing by-the-book see *by-the-book marketing.*

marketing channel see *distribution channel.*

marketing communications the combination of the elements, activities, and techniques an organization employs to connect with and persuade the target market to engage in a particular action or response, such as buying a product, using a service, or accepting an idea; the major tools include *advertising, sales promotion, public relations, direct marketing,* and *personal selling.*

marketing communications campaign a series of individual but fully integrated promotion elements, activities, and methods, with all promotional messages unified under a common theme and aimed at common objectives; also called a *promotion campaign.* See also *integrated marketing communications.*

marketing communications mix see *communications mix.*

marketing communications plan see *integrated marketing communications plan.*

marketing communications productivity audit any of the several techniques for measuring the return-on-investment in the total marketing communications program; see *return-on-investment approach (ROI).*

marketing concept a managerial philosophy that says marketing begins by identifying consumer needs and wants and then, through a series of coordinated activities, satisfies those needs and wants better than competitors while achieving organizational goals; i.e., a consumer orientation, integrated marketing activities, and organizational objectives are the key components of this market-driven philosophy.

marketing control the process and activities involved in evaluating marketing programs to determine if objectives are being met and, if not, taking corrective action.

marketing database see *database.*

marketing ethics the moral standards and values underlying and surrounding the marketer's efforts directed at the target audience; the realm of right and wrong.

marketing implementation the process of turning marketing plans into action.

marketing information system (MIS) in marketing research, a formal and structured procedure for collecting and analyzing data from a variety of key sources and systematically disseminating timely information to marketing decision makers to help them plan, execute, and control the total marketing program; a continuous program of providing key information to marketing decision makers. See also *marketing research* and *marketing research process.*

marketing intelligence the relevant data and information on the latest developments in the total marketing environment that are required for the day-to-day marketing decisions; see also *marketing information system (MIS).*

marketing logistics see *physical distribution.*

marketing metrics a broad range of quantitative measurements used to assess marketing performance; e.g., market share, advertising spending, coupon redemptions, event attendance, response rates in a direct-marketing program, number of visits to a Web site, number of clickthroughs to an advertiser's page on a Web site, and many others.

marketing mix the particular combination of ingredients that forms the marketing program an organization uses to satisfy target customer needs and wants while meeting organizational objectives; includes the blending of the four key variables that comprise marketing programs: product, price, place (distribution), and promotion activities, i.e., the controllable variables. Also known as the *4Ps*. See also *controllables* and *uncontrollables*.

marketing myopia shortsighted thinking in designing marketing programs and strategies; failure to consider the long-range consequences of marketing efforts.

marketing niche see *niche* and *niche marketing*.

marketing objectives what is to be accomplished in the performance of marketing activities and the marketing program; stated in terms of sales volume, market share, profit, return-on-investment, or other basis.

marketing management in pursuit of organizational and marketing objectives, the process of formulating marketing plans, directing the execution of the plans, and controlling each component of the implemented marketing program.

marketing on-the-edge see *on-the-edge marketing*.

marketing opportunity conditions in the marketplace that suggest it is likely that a firm can provide better, more appropriate need-satisfying solutions to prospective customers than are currently being provided.

marketing orientation steadfast adherence to the marketing concept; an approach in which customer needs and wants are the underlying determinants of an organization's direction and its marketing programs. See also *marketing concept*.

marketing plan a document, complete with rationale, that guides and directs a company's marketing effort; a formal blueprint outlining an organization's *situation analysis,* budget, objectives, marketing strategies, implementation guidelines, and measurement and control systems for the marketing of a particular product or service. Also, the sixth stage of the new-product development process, when the initial plan is designed for a new product prior to its market test. See also *new-product development process, idea generation, idea screening, concept testing, market evaluation, product development, market testing,* and *commercialization*.

marketing process the major stages in planning, designing, implementing, and monitoring marketing programs; consists of analyzing marketing

opportunities, selecting target markets, developing and integrating the *marketing mix,* managing the entire marketing program, and evaluating marketing performance.

marketing program the entire set of plans, activities, and strategies with which an organization strives to meet the requirements of its target markets while achieving organizational objectives.

marketing public relations (MPR) involves an organization's relations with consumers or other publics, such as the government, suppliers, channel members, employees, citizens action groups, or the local community, on marketing and marketing-oriented matters; specific role and scope is determined by the firm's marketing objectives. Major tool is *publicity.* See also *publicity, public relations, proactive public relations,* and *reactive public relations*.

marketing research processes and activities involved in the systematic identification, gathering, analyzing, and dissemination of data to marketing decision makers to help them render information-based decisions on problems and opportunities in marketing; the all-important link between the customer or audience and the marketer.

marketing research process the stages comprising the marketing research activity; consists of defining the problem or issue to be investigated, setting research objectives, examining secondary data, formulating a research design and methodology plan (including specific research approaches, contact methods, sampling plan and size, and data collection forms), collecting primary data, analyzing and interpreting the findings, producing recommendations, and following up on implementation. Not necessarily a step-by-step sequence, since some stages may be worked on simultaneously.

marketing strategy an action plan detailing the *marketing mix* aimed at a specific target market; how the product, price, distribution, and promotion variables will be used to attract a particular customer group and allow the organization to achieve its objectives.

markup a percentage or dollar amount added to the cost of a product to get the selling price.

markup chain the series of markups that occur at each stage in the distribution channel, as the individual channel members charge for services rendered.

markup charge an element of *advertising agency compensation* in which the agency adds a percentage charge, usually *17.65 percent* to services it buys from outside suppliers, e.g., research or production; also called *percentage charge* or *gross-up*. See also *production add-on* and *17.65 percent*.

marquee a *billboard* on an edifice, such as a movie theater.

masked identification test in advertising research, a technique whereby respondents are asked to name the sponsor of a commercial or advertisement, in which the sponsor's name, brand name, logo, or any other identifying element is bleeped out or blocked out; a test of the *memorability* of advertising.

Maslow's hierarchy of needs see *hierarchy of needs*.

mass communications reaching a widespread audience of many individuals with any of the promotional media, methods, or tools available to the advertiser for delivering its message; generally, there is no direct and personal interaction between the sender of such a message and the receiver. Sometimes called *impersonal communications* or *nonpersonal communications*. See also *nonpersonal communications*.

mass distribution see *intensive distribution*.

mass marketing using a single basic *marketing mix* or program to reach the entire market, as opposed to a specific market target, which calls for a separate marketing program for each target segment; also called *undifferentiated marketing*. See also *concentrated marketing* and *differentiated marketing*.

mass media forms or channels of nonpersonal communications that allow the advertiser to reach a large widespread audience of many individuals simultaneously with its message, as opposed to forms of media geared to a specialized audience; e.g., television or newspapers. Also called *nonpersonal media*. See also *advertising, personal selling, general-interest magazine,* and *special-interest magazine*.

mass medium the singular of *mass media;* a communications medium, e.g., television or magazines directed to the broad interests of the general public.

mass merchandiser a very large retail store selling an extremely wide and deep assortment of products; typically a self-service store that operates on a low-margin, high-turnover philosophy.

mass publication a publication edited for the general public; also called a *mass magazine*. See also *general-interest magazine*.

mass selling communicating and promoting a basic message to a large number of potential consumers at the same time.

master agency see *agency of record (AOR)*.

master tape in radio and television advertising production, the final complete recording of the commercial from which duplicates are made and sent to the stations for airing; see also *dubs* and *dupes*.

masthead in a periodical, a short section on a page listing the publication's owner, publisher, editorial and business staff members, addresses and telephone numbers of offices, and frequency of publication, generally in a portrait format, height greater than width; in newspapers, usually located on the editorial page, and in magazines, on or near the table of contents page. See also *portrait format*.

mat a printing plate mold of papier-mâché or similar substance that is made by pressing a sheet of the paper into the engraving plate; molten lead is then poured into it, forming a duplicate of the original plate; known as a *stereotype*. Mainly used by newspapers. Short for *matrix*.

matrix see *mat*.

mat service a company that specializes in producing mats and supplying newspapers with the resulting images for use as advertisements; see *mat*.

matchbook advertising an advertising message on the cover of a book of matches.

matched samples in marketing and advertising research, two identical groups according to the demographic, lifestyle, or other characteristics desired by the researcher; for testing purposes, a condition or stimulus is varied in one group, and then results are compared to determine the effect of the stimulus. For example, one group may be exposed to a hard-sell advertising message, the other to a decidedly softer-sell message, and then results are compared, either by sales levels or by questioning centered around the communications effect of each approach.

maturity stage the third stage of the product life cycle, in which sales slow dramatically, still increasing very early in the stage, but at a markedly decreasing rate, followed by a leveling off; only the strong marketers survive through this stage, with a decrease in the number of competitors, but an increase in the intensity of the competition. The vital relationships with the dealers are especially critical in this stage. Profit levels are relatively steady, although they may decline slowly. See also *product life cycle, introduction stage, growth stage,* and *decline stage.*

maximil rate   in newspaper advertising, the cost of an *agate line* of space at the highest *milline rate,* i.e., without any discounts; see *agate line, milline rate,* and *minimil rate.*

maximum depth requirement   in newspaper advertising, the maximum amount of advertising space allowed per column that also contains non-advertising or editorial material; beyond allotted amount, an advertiser must pay for a full column. See also *minimum depth requirement.*

maximum profit rule   the highest profit level is achieved with a price where marginal cost equals marginal revenue; i.e., the point at which the extra cost of producing and marketing the last unit is equal to the extra revenue earned from that unit.

McCollum-Spielman Worldwide (MSW)   a premier advertising research organization with capabilities spanning the entire range of pretesting, concurrent testing, and posttesting studies to help marketers and advertisers develop effective strategies.

mean   in a series of numbers, the average; determined by the sum of all the numbers divided by the total quantity of separate number entries on the list. Example: 22 for the series 30, 25, 21, 18, 16 (i.e., 110 divided by 5). Also called the *average.* See also *median* and *mode.*

measured media   refers to the estimated advertising expenditures in national consumer media, as monitored by *Competitive Media Reporting;* includes advertising spending in newspapers, magazines (and Sunday magazines), outdoor, network television, spot television, syndicated television, cable television, network radio, and spot radio. Expenditures are published annually by *Advertising Age* in its *100 Leading National Advertisers* issue, as well as at periodic intervals throughout the year. See also *unmeasured media.*

measurement   using a variety of methods, determination of the impact of an advertisement, sales promotion

activity, public relations effort, direct-marketing program, or any other promotion program activity or element; also pertains to determining the impact of the advertising or promotion program in its entirety. See also *marketing metrics.*

mechanical   the final version of an advertisement in all its precise detail, which will be sent to the printer upon approval by the client, who even at this point in the *layout development process* can suggest changes; typically computer-generated and sent to the printer electronically. Also called *camera-ready artwork* and *paste-up.* See also *layout development process, thumbnail, rough layout,* and *comprehensive.*

mechanical requirements   in print advertising, the specifications that must be met by the advertiser or agency when submitting advertising material; specifications are enumerated on the rate card.

media   the aggregate means, carriers, or channels of communications through which advertisers get their messages to their intended audiences; see also *media, media class, media subclass, media vehicle,* and *media unit.*

media association   an organization consisting of the individuals and companies involved with a particular advertising medium, such as magazine publishers, billboard companies, transit firms, newspaper publishers, television or radio networks, and virtually every advertising medium; common purpose is to promote the attractiveness of the particular medium as an advertising carrier. Examples: *Magazine Publishers Association (MPA), Outdoor Advertising Association of America (OAAA),* or *Radio Advertising Bureau (RAB).*

media bank   a media buying service's inventory of media available for sale to advertisers and agencies; see also *space bank* and *time bank.*

media blitz   an intensive, greater-than-normal use of a variety of media by an advertiser over its entire market or in a particular region; most often used for new-product introductions, to counter competitive moves, to advertise or push a special event or promotion, or in a public relations effort. See also *heavy-up.*

media broker   an individual or organization that accumulates time and space for sale to advertisers and agencies; also refers to a person or company that arranges for a connection between a buyer and a seller of media.

media budget   the amount of money allocated to the combination of communications carriers used to deliver an advertiser's message to its target audience.

media buy   the advertising time or space purchased from a media vehicle; often referred to simply as a *buy*.

media buyback   in sponsorship marketing, when a property buys television or radio time from an event's broadcaster and, in turn, gives the commercial time to a sponsor as part of the total package to make the sponsorship a more attractive deal; may also apply to space or time in other media purchased and used for the same purpose.

media buyer   an individual who purchases advertising time and space; may work for an advertising agency or for a *media buying service.*

media buying   the process of negotiating, ordering, securing, and confirming the purchase of advertising time or space from a media vehicle.

media buying service   an independent organization that specializes in purchasing large quantities of advertising time and space, and then selling it in blocks to individual advertisers; deals mostly with television and radio. In addition to the buying activity, may also engage in *media planning* and the actual placement.

media buy sheet   a formal record sheet containing all key details used by the *media buyer;* a formal record-keeping sheet containing all relevant details and information about a particular purchase of time or space, i.e., *buy,* from a media vehicle. Also referred to as a *buy detail report.*

media class   any one in a broad category of media such as print, electronic, out-of-home, interactive, or direct mail; sometimes a given class may be referred to as a *medium,* e.g., the *print* medium. See also *media, media subclass, media vehicle,* and *media unit.*

media commission   compensation paid by a media vehicle to a recognized advertising agency, usually 15 percent; see also *advertising agency commission.*

media company   an organization that owns a *media vehicle* or multiple media.

media department   the section of the advertising agency that develops media plans and strategies to best convey the advertising message to the target audience; also buys the advertising time and space or works closely with the *media buying service* in that regard.

media discount   any of several forms of a reduction in the *rate card*'s basic advertising cost, based on volume of time or space purchased or prompt payment.

media distribution   refers to where and when advertising is deployed.

media environment   the "atmosphere" in which the advertising appears—the image and content of the media vehicle that carries the advertising; in general, the "look" of the media vehicle.

media equivalency   in sponsorship marketing, a sponsor's measurement of the amount of time or space generated by coverage and exposure of the sponsor's name, and calculating what that time or space would have cost if the sponsor had purchased it based on the medium's or media vehicle's *rate card;* see also *in-focus exposure time, Joyce Julius Associates,* and *Sponsors Report.*

media flowchart   a grid format or bar chart that shows the media schedule over the duration of the advertising campaign; i.e., the timing of each media vehicle's use in the campaign. On the vertical axis is a list of the media vehicles and on the horizontal axis are the months of the campaign broken into weeks, with a bar running from left to right indicating which vehicles will be used in each week of the campaign. An at-a-glance picture or summary of the media schedule. See also *campaign flowchart, work flowchart,* and *media schedule.*

media impact   the impact or *memorability* created by an advertising medium, media vehicle, or any combination of media carrying an advertiser's message; the impression created by the *media mix* in an advertiser's *media schedule.*

media imperative   an expression of the extent to which one advertising medium commands more attention than another from different groups or audiences; e.g., in a comparison between magazines and radio, a *magazine imperative* indicates that the particular audience has a higher level of magazine reading than it does radio listening. A measure of the *Study of Media & Markets* done by *Simmons Market Research Bureau.*

media insertion schedule see *insertion schedule.*

media kit a media vehicle's package of materials, prepared for advertisers, containing information about the demographics, lifestyles, and buying behavior of the vehicle's audience, as well as information about the vehicle's circulation, geographical coverage, reach, frequency of publication, advertising rates, specifications, cost efficiency, comparisons with competing media or vehicles, deadlines, editorial calendar, special features, and other material relevant to the advertiser's media selection decision; not to be confused with a *press kit.* See also *press kit.*

Media Market Guide see *SQAD (Service Quality Analytics Data).*

media mix the combination or blend of *media* (*classes, subclasses,* and specific *vehicles*) used together, i.e., in the *media schedule,* to reach the target audience in a particular advertising campaign and meet the objectives of a *media plan.*

media menu the totality of all communications methods and vehicles that are available to the consumer or for use by the marketer.

media objectives the specific goals for the media portion of the advertising program; usually stated in terms of *reach* and *frequency* levels.

media pack see *media kit.*

media plan a formal blueprint outlining the *media objectives, strategy, mix, schedule, vehicles, weight, cost efficiency,* and other media issues involved in an advertising or communications campaign, including, for example, specifications of the media in which the advertising messages are to be placed to reach the intended target audience; an outline of the entire media component of an *advertising* or *communications campaign.*

media planner the individual who produces the media plan for how best to convey the advertising message to the target audience; among other things, decides the objectives to seek with the media, the strategy that will work best, how to allocate the media budget, which media vehicles will be the most effective and cost-efficient given the objectives, and how to schedule the media for maximum impact. See also *media plan.*

media planning working to make sure that the advertising message is delivered to the target audience

through the right channels at the right time; the process of making sure that all details relating to the media portion of the campaign are given proper attention. The process of developing media objectives, strategies, and tactics to employ in an *advertising* or *communications campaign.*

media quintiles in advertising media research, putting a sample of respondents into five groups of equal size to show the different exposure levels to a medium or media vehicle; e.g., ranges from heavy exposure or readership to light exposure or readership. See also *quintile* and *quintile analysis.*

media reach see *reach.*

media regulation self-regulatory programs and efforts by the television, radio, magazine, newspaper, and other media industries that are aimed at monitoring and regulating advertising by screening ads and accepting only those that are truthful, fair, and in good taste, rejecting all others; criteria and standards are established by individual media vehicles, as well as by media associations for the entire membership. Ultimately, each media vehicle makes the decision to accept or reject an advertising message. See also *self-regulation.*

media relations the dealings between an organization and the communications channels it uses in its advertising or promotion efforts; often refers specifically to the efforts by the public relations function to make an effective connection with the media.

media release see *news release* and *press release.*

media representative an individual who works for or on behalf of an advertising medium or media vehicle, typically selling the medium or vehicle as an advertising channel; often called a *media rep* or simply a *rep.* See also *rep firm.*

media research gathering and interpreting data related to the reach and effectiveness of advertising media and media vehicles to facilitate information-based media decisions on budget allocations, selection of media vehicles to reach the target audience, scheduling, and other decisions.

media schedule the chronology of a media plan showing what media vehicles will carry the advertising and exactly when the commercials and advertisements will appear in those vehicles; a media calendar; also called *schedule.*

media scheduling the process of determining a *media schedule;* also called *scheduling.* See also *continuous scheduling, flighting,* and *pulsing.*

media share see *share.*

media spillover occurs when a media vehicle's signal or circulation goes beyond the geographical boundaries of one market area into another; see also *spill-in* and *spill-out.*

media strategy statement a formal statement of the specific course of action that will be used to achieve media objectives; includes which media and media vehicles will be used, how the advertising budget will be allocated, how the media will be scheduled over the duration of the campaign, the reach and frequency that will be achieved, and other issues important to attaining the advertising goals established for the campaign. Also includes the rationale for each strategy element.

media subclass a type of media within a *media class,* such as magazines, newspapers, television, radio, or billboards; the particular type of media may be referred to as a *medium.* See also *media, media class, media vehicle,* and *media unit.*

media translation with a national or large *media plan* as the starting point, reducing it proportionally for a local market to test the plan on a smaller scale; a miniature replica of the big market media plan in a small market. Can also mean the reverse—going from the local market to the larger market by increasing the media plan proportionally. See also *as-it-falls method* and *little America method.*

media unit refers to the specific size or length of an advertisement or commercial; e.g., half-page, full-page, 30-second commercial, 60-second commercial, or 30-sheet poster or bulletin. See also *media, media class, media subclass,* and *media vehicle.*

media vehicle the specific individual means by which an advertiser's message is transmitted to the intended audience; the particular individual publication, program, or delivery mechanism used to carry or deliver an advertising message to the target audience. For example, a specific magazine (*Good Housekeeping*), newspaper (*The Washington Post*), or television program (*60 Minutes*). See also *media, media class, media subclass,* and *media unit.*

media waste see *waste audience* and *waste circulation.*

media weight the total pressure or force of a *media plan,* as measured by the collection of elements such as media expenditures, reach, and frequency; essentially, the audience delivered by the *media plan.*

Mediamark Research, Inc. (MRI) a leading supplier of multimedia audience research and information for use by advertisers, advertising agencies, magazines, television, radio, and other media; based on more than 26,000 personal interviews throughout the United States, and provides comprehensive data on demographics, lifestyles, product usage, and exposure to virtually all forms of advertising media from a single sample. Especially useful for media planning.

median in a series of numbers, the point at which one-half of the numbers are above and one-half below; e.g., 22 in the series 26, 24, 23, 22, 20, 19, 17. See also *mean* and *mode.*

MediaWatch a consumer advocacy organization whose goal is to challenge what it considers to be abusive stereotypes and biased images found in the media, including advertising; according to its mission statement, the organization aims to create more informed consumers of the mass media by "challenging racism, sexism, and violence in the media through education and action." Very often, advertising is the object of the group's attention.

MediaWeek a weekly trade magazine focusing on all aspects of media, including cost and audience data, news, insights, opinions, analysis, and research results; features both local and national media news and information. See also *AdWeek* and *BrandWeek.*

MediaWeek Directory an annual publication that provides detailed reports, profiles, data, and information on local media in the top 100 markets in the United States, plus reports on national media; see also *AdWeek Directory* and *BrandWeek Directory.*

Medical Device Regulation Act a 1976 law banning dangerous medical devices and requiring that all information be made public when a device is approved or banned.

medium generally refers to a particular *media class* (e.g., print), but may refer to a *media subclass* (e.g., magazines); the singular of *media.*

medium rectangle ad see *rectangle ad.*

meeting competition price objective setting price at the same level as competition; see also *target return, profit maximization, sales growth,* and *market share price objectives.*

megabrand the superbrand or umbrella brand name under which there are individual brands; so classified by virtue of a combination of elements such as size, sales volume, market share, profit, advertising dollars, and other factors that make the organization a giant in its field. Concept may apply to a company, product, or an advertising agency. See also *agency megabrand, agency network, agency brand,* and *product megabrand.*

megabrand strategy when a company with several brands in a product category streamlines its offering by eliminating the weaker-performing brands and focuses its budget and marketing program efforts only on those brands that have a reasonable shot to reach a top-echelon market share position in their product categories.

membership group a group of people with which an individual regularly interacts on a personal basis.

memorability the extent to which a particular advertising execution or campaign registers a lasting impression on and is recallable by the consumer.

Mendelsohn Media Research see *Monroe Mendelsohn Research.*

mention in any media, a brief acknowledgment of a company, product, or service.

merchandise pack a product package with a *premium* attached to it (*on-pack premium*) or inside it (*in-pack premium*); see also *premium, in-pack premium,* and *on-pack premium.*

merchandising a general term to describe the variety of in-store promotional activities and materials that complement and support the advertising effort; very often provided free or at a minimal charge. The totality of activities, other than advertising, that work together to make advertising and other promotion more effective at the retail level. For example, a combination of promotion activities for a product at the retail store, involving the use of literature, coupons, and sampling, along with a *point-of-purchase display* of the product.

merchandising allowance free merchandise or payment by the advertiser to the dealer for promotional support other than advertising, such as displays, in-store promotions, and other activities provided by the dealer on behalf of the advertiser; see also *advertising allowance, dealer allowance,* and *promotional allowance.*

merchandising service a broad range of advice and help made available to advertisers and agencies by the media in which the advertising is to appear; e.g., suggestions for the type of copy, position within the vehicle, use of color, viewer or reader tastes, and other matters related to advertising effectiveness.

merchant wholesaler in the *distribution channel,* a wholesaler who takes title to the products it sells; see also *agent middleman.*

merge & purge the process of taking two or more mailing lists and eliminating duplicate names; used in direct marketing or other advertising or promotion efforts that utilize different mailing lists for the same mailing or for the same purpose.

message the communication of information via words, symbols, and tone from the sender to the receiver, i.e., from the advertiser to the target audience; consists of persuasive verbal and nonverbal communications designed to influence the target audience. See also *encoding.*

message channel see *media, media vehicle,* and *medium.*

message development the activities and process by which an advertising message is ultimately created in accordance with the established objectives, from the idea stage to the point of execution.

message distribution generally, the pattern by which an advertising message is disseminated to the audience, including timing, and geographical and media dispersion.

message research an orderly investigation into the effectiveness of advertising communications, including the gathering and analysis of data relating to the different message variables, the different ways of presenting information, what types of messages influence and persuade the receiver under what conditions, why some message content and formats work better than others, and so forth; the ultimate purpose is to facilitate the design and execution of results-producing advertising. Also called *copytesting.* Along with *media* *research,* constitutes the discipline of *advertising research.* See also *advertising research, copytesting,* and *media research.* Also see *focus group* and *depth interview.*

message sidedness   see *one-sided message* and *two-sided message.*

message strategy   in achieving advertising goals and objectives, what the advertising will say and how it will say it; see also *creative brief.*

message wearout   see *wearout.*

message weight   the gross number or sum of advertising messages delivered by all the media vehicles in a complete media schedule; i.e., the size of the combined target audiences reached by all media vehicles in a single media plan. May be expressed as *gross impressions* or *gross rating points.* May be determined for individual media vehicles. Also referred to as *advertising weight.* See *gross impressions* and *gross rating points (GRP).*

metaphor marketing   in advertising research, a technique in which respondents are asked to make a collage or select pictures (provided by the researcher) that describe their attitudes toward something such as a brand, or are simply asked a question such as, "If Nike were a dog, what kind of dog would it be? Reebok? Adidas? Puma? New Balance? Asics? Converse?" Another example: "If Nokia were a particular style of house, what would it be? Nextel? Samsung? Sprint? Ericsson? Radio Shack? Sanyo?" An attempt to elicit a comparison of brands by having consumers reference images of other things.

meter   a device attached to a television set that automatically monitors and records whether the set is on or off, the station to which the set is tuned, and the time of day.

metered-market overnights   refers specifically to Nielsen's local metered-market television ratings from the 55 television markets nationwide that have households with set-tuning meters; these ratings are available the morning after the day or evening of a telecast. See also *Nielsen Media Research, metered markets, overnight ratings, People Meter, set-tuning meter, diary method, telephone coincidental,* and *sweeps.* (Additional television markets are added periodically.)

metered markets   the 55 (and increasing) local markets where *Nielsen Media Research* uses set-tuning

meters (not *People Meters*) to report household television ratings; the set-tuning meters used in these local markets are supplemented with diary data. See *diary method, metered-market overnights, Nielsen Media Research, People Meter, set-tuning meter, overnight ratings, telephone coincidental,* and *sweeps.*

methodology   see *research methodology.*

me-too marketing   see *copycat marketer.*

me-too product   a product very similar to that of another brand, offering no distinct features, except possibly a lower price; often patterned after the market leader. Sometimes referred to as a knockoff, except that a *knockoff* always has a lower price, whereas the me-too product may not. Also called a *parity product.*

metrics   see *marketing metrics.*

metro area   see *metropolitan area.*

metro edition   an edition of a national magazine that is distributed only to a particular city in the United States, i.e., *Newsweek* has editions that go to 40 of the major cities in the United States; the advertiser can buy space in the metro edition of a particular city without having to purchase any larger circulation. A type of *partial-run edition.* See also *demographic edition, regional edition,* and *state edition.*

metro rating   in television and radio advertising, a program's rating in a metropolitan area; see also *metropolitan area.*

metro rating area (MRA)   metropolitan television or radio coverage area for television and radio ratings purposes; see also *Metropolitan Area (MA).*

metro survey area   in radio audience research, the primary reporting area for local radio used by *Arbitron.*

Metropolitan Area (MA)   a core area containing a large population nucleus (i.e., a central city with a population of 50,000 or more), together with adjacent communities having a high degree of economic and social integration with that core; a definition of the U.S. Office of Management and Budget (OMB). Often referred to as *metro area.* See also *Metropolitan Statistical Area (MSA), Consolidated Metropolitan Statistical Area (CMSA), Primary Metropolitan Statistical Area (PMSA), metro rating,* and *metro rating area.*

Metropolitan Statistical Area (MSA)   a geographical area that includes a city of at least 50,000 population or an urbanized area of at least 50,000 with a total metropolitan area population of at least 100,000; a definition of the U.S. Office of Management and Budget (OMB). See also *Metropolitan Area (MA), Consolidated Metropolitan Statistical Area (CMSA),* and *Primary Metropolitan Statistical Area (PMSA).*

microenvironment   the forces in the immediate realm of an organization that greatly influence both its short- and long-term marketing efforts; includes forces such as consumers, trade customers, the distribution channel network, suppliers, competitors, various publics, and the company itself. See also *macroenvironment.*

micromarketing   custom-designed products, strategies, and marketing programs aimed at satisfying the needs, wants, and tastes of a very specific target market; the focus may be individuals or geographic locations. The opposite of *mass marketing.* See also *mass marketing, differentiation, market segmentation, target marketing,* and *niche marketing.*

microsite   on the Web, a miniature, stand-alone Web site within a Web site; e.g., a separate Web site for a specific product or brand that exists along with the corporate Web site, accessible via its own URL or from the main corporate Web site. Can be a good way to reach and tailor a site to key customer segments, especially smaller ones, without subjecting them to the large volumes of information on the company's main Web site.

middle billboard   a brief announcement somewhere in the middle of a broadcast program in the form of, "The following portion of this program is brought to you by (sponsor's name)." See also *open billboard* and *close billboard.*

middle break   in television, a station identification or a commercial at the midpoint of a program.

middleman   an intermediary or firm between the manufacturer and the customer that facilitates the flow of goods from producer to user by performing a variety of functions; a wholesaler, distributor, broker, agent, dealer, retailer, or other intermediary that buys products for the purpose of reselling them. Also called an *intermediary* or *reseller.*

middleman functions   in *distribution channels,* the several roles played by intermediaries in getting the product from manufacturer to customer; functions involve activities related to information, promotion, contact, relationships, matching, negotiation, physical distribution, financing, and risk-taking. See also *middleman, service wholesaler, limited-function wholesaler,* and *retailer.*

Miller-Tydings Act   a federal fair trade law, enacted in 1937, that allowed manufacturers to dictate the resale price of a product; although price-fixing *per se* was unlawful under the Sherman Act, this law exempted from the Sherman Act contracts and agreements between manufacturers and resellers that prescribed minimum prices for resale of the manufacturer's products, thereby allowing manufacturers to establish the price at which retailers were to sell the product to consumers. Declared unconstitutional and repealed in 1975, by passage of the *Consumer Goods Pricing Act.* See also *fair trade.*

milline rate   in newspaper advertising, the cost of one *agate line* reaching one million readers; an expression of the rate for advertising space relative to *circulation.* To calculate: agate line rate divided by the circulation times 1,000,000. Facilitates cost-efficiency comparisons of newspapers with different circulations. See also *agate line.*

minimil rate   in newspaper advertising, the cost of an *agate line* of space at the lowest *milline rate,* i.e., after all discounts; see *agate line, maximil rate,* and *milline rate.*

minimum depth requirement   a requirement of some newspapers that calls for an advertisement having certain height-width proportions, such as an ad being at least one inch high for every column it is wide; for example, an ad that is three columns wide must be at least three inches high. See also *maximum depth requirement.*

minimum frequency   the lowest level of audience exposure needed for the advertising to have effect or achieve its objectives; see also *three-hit theory.*

minimum showing   in outdoor advertising, the smallest *showing* an advertiser may purchase without being charged on a per-ad basis, which is generally more expensive; see also *showing.*

minority marketing   marketing programs and efforts directed specifically to minority groups within the total population; also referred to as *diversity* *marketing, ethnic marketing,* or *special-interest marketing.*

minute-by-minute profile television program audience data that show viewership during specific minutes of a particular program, and the increases and decreases that occur in each minute or block of minutes of the program; a service of *Nielsen Media Research.*

misleading advertising   see *deceptive advertising.*

misredemption   reimbursement for a *coupon* (face value for the consumer or handling charge for the retailer) without sale of the product to which the coupon applied; sometimes a result of consumer or retailer fraud. Examples: use of a coupon whose expiration date has passed, purchasing a size other than that stipulated on the coupon, passing counterfeit coupons, or the retailer amassing coupons and sending them to the manufacturer for reimbursement without having sold the product.

misrepresentation   an advertisement, promotion, or other marketing practice in which a message is misleading to a reasonable consumer and is a factor that confuses the consumer's decision-making process, perhaps resulting in a purchase decision that would have been different were it not for the deceptive information conveyed by the message or presentation. See also *deceptive advertising.*

missionary selling   a sales position or effort dedicated primarily to providing support services for the dealer, as opposed to seeking orders; such nonselling activities may include sales training for retail salespeople, help with in-store layout and merchandising programs, or assistance with the retailer's advertising and promotion efforts on behalf of a particular product. See also *field marketing* and *nonselling activities.*

mixed-media approach   the use of a combination of several different media types in the same advertising campaign; see also *media mix.*

mnemonic device   visual devices or other cues in advertising that are intended to facilitate the audience's memory about a particular product or benefit; an attempt to make the advertising memorable by use of symbols, pictures, rhymes, characters, associations, sounds, and other cues. For example: Aunt Jemima, the Jolly Green Giant, Charlie the tuna for Starkist, Tony the tiger for Kellogg's Frosted Flakes, or the NBC chimes.

mobile advertising   an advertising message that is moved from one location to another; see also *mobile billboard* and *mobile media.*

mobile billboard   an advertising sign that is transported by a motor vehicle from one location to another; e.g., a sign painted on or affixed to an automobile that is driven to a particular event and parked at that location, or a flatbed truck with a billboard that goes from event to event. The sign may be parked at a specific venue or may be driven around to particular locales or simply back and forth on busy roads and highways. Also a popular term, along with *rolling billboard,* referring to an auto race car with signs and decals affixed to it. See also *rolling billboard* and *truckside advertising.*

mobile media   any advertising medium or vehicle capable of moving from one location to another while displaying an advertiser's message; see also *mobile billboard.*

mobile sampling   a sales promotion activity consisting of a vehicle being driven around from which samples, coupons, and other promotions are distributed to consumers; the vehicle, usually with the company logo, brand name and colors, campaign slogan, and the like painted on it, makes visits to shopping malls, recreational areas, sports venues, fairgrounds, and other areas where crowds gather.

mockup   a close representation or simulation of the real thing, such as an advertisement, a package, or a *point-of-purchase display;* a model produced to scale.

mode   in a series of numbers, the one number that appears most often; 33 in the series 42, 38, 34, 34, 33, 33, 33, 33, 31, 29, 27. See also *mean* and *median.*

modem   an electronic device that can be used to connect computers and terminals over communication lines; permits incoming signals to be read by a computer and outgoing signals to be read by a telephone line for transmission. Used to connect computers to the Internet.

moderate (medium) users   consumers who purchase and use a product or service in medium quantities, somewhere between heavy usage and light usage; in contrast to *heavy users, light users,* or *nonusers.*

moderator   see *focus group moderator.*

monadic communications   nonpersonal and indirect communications between two parties; e.g., the advertiser placing its message in a magazine. See also *dyadic communications.*

monitoring constant vigilance of markets and marketing activities to ascertain current conditions, trends, and any relevant change; see also *tracking.*

monitoring service an organization that continuously examines magazines, newspapers, and other publications for mention of a company's name; typically employed by the advertiser on a contract basis. Also called a *clipping service.* The broadcast media equivalent is called a *broadcast monitoring service.* See also *clipping service.*

monopole in out-of-home advertising, a display mounted on a single pole; also called a *unipole.*

monopolistic competition a market structure characterized by a relatively large number of competitors (the great majority of which have a small market share), reasonably easy entry to the market, differentiated products, limited control over price, heavy emphasis on nonprice competition such as advertising, sales promotion, personal selling, branding, distribution, product, and service; e.g., most apparel, household furniture—virtually the entire retail trade in metropolitan areas. See also *pure competition, pure monopoly,* and *oligopolistic competition.*

Monroe Mendelsohn Research a leading provider of a very wide range of custom and syndicated research in all phases of marketing and advertising; among its research efforts are studies relating to new and existing products, customer satisfaction, package testing, positioning, market segmentation, concept testing, test market evaluation, advertising and promotion program evaluation, tracking, copytesting, and all types of media research. Known simply as Mendelsohn.

month preceding in magazine advertising, a closing date specification indicating one month before the publication date of the magazine; see also *closing date.*

monthly promotional calendar a retailer's month-by-month schedule of sales, special events, and other promotions and events; used as a planning device and to coordinate appropriate media advertising efforts with store promotions.

morning in the television broadcast day, the time period from 6:00 A.M.–9:00 A.M.; see also *dayparts (television).*

morning drive time in the radio broadcast day, the time period from 6:00 A.M.–10:00 A.M.; see also *dayparts (radio).*

morphing a computer-driven technique by which the form or image of an object or person is transformed into another form or image as part of the television commercial; e.g., transforming the face of an ordinary individual to that of an instantly recognized celebrity, such as a young boy on a golf course transformed into Tiger Woods.

motive the particular stimulus or driving force that causes an individual to take action toward a goal; see also *emotional motives* and *rational motives.*

motivation the process by which consumers internally initiate action to satisfy needs, wants, and desires; the individual's inner drive that moves him or her to goal-directed behavior.

motivation research in marketing and advertising research, a qualitative investigation of how and why individuals act as they do in making marketplace decisions; an attempt to determine the inner drive and reasons underlying a consumer's marketplace behavior and actions.

moving letter sign a horizontal panel containing lights that, when illuminated successively, or in a streaming fashion, give the impression that they are moving.

multibranding a brand strategy in which the marketer introduces a new brand in the same product category it currently serves; e.g., Black & Decker power tools with its DeWalt power tool line, Seiko watches with its Pulsar line, Bulova watches with its Accutron line, Procter & Gamble and its many detergent brands, as well as ConAgra with its many meal entrée brands; other examples are Sara Lee Company with an intimate apparel line that includes Hanes, Wonderbra, Bali, Playtex, Lovable, JustMySize, and Dim, in addition to a packaged meats line that includes a Sara Lee brand along with the Jimmy Dean, Hillshire Farm, Bryan Foods, and Ball Park Foods brands. Also called a *flanker brand.* See also *brand strategy, line extension, brand extension,* and *new-brand strategy.*

multichannel distribution system a distribution system in which a producer uses two or more marketing channels to get its product to market, either to different markets or the same target market; see also *dual distribution* and *hybrid marketing system.*

multicultural agency an advertising agency with capabilities for serving two or more distinct ethnic markets, national origins, or markets with different social and value systems; e.g., a U.S. agency that also serves the Hispanic market, African American market, and international markets.

multimagazine deal when two or more publishers give an advertiser the opportunity to buy space in their magazines with one *media buy* rather than separate transactions; e.g., Conde Nast and Fairchild publications collaborate for the benefit of advertisers wishing to appeal to fashion-conscious women. Also called *cross-magazine advertising deal.* See also *magazine network.*

multimedia buy whenever an advertiser uses a variety of media in its schedule; the purchase of advertising time and/or space in more than one medium or media vehicle owned by a media supplier, e.g., buying television time and magazine space from a media supplier who owns both, or buying space in several magazines owned by the same media supplier. Examples: buying commercial time and advertising space with News Corp's (Murdoch) cable television stations Fox Movie Channel, Fox Sports World, Fox News Channel, National Geographic Channel, along with *The Weekly Standard* magazine, and the *New York Post* newspaper; or buying advertising space in Conde Nast's *House & Garden, The New Yorker, GQ, Wired,* and *Self.* On a smaller scale, in a given local market, the same company may own a television station, radio station, and a local newspaper. Also called *cross-media advertising.*

multimedia promotion program a marketing communications program that uses a broad range of delivery mechanisms for the advertising, sales promotion, direct marketing (including Internet), public relations, and personal selling components of the program; a campaign involving a mix of traditional and nontraditional media—rich media, videos, CDs, displays, the Internet, and others.

multinational advertising see *international advertising.*

multiple buying influence a situation in which more than one individual has input and weight in a purchase decision; generally refers to the purchase

decisions involving business products, but also includes consumer product decisions.

multiple distribution channels system see *multichannel distribution system.*

multiple target market approach identifying, evaluating, selecting, and then marketing to two or more market segments with a different *marketing mix* for each target segment; see also *differentiated marketing* and *single target market approach.*

multiple-choice questions structured research questions in which each question provides several possible answers and the respondent must select the one that he or she thinks best answers the question.

multiple-facing in outdoor advertising, one location where there are two or more displays within 25 feet of each other and facing the same direction; may be used by the same advertiser for two different product messages or by two different advertisers.

multiple-rating list on a research questionnaire, a format that allows several factors or items to be rated using the same scale; done to save questionnaire space and respondent time. Example: a list of items for which ratings are sought in the far left column, with four other columns to the right, with each of the four headed by a different response category (the four columns may be titled *strongly agree, agree, disagree,* and *strongly disagree*) to make it easy and convenient for the respondent to place a checkmark in the appropriate place for each item.

multiple-response questions structured research questions in which each question has several possible answers provided and the respondent may select as many of the answers as he or she sees fit or thinks apply.

multiplexing in cable television, when several channels are transmitted by the same cable network; e.g., Disney, with The Disney Channel, ESPN, ESPN2, Classic Sports Network, A & E Television, The History Channel, and Lifetime Television, or Discover Communications, with The Discover Channel, The Learning Channel, The Travel Channel, Animal Planet, and Bravo.

municipal marketing a company's advertising and promotion efforts that are linked to community activities and services, such as sponsorship of local parks and recreation programs; Pepsi's or Reebok's association with an inner-city neighborhood summer basketball league or Titleist's or Callaway's sponsorship of a "Learn to Play Golf" summer program for a city's teenagers.

musical commercial   see *jingle*.

musical logo   a *jingle* that immediately identifies a particular company or product in the mind of the consumer; e.g., "Campbell's soup is mmmm, mmmm good," the "In the valley of the, ho-ho-ho, Green Giant"

for Jolly Green Giant foods, or the Doublemint gum song. See also *jingle*.

mystery shopper   the practice of professional shoppers making shopping trips to stores to evaluate the quality of the personal selling effort and other service factors; a research technique used by manufacturers to see how effectively their products (and competing products) are being handled at the retail level, as well as by retailers interested in assessing competing stores' selling efforts. Also referred to as *shadow shopping*.

N

NAA   see *Newspaper Association of America.*

NAAG   see *National Association of Attorneys General.*

NAB   see *National Association of Broadcasters.*

NAD   see *National Advertising Division.*

NAICS   see *North American Industry Classification System.*

NARB   see *National Advertising Review Board.*

NARC   see *National Advertising Review Council.*

NCTA   see *National Cable and Telecommunications Association.*

NHI   see *Nielsen Homevideo Index.*

NMR   see *Nielsen Media Research.*

NPD   see *new-product development process.*

NRF   see *National Retail Federation.*

NSI   see *Nielsen Station Index.*

NSS   see *Nielsen Syndication Service.*

NTI   see *Nielsen Television Index.*

NAB Code   in television and radio, a self-regulatory "Code of Conduct" aimed at promoting a steadfast commitment to the highest standards of broadcasting in the public interest; includes guidelines and standards relating to program content, advertising content, types of products that should or should not be advertised on programs, time limits for advertising, a special sensitivity to programming and advertising directed to children, and other standards in the public interest.

name recognition   the extent to which a company, organization, or brand registers with and has meaning for the consumer; see also *brand recognition.*

naming rights   in sponsorship marketing, the privilege or claim a marketer has to put its name on the title of an event or other sponsorship; e.g., the FedEx Orange Bowl in college football, the Mercedes Championship in professional golf, or Gillette Stadium for the home field of the New England Patriots professional football team.

narrative copy   advertising copy that tells a story as it attempts to influence the audience; the product's selling points are delivered by means of a series of statements. Often uses a problem-solution execution format. See also *dialogue copy* and *problem-solution format.*

narrowcasting   in television or radio, in contrast to broadcasting, a specialized program tailored to smaller, more defined audiences with specific interests or particular demographics; e.g., cable television networks devoted to food, golf, finances, or history, or radio programming that caters to sports enthusiasts. The broadcast equivalent of *special-interest magazines.* See also *broadcasting.*

national advertiser   a company or other organization whose advertising is aimed at a nationwide or multiregion target audience.

national advertising   advertising directed at target audiences nationwide or in geographic regions, as opposed to local advertising; see also *local advertising.*

National Advertising Division (NAD)   a division of the *Council of Better Business Bureaus (CBBB);* along with the *National Advertising Review Board (NARB),* one of two operating arms of the *National Advertising Review Council (NARC),* this body is the advertising industry's primary voluntary self-regulation force. Monitors national advertising practices and reviews complaints from competitors, local Better Business Bureaus (BBBs), consumer groups, trade associations, and those emanating from its own monitoring efforts. After a complete review of the alleged advertising abuse, the NAD issues a finding, which may be that the contested claims were substantiated (in which case the advertising may continue as it was) or that the advertising claims were unsubstantiated and, therefore, the advertising should be modified or discontinued. When its nonbinding decision is not agreed to by the advertiser in question, and the matter of modifying or discontinuing the advertising cannot be resolved, the advertiser has the option of abiding by the NAD decision or appealing to the NARB, a rare occurrence. See also *Council of Better Business Bureaus (CBBB), National Advertising Review Board (NARB),* and *National Advertising Review Council (NARC).*

National Advertising Review Board (NARB) a division of the *National Advertising Review Council (NARC),* this body serves as the appeals board for *National Advertising Division (NAD)* decisions in the self-regulatory mechanism of the advertising industry; when a NAD decision is appealed, the NARB reviews the complaint and the NAD findings, conducts a hearing in which the advertiser presents its case, and then issues a nonbinding decision. The next step if an advertiser refuses to abide by the NARB decision to either modify or discontinue the questionable advertising is government intervention by the Federal Trade Commission (FTC), an extremely rare occurrence. See also *Federal Trade Commission (FTC), National Advertising Division (NAD),* and *National Advertising Review Council (NARC).*

National Advertising Review Council (NARC) the council consists of two divisions that together form the advertising industry's primary voluntary self-regulation mechanism—the *National Advertising Division (NAD)* and the *Children's Advertising Review Unit (CARU);* this body's mission is to maintain high standards of truth, accuracy, and social responsibility in national advertising. Established by the cooperative efforts of the *American Advertising Federation (AAF),* the *American Association of Advertising Agencies (AAAA),* the *Association of National Advertisers (ANA),* and the *Council of Better Business Bureaus (CBBB).* See also *National Advertising Division (NAD)* and *Children's Advertising Review Unit (CARU).*

National Association of Attorneys General (NAAG) an association composed of the states' attorneys general; has considerable impact on the way in which the states regulate business practices, including advertising.

National Association of Broadcasters (NAB) the industry association that represents the interests of free, over-the-air television and radio broadcasters; promotes and protects interests at the federal level, does industry research for the betterment of practice, and keeps members current on policy issues, technological developments, and management trends. See also *NAB Code.*

national agency an advertising agency with the capability to prepare and place advertising throughout the entire country or at least several geographic regions of the country.

national brand see *manufacturer's brand.*

national buy in magazine and newspaper advertising, the purchase of advertising space in the national edition of the publication, as opposed to buying space in individual markets in regional or metro editions, one market at a time as in the case of a market-by-market buy; see also *market-by-market buy* and *network buy.*

National Cable and Telecommunications Association (NCTA) the major trade association of the cable television industry dedicated to providing a single voice on issues affecting the cable and telecommunications industry; represents cable networks, cable system operators, equipment suppliers, and providers of other services to the cable industry. Heavily involved with public affairs and government relations, as well as a broad range of activities and initiatives to advance the causes of cable television and telecommunications

national magazine a magazine with nationwide circulation.

national newspaper a newspaper whose circulation covers the entire country; e.g., *USA Today, The Wall Street Journal, The New York Times.*

national media media whose audience or circulation covers the entire country.

National Outdoor Advertising Association (NOAA) see *Outdoor Advertising Association of America (OAAA).*

national plan an advertising and media plan aimed at the entire country (or more than one region), as opposed to a local plan covering only the immediate local or regional area.

national rate   an advertising rate charged by local media vehicles, such as newspapers, to national or regional advertisers; higher than the local rate charged to local retailers. Also called a *general rate.* See also *general rate* and *local rate.*

national ratings   see *People Meter.*

National Retail Federation (NRF)   the major retail industry association for department, specialty, and discount chain stores, plus nearly two million smaller retailers; conducts extensive and timely conferences and educational programs to assist retailers in their marketing and operational programs, and collects and distributes statistical information on every aspect of retailing. Formed by a merger of the National Retail Merchants Association with the American Retail Federation.

national spot advertising   in television or radio, a national advertiser's nonnetwork or local advertising time purchased from a local station; i.e., local advertising time bought by a national advertiser. See also *spot* and *local spot advertising.*

national supplement   see *Sunday supplement.*

National Traffic and Motor Vehicle Safety Act   the major federal legislation governing all aspects of highway safety, via the *National Highway Traffic Safety Administration (NHTSA).*

navigation   on the Internet, the way in which a user travels to, around, and from a Web site and its pages.

near-pack premium   in consumer sales promotion, a *premium* that is located away from but close to the product rather than in the package or on it; so placed because the premium is too large for the product's package or it is otherwise not economically feasible to insert or affix it to the package. See *in-pack premium, on-pack premium,* and *premium.*

neckhanger   promotional material that is slipped over and hung from the neck of a bottle.

need   the difference between an individual's actual situation and desired situation; the lack of something useful or desired. See also *need recognition* and *wants.*

need recognition   a consumer's awareness or realization of a discrepancy between his or her current state and that which is desired; the first stage of the consumer

decision process. To the extent the recognition of a need stimulates behavior to fill that need, there is *motivation.* See also *consumer decision process.*

needs   the composite of the consumer's requirements; see also *hierarchy of needs.*

negative advertising   advertising whose focus is almost entirely on the dire consequences of not having the advertiser's product; sometimes the approach when fear appeals are employed. Also a term for advertising that attacks or slams the competition (i.e., *comparison advertising*) with extremely hard-hitting copy. See also *negative appeals, fear appeals,* and *comparison advertising.*

negative appeals   an advertising copy approach in which virtually the entire emphasis is on problems consumers will face without a particular product or service and how their lives will be difficult if they do not buy the product or service; the intent is to create such anxiety in the consumer that he or she perceives a big void. See also *positive appeals.*

negotiated commission   advertising agency compensation that is the result of the advertiser and the agency bargaining and agreeing to a rate structure other than the usual 15 percent commission on all billings, or time and space purchased by the agency on behalf of the advertiser; often results in a sliding scale, with the commission rate decreasing as the media purchases increase. See also *agency compensation method, agency commission, fee method, commission method, combination method, performance-based method, sliding rate,* and *billings.*

negotiated price   a product or service price determined by bargaining between the buyer and seller.

neighborhood showing   a small group of outdoor posters, in close proximity to one another, featuring a product available in the area or neighborhood in which the posters are located.

neon bulletin   an outdoor advertising poster illuminated by neon lights.

net   in buying advertising time or space, the money actually paid to a media vehicle by an advertising agency after deducting the agency's commission; also short for *network.*

net amount   generally, what remains, i.e., the gain, after any reductions or adjustments in the grand total; see also *gross amount.*

net audience the total unduplicated audience (individuals or households) reached by all media in a complete media schedule; can also refer to the unduplicated audience reached by a particular medium or by a specific *media vehicle* over the entire *media schedule* (i.e., the total number of different people or households reached at least once in a media schedule). Also known as *net unduplicated audience* or *unduplicated audience.*

net circulation in periodicals, the total number of copies actually distributed to all individuals, regardless of whether or not the copies are paid for.

net controlled circulation in controlled circulation periodicals, the number of copies bought, as well as those not bought but received by individuals on the controlled-circulation distribution list; i.e., the number of copies of a controlled-circulation publication actually distributed. See also *controlled circulation.*

net cost an advertiser's cost of using the services of an advertising agency, after the agency commission has been deducted; also an advertising media rate after all discounts, including the agency commission, have been deducted from the *base rate.*

net coverage see *net audience.*

net earnings see *net profit.*

net income see *net profit.*

net paid circulation in periodicals, the number of copies actually sold, i.e., the total number of purchasers of an average issue of a periodical, including subscription and newsstand sales; same as *paid circulation.*

net profit gross sales less taxes, interest, depreciation, and other expenses in operating the business; also called *net earnings* or *net income. See also gross sales, gross profit, gross margin, net sales,* and *cost of goods sold.*

net rating in television or radio, the percentage of the total potential audience exposed to a program, without duplication; see also *reach.*

net rating point in television or radio, one percent of the total potential audience that is exposed to a program, without duplication; see also *gross rating point.*

net reach see *net audience.*

net sales gross sales less discounts, returns, and allowances; i.e., the actual sales dollars received by the company. See also *gross sales, gross profit, gross margin, net profit,* and *cost of goods sold.*

net single-copy sales for a particular publication or the total number of copies sold through retail locations, such as newsstands, minus any returns from the retailer.

net unduplicated audience see *net audience.*

net weekly audience in television or radio, the number of individuals or households that tune in to a program that is broadcast more than once a week, over a period of time.

net weekly circulation in television or radio, the number of individuals or households tuned to a particular station for a minimum of five minutes during a week, over a period of time.

network in television or radio, a group of interconnected stations, i.e., affiliates, bound together by contract, that broadcast the same programs simultaneously in many different markets; stations are interconnected for the distribution of programming. Can also refer to a group of magazines that sell advertising space in the different publications as a single unit. Examples: ABC, CBS, NBC, Fox, WB, or UPN in television and Westwood One or Premiere Radio in radio. See also *broadcast network* and *network affiliate.*

network affiliate a local television or radio station, not owned by the *network* but which is formally a part of the network group, that makes specific time periods available for network-supplied programs and advertising; in contrast to an "*owned-and-operated*" station. See also *O & O station* and *network.*

network buy in television and radio advertising, the purchase of commercial time directly from the *network,* resulting in the commercial being aired on all affiliate stations, as opposed to buying time in individual markets as in the case of a market-by-market buy; see also *market-by-market buy* and *national buy.*

network commercial review board in television advertising, a TV network's committee charged with the responsibility of reviewing all advertising scheduled for broadcast, to ensure it meets the network's acceptability standards for airing commercial messages.

network compensation in television advertising, when broadcast networks pay their affiliated stations in each local market to air the network offerings and, in return, the networks retain the bulk of the commercial time for sale to national advertisers; also called *station compensation.*

network cooperative program   a broadcast network program that allows local commercials to be aired.

network identification   in television or radio, a brief announcement identifying the network made during a program, usually at the beginning or the end; see also *station identification.*

network option time   see *network time.*

network participation   see *participation basis.*

network promo   a commercial by a television or radio network that airs on its own stations and promotes the network or a particular program or program lineup.

network radio   see *network.*

network spot buy   a spot or an entire schedule of spots purchased on network programs; see also *spot* and *spot advertising.*

network television   see *network.*

network time   a time period in the broadcast day when a local television or radio station agrees it will broadcast network programs and for which the networks have the option of selling the advertising time (rather than the individual stations having the option); e.g., *prime time.* Also called *network option time.* See also *station option time.*

new media   any of the variety of media developed and utilized relatively recently, especially those made possible by technological advances; e.g., the Internet, interactive kiosks, CD-ROMs, interactive television, videotapes.

new unsought products   consumer products that the potential customer simply does not know exist on the market and, as a result, is making no attempt to find; see also *unsought products* and *regularly unsought products.*

new-brand strategy   a strategy in which the marketer uses an entirely new brand name, entering a new product category for the company; e.g., Black & Decker home-improvement power tools company entering the lawncare market with its GrassHog edge trimmer, LeafHog blower, HedgeHog hedge trimmer, EdgeHog edge trimmer, the kitchen appliance market with its ArcticTwister ice cream maker, SmartBrew coffeemaker, and Gizmo can opener, as well as the home cleaning market with its DustBuster cordless vacuum. Another example is Unilever with its Dove soap, Lipton tea, Bird's Eye frozen foods, Close Up toothpaste, Slim Fast wellness products, Hellmann's dressings, Vaseline personal care products, and many others. See also *brand strategy, line extension, brand extension,* and *multibranding.*

new-product development process (NPD)   a series of stages describing how an idea for a product or service ultimately becomes an official entry into the marketplace; full process consists of *idea generation, idea screening, concept testing, market evaluation, product development, marketing plan, market testing,* and *commercialization.* For the most part, this is a sequential series of stages, although some stages are worked on simultaneously.

news format   in advertising, a creative *execution format* that presents the message in an announcement or reporting style; e.g., an advertisement announcing a new product or the grand opening of a new store. See *straightforward factual, demonstration, problem-solution, slice-of-life, dramatization, symbolic association, fantasy, animation, still-life, humor, spokesperson, testimonial,* and *comparison formats.*

news release   formally prepared information distributed by the organization to print and broadcast media for appearance in the media outlets for the purpose of gaining publicity for the organization's products, its people, an occurrence, an issue, or other matter of importance to the organization; a public relations activity. Also known as a *press release.*

newsgroup   on the Internet, a system for conducting discussions; essentially, a worldwide bulletin board.

news-information headline   a type of headline for an advertisement or commercial in which the advertiser makes an announcement or an informative statement that causes the audience to take notice; e.g. "A surprising ally in the fight to save the environment— an oil company." (Sunoco oil) or "Introducing a new way to lower your cholesterol. Without drugs." (Cholestin capsules). See also *headline,* as well as *benefit headline, command headline, curiosity headline,* and *question headline.*

newspaper   an advertising-dependent daily or weekly publication containing news, current events, articles on a variety of topics, and generally organized into major sections such as national news, metropolitan and local news, arts and entertainment, business and finance, sports, and so on; see also *broadsheet* and *tabloid*.

Newspaper Association of America (NAA)   the major professional association for the newspaper industry, with a focus on strategic priorities collectively affecting the entire industry, including marketing, public policy, diversity, industry development, newspaper operations, and readership; an important effort is made by the NAA to increase newspapers' share of advertising dollars, as well as to improve sales and marketing capabilities. Formed by a merger of the American Newspaper Publishers Association, the Newspaper Advertising Bureau, and five other industry associations.

newspaper insert   see *insert*.

newspaper network   a group of newspapers that sell advertising space to advertisers, who can buy space in several of the group's newspapers at the same time with just one insertion order, i.e., buy space as a single purchase transaction.

newspaper sampling   a method of sampling in which the trial-size samples are distributed via newspapers; see also *sampling, polybag,* and *billboard bag*.

newspaper supplement   see *Sunday supplement*.

newspaper syndicate   an organization that sells features, comic strips, cartoons, and other special materials for publication in newspapers.

newsstand circulation   a periodical's sales through retail outlets.

newsweekly   a weekly publication devoted mainly to news and current events; e.g., *Newsweek, Time*.

next-to-reading-matter   when ordering space in a publication, an instruction or request from the advertiser to the publication to have an advertisement placed next to editorial matter on a page, as opposed to having other advertisements on its borders; sometimes sold at a premium rate.

niche   a narrowly defined market segment with a very distinct set of characteristics or needs; often willing to pay a premium price to have its specific needs met and satisfied. See also *niche marketing*.

niche magazine   see *special-interest magazine* and *custom magazine*.

niche marketing   marketing, advertising, and promotion to a small and distinct segment of a broader market, with the marketer often facing little or no competition, because the segment is overlooked or simply ignored by competitors; see also *niche*.

niche network   in television, a *network* aimed at a very specific audience; e.g., cable TV's The Golf Channel. The television equivalent of a *special-interest magazine* or *custom magazine*.

nighttime   in the radio broadcast day, the time period from 7:00 P.M.–12:00 A.M.; see also *dayparts (radio)*.

Nielsen families   the households and people comprising the representative sample from which *Nielsen Media Research* provides television audience estimates; there are approximately 5,000 households in the national *People Meter* sample and 18,000 households with *set-tuning meters* in the local television market samples, plus there are about 1.5 million diaries from the 210 television markets in the United States reviewed and tabulated each year. See also *diary method, People Meter,* and *set-tuning meter*.

Nielsen Hispanic Station Index   a service of *Nielsen Media Research* that provides viewing information in 16 local television markets with significant Hispanic population (via metered-market measurement and diary measurement).

Nielsen Hispanic Television Index   a service of *Nielsen Media Research* that provides audience measurement and estimates of the Hispanic audience on a national basis (via *People Meters*).

Nielsen Homevideo Index (NHI)   a service of *Nielsen Media Research* that provides measurement of cable television, pay cable, VCRs, video discs, and other television technologies (via *People Meters, set-tuning meters,* and *diaries*).

Nielsen Interactive Services   a service of *Nielsen Media Research* that provides auditing and measurement of Web site traffic, including the number of visits by different people and the length of each visit.

Nielsen Market Research   see *A.C. Nielsen*.

Nielsen Media Research (NMR)   the leading provider of television audience data and information services to worldwide, national, and local customers, including television networks and local affiliates, cable networks and local cable systems, independent stations, syndicators, satellite distributors, advertisers, advertising agencies, media buying services, station representatives, and program producers; also provides a wide range of research services, such as audience estimates for the Internet, sports marketing organizations, and interactive marketing organizations. See also *VNU Media Measurement & Information Group* and *A.C. Nielsen.*

Nielsen Monitor-Plus a service of *Nielsen Media Research* that uses advanced data collection technology and information delivery systems to gather, manage, and distribute information on advertisements from a wide variety of media; includes cost estimates and other data to give a comprehensive view of the reach and cost-effectiveness of advertising, along with a means to evaluate competitors' advertising strategies. Media planners can compare advertising schedules and actual audience delivery to gain insight into how well their advertising reaches target audiences compared to the competition.

Nielsen/Net Ratings a service of *Nielsen Media Research* that provides data on Internet audiences and usage, as well as Internet advertising measurement; Web site ratings are based on a sample of more than 225,000 individuals worldwide. Results are compiled from real-time meters on the individuals' computers, which monitor the sites they visit.

Nielsen People Meter see *People Meter.*

Nielsen Retail Index a compilation of retail statistics coming from store audits done by *A.C. Nielsen;* stores include those involved with household and food products, cosmetics, and over-the-counter (OTC) drugs. See also *store audit.*

Nielsen Sports Marketing Service a service of *Nielsen Media Research* that provides a wide range of tracking data on sports leagues, teams, and marketers, including measurement and estimates of broadcast and cable television audiences.

Nielsen Station Index (NSI) a service of *Nielsen Media Research* that provides local market television audience measurement in 55 major markets (via metered-market overnight measurement) and 210 *Designated Market Areas (DMAs)* (via *diary* measurement); see also *Nielsen Television Index (NTI).*

Nielsen Syndication Service (NSS) a service of *Nielsen Media Research* that provides measurement of the syndication programming segment of the television industry (via *People Meters, set-tuning meters,* and *diaries*).

Nielsen Television Index (NTI) a service of *Nielsen Media Research* that provides television audience measurement and estimates for all national broadcast television programs (via *People Meters*); see also *Nielsen Station Index (NSI).*

Nielsen TV ratings the catch-all for the entire range of television ratings services provided by *Nielsen Media Research;* see also the individual *Nielsen* entries.

90-day cancellation in outdoor advertising, the advertiser's right to cancel scheduled advertising, with at least 90 days' notice.

no-change rate a special rate for space or time offered to an advertiser by some media vehicles when the advertiser uses the same advertisement or commercial for an extended period of time.

noise interference or extraneous stimuli along the communications channel that is a distraction and reduces the clarity, accuracy, or intended meaning of a message from the sender to the receiver; anything that serves to disrupt the free flow of communications or diminishes the effectiveness of the message.

nonadvertising promotion promotion activities other than advertising, especially those activities used in a public relations program.

nonbusiness advertising see *noncommercial advertising.*

noncommercial advertising advertising done by a not-for-profit organization to promote a charity, cause, idea, attitude, philosophy, or other similar purpose; e.g., advertising done by a charitable institution, civic group, college or university, a specific-purpose cause organization, a political party, or other not-for-profit organization.

noncommercial broadcasting television and radio stations whose major sources of funds are viewers, listeners, grants from foundations, companies, government, and other sources, as opposed to advertisers; see also *advertiser-supported broadcasting, cable television (CATV),* and *public broadcasting.*

noncommissionable media media and services bought by an advertising agency that, unlike magazine and other traditional media vehicles, do not grant the agency a *commission* or discount on the purchase; e.g., sales literature created for dealers to distribute to prospects as part of a campaign. See also *collateral materials, collateral services,* and *commissionable media.*

noncompensatory decision rule a *decision rule* in which the consumer, in choosing between two or more alternatives, rules out a product that scores low on any one relevant attribute, because a particular brand's weakness on one attribute is not offset by its strength on another attribute; a choice process wherein each product attribute is considered separately, and a favorable evaluation on one attribute of a particular brand does not compensate for an unfavorable evaluation on some other attribute of the same brand where it does not meet the minimum standard on that attribute. See also *compensatory decision rule, lexicographic decision rule, consumer decision rules,* and *evoked set.*

noncumulative quantity discount a reduction in price offered to a customer on the basis of amount purchased on that particular order only; see also *cumulative quantity discount.*

nondeal-prone consumers individuals who are either loyal to a particular brand in a product category or who actually may engage in brand-switching behavior but are not, under any circumstance, drawn to a brand by any deal or sales promotion activity; consumers who are not responsive to deals. See also *deal-prone consumers.*

nondirective interview a type of *depth interview* in which the respondent is given wide latitude and freedom to express thoughts on the subjects central to the research and of interest to the interviewer; see *depth interview.*

nondisguised research in marketing and advertising research, asking respondents questions in a very clear and straightforward manner, with each respondent knowing the purpose of the questions; also called *direct questioning.* See also *disguised research.*

nondurable goods consumer goods that are consumed in one or very few uses and that are bought frequently; e.g., breakfast cereal, photographic film, or toothpaste. Sometimes referred to as *soft goods.* See also *durable goods.*

nonfinal art in the creative phase of the advertising design process, any of the various sketches done in stages prior to the *mechanical,* or final artwork; e.g., *thumbnail, rough layout,* or *comprehensive.*

nonfoods products other than food that are commonly sold in supermarkets and other food stores; e.g., baking supplies, magazines, photographic film.

nonfranchise-building promotions sales promotion activities whose primary purpose is to induce immediate consumer action rather than attempting to enhance a brand's image over the long run; e.g., a one-time consumer deal or a coupon program. See also *franchise-building promotions.*

nongovernment regulation see *self-regulation.*

nonguaranteed rate base in print media, the circulation number that is the basis for a periodical's advertising, but is not officially verified by an audit, such as that done by the *Audit Bureau of Circulations (ABC);* see also *rate base* and *Audit Bureau of Circulations (ABC).*

nonilluminated panel an outdoor poster without lighting.

nonmeasured media see *unmeasured media.*

nonnetwork program in television and radio, any programming that is not created by or does not originate from a broadcast network; e.g., local programming or syndication. See also *local programming* and *syndication program.*

nonpaid circulation number of copies of a subscription-type publication that are distributed free-of-charge; usually, recipients must be qualified to receive the publication. Not to be confused with *free publication.* Also called *free circulation.* See also *circulation, controlled circulation, paid circulation,* and *qualified circulation.*

nonpersonal channels see *nonpersonal media.*

nonpersonal communications communications in which there is no direct and personal interaction between the sender and the receiver; e.g., *advertising, public relations, direct marketing,* or *sales promotion.* Sometimes referred to as *impersonal communications* or *mass communications.*

nonpersonal influences in the consumer decision-making process, those factors beyond the individual's own inner self or beyond his or her control that affect marketplace decisions; e.g., time or place.

nonpersonal media communications channels in which there is no personal contact between the sender of a message and the receiver; e.g., magazines or radio. Also called *mass media.* See also *nonpersonal communications.*

nonpersonal selling see *nonpersonal communications.*

nonprice competition challenging competitors for consumer patronage by emphasizing product, promotion, and distribution strategies and actions, as opposed to playing up price; see also *price competition.*

nonprobability sample in survey research for marketing and advertising, an approach to sample selection where the units of the population of interest are chosen based on factors such as convenience, judgment, or meeting a specified quota of responses; i.e., selection is not based on random chance and individuals in the particular population being sampled do not have an equal chance of being selected for inclusion in the sample. See also *nonprobability sample, convenience sample, judgment sample, quota sample, probability sample,* and *survey method.*

nonproduct advertising advertising whose purpose is to sell ideas or images, rather than products or services; e.g., gun control, anti-drug abuse, reading for pleasure, or environmental issues. See also *services advertising* and *product advertising.*

nonprogram material in television and radio, content aside from the specific program itself, such as commercials, public service announcements, or promotions for other shows on that station; see also *clutter.*

nonrenewal when an advertiser in a media vehicle does not continue beyond the current contract agreement.

nonresponse error in survey research, the error resulting from failure to obtain information from a respondent predetermined to be included in the survey's sample; see also *sampling error.*

nonselling activities the activities a salesperson engages in that are not directly concerned with order-getting or order-taking; e.g., reports to the home office, meetings, or the many activities involved in *missionary selling.* See also *missionary selling.*

nontraditional advertising agency an advertising agency or other organization that does not offer its advertisers-clients the broad range of advertising services normally found at a full-service or even a limited-service advertising agency, instead tending to specialize in other areas, such as music or talent, perhaps in combination with creative writing; does not handle all the promotional needs of its clients. See also *creative boutique, full-service advertising agency,* and *limited-service advertising agency.* Also see *Creative Artists Agency.*

nontraditional media refers to any of a variety of advertising media that typically do not carry the bulk of the media load for most advertisers, especially in a particular product category; generally considered to be support media that are often used to make a full impact. Usually, the media for which the fewest dollars are spent by the majority of advertisers. See also *support media* and *unmeasured media.*

nonusers a market segment consisting of consumers who do not purchase or use a particular product or service, in contrast to those who are *heavy users, moderate users,* or *light users.*

nonverbal communications advertising or communications through visual means rather than words; e.g., a picture or illustration in advertising or body language in personal selling situations.

nonwired network a group of television or radio stations that sells advertising time on several of the stations as a single unit, with only one purchase transaction needed; not a network in the legal sense, thus referred to as "nonwired."

norms within a group, beliefs held by a consensus of individuals about the rules of behavior for the group's members; also refers to benchmarks used for purposes of advertising measurement and testing. See also *benchmark.*

North American Industry Classification System (NAICS) a six-digit hierarchical coding system to classify all economic activity into 20 industry sectors; 5 sectors are primarily goods-producing sectors and 15 are entirely services-producing sectors; replaced the long-used four-digit *Standard Industrial Classification System (SIC),* to permit greater coding flexibility.

nostalgia-prone consumer a consumer with a special liking or preference for products, advertising, and icons from his or her younger days.

not-for-profit marketing   the marketing programs and activities of non-profit-seeking organizations, such as government agencies, colleges and universities, museums, social service agencies, or trade associations.

Noted score   in magazine readership studies, the percentage of the readers of a specific issue of a magazine who remember having previously seen a particular advertisement at the time of reading the magazine; a measure of *The Starch Readership Report.* See also *Associated score, Read Most score,* and *Read Some score.*

notification date   in television or radio advertising, the deadline for the advertiser to inform the network or station that it will become or will remain a sponsor of a particular program.

NTIV Analysis (National Television Impression Value)   a comprehensive measurement and evaluation of a corporate sponsor's total sponsorship program in sports and special events, including not only the sponsor's exposure during the actual event television broadcast (i.e., *Sponsors Report*) but also the exposure in other media such as TV news programs, radio, print, and the event site; a service of *Joyce Julius & Associates.* See also *Sponsors Report, in-focus exposure time,* and *Joyce Julius & Associates.*

Nutrition Labeling and Education Act (NLEA)   a 1990 law that requires food producers and distributors to display certain nutritional information on the package (e.g., amount of fat, cholesterol, sodium), as well as requiring that all nutritional claims on the package (e.g., "low-fat," "light," or "reduced calories") are substantiated according to government standards; see also *Federal Food, Drug, and Cosmetic Act.*

O

OAAA see *Outdoor Advertising Association of America.*

ORC see *Opinion Research Corporation.*

OTO see *one-time-only.*

OTS see *opportunity-to-see.*

O & O station a television or radio station "owned and operated" by a network. See *network affiliate.*

Obie Award in the outdoor advertising industry, an annual award that recognizes creative excellence; administered by the *Outdoor Advertising Association of America (OAAA).*

objections the obstacles and resistance shown by a prospective buyer during the personal selling process; may be stated or unstated, rational or emotional. See also *handling objections,* as well as *prospecting, preapproach, approach, presentation, closing,* and *follow-up.*

objective the goal toward which a particular effort is directed; the result being sought, for example, a 5% increase in sales, a 2% increase in market share, a 10% increase in brand awareness, or a 4% coupon redemption rate. A well-stated objective identifies a specific communications *task* to be accomplished with a specific *target audience* during a specific *time period* to achieve a particular *degree of change* as evaluated by a specific *measurement.*

objective-and-task method an approach to determining the advertising (or promotion) budget that starts with setting the objectives, followed by identification of the tasks required to attain those objectives, cost estimates for the tasks, and, finally, a summing up of the costs to arrive at the total budget; a build-up approach to budgeting. See also *affordable method, arbitrary method, competitive parity method, percentage-of-sales method,* and *unit-of-sales method.* See also *build-up approach to budgeting* and *top-down approach to budgeting.*

observation method a research technique that focuses on observing consumers as they go through the decision process and make marketplace choices; used primarily in the *information search* stage of the decision process, but may be used in other stages, and may also include observing their consumption behavior. See also *experimental method* and *survey method.*

off-camera see *voice-over.*

off-card television or radio advertising time sold at a special rate not shown on the station's official *rate card.*

offensive marketing marketing programs, strategies, and tactics used by an organization in its attempt to win market share away from competitors; see also *defensive marketing.*

offensive spending increased advertising and promotion spending intended to make an impression, secure new business, or put a burst of pressure on competitors; may refer to a long-term strategy of heavy promotion expenditures or to a short-term tactic designed for a specific purpose. See also *defensive spending, heavy-up scheduling, bursting,* and *pulsing.*

offer an invitation or proposal made by a seller to a buyer for an exchange of values, such as those involving a product, service, exhibit space, cooperative advertising program, or an event sponsorship; most often, advertising is an offer to sell something.

offer test in testing direct-marketing or sales-promotion activities and programs, a measure and evaluation of the responses generated by a particular proposition vs. another; e.g., offering cash vs. a vacation trip as an inducement to participation by dealers in a trade contest, offering a two-year magazine subscription at a savings compared with a one-year subscription, offering a consumer deal involving a free premium with the product at the regular price vs. a reduced price for the product alone, or a direct-mail offer of a premium fountain pen with a purchase vs. personalized stationery.

offering the combination package that the marketer makes available to the consumer in an attempt to provide need-satisfying benefits; the products, services, information, as well as the experiences the consumer will gain from acquisition of the offering. See also *value proposition.*

official count in out-of-home advertising, a traffic count for an advertising structure taken by a certified and approved governmental source such as a municipal, city, county, or state agency; e.g., a department of transportation at any one of those agencies. See also *traffic count, hand count,* and *counting station.*

official organ a periodical owned and issued by an association or group whose purpose is not simply to publish the periodical but to use it to carry the organization's message; similar to a house publication or house organ, except it is the property of an association, not a company. See also *house publication.*

Office of Consumer Affairs a federal agency charged with the responsibility to oversee programs and efforts to educate, inform, and protect consumer interests; heightens public awareness of key consumer issues, helps to enforce product safety standards, handles consumer complaints, and generally serves as a watchdog for consumer interests.

off-invoice allowance a promotional reimbursement from the advertiser to the retailer, in the form of a reduced price on the bill rather than payment being made by check at a later date; retailer often gets a lower bill for performing certain promotional activities on behalf of the manufacturer.

offline no connection between computers; see *online.*

off-network syndication television programs that originally were produced for and ran on a network in *prime time,* and that are sold as reruns in the syndication market; e.g., *Seinfeld, Frasier, Friends, Everybody Loves Raymond, Home Improvement.* See also *first-run syndication* and *syndication.*

off-premises sign in out-of-home advertising, a sign that features products or services not produced, marketed, or otherwise available on the property where the sign is located; e.g., an *outdoor bulletin.* See also *on-premises sign.*

off-screen announcer see *voice-over.*

offset lithography in print production, a process in which the printing surface is flat, i.e., not raised (as in letterpress printing) or etched into a printing plate (as in rotogravure printing); a popular method for printing large quantities, e.g., posters for out-of-home advertising. See also *letterpress* and *rotogravure.*

oligopolistic competition a market structure characterized by relatively few producers, substantial barriers to entry, either a standardized or differentiated product, considerable control over price, significant reliance on nonprice competition, especially product differentiation (although any price or nonprice strategies must carefully consider any possible competitive reaction or counterstrategy); e.g., steel, aluminum, automobiles, refrigerators, lawnmowers, photographic equipment, computers. See also *pure competition, pure monopoly,* and *monopolistic competition.*

omnibus layout see *circus layout.*

on-air test in television advertising research, a test commercial shown during a regular program telecast in a test market(s); purpose is to determine the effectiveness of the commercial.

on-camera refers to an individual appearing on the television screen during a commercial, as opposed to being *off-camera* or *off-screen;* e.g., a *spokesperson* or an actor. See also *voice-over.*

100 showing in outdoor advertising, an expression indicating that 100 percent of a given market's population will be reached by (i.e., will have the opportunity to see) a particular advertising message by virtue of the number and placement of an advertiser's billboard panels in the market, in a 30-day period; in *transit advertising,* an advertiser's car card in every vehicle in a transit line's system. Also called a *full showing.* See also *outdoor advertising, showing, 25 showing, 50 showing,* and *75 showing.*

one-on-one interview collecting market research data by interviews with individual consumers, as opposed to in a group setting; see also *focus group.*

one-sheet poster an advertising poster or sign, measuring approximately 46″ high × 30″ wide, especially common in rapid-transit train and subway station platforms in downtown business and shopping districts; also used near entrances of *point-of-sale* locations. See also *two-sheet poster* and *terminal poster.*

one-sided message an advertising, sales, or other promotion message that focuses only on the favorable or positive aspects, i.e., benefits of an advertiser's product, with no mention of limitations; see also *two-sided message.*

one-time-only (OTO) a television or radio commercial that airs one time, and no more.

one-time rate see *open rate.*

one-time use in direct marketing, the understanding that the individual or organization that rents a mailing list will use it only one time, unless granted prior approval by the list owner.

online a live connection to another computer; the state of being connected to the Internet. See also *offline.*

online advertising commercial messages delivered via the Internet and Web sites.

online jargon the technical language used to describe online activities and that is used in online communications; any vocabulary pertaining to the online world. Also called *cyberspeak, cyberslang,* or *geekspeak.*

online marketing a type of marketing that combines traditional marketing principles and practices with the interactive features of the Internet, for the purpose of delivering need-satisfying products and services to consumers; organizations conducting marketing by communicating with consumers on the World Wide Web or the Internet by means of personal computers and modems. Also called *Web marketing, Internet marketing, and I-marketing.* See also *interactive advertising, interactive marketing,* and *interactive media.*

online reverse auction in a media buying or creative review conducted by an advertiser, a situation in which agencies compete with one another online, as opposed to negotiating one-on-one with the client; essentially, it involves competitive bidding using technology. Similar to eBay-type auctions, except that one buyer (the client) reviews bids from multiple sellers (agencies) to evaluate what it will cost to service the account.

on-location in television advertising production, shooting a commercial at a site away from the production studio; see also *location shoot* and *production stage.*

on-pack any of a variety of promotional offers that are attached to a product's package; e.g., a *premium, coupon,* advertisement, recipe, or fitness club application.

on-pack premium a promotional item affixed to a product's package, as opposed to being inside or near the package; sometimes called a *banded premium.* See also *in-pack premium, near-pack premium,* and *premium.*

on-package sampling in sales promotion, a version of sampling in which a trial-size product is attached to another product's package; generally, both the packaged and the trial-size product are produced by the same company. See also *sampling.*

on-page coupon a *cents-off coupon* that is part of a print advertisement, and that can be cut out and then redeemed.

on-premises sign in out-of-home advertising, a sign that features products or services produced, marketed, or otherwise available on the property where the sign is located; e.g., a Rockport shoes sign at the Rockport factory outlet or at an independent shoe store that carries Rockports. See also *off-premises sign.*

on-sale date the date on which a magazine is available for sale at retail outlets; generally, a few days before the cover date for a weekly and several weeks before the cover date for a monthly; see also *cover date.*

on-site order an order for goods placed at the booth or location of a trade show; also called an *at-site order.*

on-the-edge marketing a marketing approach driven by unconventional methods and nontraditional practices, with the emphasis on taking a different, sometimes risky, path to attracting consumers, and standing out from others in the industry.

open billboard a brief announcement at the beginning of a broadcast program in the form of, "The following portion of this program is brought to you by (sponsor's name)." See also *middle billboard* and *close billboard.*

open end in television and radio advertising, the very end of a program or commercial that is left blank to allow local advertising to be inserted, i.e., time at the end given over to local advertisers.

open rate in print advertising, the basic, highest rate charged to an advertiser for a single insertion (i.e., a one-time rate), without the agency commission or other media discounts of any kind; the full rate as quoted on the rate card, subject to no discount. Also called *base rate, card rate, gross rate, one-time rate,* or *transient rate.* See also *agency commission, media discount,* and *rate card.*

open-end cooperative advertising a cooperative advertising program in which the manufacturer's contribution or reimbursement to the retailer for the advertising cost is not contingent on the amount of product bought by the retailer; see also *cooperative advertising.*

open-end questions in survey research, questions in which no alternative answers are provided, requiring the respondent to answer in his or her own words or to "ad lib" a response; also called *unstructured questions.* See also *closed-end questions.*

opening rate in direct-mail marketing, the percentage of mail recipients who open the envelope and investigate its contents.

opinion leader an individual who has a disproportionate amount of influence over consumers in their exposure to advertising and promotional efforts of marketers, and in their marketplace decision making; i.e., one who greatly influences the attitudes, opinions, and behavior of others. See also *personal influence.*

Opinion Research Corporation (ORC) a leading market research firm that provides global marketing research and services for a wide range of corporate customers; organization was a pathfinder in applying public opinion polling methods and techniques to marketing issues.

opinion sampling in public relations research, seeking consumer or other public's feedback relative to an issue or situation via formal or informal research methods.

opportunity cost in marketing decision making (assuming scarcity of resources and that choices have to be made on how to allocate funds), the value or worth of the best alternative use for a particular resource, i.e., the next best choice or what must be given up in taking a particular course of action; e.g., the value of a sports event sponsorship that was forfeited for a traveling art exhibit sponsorship, or the value of a sales promotion activity that was given up when the available funds were allocated to advertising. Also known as *economic cost.*

opportunity-to-see (OTS) a term used to describe the reality of the reach figure, in that *reach* is the number of individuals or households in the target audience who are exposed to a media vehicle (as opposed to actual contact with the commercial or advertisement itself); i.e., those who are exposed to the vehicle are in a position to see or hear a particular advertising message. See also *reach.*

opticals in television advertising, the different visual effects used in commercials; e.g., *dissolves, fades, wipes.*

optimum advertising level the level of advertising that yields the best return to the advertiser.

optimum promotion level the level of any individual promotion program element or the level of promotion activity in its entirety that yields the best return to the firm.

opt-in in Internet or online marketing or advertising, permission granted by consumers to Web site marketers to collect their personal information and to send them unsolicited e-mail messages; also referred to as *permission marketing.* See also *opt-out.*

option time in television and radio, a specific time slot for use by a network or station if it so chooses, i.e., if it elects to exercise its option; time reserved in advance or available on demand.

option to renew the contractual right to renew a sponsorship agreement on previously specified terms; see also *right-of-first-refusal.*

opt-out in Internet or online marketing or advertising, an option for consumers to tell Web sites (or other media) not to collect their personal information or have unsolicited e-mail messages sent; see also *opt-in.*

orbit an advertiser's strategy of scheduling television commercials by rotating them among several different programs or time periods; sometimes called a *rotation.*

order card   a card enclosed in a direct mailing for the consumer to fill out with all information required to place an order or inquiry with the advertiser.

order getting   personal selling efforts in which the salesperson has to go through the entire formal selling process to land a new customer; see also *order taking.*

order taking   personal selling efforts in which the salesperson has only to take the customer's order, with no selling per se required; often done in routine fashion. See also *order getting.*

order-of-merit test   in print advertising research, a method by which respondents are exposed to two or more advertisements and asked to rank the ads from the best to the worst; testing can be done on the advertisement as a whole, as well as on individual elements of the ad, such as headline, color, readability, illustrations, and other factors.

organizational buyers   individuals who buy the goods and services for firms or businesses to use in the manufacture, distribution, or resale of other products, or for use in the conduct of operations of institutions whose "product" is a service, such as educational institutions, hospitals, or government agencies.

organizational goods   see *business products.*

organizational market   see *business market* and *organizational marketing.*

organizational marketing   marketing programs aimed at firms engaged in the manufacture, distribution, or resale of products, as well as institutions providing services, such as social service agencies, sports organizations, or entertainment and recreation organizations; as opposed to *consumer* marketing. Sometimes may be used to refer to the marketing activities, including advertising and promotion, done by the company or organization on behalf of itself, e.g., *corporate advertising.* See also *business marketing* and *consumer marketing.*

Osgood Scale   see *semantic differential scale.*

out period   in a *flighting* pattern of media scheduling, the time period in which there is no advertising activity; see also *flighting, hiatus,* and *in period.*

outbound telemarketing   when the marketer or seller telephones a prospect in the attempt to make a sale, or to interest the individual in a product or service, offer sales materials, or gather information for marketing research purposes; see also *inbound telemarketing* and *telemarketing.*

outdoor advertising   advertising at outdoor locations, using billboards, posters, panels, signs, and other means used specifically to reach consumers outside the home; often used synonymously with *out-of-home advertising,* but is not quite as inclusive as out-of-home and does not utilize as wide a range of media to reach audiences. See also *out-of-home advertising* and *out-of-home media.*

Outdoor Advertising Association of America (OAAA)   the trade association for the outdoor advertising industry; involved with a wide range of activities such as research, government regulations, outdoor plant standards, and display standards. The mission is to promote, protect, and improve the outdoor advertising medium by focusing on legislation, marketing, product improvement, new technologies, and industry unity with the ultimate goal of making outdoor advertising an attractive medium for advertisers, agencies, and consumers. Sponsors a voluntary Code of Advertising Practice for outdoor companies. Formerly called the *National Outdoor Advertising Association (NOAA).* See also *outdoor advertising* and *out-of-home advertising.* Also see *exclusionary zone.*

outdoor advertising plant   the physical structure on which the outdoor advertising poster is affixed; term may be used to refer to the entire group of outdoor structures in a given market that are operated by one company or to the out-of-home advertising company itself. See also *plant operator.*

outdoor bulletin   see *bulletin.*

outdoor network   a group of outdoor advertising companies that have banded together to sell advertising space in several markets with one *insertion order* and one invoice.

outdoor poster   the most popular form of outdoor advertising and the smaller of the two standard *billboard* sizes, measuring 12′ high × 25′ wide, compared with the *bulletin,* whose dimensions are 14′ high × 48′ wide. Typically a multiple-unit buy for an advertiser to achieve market penetration. Standard showing sizes are #25, #50, #75, and #100. See also *poster panel, bulletin,* and *showing.*

outgoing posters   the outdoor advertising posters seen by the traffic leaving a central business district; as opposed to *incoming posters.*

out-of-home advertising   all advertising whose specific aim is to reach consumers outside the home; often used synonymously with *outdoor advertising* but is more inclusive than outdoor and uses a wider range of media. See also *out-of-home media* and *outdoor advertising.*

Out-of-Home Advertising Source   see *SRDS Out-of-Home Advertising Source.*

out-of-home audience   the individuals who are reached by advertising media outside their homes, e.g., going to and coming from work, traveling through airport terminals or train stations, shopping at malls; see also *out-of-home media.*

out-of-home media   a wide range of advertising media outside the home, such as billboards and posters on highways, panels on transit vehicles, train or bus stations and in airports, signs at shopping malls, or signs at stadiums; see also *outdoor advertising* and *transit advertising.*

out-of-store promotions   a catch-all term for the sales promotion and advertising efforts that occur outside the retail location; includes activities such as *couponing, direct marketing,* or *sampling* or other programs done off-premises. See also *in-store promotions.*

outsert   a promotional message or material that is attached to the exterior of a product's package.

outside back cover   the outside of the back cover of a magazine, an advertising position that commands a premium rate; generally, the most expensive page in a magazine; also called the *fourth cover.* See also *inside front cover* and *inside back cover.*

outside panel   in a multiposter *showing* at a given location where two or more panels are positioned side by side, the *billboard* that is closest to the traffic or edge of the street; see also *inside panel.*

outside poster   any of a variety of transit advertisements on the outside of buses, trains, and taxis; e.g., front, rear, and sides of the vehicle. See also *exterior bus, headlight poster, taillight poster, queen-size poster,* and *king-size poster.*

outside producer   in television or radio advertising production, the individual or company hired by the advertising agency producer to make the commercial as specified by the advertising agency; see also *producer.*

over-delivery   when a *media vehicle* delivers more than the promised number of *impressions* in a particular campaign or time period.

over-door display   in transit advertising, a *car card* advertisement above the door, on the inside of the vehicle; also called a *top-end display.*

overlapping circulation   see *duplication.*

overlay   see *snipe.*

overlay program   see *combination program.*

overnight ratings   a local, metered-market rating service of *Nielsen Station Index (NSI);* the television program ratings that are available the day after a program has run. The so-called "early ratings" are available from Nielsen's local *metered markets* that have television households with *set-tuning meters* (these ratings are available the morning after the day or evening of a telecast), as well as being available for network audience estimates based on *People Meter* households (these results are available in the afternoon following telecast). Often referred to as *overnights.* Also see *diary method, metered markets, telephone coincidental,* and *sweeps.*

override   in outdoor advertising, continuation of advertising past the time stated in the contract, free of charge.

overrun   see *renewal paper.*

over-spin   see *spin.*

over-the-air station   a broadcast television station whose signal is transmitted through the air, rather than via wires, i.e., cable, as in the case of cable television.

owned-and-operated station (O&O)   in television or radio, a station owned and operated by a *network;* in contrast to a *network affiliate.* See also *network affiliate.*

P

PBS   see *Public Broadcasting Service.*

PACT   see *Position Advertising Copytesting.*

PDF   see *Portable Document Format.*

PIB   see *Publishers Information Bureau.*

PLC   see *product life cycle.*

PMs   see *push money.*

PMA   see *Promotion Marketing Association, Inc.*

PMS   see *PANTONE Matching System.*

PMSA   see *Primary Metropolitan Statistical Area.*

POP   see *point-of-purchase advertising.*

POPAI   see *Point-of-Purchase Advertising Institute.*

PPAI   see *Promotional Products Association International.*

PPM   see *Personal People Meter.*

PPV   see *pay-per-view.*

PR   see *public relations.*

PRM   see *partner relationship management.*

PRSA   see *Public Relations Society of America.*

PSA   see *public service announcement.*

PUR   see *people using radio.*

PUT   see *people using television.*

PVR   see *personal video recording device.*

package   the container for a product, including the size, shape, design, color, imprinted information, and other physical and graphic features affecting its appearance and effectiveness as a selling tool; in *direct marketing,* the term refers to the complete set of enclosures in a mailing. For term's use in television or radio advertising, see *package plan.* Also see *packaging.*

package insert   any advertising or promotional material placed inside a product's package; also called a *package stuffer.* See also *outsert.*

package plan   in television or radio, a combination or group of commercial units on one or multiple programs offered to an advertiser by a *network* or individual station so the advertiser may sponsor them as a "single unit"; usually priced lower than if each commercial unit was purchased separately. Also known as a *package* and *program package.* See also *syndication.*

package stuffer   see *package insert.*

package test   in direct marketing, research to determine the effectiveness of different combinations of elements or enclosures in a direct-mail package; also refers to the research done on a product's container to determine its effectiveness in helping to promote and sell the product.

packager   see *syndicator* and *syndication;* sometimes refers to the company that owns a branded product sold in a consumer-unit package.

packaging   see *package.*

packaging concept   the package's role in the marketing of a product; involves thinking about the functions of the package and what the package should do to provide information, selling ability, and product protection.

page unit   in magazine advertising, the basis on which advertising is sold, as opposed to column inches (newspapers); e.g., full-page, half-page, quarter-page, and other units.

page views   on the Internet, the number of times a user requests a given page on a particular Web site;

e.g., the number of hits on a specific advertisement on a Web site page.

pages-per-person on the Internet, a measure of the average number of pages a unique visitor (i.e., a single person) views on a particular Web site; an indication of the user's interest level in a given site. See also *unique visitor.*

paid circulation the total number of copies of a publication bought by subscription and at newsstands or retail outlets; based on an average issue. See *circulation, controlled circulation, nonpaid circulation,* and *qualified circulation,* as well as *Audit Bureau of Circulations (ABC).* Same as *net paid circulation.*

paid programming see *infomercial.*

painted bulletin in outdoor advertising, a *billboard* whose advertising message is usually painted, as opposed to printed on paper; at 14′ high × 48′ wide, the larger and more expensive of the two standard-size billboards or outdoor bulletins. Used in prime, high-traffic locations on a long-term basis. Artwork is painted onto a piece of vinyl, which is then affixed to the structure, or the art is painted onto the structure itself. Also referred to as a *permanent bulletin* or *rotary bulletin.* See also *billboard, outdoor bulletin, poster panel,* and *spectacular.*

painted wall in outdoor advertising, an advertising message painted on the side of a building; also called a *permanent bulletin.*

paired comparison test in marketing and advertising research, a technique where respondents are presented with two alternatives (e.g., product features, product benefits) and asked to choose one based on a particular criterion; any number of questions or combinations may be used, but each particular question involves just two alternatives.

panel in outdoor advertising, a single unit or "board"; also refers to a continuing sample of individuals or households whose actions and behavior are measured over time. See also *consumer panel.*

panel data collection in advertising research, information gathered from a semipermanent group of sample respondents (individuals or stores) who participate in ongoing and continuous research sponsored by the advertiser, and who are monitored or periodically report their activities, experiences, opinions,

decision-making behavior, and other matters of importance to the advertiser. See also *consumer panel.*

panel number in outdoor advertising, a number given to each *panel* to serve as location-specific identification to aid the buying and selling transaction; also helps employees (e.g., painters, installers) identify specific structures.

panel study see *consumer panel.*

PANTONE Matching System (PMS) the authoritative source and universal standard for specifying, selecting, and matching color systems; assures that any communication pertaining to color, such as that pertaining to a billboard, is accurate and consistent.

paper diary see *diary method.*

paperless coupon an instant *coupon* dispensed at the time of purchase at the checkout counter.

parallel location in billboard or outdoor advertising, a *panel* that is parallel or very slightly angled to the street or highway, making it clearly visible to traffic in both directions; see also *angled poster.*

parent station in broadcast television, a station that supplies programming to another station (i.e., a satellite station) to achieve greater coverage than it would get alone; see also *satellite station.*

Pareto rule see *80–20 rule.*

parity marketing see *copycat marketing.*

parity product see *me-too product.*

parody advertising advertising that is an imitation or spoof of a common and well-known situation, issue, or person, typically in an attempt to be humorous through ridicule that is in acceptable taste; e.g., the advertising may mirror the travails of corporate life, the endless quest to keep up with the neighbors, or a swashbuckling high-stakes attorney.

partial showing in outdoor and transit advertising, anything less than a *full showing;* see also *full showing, half run,* and *half showing.*

partial sponsorship in television or radio advertising, sponsorship of a program shared by several advertisers; sometimes called *segment sponsorship.* Also may refer to *event sponsorship* in which there are several sponsors of a particular event. See also *cosponsorship.*

partial-run edition in magazine advertising, something less than the total circulation offered to advertisers, for which the advertiser pays a lower rate than for the entire circulation; e.g., a *demographic edition, metro edition, regional edition, or state edition.*

participating announcement in television or radio, a commercial from one of the advertisers that has bought time on a particular program; see also *participation basis* and *participation program.*

participation basis in television and radio, the way in which most network advertising time is sold, with several different advertisers buying commercial time on a particular program. See also *participation program* and *participating announcement.*

participation program a television or radio program sponsored by several advertisers; i.e., a cosponsored program; see also *participation basis* and *participating announcement.*

participation rate in *cooperative advertising,* the dollar amount the manufacturer reimburses the retailer for advertising; also called *payment share.* See also *cooperative advertising.*

partner relationship management all activities designed to launch, preserve, and enhance a long-term bond and mutually beneficial connection between a company and its business and industry partners; e.g., a manufacturer's efforts to secure its relationship with its suppliers, distributors, retailers, advertising agency, or other manufacturers with which it has joint programs. See also *customer relationship management (CRM).*

partnership marketing see *comarketing.*

partnership promotion see *tie-in promotion.*

part-time station see *limited-time station.*

pass-along audience see *pass-along readership.*

pass-along deal in trade sales promotion, a promotional deal extended to a retailer by an advertiser, with the expectation that the retailer will pass the savings, or at least a portion of them, on to the consumer.

pass-along readership readers of a publication other than the subscriber or newsstand buyer, i.e., a reader of a publication he or she has not purchased; e.g., family members other than the subscriber, or readers in professional office waiting rooms. An estimated number or rate. Also called *pass-along audience.*

paste-up see *mechanical.*

patch primarily in sports marketing, an advertiser's logo, insignia, or other identification of the advertiser affixed to a player's uniform; e.g., the "R" on a major-league baseball player's uniform, standing for Russell Athletic, or the "CCM" on a college ice hockey player's uniform, standing for the company that supplied the uniform.

Patent and Trademark Office see *U.S. Patent and Trademark Office.*

patronage reward free merchandise or some other consideration given by a marketer to a customer in recognition of the customer's regular use of a product or service; a minor-league baseball team's gift of a team logo jacket to season-ticket holders of five years or longer, an art museum's gift of an art history book to attendees of three or more art exhibits, or an automobile dealer offering a free oil change with every five oil changes. See also *frequency program.*

pay cable see *pay television.*

pay television refers primarily to cable television programming that subscriber households must pay for in addition to the basic cable fee; may also be used as an all-inclusive term for cable television, since any cable television must be paid for, whether it is the basic service or a premium service. Also called *pay cable* or *subscription television.*

payback the time period until a product, advertising campaign, or other marketing-related activity or program has fully recovered its costs; see also *payout.*

pay-for-performance in trade sales promotion, a method in which the manufacturer pays off on a trade deal according to the number of units sold by the retailer; i.e., the manufacturer rewards the retailer based on the retailer's success in selling the deal product; not to be confused with *pay-for-results agency compensation plan* or *performance-based agency compensation plan.*

pay-for-results agency compensation plan see *incentive-based agency compensation system.*

payment share see *participation rate.*

payoff the final results of an advertising campaign or a marketing program.

payout the profit or value resulting from investment in an advertising or promotion campaign; i.e., the *return-on-investment (ROI)*. Can also refer to other returns from a campaign, such as the impact on sales, market share, or even awareness levels and other qualitative measures. See also *payback*.

pay-per-click advertising in Internet advertising, when the rate paid by an advertiser is based on the number of *clickthroughs* to the advertiser's Web site; see also *clickthrough*.

pay-per-lead advertising in Internet advertising, when the rate paid by the advertiser is based on the number of sales leads generated by the advertising.

pay-per-sale advertising in Internet advertising, when the rate paid by the advertiser is based on sales of the advertiser's product as a direct result of the Web site advertising; quite common in *affiliate marketing*.

pay-per-view advertising in Internet advertising, when the rate paid by the advertiser is based on the number of times a visitor arrives at the Web page that has its advertisement on it, whether or not the visitor clicks on the advertisement to go to the advertiser's Web site or destination point; i.e., the advertising rate is based on the number of *impressions*. See also *impressions*.

pay-per-view television (PPV) television programming for which viewers pay a fee for a single showing of a particular program, e.g., a championship boxing match or a movie.

pay-to-stay fee in trade promotion, a manufacturer's payment to a retailer to continue stocking and displaying a product.

PC a personal computer.

pencil drawing see *rough*.

pencil-and-paper diary see *diary method*.

penetration the effectiveness with which a commercial, advertisement, or advertising campaign not only reaches but also has a measurable impact on (i.e., convinces) the target audience; also refers to the percentage of different people or homes within a defined population or market that can be exposed to a medium, a media vehicle, or a media schedule, e.g., the proportion of households owning televisions or subscribing to cable TV. See also *reach*.

penetration price policy a new-product pricing policy in which a low price is set for the product; used when demand is elastic, i.e., high price sensitivity exhibited by the consumer. Unlike *introductory price dealing*, the low price level is permanent. See also *skimming price policy, introductory price dealing, elastic demand*, and *inelastic demand*.

pennysaver see *shopping newspaper*.

People Meter an electronic device or "box" hooked up to each television set in a particular household that records the specific program or channel being watched and who is watching; collects data and measures audiences for programs on broadcast and cable networks, nationally distributed syndicated programs, and satellite distributors over the entire United States. The meters are installed in more than 5,000 television households nationwide (involving more than 13,000 persons). *Nielsen* households are randomly selected and recruited by the company. The meters remain in the selected households for about two years. Data accumulated from the meters provide the basis for Nielsen's national ratings estimates. A sample of People Meters in the largest television markets provides the data for the *overnight ratings*. See also *Nielsen Media Research, diary method, metered markets, overnight ratings, set-tuning meter, telephone coincidental*, and *sweeps*.

people using radio (PUR) the number or percentage of people listening to radio at a particular time.

people using television (PUT) the number or percentage of people viewing television at a particular time.

perceived risk the level of uncertainty the consumer believes exists in a particular purchase decision; the consumer's estimate of the consequences of a poor decision and that the outcome will not be favorable.

perceived value the extent to which the satisfaction with a product is greater than the cost of obtaining it, as measured by consumer perception; the consumer's view of the difference between the cost incurred to purchase a product or service and the satisfaction derived from its ownership and use. The consumer will favor the company or brand that he or she perceives to offer the highest delivered value.

perceived value pricing the practice of pricing a product or service at the level believed to represent the value placed on it by the consumer (i.e., perceived benefits), without regard to the costs incurred in making the product or creating the service.

percent return   see *response rate.*

percentage accrual   an approach to establishing a cooperative advertising fund in which, for the specified length of the cooperative advertising program, the advertising fund grows by a percentage of the value of purchases by the retailer from the particular manufacturer; e.g., if a digital camera manufacturer provides 5% of a retailer's purchases to accrue to the retailer's cooperative advertising fund, and the retailer purchases $300,000 worth of cameras during the period, the funds available from the manufacturer for cooperative advertising total $15,000. See also *accrual account, percentage accrual,* and *cooperative advertising.*

percentage charge   see *markup charge.*

percentage-of-sales method   a way of determining the advertising or promotion budget based on a predetermined percentage of expected sales; commonly used because it is simple and straightforward, but has a major drawback in that it treats advertising as a result of sales rather than a cause of sales. A top-down approach to budgeting. See also *affordable method, arbitrary method, competitive parity method, objective-and-task method,* and *unit-of-sales method.* See also *build-up approach to budgeting* and *top-down approach to budgeting.*

perceptible differences   differences among products that are visibly recognizable to the consumer.

perception   the process by which individuals select, organize, and interpret stimuli to form a picture of the world around them; see also *selective attention, selective comprehension, selective distortion, selective exposure,* and *selective retention.*

perception management   a coined term for *public relations;* guidance of efforts designed to influence someone's view or outlook toward something. See also *public relations.*

perceptual map   a graph that shows consumers' perceptions of competing brands and how the brands compare with each other on certain product attributes, such as comfort, durability, ease of use, and status; the result of perceptual mapping research. A research tool to help understand how a particular brand is positioned relative to competitors' brands, in the minds of consumers. See also *perception* and *perceptual mapping.*

perceptual mapping   a research technique that asks consumers to rate different brands on certain product attributes, such as styling and durability; i.e., their perceptions of different brands. The ratings are then plotted on a graph and the result is a *perceptual map.* Particularly useful when assessing opportunities and deciding on marketing communications goals and objectives. See also *perception* and *perceptual map.*

performance allowance   a purchase price rebate given by an advertiser to a retailer who agrees to and carries through agreed-upon promotional services on behalf of the advertiser's product, such as advertising, display of the goods, or other merchandising activities; retailer must submit *proof of performance.* See also *proof of performance.*

performance analysis   comparing actual vs. planned accomplishments, and investigating the reasons underlying variations between the two.

performance index   in television, a station's revenue-share relative to audience-share; generally, a number that describes one factor relative to another number, or base. See also *index number.*

performance measures   the various criteria used to evaluate an individual, organization, product, advertisement, or any other marketing activity or program.

performance risk   in consumer decision making, the chance that a product will not work or function as expected by the consumer; also called *functional risk.* See also *risk-taking, financial risk, physical risk, social risk,* and *time-loss risk.*

performance-based method of agency compensation an advertising agency compensation method in which the advertiser-client pays the agency according to the results achieved by the advertising; when used, it normally is part of a combination plan for agency compensation that also involves a fee and/or commission. The results that serve as the incentive are based on criteria agreed upon in advance by client and agency, and these criteria generally involve performance goals, such as sales volume or market share. Also called *incentive-based method, results-based method,* or *pay-for-results agency compensation plan.* See also *fee method, commission method,* and *combination method.* Also see *agency commission* and *sliding rate.*

peripheral cues elements or features of an advertisement or commercial other than the actual statements about the product itself; e.g., music, scenery, or the presence of a celebrity spokesperson. See also *cue*.

perimeter advertising signage around the perimeter of an event site.

per-inquiry advertising an agreement between a media vehicle and an advertiser that payment for the space or time will be based on the number of inquiries or sales resulting from the particular promotional effort in that vehicle.

per-issue rate in magazine advertising, a special rate for an advertiser based on the number of issues it advertises in during a contract period; somewhat like a *frequency discount,* but based on the number of issues in which the advertising appears, not the number of advertisements placed; see also *frequency discount.*

permanent bulletin in outdoor advertising, a display that remains at one location for the entire term of the advertiser's contract; see also *painted bulletin.*

permanent display a display such as a *point-of-purchase display* that is in service for six months or longer.

permission marketing in Internet or online marketing or advertising, permission granted by consumers to Web sites to collect their personal information; also refers to Web users who agree to receive e-mail communications from organizations. Also referred to as *opt-in.* See also *opt-out.*

personal communications communications in which there is a direct and personal interaction between the sender and the receiver; see also *personal selling* and *nonpersonal communications.*

personal influence the ability of an individual to affect marketplace behavior by shaping another person's attitudes, opinions, motivations, and other factors associated with consumer decision making; see also *opinion leader.*

personal interview a *survey method* of *data collection* by means of a trained interviewer questioning a respondent in face-to-face contact.

Personal People Meter (PPM) in television and radio audience measurement, a device about the size of a pager that consumers carry throughout the day to monitor their viewing or listening habits. The device detects inaudible codes that broadcasters embed in the audio portion of the television or radio program, thereby measuring viewership or listenership. A product of *Arbitron.*

personal selling one-to-one selling by a salesperson to a prospect or customer; personally persuading or assisting the target audience to take a particular action that has commercial significance to the seller. Communications involving direct, face-to-face contact between a company representative and a customer.

personal selling process the sequential steps a salesperson goes through in selling a product or service; see also *prospecting, preapproach, approach, presentation, handling objections, closing,* and *follow-up.*

personal video recording device (PVR) an interactive television recording device that can record a television program and replay it virtually immediately; see also *digital video recorder (DVR).*

personality the totality of an individual, comprising all the distinctive behavioral and emotional forces that set him or her apart from others, and that have great influence in shaping marketplace behavior; in advertising, the individual *spokesperson* speaking on behalf of the advertiser's product or service.

persons-using-radio (PUR) the number or percentage of an area's or market's population who are listening to the radio at a particular time; a measure of audience size. See also *households-using-radio (HUR).*

persons-using-television (PUT) the number or percentage of an area's or market's population who are viewing television at a particular time; a measure of audience size. See also *households-using-television (HUT).*

persuasion a means by which an advertiser influences a target audience to believe something or to do something, using reasoning and coaxing in a compelling and convincing way; accomplished via communications such as advertising and personal selling.

persuasive advertising advertising whose purpose is to convince the target audience of the merits of the advertiser's product or service or to induce someone to take a particular action; often attempts to build *selective demand* for the advertiser's product. See also *informative advertising* and *reminder advertising.*

persuasive communications the attempt to change consumers' opinions, attitudes, or behavior as a result of a particular form or combination of forms of marketing communications.

PEST analysis in the *situation analysis* stage of the marketing communications planning process, a framework for investigating the macroenvironment; an acronym for Political, Economic, Sociocultural, and Technological forces that impact the planning process. See also *macroenvironment* and *situation analysis.*

phantom cume in radio advertising, an industry expression to describe unreported listening of people who are recording their radio listening via an *Arbitron* diary. Those using the diaries often neglect to put the data in the diaries, especially their second- and third-choice radio stations. See also *Arbitron* and *cume.*

phone kiosk in out-of-home advertising, a display affixed to a pay telephone.

photoanimation a technique of creating animation using a series of still photographs; see also *animation format.*

photoboard displayed on a single sheet of paper, a series of still photographs (and the audio script) made from a television commercial; it is used for record-keeping or promotional purposes (e.g., merchandising the advertisement to the trade).

photomatic in *pretesting* a television commercial in preliminary form, a rough commercial produced from a series of still photographs shot in sequence; used to give the client an idea of what to expect in the finished commercial. See also *pretesting, liveamatic, ripomatic, storyboard,* and *rough.*

physical distribution all the activities involved in the physical flow of materials and products through the entire distribution network, to and from producers and intermediaries; transportation, storage, and handling of the products every step of the way, from raw materials to matching customer requirements throughout the entire distribution network. Also referred to as *marketing logistics* or simply *logistics.*

physical risk in consumer decision making, the chance a product will be harmful to the health or safety of the user; also called *safety risk* or *health and safety risk.* See also *risk-taking, performance risk, financial risk, social risk,* and *time-loss risk.*

physiological testing measures in advertising research, pretesting methods that use a variety of means and devices to measure consumers' physical responses to advertising, or the physiological functions controlled by the central nervous system and over which the individual has little or no voluntary control; see also *galvanometer, pupillometer,* and *voice-pitch analysis (VOPAN).*

picture caption copy in print advertising, a layout that features a series of pictures, each with a caption, to deliver the advertising message; can be effective in showing time-related effects of a product's use; e.g., a series of pictures with captions showing the results of a lawn fertilizer or grass seed brand from spring to fall or a "before-after," or an "ours vs. theirs" sequence utilized to advertise many types of products such as exercise machines or house paint.

picture response test in qualitative advertising research, a projective technique in which a person is shown a picture and asked to describe what is happening, what the people and/or objects in the picture are all about, and what thoughts come to mind. See also *word association test, sentence completion test, story completion test, cartoon method,* and *third-person method,* as well as *qualitative research* and *projective research techniques.*

piggyback commercial the back-to-back airing of two television (or radio) commercials for the same advertiser but for different products; e.g., a commercial for Folger's coffee followed immediately by a Pringles potato chips commercial, both products of Procter & Gamble. Also referred to as *double spotting* or *back-to-back.*

pilot in television or radio, a trial or sample production of a proposed broadcast program made for testing and review; sometimes may be used for advertising testing purposes, such as for a *theater test.*

pioneering advertising advertising messages that seek to educate the consumer about a product, service, or idea, or the focus may be on a specific brand; the message may aim to stimulate *primary demand* for a product category or to inform consumers about a new brand. See also *informative advertising* and *primary demand advertising.*

pitch the oral presentation made by the advertising agency to the advertiser, either in an attempt to win a new account or to propose a new campaign for an existing client; also can refer to any type of message whose aim is to persuade, convince, or sell.

pixel   in Internet advertising, a dot that represents the smallest graphic unit of measurement on a computer screen; a descriptive term for measuring a graphic in online advertising, it is the online equivalent of inches in print media advertising. Typically, a full screen is 640 × 480 (640 pixels wide × 480 pixels high). A common *banner ad* measures 468 pixels wide × 60 pixels high (i.e., a 468 × 60 banner ad). Short for "picture element."

place   the distribution component of the marketing program, or making products and services available to customers in the right quantities, at the right locations, at the right time; along with *product, price,* and *promotion,* one of the 4Ps of the marketing mix.

placement   in *public relations,* getting an article or other release accepted for publication or airing in the media desired; not to be confused with *product placement.*

place utility   the benefits to a consumer of the marketer making a product or service available where the consumer wants it; see also *utility, possession utility, form utility,* and *time utility.*

place-based media   the variety of fixed locations in which posters and other advertising messages can be displayed, and that require the audience to come to the site, as opposed to the advertising coming to them; e.g., *outdoor advertising* locations, airports, stores, and stadiums.

planogram   a retailer's diagram of a product or group of products as it should appear on the store shelves for maximum visibility and impact, while providing efficient utilization of space.

plans board   a blue-ribbon management committee at the advertising agency whose work involves review of creative plans and strategies and, ultimately, approval of the proposed advertising before it goes to the advertiser.

plant   see *outdoor advertising plant.*

plant capacity   in out-of-home advertising, the total supply of advertising structure or *faces* owned by and available through a particular company.

plant operator   in *outdoor advertising,* the company that owns and maintains poster panels and other out-of-home media, and rents the space to advertisers, generally in 30-day time blocks, though some locations are contracted for longer periods; see *outdoor advertising plant.*

plug in   in television or radio mainly, but may be in any media, the mention of a company's product, service, cause, or other activity, free of charge; sometimes used to generally describe any broadcast advertising.

Pocketpiece   a condensed weekly ratings report issued by *Nielsen Media Research;* so named because it is much smaller than the typical Nielsen report (i.e., pocket-size vs. booklet-size).

pod   in television, a group of back-to-back commercials aired during a break in a program; e.g., four :30s in a 2-minute span between segments of a particular program. See also *ad pod rating.*

point-of-purchase advertising (POP)   floor displays, counter-top displays, window displays, wall displays, signs, banners, and other promotional materials at the location, most commonly the retail store, where the consumer meets and considers buying a product; aim is to influence the consumer's buying decision at the action stage, often as an *impulse purchase.* See also *point-of-sale.*

Point-of-Purchase Advertising Institute (POPAI)   a trade association dedicated to serving organizations involved with *point-of-purchase,* including the advertisers, retailers, producers, suppliers, as well as advertising and sales promotion agencies; protects and advances the industry members' interests through programs of research, education, trade forums, and legislative efforts, all directed toward making point-of-purchase an integral part of marketing communications strategy to influence consumers' buying decisions.

point-of-purchase display   see *point-of-purchase advertising (POP).*

point-of-sale   the site or location where the customer meets the product and where the product is bought and sold; e.g., the retail store. See also *point-of-purchase advertising (POP).*

point program   a sales promotion program offered to consumers and the trade in which points are awarded for purchases or activities and accumulated over time for redemption for merchandise, travel, or some other incentive.

political advertising   advertising messages used to influence the outcome of an election or vote on a political issue or matter.

polybag   a plastic film bag containing a product sample or other promotional item, home-delivered with a newspaper or magazine; see also *billboard bag*.

pony spread   see *junior panel*.

population   in marketing and advertising research, the complete count of all members of a group of interest to the researcher; also called the *universe*. See also *sample* and *census*.

pop-up   in magazine advertising, a specially designed three-dimensional advertisement or promotional piece that rises up and takes form when a reader turns to the page the display is on or otherwise opens the display by hand.

pop-up advertising   in Internet advertising, an advertiser's pitch that suddenly appears out of nowhere in a separate window on the computer screen while a page loads, and that is superimposed on top of what the Web site content the user is trying to view; see *pop-under advertising, square pop-up ad, banner ad, skyscraper ad,* and *rectangle ad.*

pop-under advertising   in Internet advertising, an advertiser's pitch that appears under what the user is viewing, rather than being superimposed on top of the Web site content, and that comes into full view on the computer screen when the user exits the Web site; see *pop-up advertising, square pop-up ad, banner ad, skyscraper ad,* and *rectangle ad.*

portable display   a floor display, generally with folding legs, that is easily transportable from one location to another.

Portable Document Format (PDF)   on the Internet, a file format that enables the sending of documents (especially graphics files) from one user to another.

portal   an entry point to the World Wide Web, accessed through Web browsers such as Internet Explorer or Netscape Navigator; for example, Google, Yahoo!, Lycos, or Excite.

Porter's Five Forces   a framework for evaluating the state of competition in an industry; involves assessment of the bargaining power of *buyers,* the intensity of the rivalry among existing *competitors,* the threat of *potential entrants* joining the industry, the bargaining power of *suppliers,* and the threat posed by *substitutes* for the existing product or service. An essential part of the *situation analysis* in designing a marketing plan or a marketing communications plan.

portfolio   see *sample book.*

portfolio test   in advertising research, a laboratory technique used to measure print advertising effectiveness, in which respondents are given a collection of advertisements, both control ads and test ads, and asked to evaluate them; a test advertisement is hidden within the mix of other ads. See also *jury test.*

portrait format   a layout of an advertisement in which the height is greater than the width; more common than the *landscape format* where the width is greater than the height. See also *landscape format.*

position   the specific location of an advertising message in print or broadcast media; e.g., in magazines or newspapers, the particular page and the place on that page, or in television or radio, the particular part of the program. Also refers to the particular place a product occupies in the mind of a consumer, or the way in which the consumer thinks about and ranks the product relative to competitors' products. See also *positioning.*

Position Advertising Copytesting (PACT)   a document consisting of nine fundamental *copytesting* principles, representing the advertising industry's consensus of the guidelines for how copytesting research should be conducted or supervised; a statement prepared and issued by 21 leading U.S. advertising agencies, focusing on what constitutes good copytesting practice. See *copytesting.*

position charge   an extra fee levied by a media vehicle for advertising space or time when the advertiser wants to specify exactly where the advertisement or commercial will appear; typically a percentage of the basic charge. See also *preferred position* and *preferred position rate.*

positioning   the process of differentiating—and then communicating—a firm's product or service offering so that it occupies a meaningful and competitively distinct place in the minds of target customers; refers to how consumers think about a company's product or service.

positioning by attribute   in an advertiser's attempt to make its product offering distinct from competitors in consumers' minds, a promotional strategy that focuses on a product's physical feature(s) that sets it apart from the competition.

positioning by benefit   in an advertiser's attempt to make its product offering distinct from competitors in consumers' minds, a promotional strategy that focuses on how the advertiser delivers a particular benefit or set of benefits better than anyone else.

positioning by competitor   in an advertiser's attempt to make its product offering distinct from competitors in consumers' minds, a promotional strategy that focuses on how the advertiser's product is better than a directly or indirectly named competitor; a positioning strategy by which an advertiser sets itself apart from the competition by establishing a distinctive and important difference between its product and those of the competition. The advertiser's claims are presented relative to the competition.

positioning by price   in an advertiser's attempt to make its product offering distinct from competitors in consumers' minds, a promotional strategy that focuses on providing the best value relative to competitors.

positioning by product class   in an advertiser's attempt to make its product offering distinct from competitors in consumers' minds, a promotional strategy that focuses on how the advertiser's product is better than another product in another category or the entire range of products in another product category; e.g., Amtrak passenger rail service vs. the entire product category of airline travel.

positioning by quality   in an advertiser's attempt to make its product offering distinct from competitors in consumers' minds, a promotional strategy that focuses on the superior craftsmanship of the advertiser's product relative to what is available from the competition.

positioning by use   in an advertiser's attempt to make its product offering distinct from competitors in consumers' minds, a promotional strategy that focuses on its superiority in a particular use or application relative to the competition; sometimes referred to as *positioning by application.*

positioning by user   in an advertiser's attempt to make its product offering distinct from competitors in consumers' minds, a promotional strategy that focuses on the individuals who use the product and how this product is "the one" for this particular user, relative to what is offered by the competition.

positioning map   see *perceptual map.*

positioning statement   a formal declaration of what a brand is intended to mean or represent in the target customer's mind; see also *positioning.*

positioning strategy   the particular approach or concept an advertiser uses to communicate the distinctive and noteworthy nature of its product or service to the target market; see also *positioning, positioning by attribute, positioning by benefit, positioning by competitor, positioning by price, positioning by product class, positioning by quality, positioning by use,* and *positioning by user.*

positive appeals   in advertising copy, an approach that places sole emphasis on the favorable results for the consumer in purchasing a particular product or service, without mention of the downside of not having the product or service; a very sunny approach. See also *negative appeals.*

possession utility   the benefits, satisfaction, and pleasure a consumer receives from a product or service by owning, consuming, or using it; see also *utility, form utility, place utility,* and *time utility.*

post analysis   generally, any after-the-fact evaluation of advertising or other marketing activity; see also *postbuy analysis.*

postbuy analysis   an examination of a *media schedule* after it runs; usually based on physical evidence of the schedule running as planned (e.g., *tearsheets, affidavits of performance*) and audience delivery data during the time the schedule ran. See also *tearsheet, affidavit of performance,* and *prebuy analysis.*

postbuy ride   see *postride.*

postdecision evaluation stage   the fifth and final stage of the consumer decision process, in which the consumer assesses the decision in terms of its appropriateness and effectiveness in satisfying the need that put the consumer into the market in the first place; a more appropriate term for the phenomenon vs. *postpurchase evaluation,* since the consumer's decision may have been to *not* purchase, a decision that, like a decision to purchase, is evaluated by the consumer. See also *consumer decision process* and *cognitive dissonance.*

poster an advertising message printed on paper and affixed to a large surface as a sign in a public location; a general term for advertising messages that are posted on advertising structures. Also called a *bill.*

poster bench a seat on which an advertising message is painted or a sign is attached; e.g., bus stop or terminal bench, golf course bench, or park bench.

poster panel a *billboard,* or sheet metal surface, on which a printed (vs. painted) advertising message is mounted; the smaller of the two standard billboard sizes, measuring 12′ high × 25′ wide, compared with the bulletin, whose dimensions are 14′ high × 48′ wide. The most popular form of *outdoor advertising.* An outdoor unit that can accommodate a *30-sheet* or *8-sheet poster* display. See also *outdoor advertising, outdoor poster, bulletin, painted bulletin, permanent bulletin, rotary bulletin, 30-sheet poster, 8-sheet poster,* and *spectacular.*

poster plant a company whose work is in the *outdoor advertising* industry.

poster showing see *showing.*

posting the actual raising of the outdoor advertisement; sometimes may refer generally to when advertising actually appears in the media.

posting date the date on which the advertiser's outdoor *showing* is to begin; see also *posting leeway.*

posting instructions the details about the display of a particular outdoor poster such as objectives, location selection; sent to the *plant operator* by the advertiser or the advertising agency.

posting leeway in *outdoor advertising,* a margin of time beyond the *posting date* for the *plant operator* to actually post the advertisement without penalty; i.e., a grace period. Used to allow for inclement weather, holidays, or other factors beyond the plant operator's control. Typically, five working days. See also *posting date* and *plant operator.*

posting period in *out-of-home advertising,* the length of time bought by the outdoor or transit advertiser for the advertising to be displayed; usually 30 days.

post-media buy analysis see *postbuy analysis.*

postproduction stage all the work done after the shooting to finish a television commercial (or a radio commercial); includes editing, film processing, recording the sound effects, coordinating (mixing) the music and sound effects, making duplicates, and other activities to put the finishing touch on the commercial. See also *preproduction stage* and *production stage.*

postpurchase dissonance see *postdecision evaluation stage.*

postpurchase evaluation see *postdecision evaluation stage.*

postride in *out-of-home advertising,* an in-the-field check of outdoor poster or billboard locations when the advertising copy is already in place, although it could refer to checking locations prior to contracting for specific locations; also called *riding the showing.* See also *preride* and *riding the showing.*

posttesting part of *copytesting;* measuring the effectiveness of an advertising message after it appears in the media, i.e., anytime after the *launch* of an advertising campaign; done to see if the advertisements and the campaign have accomplished their objectives and to serve as input into the planning stages for a subsequent campaign. See also *copytesting, message research,* and *pretesting.*

postturn see *trivision.*

potential audience the number of individuals or households in a position to be exposed to an advertising medium or media vehicle by any means, whether purchased or not; essentially, the maximum possible audience.

potential buyer see *prospect.*

Power, J.D. the leading marketing information services firm specializing in customer satisfaction research across many industries; provides quality and customer satisfaction ratings for the automotive, boating, financial services, travel (hotel, airline, airport, rental car), telecommunications (television, Internet, telephone), health care, and home (builders, insurance, lenders) industries. Officially, the *J.D. Power Consumer Center.*

preapproach the stage in the personal selling process in which the sales representative does a thorough investigation to learn as much as needed to be knowledgeable about the potential buyer and the organization, as well as to know the most effective way to approach the prospect; see also *prospecting, approach, presentation, handling objections, closing,* and *follow-up.*

prebuy analysis   in media buying, the research and analysis that go into a media plan prior to actually buying time and space; e.g., determining the *reach* and *frequency* objectives, the optimum number of *GRPs,* and the combination of media vehicles that will work best. See also *postbuy analysis.*

prebuy ride   see *preride.*

preemptible rate   in broadcast advertising, a special discount rate for advertising time given by a television network or station to an advertiser on the condition that the network or station can resell that same exact time to another advertiser at a higher rate, thereby bumping the original buyer from the spot; i.e., an advertising rate subject to cancellation when another advertiser agrees to pay a higher rate for the same broadcast time. See also *fixed rate.*

preemption   in broadcasting, the act of a network or station taking back or displacing a scheduled program and/or its advertising time to air a special program of major importance to the public interest; e.g., breaking news of a major disaster or the president of the United States giving a major address. Also, the act of taking paid-for advertising time away from an advertiser and selling the time to another advertiser for a higher rate. May involve the use of a *make-good* or a *credit.* See also *preemptible rate.*

preemptive claim   an advertiser's assertion about its product that competitors either cannot duplicate with their own products or choose not to contest directly; such an assertion may put an advertiser in the advantageous position of "owning" that particular difference.

preferred position   a specific location for an advertisement or commercial desired by an advertiser; e.g., the location may be on a particular page of a publication, a specific place on a page, in a particular section of a publication, at a certain spot during a broadcast program, or at a given time. A premium price is charged by the *media vehicle.* In a sense, the opposite of *run-of-press (ROP).* See also *preferred position rate, run-of-book (ROB), run-of-press (ROP),* and *run-of-schedule (ROS).*

preferred position rate   a premium rate charged by a *media vehicle* for placing an advertisement or a commercial in a special location, or *preferred position,* ordered by an advertiser; also called a *position charge.* See also *preferred position.*

preliminary investigation   see *situation analysis.*

pre-media buy analysis   see *prebuy analysis.*

premiere panel   in *outdoor advertising,* a standard display format measuring $12'3'' \times 24'6''$ in overall size.

premiere square   a standard display format measuring $25'5'' \times 24'6''$ in overall size; a single-sheet vinyl face is stretched over two stacked *30-sheet* poster panels. Same technique can be used with *8-sheet* poster panels. See also *stacked panels.*

premium   a merchandise offer made by an advertiser as an incentive to purchase a particular product; may be offered free or at a reduced price. See also *in-pack premium, near-pack premium,* and *on-pack premium.*

premium pack   a product package that includes a free promotional item inside the package (*in-pack premium*) or affixed to the outside of the package (*on-pack premium*). See also *in-pack premium* and *on-pack premium.* Also see *near-pack premium.*

premium rate   a higher-than-normal or extra charge for advertising that appears in a *preferred position* or for advertising services not considered part of the customary package offered by the supplier; see also *preferred position.*

prepack display   a promotional display unit that arrives at the retail store already packed with the featured merchandise, so all the store operator has to do is open the shipping container and place the display.

prepared sales presentation   see *canned presentation.*

preprint   in print advertising, a prepublication copy of an advertisement; often used for publicity or promotional purposes. For example, an advance copy of an advertisement sent to retailers to inform them about an upcoming campaign.

preprinted insert   an advertising message or other promotional material printed in advance by the advertiser and then sent to the publisher for insertion into the newspaper prior to delivery; not a part of the newspaper.

preproduction meeting in television advertising production, a meeting at which the final plans are set for the production of the commercial; involves the producer, creatives, account management team, client, and the people responsible for actual production of the commercial. See also *preproduction stage, production stage,* and *postproduction stage.*

preproduction stage in television advertising, all of the planning and organizing activities done in preparation for the actual shooting of a television commercial (or a radio commercial); includes activities such as selecting a director, hiring a production company, cost estimation, finding a location, securing the talent, casting, securing props, getting permissions, establishing a production timetable, tending to legal matters, and other considerations. See also *production stage* and *postproduction stage.*

preride in *out-of-home advertising,* a physical in-market inspection tour of the available *billboard* advertising locations and *panels* prior to an advertiser's selection and commitment to use them; see also *postride* and *riding the showing.*

presentation the stage in the personal selling process in which the sales representative convincingly relates and demonstrates, if possible, the key features of the product or service and translates the features into benefits for the prospective buyer; important to convey that what is being sold is a solution to a problem or need, not just a physical object or a service itself. See also *prospecting, preapproach, approach, handling objections, closing,* and *follow-up.*

presentation fee see *hello money.*

presenter commercial see *spokesperson.*

presenting sponsor a sponsor whose company name is affixed immediately below the name of the sponsored property; for example, on the Professional Golf Association (PGA) Tour—the Bay Hill Invitational presented by Cooper Tires. See also *primary sponsor.*

press kit a collection of public relations materials provided by an advertiser to the media, as company background information for use in articles or programs done about the company, its people, products, or other matters; e.g., a press kit is often given to the media covering a special event sponsored by the advertiser. Not the same as a *media kit.*

press release a formal statement given to the media by an advertiser containing information about the advertiser's organization, its products, its people, or other matter of importance at that particular time; also called a *news release.* See also *news release.*

prestige pricing setting an elevated price for a product or service to connote high status or a lofty image.

pretest in survey research, a small-scale trial run of a completed questionnaire to determine its appropriateness for full-scale use; provides opportunity to make changes and fine-tune the instrument prior to actual use. Not to be confused with *pretesting.* See also *pretesting* and *rough.*

pretesting in advertising research, part of *copytesting;* done to evaluate the elements and determine the effectiveness of an advertising message during its development stage and prior to its appearance in the final version ready for use in a campaign; typically done before the advertising agency submits it to the client as a recommendation. See also *rough, copytesting, message research,* and *posttesting.*

price the amount of money a customer is willing to pay for a product or service, as a measure of the value and benefits of having that product or service; along with *product, place,* and *promotion,* one of the 4Ps of the *marketing mix.*

price allowance in sales promotion or media buying, any of several different price-reduction plans offered by the marketer or seller as an inducement to the buyer to make a purchase; see also *quantity discount.*

price competition using an aggressive pricing approach to challenge competitors for consumer patronage, as opposed to putting the major emphasis on product, promotion, and distribution strategies and actions; see also *nonprice competition.*

price discrimination when, for the exact same product, a marketer charges different prices to different buyers; a legal tactic if the price difference is supported by a difference in cost of serving the buyer (e.g., a quantity discount) or when there is a need to meet competition in a particular market. Otherwise, it is considered *undue price discrimination,* and unsubstantiated price differences are judged to "injure competition" and are in violation of the *Robinson-Patman Act.*

price elasticity the relationship between the percentage change in price of a product or service and the percentage change in the quantity demanded for the product or service; i.e., the market's sensitivity or responsiveness to a change in the price of a product or service.

price follower a firm that changes its price only in response to a competitor's price change; see also *price leader.*

price leader a firm in a particular industry that initiates a price change and other firms follow; see also *price follower.*

price pack a product package that features a special price or "cents-off" deal imprinted on the package by the advertiser; also called a *cents-off deal.* See also *price-off deal.*

price positioning see *positioning by price.*

price objectives see *target return, profit maximization, sales growth, market share growth,* and *meeting competition price objectives.*

price sensitivity the degree to which a product's demand is affected by a change in its price.

price-based trade deals in trade sales promotion, incentives offered by the marketer to its dealers that involve price reductions on dealer purchases of the product, as opposed to activities such as display materials, a contest, or an in-store sampling program sponsored by the marketer.

price-off deal a consumer sales promotion that offers the buyer a limited-time reduction in the regular price of an advertiser's brand; see also *price pack.*

primacy effect a theoretical notion that information presented first or at the beginning of an advertising message will have greater impact and effect on the audience and will be the information most remembered from the message; see also *recency effect.*

primary audience see *primary readership.*

primary circulation see *primary readership.*

primary data original data collected for the specific information needs of the current research effort, as opposed to data that already exists; research collected directly from the marketplace. See also *secondary data.*

primary demand the demand for a type or category of product; e.g., the demand for digital cameras, microwave ovens, or house paint. Sometimes called *generic demand.* See also *selective demand.*

primary demand advertising an advertising message designed to promote and stimulate demand for a product category (computers, insurance, digital cameras), as opposed to a specific brand (Compaq, Kemper, Kodak); sometimes called *generic advertising.* See also *selective demand advertising.*

primary group generally consisting of relatively few individuals, a group characterized by frequent interpersonal contact, cohesiveness, and similarities in beliefs and behavior; quite influential in shaping an individual's behavior. Example: the family. See also *secondary group, formal group, informal group,* and *reference group.*

primary household a household in which there is an individual who is a subscriber to or newsstand buyer of a periodical.

primary listener an individual who is a regular listener to a particular radio program or station.

primary listening area in television or radio broadcasting, the geographic area in which a station's broadcast signal is perfectly clear, with no interference or static.

primary market see *primary target market.*

Primary Metropolitan Statistical Area (PMSA) a geographical area composed of one or more counties within a metropolitan area that have a population of 1,000,000 or more; a definition of the U.S. Office of Management and Budget (OMB). When PMSAs are established, the larger area of which they are component parts is designated a Consolidated Metropolitan Statistical Area (CMSA). See also *Metropolitan Area (MA), Metropolitan Statistical Area (MSA),* and *Consolidated Metropolitan Statistical Area (CMSA).*

primary readership the individuals who subscribe to or purchase a particular publication.

primary sponsor the sponsor that pays the largest rights fee and is the most prominently identified and featured; would be called the *title sponsor* if the sponsored property had sold the naming rights to the sponsor. For example, John Hancock's major commitment to sponsorship of the Boston Marathon, without its company name in the title of the event. See also *title sponsor, associate sponsor,* and *presenting sponsor.*

primary target market   the individuals, households, or market segment that a marketer considers its most attractive opportunity for sales and profit, and which is the main focus of its marketing and promotion program; see also *target market, target marketing,* and *secondary target market.*

primary viewer   an individual who is a regular viewer of a particular television program or station.

prime access   in the television broadcast day, the time period from 7:00 P.M.–8:00 P.M.; see also *dayparts (television)* and *prime access rule.*

prime access rule   in broadcast television, a rule prohibiting network-affiliated stations from broadcasting more than three hours of network programs between the hours of 7:00 P.M. and 11:00 P.M., Monday to Friday, with the intent that one hour of the four would be at the individual station's discretion and that it would be used to air programs of local interest; the hour from 7:00 P.M.–8:00 P.M. became almost universal in its use for local stations. Mandated by the *Federal Communications Commission (FCC)* in 1970 and repealed in 1996. See also *prime access.*

prime location   a superior location conducive to an advertising message achieving maximum impact on the target audience; e.g., in *outdoor advertising,* an exceptional location, based on the audience it delivers.

prime time   in the television broadcast day, the time period from 8:00 P.M.–11:00 P.M., except Sunday when it is 7:00 P.M.–11:00 P.M.; time during which networks broadcast the most high-profile programs. See also *dayparts (television).*

prime-time access rule   see *prime access.*

print media   commercially published media, i.e., *newspapers* and *magazines,* that sell advertising space to companies and organizations that have an advertising message to deliver to their target audiences; see also *broadcast media.*

print production   see *production.*

printing plate   a prepared plate of the image to be printed, which is applied directly to the paper; see also *mat.*

prior knowledge   the information a consumer has in his or her memory when entering the consumer decision process.

private brand   see *dealer brand.*

private label   see *dealer brand.*

PRIZM (Potential Rating Index by Zip Market)   a *geodemographic* market segmentation system in which each neighborhood of the United States is classified into one of 64 distinct clusters based on lifestyle; to determine proper placement of each neighborhood, a number of characteristics are analyzed, including household size and makeup, age, gender, education, occupation, income, housing data, marital status, ethnicity, interests, media habits, financial data, and other factors contributing to audience profiles. A product of *Claritas, Inc.,* designed to aid marketers and advertisers in targeting consumers by lifestyle. See also *geodemographics.*

proactive marketing   marketing strategies and tactics designed and implemented in anticipation of competitive action, with the intent to dilute or forestall it; an *offensive approach.* See also *reactive marketing.*

proactive public relations   marketing and public relations activities and programs designed to continually monitor the attitudes and opinions of an organization's publics, and to address an issue before it becomes a threat to the organization's image, reputation, and public stature; identifying opportunities to enhance an organization's image and standing, and acting to create and maintain positive outcomes. Includes having a plan or set of guidelines to deal with negative publicity that occurs from conditions beyond the control of the organization. A "before-the-fact" approach or one that seeks to take the offensive. See also *marketing public relations* and *reactive public relations.*

probability sample   in survey research for marketing and advertising, an approach to choosing a sample in which all units in the population of interest have a specific and known nonzero chance of being selected; see also *simple random sample, stratified random sample, cluster sample, nonprobability sample,* and *survey method.*

problem definition   the first stage of the marketing research process, in which an attempt is made to clarify and crystallize the predicament, difficulty, question, or issue that needs attention and resolution; see also *marketing research process.*

problem solving   see *consumer decision process.*

problem-recognition stage   the first stage in the consumer decision process, when the consumer becomes aware of the need for something; sets into motion the problem-solving sequence. Every need creates a problem situation, and the problem manifests itself when there is a difference between the consumer's actual condition and his or her desired condition. See also *consumer decision process, information search stage, information evaluation stage, decision stage,* and *post-decision evaluation stage.*

problem-solution format   in advertising, a creative *execution format* in which the message spotlights a problem faced by consumers and focuses on the advertiser's product or service as the solution; e.g., a Gatorade commercial for fluid replacement after an intense workout, an Ortho Weed-B-Gon advertisement for a lawn application to eliminate and control weeds, or a Robitussin commercial for cough relief. See also *straightforward factual, news, demonstration, slice-of-life, dramatization, symbolic association, fantasy, animation, still-life, humor, spokesperson, testimonial,* and *comparison formats.*

producer   most commonly refers to the producer of a television commercial; may also refer to the individual at the advertising agency who manages the production process for a commercial or an advertisement. Individual may be from the production house or the studio. See also *outside producer.*

product   an organization's or individual's offering to a customer that contains a bundle of attributes capable of satisfying the needs and wants of the customer; the offering may take the form of a physical object, a service, an idea, a person, a place, or an organization. Along with *price, place,* and *promotion,* one of the 4Ps of the *marketing mix.* See also *actual product, augmented product,* and *core product.*

product advertising   an advertising message specifically designed to promote and stimulate demand for a product or service of the advertiser, as opposed to a message promoting an idea; see also *nonproduct advertising* and *services advertising.*

product allocation   the portion of an advertising or total promotion budget that is allotted to the individual products of a multiproduct company; also the amount of advertising time or space allotted to the individual products of a multiproduct company.

product ambassador   an individual appearing as a spokesperson or representative on behalf of a particular product, as part of the marketing and promotion program, particularly in the role of promotion goodwill; e.g., Tiger Woods for Buick or Michael Jordan for Nike. Title and role as a true ambassador often reserved for those individuals perceived by the audience as extraordinary in their field of endeavor, and who are believable, trustworthy, and of impeccable character. Same principle as *company ambassador.* See also *goodwill, spokesperson,* and *company ambassador.*

product assortment   the complete set of all products a company offers, consisting of all product lines and every individual product; e.g., Sears and Wal-Mart each stocks thousands of items in many product lines, General Electric manufactures thousands of items, Procter & Gamble, Sara Lee, and Black & Decker produce an enormous number and variety of products. See also *product assortment depth, product assortment width, product line, product line depth, product line width, individual product,* and *product item.*

product assortment depth   the number of products within all the product lines offered by a company; e.g., Sara Lee has a large number of packaged meats and bakery products in its food and beverage line, including brands such as Sara Lee, Jimmy Dean, Bryan, Hillshire Farms, Ball Park, Kahn's, and Hygrade among its nearly 50 different brands of packaged meat alone. See also *product assortment, product assortment width, product line, product line depth, product line width, individual product,* and *product item.*

product assortment width   the actual number of product lines marketed by the company; e.g., Sara Lee offers a broad mix of many product lines, including food and beverage, casual and intimate apparel, sportswear, household products, personal care products, and baby care products, and Black & Decker offers many product lines as well, among them power tools, cleaning products, outdoor power equipment, kitchen appliances, garment care, and heaters and fans. See also *product assortment depth, product line, product line depth, product line width, individual product,* and *product item.*

product bundling   see *bundling.*

product cannibalization see *cannibalization.*

product category a type or classification of products, as opposed to the individual brands comprising the classification; e.g., appliances, sporting goods, apparel, soft drinks.

product class positioning see *positioning by product class.*

product concept a detailed written description of a product idea, put forth in terms that will be meaningful and understood by the consumer; concept development is a key stage in the *new-product development process.* See also *product idea* and *new-product development process.*

product development the fifth stage of the new-product development process, in which the engineering and design of the physical product is completed, getting the product from a concept to a final form ready for market testing; see also *new-product development process, idea generation, idea screening, concept testing, market evaluation, marketing plan, market testing,* and *commercialization.* Also refers to an organization's growth strategy by which the firm attempts to increase sales and profits by offering new or modified products to its existing markets; e.g., Nike adding apparel to its running shoe line, then adding golf balls and golf clubs to its golf shoe line, or Kraft introducing low-fat salad dressings to go with its regular line of salad dressings. See also *growth strategies, market penetration, market development,* and *diversification.*

product differentiation the tangible and intangible features and characteristics of a product or service that make it distinctive from those of competitors.

product features the physical attributes of a product or service; see also *benefits.*

product fulfillment see *fulfillment.*

product idea the very basic notion or vision behind a prospective product the company might eventually market to consumers; the initial stage of the new-product development process. See also *new-product development process* and *product concept.*

product image the way consumers perceive a product; see also *perception* and *brand image.*

product immersion the practice of merging a product into a television program to the point that it seems like an integral and seamless part of the show; see also *convergence* and *product placement.*

product integration a promotional technique, similar to *product placement,* in which advertisers pay to have their products placed into the action and plots of television shows or movies; rather than being used simply as a prop, the product is built into the action of the television program right from the beginning. For example, the reality program *Survivor* featured contestants munching Doritos, guzzling Mountain Dew, wearing Reebok sneakers, and winning prizes from Dr. Scholl's or Pontiac—all as part of the content and action of the show; the 20th James Bond movie, *Die Another Day,* was the centerpiece for Norelco's launch of its Spectra Shaving System, to go along with Bond's driving an Aston Martin car, wearing an Omega watch, and drinking Finlandia vodka. See also *product placement.*

product item the very specific product, or individual unit, in a product line; e.g., each size and flavor of a ready-to-eat cereal brand. Also called *individual product.* See also *product assortment, product assortment depth, product assortment width, product line, product line depth,* and *product line width.*

product launch the formal introduction of a new product to the market.

product liability a marketer's legal obligation to compensate individuals harmed by defective or unsafe products.

product life cycle (PLC) the four stages through which a product passes during the course of its existence, including the sales and profit levels of the product over its lifetime; introduction stage, growth stage, maturity stage, decline stage. Especially relevant for advertisers in that the product's life cycle stage influences the planning, development, and implementation of the marketing, advertising, and promotion programs. An important distinction is that in its basic application, the PLC concept describes *industry* sales and profits for a product; individual product and brand sales and profits may not follow the industry pattern, but still can be the focus of PLC description and analysis. See also *introduction stage, growth stage, maturity stage,* and *decline stage.*

product life cycle management using the *product life cycle (PLC)* as the basis for managing a product and its *marketing mix* over the life of the product; see also *product life cycle (PLC)*.

product line   a set of closely related individual products; products may be considered related by their similarity in functions, target markets, and retail stores in which they are sold. Example: Sears has many product lines, among them appliances, housewares, electronics, tools, lawn and garden, automotive, fitness and recreation, jewelry and watches, computers and office, gifts, and children's products. See also *product assortment, product assortment depth, product assortment width, product line depth, product line width,* and *product item.*

product line depth   the number of specific versions of each type of product in a product line; e.g., Sears Craftsman tool and equipment line includes nine categories, among them portable power tools, bench power tools, storage chests, compressors, and others; the company's Kenmore household appliances line also includes nine categories, including laundry, refrigeration, cooking, dishwashing, grilling, compacting, and others. Beyond that, Sears Craftsman has 52 different toolset combinations in its mechanics hand tools line and six different combinations of homeowners hand tools, while its Kenmore-brand washing machines come in 64 models, and Kenmore room air conditioners come in 21 different models. See also *product assortment, product assortment depth, product assortment width, product line, product line width,* and *product item.*

product line length   see *product line depth* and *product line width.*

product line width   a measure of the number of different products in each product line in a company's offering; Sears, in its lawn and garden line, has several entries, including garden tools, grills, lawnmowers, lawn tractors, tractor attachments, patio furniture, power lawn equipment, pressure washers, snow equipment, and yard care products; the company has 19 lines within its appliances line and 10 within electronics, to mention just a few. See also *product assortment, product assortment depth, product assortment width, product line, product line depth,* and *product item.*

product management   see *brand management.*

product manager   see *brand manager.*

product marketing   all the activities and processes relating to the marketing of a physical object or tangible item, as opposed to services or something intangible; see also *services marketing.*

product megabrand   the *superbrand* or umbrella brand name under which there are individual brands; so classified by virtue of a combination of elements such as size, sales volume, market share, profit, advertising dollars, and other factors that make the organization a giant in its field. Examples: Toyota, with individual brands including Camry, Corolla, Avalon, Prius, Matrix, Tacoma, 4Runner, and Highlander, or General Mills, with Cheerios, Wheaties, Total, Lucky Charms, and Chex. See also *megabrand.*

product mix   see *product assortment.*

product placement   a promotional technique that involves arranging for an advertiser's product to appear in use or at least be clearly visible (*in-focus exposure*) during a movie or a television program; also includes products at other venues such as major-league baseball team dugouts with Gatorade buckets and cups and David sunflower seed buckets and packages. Advertiser pays a fee and/or provides free products. Also referred to as *virtual placement,* although product placement has the physical product as part of the scene, while virtual placement involves digitally inserting the product or image in a scene where there is no actual product. See also *in-focus exposure time, product integration, product immersion,* and *convergence.*

product positioning   see *positioning.*

product protection   in television or radio advertising, the amount of time between the airing of commercials for competing products; in print advertising, the number of pages separating competing advertisers' messages. Also called *competitive separation* or simply *separation.* See also *competitive separation, commercial protection,* and *piggyback.*

product release   a publicity tool used for a new-product announcement and to provide relevant information about the product.

product symbolism   an abstract meaning attached to a product or brand by the consumer; what the product or brand represents and what the consumer experiences in having and using it.

production   see *production stage.*

production add-on   a part of an advertising agency's total compensation package; a markup charge that the agency tacks on to the cost of producing work such as art, photos, illustrations, printing, market research, or other such work done on behalf of its client, whether performed by the agency itself or by outside vendors who do not allow a commission. The markup typically is *17.65 percent,* because 17.65 percent added to the cost, say, of photographytranslates to a 15 percent commission. Example: Suppose an advertising agency purchases photography services from an outside vendor at a cost of $20,000. Adding 17.65 percent as the "production add-on" gives a markup of $3,530, which, when added to the $20,000 basic cost, yields a total of $23,530 billed to the client. The $3,530 markup is 15 percent of $23,530. See also *markup charge* and *17.65 percent.*

production department the advertising agency unit responsible for the preparation of the finished commercial or advertisement; see also *production.*

production house an organization that specializes in producing television and radio commercials.

production services the advertising agency function and team that is responsible for the transformation of the creative ideas into finished advertising, direct-mail pieces, and other campaign materials.

production stage a stage in the advertising development process that involves taking an advertising idea, copy, scripts, illustrations, art, and other elements and producing a finished, ready-to-run commercial or advertisement or a brochure or other promotional material; e.g., when a commercial is actually made, including the shooting and recording. Most commonly refers to television commercials. Sometimes called the *shoot.* See also *preproduction stage, postproduction stage,* and *shoot.*

production timetable in producing a television commercial, a time schedule establishing deadlines for all the activities associated with making a commercial; includes *preproduction stage, production stage,* and *postproduction stage.*

productivity audit generally, the measure of the *return on investment* of a marketing communications program or any specific element of the program; see also *return-on-investment approach (ROI).*

professional advertising an advertising message directed to individuals engaged in the professions that influence the products and services used by their clients; e.g., doctors, dentists, architects, teachers, accountants, financial planners, lawyers.

professional journal a magazine geared to lawyers, physicians, architects, and other professionals; e.g., *Architectural Record, The Complete Lawyer, The New England Journal of Medicine.* See *business publication.*

profile refers to the characteristics of a medium's or media vehicle's audience composition; also refers to the characteristics of the customers or potential customers of a product or service. See also *audience profile* and *consumer profile.*

profit maximization price objective setting price at a level that allows the firm to gain as much profit as possible; see also *target return, sales growth, market share,* and *meeting competition price objectives.* Also see *maximum profit rule.*

program compatibility the match, suitability, or fit between a company and its product and the broadcast programming offered by a particular network or station; see also *editorial compatibility.*

program package see *package plan.*

program rating in television or radio, the percentage of households owning television sets (or radios) in a given broadcast area (national or market-by-market) that are tuned in to a particular program; calculated by dividing the number of households tuned in to a program by the number of households with television sets (or radios). Each rating point represents approximately one percent of the population. See also *time-period rating.*

program share in television or radio, the percentage of all viewing or listening households in a given broadcast area (national or market-by-market) that are tuned in to a particular program; calculated by dividing the number of households tuned in to a program by the number of households with their television set (or radio) on.

program tie-in in television advertising, the practice of integrating a product or service into a particular program; see also *product integration* and *product placement.*

program-length commercial see *infomercial.*

programming format in radio, the distinctive style of a station that separates it from other stations; e.g., news, sports, country music, classical music.

progressive proofs (progs) in advertising production, a series of proofs that show the colors of an advertisement at each stage of its development, as each new color is added; also called *progs* and *color keys.*

projected audience in television or radio, an estimate of the total number of individuals or households watching or listening to a particular program, based on ratings or results derived from a sample survey.

projective research techniques qualitative research used in the development of advertising programs in which the consumer is asked to respond to ambiguous stimuli such as vague statements or objects; designed to measure consumer feelings, opinions, attitudes, and motivations. See also *word association test, sentence completion test, story completion test, cartoon method, third-person method,* and *picture response.*

promo in television or radio, a station's announcement of its own upcoming program or other event; also, a station's or network's commercial promoting itself. The short version of a *promotional spot.*

promotion the marketing communications function of a company or organization; the process and techniques by which an organization finds, encourages, and persuades target customers toward a particular response, such as buying a product or service, or accepting an idea. Along with *product, price,* and *place,* one of the 4Ps of the *marketing mix* (among the 4Ps, promotion denotes the entire marketing communications mix, including *advertising, sales promotion, public relations, direct marketing,* and *personal selling*). See also *promotion mix, promotion element, promotion plan,* and *marketing communications.*

promotion agency a firm that specializes in handling all or some phases of *sales promotion* activities.

promotion audit see *communications audit.*

promotion budgeting see *budgeting methods.*

promotion campaign see *marketing communications campaign.*

promotion copy in print advertising, a copy of a publication sent to prospective advertisers and advertising agencies; see also *complimentary copy* and *unpaid distribution.*

promotion element any of the five major components of the marketing communications program: *advertising, sales promotion, public relations, direct marketing,* and *personal selling.*

promotion management providing leadership, coordination, and supervision of the planning, development, implementation, and control phases of the marketing communications program.

promotion mix the particular combination of promotion methods and techniques an organization uses to persuasively communicate information about its products or services to its target audience; major tools include *advertising, sales promotion, public relations* and *publicity, direct marketing,* and *personal selling.*

promotion money see *push money (PM).*

promotion objectives the goals toward which the marketing communications program is directed, as it contributes to the achievement of overall marketing objectives; e.g., a promotion objective of getting consumers to try a product for the first time would imply a different set of techniques as compared with an objective of boosting repeat purchases. See also *communications objectives* and *hierarchy of effects.*

promotion plan see *communications plan.*

promotional allowance in trade promotion, any of a wide variety of deals (e.g., discounts or free goods) given by the advertiser to the dealer for promotional support to be provided by the dealer on behalf of the advertiser's products, such as advertising or providing a special display during a sales promotion period; see also *advertising allowance, dealer allowance,* and *merchandising allowance.*

promotional crawl in television, a promotional message that runs across the screen during a program; runs from right to left and usually appears at the bottom of the screen. Also called a *crawler.*

Promotional Marketing Association, Inc. (PMA) the major voice of the promotion and promotional products industry, representing the interests of marketers, retailers, agencies, suppliers, and academics; primary goal is to foster a better understanding of how promotional products and programs build brand equity through integration with overall marketing and marketing communications strategies. See also *promotional products marketing.*

promotional partnership any of a broad range of cooperative efforts or alliances between marketers for the purpose of promotion; see also *comarketing.*

promotional pricing a temporary price reduction as part of a special promotional effort for a product or service.

Promotional Products Association International (PPAI) an international trade association serving the promotional products industry through efforts designed to enhance the professionalism of the industry, such as establishing standards and guidelines for members' promotional programs, sponsoring expositions and forums, administering certification programs, and collecting and disseminating research data and information.

promotional products marketing a promotion method that uses promotional products such as specialties, premiums, prizes, or other sales promotion tools to attract or keep customers. See also *specialty advertising* and *advertising promotional products.*

promotional pull strategy see *pull strategy.*

promotional push strategy see *push strategy.*

promotional spot see *promo.*

promotional stock products and merchandise offered to retailers at a reduced price as part of a special promotion, such as that accompanying a special event or a seasonal promotion.

prompted recall see *aided recall.*

proof a copy of an advertisement given to the advertiser by the advertising agency for final checking before it is run as scheduled.

proof copy in newspaper advertising, a copy of an advertisement that was prepared by the newspaper's advertising department, given to the advertiser (usually a local retailer) for proofreading before the advertisement appears in the newspaper; often used more generally to refer to a copy of any completed advertisement or commercial that is used for a final check for errors.

proof of performance certification that an advertisement or commercial was actually run as scheduled and contracted for; common to all media. See also *affidavit of performance* (broadcast media) and *tearsheet* (print media).

proof-of-purchase a requirement that the consumer must submit to the marketer in order to be eligible for a promotional offer; can be a UPC symbol, cash register receipt, or some other proof that a particular product was purchased.

propaganda information and opinions, typically heavily slanted, disseminated by the sender to influence a particular audience on an idea, belief, or view; essentially, what public relations, advertising, and other promotion activities are all about. Term has negative connotations stemming from the distortion of facts and the zeal of some users of the technique, such as marketers, whose motives may tend to be subversive or questionable, far removed from the professional goals and standards of marketing communications.

property in sponsorship marketing, a specific entity that makes itself available to a company or marketer for it to become involved as a sponsor; e.g., an entity engaged in the arts, sports, causes, entertainment, or a nonprofit organization that makes it known that it is available sponsorship. For example: a youth summer basketball league, Little League baseball, a convention center, a theater, a golf tournament, a music festival, or an art exhibit.

proportion in a print advertisement, the size relationship of one element to another; e.g., an advertisement is in proportion when the sizes of the elements relative to one another make sense visually and are balanced.

proprietary panel see *consumer panel.*

props in advertising production, the broad range of structures, objects, devices, and aids needed to provide the staging, scenery, and décor for shooting a television or radio commercial or for photographing a print advertisement.

prospect a legitimate potential buyer who has a need for the particular product or service being offered, the ability to pay for it, and the authority and willingness to consummate the deal; see also *suspect.*

prospecting the stage in the personal selling process in which the sales representative, using several sources to generate leads, identifies solid, bona fide potential customers for the product or service; see also *preapproach, approach, presentation, handling objections, closing,* and *follow-up.*

prospective customer (buyer) see *prospect.*

provocative headline see *curiosity headline.*

psychogalvanometer see *galvanometer.*

psychographics consumer lifestyles as reflected in attitudes, interests, and opinions; used to sharpen the focus beyond demographics in developing consumer profiles. See also *psychographic segmentation* and *demographic segmentation.*

psychographic segmentation dividing buyers into groups based on variables such as activities, interests, opinions, lifestyle, values, personality, and social class; see also *attitudes, behavioristic segmentation, demographic segmentation, geographic segmentation, geodemographic segmentation,* and *lifestyle advertising.*

psychological influences in consumer behavior, the intrapersonal factors that affect an individual's buying process; i.e., the internal variables, such as needs, motives, perception, attitudes, and others. See also *social influences.*

psychosocial consequences the various results of a consumer's decision-making behavior that involve intangible and personal dimensions.

public access in cable television, the availability of broadcast facilities for use by local groups in the community interest.

public access channel in cable television, a non-commercial channel set aside by the cable operator exclusively for public use and community-interest programming, especially that of not-for-profit organizations.

public affairs all the activities having to do with an organization's relationships with the community (city, state, or region) in which it operates; involves working with community officials, governmental bodies, lawmaking and law-enforcing agencies, and other groups.

public broadcasting not-for-profit television and radio stations whose primary focus is high-quality educational programming; in contrast to advertiser-supported broadcasting, funding comes from individuals, foundations, government, corporate grants, and other nonadvertiser sources. Also called *noncommercial broadcasting.* See also *advertiser-supported broadcasting.*

Public Broadcasting Service (PBS) an organization of noncommercial stations that, working with member stations nationwide, produces and distributes a wide variety of high-quality educational programs.

public radio see *public broadcasting.*

public relations the relationship between an organization and the publics with which it is associated, including customers, dealers, suppliers, investors, government, the community, and others; all the activities undertaken to understand the attitudes and opinions of the various publics and to bring the organization into alignment with its relevant publics. Involves systematic planning and distribution of information to establish and maintain a positive image on all fronts. An attempt to manage and control the firm's image. Among the means used to influence the different publics and to promote and protect the organization's credibility, image, and goodwill are publications, speeches, public service activities, events, and advertising. Involves both paid and unpaid forms of communications. A much broader concept than *publicity.* See also *engineering of consent, publicity, marketing public relations, proactive public relations,* and *reactive public relations.*

public relations advertising see *corporate advertising.*

public relations agency a company that masterminds an organization's relationships with its publics, such as consumers, employees, suppliers, dealers, stockholders, the financial community, legislators, and the community at-large.

public relations audit a comprehensive internal study and accounting of an organization's standing and reputation among its publics; study focuses on the firm's characteristics and activities that result in particular feelings and attitudes, positive or negative, of its publics.

Public Relations Society of America (PRSA) the primary organization for public relations practitioners, representing business and industry, public relations counseling firms, government, associations, hospitals, schools, professional services firms, and not-for-profit organizations; dedicated to building value, demand, and understanding for public relations through programs to advance industry standards, information exchanges, research projects, and continuing education, as well as promulgating an industry code of ethics.

public television   see *public broadcasting.*

publication life   in print media, the length of time a publication is kept by its subscribers and buyers before being discarded.

publication-set   see *pub-set.*

publicity   a specific activity and tool of an organization's marketing *public relations* efforts that involves generating media coverage and goodwill about the organization, its image, its products, people, ideas, and whatever else is important to the public standing of the organization; nonpersonal communications regarding an organization, its products, services, or ideas. Not directly paid for by the company. See also *public relations* and *marketing public relations.*

publics   the different groups of people in whom a company or organization has a special interest by virtue of the relationship each group has with the firm; e.g., customers, employees, suppliers, public interest groups, government agencies, stockholders, financial institutions, and the media. Also referred to as *stakeholders.*

public service advertising   an advertising message that is in the public interest or promotes the general welfare, delivered by a not-for-profit organization, a company, or other sponsor; the message may focus on social issues, pollution, education, civic, philanthropic, or other matters of public interest. Advertising time and space are donated by the media or offered at a greatly reduced rate. See also *Advertising Council* and *corporate advertising.*

public service announcement (PSA)   an announcement containing information in the public interest that is broadcast by a television or radio station, free of charge; involves a variety of social issues important for the public welfare.

Publishers Information Bureau (PIB)   a leading source of detailed consumer magazine advertising spending data, tracking the number of pages and type of advertising carried by consumer magazines, sorted by publication title, type, company, and brand; serves advertisers, agencies, media buyers, and the consumer magazine sales staffs.

publisher's statement   a certified report of a publication's circulation statistics, such as total circulation, the geographic distribution, paid and free circulation, subscription and newsstand circulation, and other data;

subject to audit, it serves as the basis for advertising space rates. Usually included in a publication's *media kit.* See also *Audit Bureau of Circulation (ABC), rate base,* and *media kit.*

pub-set   in print advertising, an advertisement in which the copy is set by the newspaper or magazine where the ad will appear, as opposed to another source that sets the type for the ad and supplies the publication with the type already set (e.g., an outside compositor or the advertising agency); short for *publication-set.*

puffery   advertising or other sales representations that praise the item to be sold with subjective opinions, superlatives, or exaggerations, vaguely and generally stating no specific facts; i.e., exaggerated and overstated but legitimate expressions of praise for a product, based not on factual claim but on the advertiser's biased opinion. Examples: "We provide the best service in the industry" or "Our product will give you more satisfaction than any other brand on the market" or "This is the only pair of sunglasses good enough for you."

pull strategy   advertising and promotion activities by the manufacturer aimed at the ultimate consumer, to influence and encourage acceptance and to generate consumer demand causing the retailer to carry the product, which in turn causes the wholesaler to carry the product; a large amount of advertising and sales promotion directed to the consumer to stimulate a "pulling" effect through the distribution channel. See also *push strategy.*

pulling power   the ability of advertising, sales promotion, direct mail, or any marketing communications activity to capture the audience's attention and move them to the action desired by the marketer.

pullout   in print advertising, a special self-contained section that is easily removed from the publication for saving and referencing; e.g., a special Presidents Day automobile advertising section in a newspaper, featuring the local dealers' inventory for the big auto-selling weekend.

pulsing   an advertising scheduling pattern that combines a steady pattern of continuous advertising at relatively low levels with intermittent *bursts* of heavy advertising activity; in contrast to a *flighting* pattern, which has periods of no activity (hiatuses), there is a continuous base of advertising support and always some advertising activity. A combination of *flighting* and *continuous scheduling*. See also *blinking, bursting, continuous scheduling, flight, flighting,* and *hiatus*.

pupillometer   a device that measures the dilation of the pupil of a person's eye in response to a visual stimulus; used to measure advertising effectiveness and is based on the idea that the pupil dilates or becomes larger when it encounters something noteworthy in an ad, such as a headline, a particular word, or an illustration. See also *physiological testing measures.*

pure competition   a market structure characterized by large numbers of buyers and sellers, ease of entry, a standardized or homogenous product, very little control over price, and virtually no *nonprice competition;* e.g., agriculture, the stock market. See also *pure monopoly, monopolistic competition,* and *oligopolistic competition.*

pure monopoly   a market structure characterized by a single seller, extreme barriers to entry (essentially blocked), no close substitutes, considerable control over price, and public relations advertising is about the only form of nonprice competition; e.g., local utilities, government-owned or -regulated monopolies (as well as those privately owned or regulated), professional sports teams. See also *pure competition, monopolistic competition,* and *oligopolistic competition.*

purchase criteria   the factors and standards the prospective consumer uses to make product or service choices in the *buying decision;* also called *buying criteria.*

purchase decision   see *buying decision.*

purchase influences   all the factors, personal and nonpersonal, that affect the consumer's decision to buy a particular product, or the decision not to buy.

purchase intention   an individual's predisposition toward a particular product or brand after information search and evaluation, or at any time prior to actual purchase; see also *consumer decision process.*

purchase occasion   a type of *market segmentation* based on the time or situation for which the consumer enters the marketplace to buy a product or service; e.g., an anniversary, birthday, wedding, or graduation. See also *market segmentation* and *behavioristic segmentation.*

push money (PM)   a cash payment made by the advertiser directly to trade salespeople, such as those at the retail store, whenever they sell the advertiser's product; an inducement to give special attention to selling a particular product. Also called *promotion money* or *spiffs.* See also *street money.*

push strategy   advertising and promotion activities aimed at the trade and dealers, for the purpose of getting products down through the distribution channel, all the way to the ultimate consumer, by generating selling support on the part of channel members; a large amount of advertising and sales promotion directed at encouraging the trade to buy from a marketer and therefore helping to "push" the product from the top of the distribution channel, all the way through to the consumer. See also *pull strategy.*

Q

qualified access in Internet marketing, admission to a Web site or particular Web site feature by meeting certain requirements; e.g., an official subscriber with a login name and password or the user is required to answer some questions to gain access. Can be used by the Web site to collect audience user data; e.g., a person going to the "Scores" link on *www.usatoday.com* may be stopped and allowed to gain access only by filling out a dialogue box asking for gender and age, allowing the sponsor of the Web site to get a better picture of who is using that particular feature.

qualified circulation individuals eligible to receive a controlled circulation publication; may be paid or nonpaid. See also *circulation, controlled circulation, nonpaid circulation,* and *paid circulation.*

qualified lead see *qualified prospect (buyer).*

qualified prospect (buyer) an individual who meets all requirements to be considered a bona fide or legitimate candidate to buy a product or service.

qualified reader in advertising research, an individual who has given evidence of having read a particular issue of a magazine that is being studied (e.g., by correctly describing an article in the publication as proof of readership) and, therefore, is eligible to be interviewed about the magazine's advertisements; also called *qualified issue reader.*

qualified respondent an individual who meets all the criteria and requirements that have been established for selecting participants in an advertising research project.

qualified viewer in advertising research, an individual who has demonstrated viewing of a particular television program (by correctly recalling some part of the program) and who, therefore, is acceptable as a respondent to be interviewed about the program's commercials.

qualitative media effect the symbolic impact a medium or media vehicle has on an advertiser's message by virtue of it appearing in that medium or vehicle.

qualitative objectives subjective, unquantifiable goals established for the overall promotion program or for each element of the promotion mix; e.g., to produce more informative advertising to help consumers make better marketplace decisions or to improve an organization's reputation for being socially responsible. See also *quantitative objectives.*

qualitative research subjective research done primarily for exploratory purposes and to better understand a problem; e.g., a consumer's perceived image of a particular brand vs. a competing brand, why consumers like or dislike comparison advertising, the conditions under which it works best for them, and what they would do to improve it, or what particular sales promotion activities are best under different conditions and why. Investigates consumer variables that are unquantifiable, such as attitudes, perceptions, and lifestyle. Often makes use of *focus groups.* See also *quantitative research.*

quality positioning see *positioning by quality.*

quantitative objectives goals that are established in numbers and percents and that set finite yardsticks against which results are measured; e.g., to achieve a 15 percent increase in awareness of a product's special feature, to generate a 10 percent response rate for a promotional offer, or to gain a 25 percent *share of voice.* Profit, sales, market share, reach, GRPs, and the like, are common goals. See also *qualitative objectives.*

quantitative research objective research that seeks information that can be expressed in numbers and statistical terms; e.g., the number of individuals in each of several age brackets who rely heavily on advertising in making high-involvement product decisions, or consumers' ratings of a brand's performance. Typically uses formal research design and methodology. See also *qualitative research.*

quantity discount   a lower rate offered to an advertiser by a media vehicle for the purchase of a given amount of advertising time or space; a *price allowance* based on time or space bought at one time or over a period of time. See also *frequency discount.* Regarding product purchase, a price reduction based on the amount bought by the customer; see also *cumulative quantity discount* and *noncumulative quantity discount.*

quarter run   in *car card* advertising, placing a card in every fourth vehicle in the transit system; see also *full run* and *full showing.*

quarter showing   in outdoor and transit advertising, one-fourth of a full showing; i.e., a *partial showing.* See also *full run, full showing, half run,* and *half showing.*

queen-size poster   an advertising sign placed on the sides of a bus or transit vehicle, below the windows; advertising copy area typically measures approximately 30″ high × 88″ wide. See also *exterior bus, headlight poster, taillight poster,* and *king-size poster.*

question headline   a type of headline for an advertisement or a commercial that is designed to encourage the audience to search for the answer in the body copy; e.g., "Can your eyeglasses pass this test?" (Corning, Inc.) or "Does your suit contradict every intelligent thing you say?" (Paul Stuart clothes). See also *headline,* as well as *benefit headline, command headline, curiosity headline,* and *news-information headline.*

quintile   one-fifth of a given population; e.g., the audience of a media class, subclass, or media vehicle may be divided into five roughly equal groups based on usage such as readership of a specific periodical, with the groups ranging from very heavy usage to very light readership of the periodical. See also *quintile analysis.*

quintile analysis   examination and interpretation of a particular population that has been divided into five roughly equal groups, focusing on comparison between and among the groups; see also *quintile.*

quota   a specific sales or activity goal assigned to an individual, department, or other marketing unit for purposes of managing sales and marketing efforts; e.g., the specific sales figure a sales representative is expected to attain, or the number of new accounts the salesperson is expected to gain for the company.

quota sample   in survey research for marketing and advertising, a type of *nonprobability sample* that uses a method of choosing respondents from the population based on a predetermined desired number of individuals to include for questioning; see also *nonprobability sample, convenience sample, judgment sample, probability sample,* and *survey method.*

R

RAB   see *Radio Advertising Bureau.*

RADAR   see *Radio All Dimension Audience Research.*

ROB   see *run-of-book.*

ROI   see *return-on-investment approach.*

ROP   see *run-of-press.*

ROS   see *run-of-schedule.*

radio   an advertising *medium* in which messages are transmitted via electromagnetic waves, ultimately to a receiving radio set.

radio households   households with radio sets.

radio network   see *network.*

Radio Advertising Bureau (RAB)   a trade organization serving the radio advertising business by promoting radio as an effective medium for national and local advertisers.

Radio All Dimension Audience Research (RADAR) in radio audience research and measurement, the standard for radio ratings; an important goal of RADAR is to generate reliable audience estimates for local and network buying and selling. A service of *Arbitron.*

radio dayparts   see *dayparts.*

radio format   the subject or style that characterizes a radio station's programs; e.g., country, classical, oldies, rock, or adult contemporary music, or news, talk, or sports.

Radio Market Report   see *Arbitron.*

radio network   see *network.*

radio syndication   see *syndication* and *syndication program.*

ragged   in print advertising, printed matter (i.e., *copy*) that is unaligned or uneven on the left side (*ragged left*

and aligned on the right), the right side (*ragged right* and aligned on the left), or on both sides (*ragged left and right*); see also *flush.*

railroad showing   an advertising poster at a railroad station or along the tracks of a train line.

random sample   in marketing and advertising research, a probability sample in which all individuals have an equal and known chance of being selected using a random selection process; see also *probability sample.*

ranking   see *forced-ranking question.*

rank-order scale   see *forced-ranking question.*

rate   the amount charged per unit of space or time by a *media vehicle* to an advertiser for placing an advertisement or commercial in that vehicle; e.g., the amount charged per full page, half page, column inch, :30, :60, and the like.

rate base   the circulation number that is the basis for a periodical's advertising rates; may be guaranteed or nonguaranteed. See also *circulation rate base, guaranteed rate base,* and *nonguaranteed rate base.*

rate book   a publication that presents advertising rates for a wide variety of media; e.g., *Standard Rate and Data Service* volumes or *Marketer's Guide to Media.*

rate card   a published listing of the relevant information about placing advertising in a particular *media vehicle,* issued by the media vehicle to the advertiser; contains information such as advertising rates, availability of discounts, mechanical requirements, copy requirements, closing dates, circulation data, availability of regional editions, special issue information, special services (e.g., split-runs), and other information the advertiser needs before ordering space or time. An important part of a *media kit.* Used by print media, out-of-home media, and broadcast media. See also *media kit.*

rate class   in television or radio, the particular type of rate that is in effect during a given time period; e.g., *prime-time rate* or *daytime rate.* See also *dayparts.*

rate differential   in newspaper advertising, the difference between the national rate and the local rate; see also *national rate* and *local rate.*

rate guarantee   see *rate protection.*

rate holder   an advertisement or commercial that an advertiser runs solely for the purpose of qualifying for or meeting the requirements to earn a *quantity* or *frequency discount* from the *media vehicle,* during a contract period.

rate protection   a guarantee given by a *media vehicle* to an advertiser who has a contract for space or time that the agreed-upon rate will not change during the life of the contract, even if the media vehicle raises its rates during that period; in the absence of a contract, there still may be an agreement that a rate will be guaranteed for a given period of time, even if a rate increase occurs. Also called a *rate guarantee.*

rated structure   in out-of-home advertising, a structure such as a *billboard* that has been judged and gauged for location, visibility, type and amount of traffic, competition, and other factors; see also *space position value (SPV).*

rating   in television and radio, an expression of the percentage of households with television sets or radios that viewed or listened to a particular program; can also be applied to a network's or station's entire slate of programs collectively, or to a specific *daypart.* Most often used for broadcast media, but can be used for any medium as the percentage of homes or individuals exposed to the medium or a particular vehicle. Example: in television, a 9 rating for women 25–54 signifies that 9 percent of all women 25–54 in a specific geographic area were viewing a particular program or station. See also *program rating, rating point,* and *share.*

rating point   in television and radio, a measure of the audience watching or listening to a given program, where one rating point is equivalent to one percent of the population that owns a television or radio. With approximately 106.6 million television households in the United States, for example, each rating point is

equal to about 1,006,600 households. Can be done on a national, regional, or local basis, appropriately adjusting the population figure. In *outdoor advertising,* a rating point is a percentage of the area population potentially exposed to an advertiser's message either in the course of one day or over a 30-day period. See also *program rating, 100-showing,* and *share.*

rating service   an organization that measures audiences for television or radio programs, using a representative sample of the given population (national, regional, or local); service is performed for advertisers, networks, and stations. Data collected include audience size and viewer or listener characteristics. See also *Arbitron* and *Nielsen Media Research.*

rational appeals   in designing and executing advertising messages, a basis used to attract and engage the consumer through logic and pragmatic concerns, employing facts and claims related to function, dependability, economy, safety, efficiency, greater earnings, quality, price, increased leisure time, durability, and other links to the practical and reasoned judgment of the individual; also called *informational appeals* and *logical appeals.* See also *appeals* and *emotional appeals.*

rational motives   in consumer behavior, the economic or objective reasons for choosing a particular alternative or course of action; as contrasted with emotional motives, which focus on personal or objective bases in making marketplace decisions. See also *motive* and *emotional motives.*

raw data   in marketing and advertising research, the actual and specific responses to a survey, exactly as provided or stated by the respondents, with no editing.

reach   the number or percentage of different people or households in an advertiser's target audience who are exposed to a media vehicle or schedule at least once over a specific period of time (e.g., four weeks); in reality, the figure represents the audience's "opportunity-to-see" an advertisement or commercial, since the reach measure is an expression of exposure to the media vehicle or schedule, rather than to the advertising itself. A measure of *unduplicated audience.* Common to all media. Sometimes called *penetration.* See also *effective reach, opportunity-to-see (OTS), frequency, effective frequency,* and *average frequency.*

reach curve a graphical depiction of how total reach builds over the duration of an advertising and promotion campaign; see also *reach.*

reach × frequency equals gross rating points (GRPs); the total *advertising weight* of a media schedule, media vehicle, or medium. See also *reach, frequency,* and *gross rating points (GRPs).*

reactive marketing marketing strategies and tactics designed and implemented in response to competitive action and the need to combat the competitive moves or suffer market share damage; a defensive approach. See also *proactive marketing.*

reactive public relations marketing and public relations efforts undertaken in response to a developing or actual situation that if left unattended will likely result in negative consequences for the organization; a counteraction to pressure exerted on the advertiser, especially that from outside the firm, such as consumer displeasure with an event, activity, or practice of the firm, competitive actions, or change in government policy. A defensive move aimed at problem solving. An "after-the-fact" or defensive approach. Often necessitated by conditions, events, or influences beyond the control of the company. See also *marketing public relations* and *proactive public relations.*

readability index a measure of the ease with which advertising copy can be read; see also *Gunning Fog Index* and *Flesch Reading Ease Score.*

Read Most score in magazine readership studies, the percentage of readers of a specific issue of a magazine who read one-half or more of the written material in a particular advertisement's *copy;* see also *Associated score, Noted score,* and *Read Some score.* A measure of *The Starch Readership Report.*

Read Some score in magazine readership studies, the percentage of readers of a specific issue of a magazine who read any part of a particular advertisement's *copy;* see also *Associated score, Noted score,* and *Read Most score.* A measure of *The Starch Readership Report.*

reader an individual who reads a particular issue of a print publication.

readers per copy (RPC) the average number of individuals who read each copy of a particular publication, including pass-along readers; often noted in magazines' media kits to highlight cost comparisons among specific vehicles. See also *pass-along readership.*

readership the total number of individuals, including pass-along readers, who read a particular publication; i.e., readership by base circulation and pass-alongs, as calculated by a publication's circulation multiplied by the number of people who read it. Also refers to the extent to which the editorial and/or advertising content is read by the audience. See also *pass-along readership.*

readership studies in print advertising research and testing, the measurement and analysis of the performance of individual advertisements among readers; see also *Starch Readership Studies.*

readership survey in advertising research, an investigation into the readership and their reading habits concerning a specific publication and/or the advertising in that publication.

reading notice a newspaper or magazine advertisement whose format and type style is very similar to that of the publication's editorial matter; the advertisement must contain the word "advertisement," clearly visible and set apart at the top or bottom. Usually carries a higher rate than a regular advertisement.

rear-end display see *front-end display* and *taillight poster.*

reason-why copy an argument presented in an advertising message that explains why a consumer will benefit from purchasing and using a particular product; a formal statement describing exactly why a particular product or a specific feature will produce a need-satisfying benefit to the consumer. Body copy that substantiates the promise made in the headline. Should be included in the *copy platform* or blueprint outlining the creative strategy.

rebate a sales promotion tool in which a buyer receives cash back from the advertiser following purchase of a particular product and submission of proof-of-purchase; most commonly used for durable, expensive goods. Also may refer to the payment by a media vehicle to an advertiser when the advertising time or space actually used by the advertiser exceeds the original contract commitment, allowing the advertiser to qualify for and secure a lower rate. May further refer to a media practice in which there is a return payment from the media to the advertiser to compensate for less space being used than originally contracted and paid for, or because of error or less-than-promised circulation or audience delivery. See also *refund*.

rebuttal advertising   see *counteradvertising*.

recall   an individual's ability to remember specific elements or points about a particular advertisement, commercial, or campaign; see also *recall test*.

recall test   a technique for determining how well respondents remember an advertisement or other element of a promotion program; respondents may be provided with verbal or visual details to help their memory (*aided recall*), or they may be given no help at all (*unaided recall*). See also *aided recall* and *unaided recall*, as well as *recognition method*.

receiver   the recipient or target audience of a sender's message, i.e., an advertising or promotional message; see also *decoding*.

recency effect   in theory, the information presented last in an advertising message tends to have greatest impact and effect on the audience and will be remembered longest; see also *primacy effect*.

recent-reading method   a method for measuring print media exposure and readership that begins with the interviewer asking the respondent whether he or she has read a copy of a particular publication in the past week (for a weekly) or in the past month (for a monthly).

recognition   an individual's ability to remember having seen a particular advertisement, commercial, or campaign; see also *recognition method* and *recall*.

recognition method   in print advertising research, a measure of the respondent's ability to remember having seen a particular magazine advertisement; can be done on a one-time, single-issue basis or over a period of time, with a single magazine title or several titles. See also *Starch Readership Studies* and *recall test*.

recognized agency   an advertising agency that meets a media vehicle's criteria and standards of a legitimate agency and is, therefore, eligible to receive a commission (usually 15 percent) from the vehicle for the space or time it sells to advertisers.

recruitment advertising   advertising by organizations seeking qualified applicants for position openings, typically placed in the "help wanted" classified section of daily and Sunday newspapers, as well as in trade and industry publications.

rectangle ad   in Internet advertising, a rectangle ad shape with 180×150 dimensions (width $\times$ height, in pixels); a *medium rectangle ad* $= 300 \times 250$, a *large rectangle ad* $= 336 \times 280$, and a *vertical rectangle ad* $= 240 \times 400$ dimensions. See also *pixels, banner ad, skyscraper ad*, and *square pop-up ad*.

Red Books   see *Standard Directory of Advertisers, Standard Directory of Advertising Agencies,* and *Standard Directory of International Advertisers & Agencies.*

redemption   the act of submitting a *coupon* at the point-of-purchase for a reduction in price of a given product equal to the face value of the coupon.

reference group   individuals who are a point of comparison and a basis for shaping and expressing a person's attitudes, opinions, values, and behavior; a group of people who influence a consumer's decision making for products and brands in that they serve as a guide for a person's behavior in a specific situation. Those more influential individuals in a reference group are referred to as *opinion leaders*. See also *primary group, secondary group, formal group, informal group,* and *opinion leader*.

reference price   prior to a purchase situation and exploration of alternatives, the price the consumer expects to pay for a particular product or service.

refund   a sales promotion tool whereby the advertiser returns cash to the buyer of a given product, usually a nondurable, inexpensive product; also may refer to the payment by a media vehicle to an advertiser when the advertising time or space actually used by the advertiser exceeds the original contract commitment, allowing the advertiser to qualify for and secure a lower rate. May further refer to a media practice in which there is a return payment from the media to the advertiser to compensate for less space being used than originally contracted and paid for, or because of error or less-than-promised circulation or audience delivery. See also *rebate*.

Reggie Awards   in promotional marketing, annual formal recognition for superior promotional thinking, creativity, and execution across the full spectrum of promotional marketing; organized and administered by the *Promotion Marketing Association*.

regional advertiser an organization that operates in and markets exclusively to only one part of the country; see also *regional advertising* and *local advertiser.*

regional advertising advertising that covers only a specific portion or limited geographic region of the United States, for products that are sold only in that area; as opposed to *national advertising* or *local advertising*. See also *regional advertiser* and *localized campaigns.*

regional agency an advertising agency that prepares and places advertising in a limited geographic area of the country; see also *local agency.*

regional edition an edition of a national magazine (or newspaper) that is distributed only to a particular region of the United States, e.g., the Southeastern edition of *People* magazine or the West Central edition of *Newsweek* magazine; the advertiser can buy space in the regional edition without having to pay for the entire circulation. A type of *partial-run edition*. See also *demographic edition, metro edition,* and *state edition.*

regional interconnect see *interconnect.*

regional magazine see *sectional magazine.*

regional media any of several advertising media that cover only a part of the entire country, but whose circulation or audience is more than what would be considered local; typically, several states constitute the coverage area. See also *regional edition.*

regional network a broadcast network covering only a limited part of the country, and for which advertising rates are priced accordingly; can also refer to a group of magazines (a *magazine network*) offering advertising space in only a portion of the country. See also *magazine network* and *network.*

regionalization in international advertising, when the advertiser uses a single campaign to target two or more countries, rather than a different campaign for each country (*localization*) or one campaign for all countries in which the advertiser does business (*globalization*); see *globalization* and *localization.*

regularly unsought products consumer products that the potential customer knows exist, but has little or no motivation to find and even may actively avoid a search; see also *unsought products* and *new unsought products.*

regulation those attempts to govern and control marketing activities for the protection and betterment of all parties affected by marketing; see also *federal regulation, state regulation, local regulation,* and *self-regulation.*

regulatory agencies the broad spectrum of federal, state, and local bodies that, by legal empowerment and authority, have the responsibility to govern and control the practices of marketing, advertising, and the other forms and aspects of promotion; the entities whose major responsibility is to ensure that all marketing practices are conducted in the public interest. Also includes the individual industry self-regulation efforts.

reinforcement the strengthening of learning that occurs when a consumer makes a choice about a product or service and experiences satisfaction or dissatisfaction with the decision; see also *learning.*

reinforcement advertising use of media to supplement the major media used in a campaign; e.g., the main media employed in a particular campaign might be magazines and television, with billboards and radio in a supplementary or secondary role to provide additional support or reminder value to the primary media. Also refers to the advertising aimed at recent purchasers and current users to confirm and strengthen their thoughts on what a good choice they made by buying the advertiser's product.

related-recall score in television advertising research, a finding reported by a *day-after-recall test,* identifying the percentage of respondents who not only remember seeing the commercial in question but also accurately describe some of the specific details of the commercial; see also *claimed-recall score, day-after-recall test,* and *ASI Recall Test.*

relationship marketing an organization's marketing approach that revolves around building and maintaining a long-term link or bond with customers, the trade, and other groups with mutually dependent needs and goals; advertising and promotional activities, along with personal attention, play a major role in the entire process. Often a goal for a company's sponsorship marketing program. See also *sponsorship.*

relative advantage see *competitive advantage.*

relative cost the relationship between the cost of advertising space or time and the size of the target audience delivered; a measure by which media may be compared as to cost efficiency. See also *cost per point (CPP), cost per thousand (CPM),* and *cost per thousand—target audience (CPM-TA).*

relaunch the revival of a marketing or advertising campaign or even a product, after its discontinuation for an extended period of time; e.g., bringing back Tony the Tiger as the spokescharacter for Kellogg's Frosted Flakes.

release see *news release.*

release print in television advertising, the final version of the commercial or program.

reliability a measure of the extent to which the same marketing, advertising, or promotion research technique or procedure will yield similar results every time; an expression of the dependability and consistency of a research technique in the sense that it yields the same results in repeated studies time after time. Also the extent to which the sample result would be the same if the entire population had been surveyed (i.e., if a census had been taken). See also *validity.*

reminder advertising advertising whose purpose is to keep the advertiser's brand name in the target audience's mind; often used for established, familiar brands to complement the advertising efforts aimed at persuasion. See also *informative advertising* and *persuasive advertising.*

remnant space in magazine advertising, unsold space in regional and demographic editions at the time a periodical is ready to go to press; usually offered at a substantial discount to an advertiser.

renewal on or before its expiration date, the extension of a contractual agreement between an advertiser and a *media vehicle,* such as a television station or a newspaper.

renewal paper the extra outdoor posters or transit cards, beyond the number needed at one time, that are produced to replace the ones that are damaged (by natural forces or vandalism) during the course of their *showing;* also called *overrun.*

rep see *sales representative* and *media representative.*

rep firm in advertising media sales, a firm acting on behalf of a *media vehicle* to sell advertising time or space to advertisers on a national basis or in cities other than where the media vehicle is located; see also *media representative.*

repeat purchase when a consumer buys the same brand as that purchased the time before for that product category; i.e., the same brand is purchased a second consecutive time; also called *repurchase.*

repositioning changing a brand's image and the way consumers view it, often in an attempt to attract a different target market segment or audience; see also *positioning.*

repositioning the competition an advertiser's strategy that aims to get a target audience to change its opinion about or views toward a competitor; i.e., altering the way consumers think about or perceive a competitor.

representativeness the degree to which advertising research data and results generated from a sample can be generalized to a larger population; e.g., the degree to which television viewing habits found in a sample survey of television viewers can be generalized to the national television viewing audience. Also, in *test marketing,* the similarity between the *test market* and the full, large-scale market. See also *test market* and *test marketing.*

repurchase see *repeat purchase.*

reputation management in public relations, a long-term process, using a variety of tools and programs, of building and maintaining an organization's solid image and standing among its relevant publics; see also *public relations.*

request see *hit.*

resale price maintenance see *fair trade.*

rescaling see *resizing.*

research see *advertising research* and *marketing research.*

research design an overall plan or blueprint establishing the framework for collecting and analyzing data, including the details of the research techniques, procedures, and methodology to be used.

research director an individual at the advertising agency who masterminds the complete consumer research effort, and who provides input to the creative effort aimed at producing effective advertising.

research firm an independent organization capable of planning, designing, implementing, analyzing, interpreting, and reporting out on marketing research projects.

research methodology in marketing and advertising research, a complete description of the manner in which data are to be collected for the research project at hand; key methodologies involve *surveys, test markets,* and *literature searches.*

research process see *marketing research process.*

reseller see *middleman.*

residual in broadcast advertising, a payment to the talent, i.e., performers, who appear in a commercial; the payment that occurs after the original contract expires, every time the commercial is broadcast until it is no longer used. Payment to performers for repeated airings or showings of a commercial. See also *talent cost* and *session fee.*

resizing changing the dimensions of the elements in a print advertisement so the ad can appear in another size; often done to accommodate the different dimensions of a magazine. When applied to a broadcast commercial, term refers to a "reduced" or shorter time frame, e.g., a :30 becomes a :15 by eliminating some of the voice-over while retaining the essence of the commercial. Sometimes called *rescaling.*

resonance test in advertising research, an examination and evaluation of the extent to which a message scores accurately with the target audience.

respondent an individual or organization that answers or participates in an advertiser's request for action of some kind.

response an individual's reaction to an advertising message or promotional effort; i.e., the receiver's reaction to the sender's communication.

response analysis in direct mail, an evaluation of the individuals who were moved to action by a direct-mail program, as well as an examination and interpretation of different components in a direct-mail package that were subjected to testing; concept applies generally to the investigation and explanation of responses to any promotion activity or program.

response bias in marketing and advertising research, the distortion of results that occurs when a respondent, knowingly or unknowingly, provides incorrect or untruthful answers to questions posed by the researcher.

response device in direct marketing or other promotional effort, an order form or other mechanism that the recipient can return to the advertiser to show acceptance of or interest in an offer or request.

response elasticity the extent to which the target audience reacts to a marketing program or particular activity in the way the marketer intended.

response list individuals and organizations that have in the past responded to direct marketing or promotional efforts of the advertiser or other firm for products, services, or purposes similar to those of the advertiser.

response rate a measure of the positive reaction to an advertiser's efforts, e.g., the percentage of individuals who respond to a direct-marketing program, the percentage of the target audience who take action asked for by the advertiser, the percentage of individuals who participate in an advertising or marketing research survey (e.g., who complete a questionnaire), the percentage of the target audience who participate in a sales promotion (e.g., who enter a contest or redeem a coupon), and the like; also referred to as *percent return.*

response threshold the point at which an individual is moved to accept the marketer's or advertiser's call to action; the number of exposures needed or the extent to which the marketer or advertiser must deliver a message to hit an individual's *"hot button"* to elicit a response.

results-based method of agency compensation see *performance-based method.*

retail advertising advertising placed in local media by a local dealer selling directly to the consumer, i.e., a retailer; qualifies for a preferential advertising rate. See also *local advertising, local advertiser,* and *local rate.*

retail display allowance see *display allowance.*

retail rate the advertising rate paid by local retailers; lower than the national rate. Also called *local rate.* See also *national rate.*

retailing all activities involved in selling products and services to final consumers or users.

retail trading zone a geographical area, inside and outside a central city, in which most of the population does the majority of its shopping and buying; the market outside a city zone whose residents engage in trade with retail merchants located in the city zone. The entire geographical area from which a retailer draws its business.

retailer   an organization that buys products and sells them to ultimate consumers; also known as a *dealer*.

retailer coupon   a coupon distributed to the consumer by a retailer; see also *coupon* and *retailer in-ad*.

retailer in-ad   a retailer-specific advertisement containing a coupon offer that is redeemable only at that retailer's location(s).

retailer promotion   any of a variety of sales promotion tools and activities used by the retailer to generate store traffic and sales.

retainer method of agency compensation   a fee paid by the advertiser to the advertising agency for services, with the fee established by an estimate of the number of billing hours required to serve the account and then determining a series of equal payments; also called *straight-fee method*. See also *fee method, commission method, combination method,* and *performance-based method*. Also see *agency commission* and *sliding rate*.

retention rate   the extent to which a television station or network keeps a viewing audience from one program to another (i.e., *holdover audience*); the extent to which a television program, station, or network retains its viewers during commercial breaks (i.e., *ad pod rating*); or the extent to which a company retains its customers from purchase to purchase.

retentive advertising   see *reminder advertising*.

retro ads   in current-day advertising, using advertisements, themes, and approaches that proved popular decades earlier; aim is to capture the look and feel of days gone by and to capitalize on people's nostalgia, emotions, and feelings for the old days. A yesteryear approach to present-day advertising. Often involves bringing back a former spokesperson-character, e.g., Charmin's Mr. Whipple, Starkist's Charley the Tuna, or Kellogg's Frosted Flakes' Tony the Tiger. Also called *throwback ads*.

retro campaign   see *retro ads*.

retro theme   see *retro ads*.

return-on-investment approach (ROI)   considering advertising and promotion programs an investment, a method of determining payback by comparing the costs of the program and the results or value generated by it; e.g., the change in sales, revenues, or brand awareness in response to an advertising program. Very difficult to use with any degree of precision and reliability given the many factors that affect sales, market share, and other results or measures of returns.

returns   the response to a direct-marketing mailing program.

revenue-per-rating-point   the amount of advertising revenue a television network or station generates for each rating point it delivers; a common denominator and comparison tool for measuring results relative to delivery. Hypothetical example: for its college football telecasts, ESPN takes in $120 million in advertising revenue and delivers an average rating of 2.3 for the season, yielding a revenue-per-rating-point figure of $52.2 million. See also *rating point*.

reverse auction   see *online reverse auction*.

reverse timetable   see *work flowchart*.

review   see *account review*.

rich media   see *rich media advertising*.

rich media advertising   in Internet advertising, an advertisement that makes use of elaborate technology and that contains elaborate visual or interactive elements that allow a visitor to select any of a number of pages to link to on the advertiser's Web site; an advertisement more elaborate than usual, such as a banner ad with a pop-up menu from which the visitor can select a page to go to on the advertiser's Web site, a streaming video, fill-in forms, elaborate animations, sound, and other devices designed to capture the user's attention and encourage interaction.

ride-along   promotional material that is enclosed in direct mailings sent to consumers for another purpose, such as an invoice or statement; sometimes called a *hitchhiker* or a *statement stuffer*.

riding the boards   see *riding the showing*.

riding the showing   a physical inspection tour of the billboard advertising locations and panels that comprise a particular advertiser's *outdoor advertising buy;* may refer to checking posters and sites prior to or, more commonly, after posting, i.e., may be a prebuy ride or a postbuy ride. See also *preride* and *postride*.

right-of-first-negotiation   see *right-of-first-refusal*.

right-of-first-refusal in sponsorship marketing, a contractual agreement giving a property's sponsor the right to match any offer the *property* receives in a particular category or level of sponsorship when it is up for renewal; sometimes referred to as *right-of-first-negotiation*. See also *option-to-renew*.

ripomatic a technique used to pretest a rough, unfinished television commercial produced by "ripping off" or taking parts of other commercials and piecing them together to give an idea of what the new commercial will look like; used to show to the advertiser and to gain approval before production of the finished commercial. Also called a *stealomatic*. See also *pretesting, liveamatic, photomatic, storyboard, rough,* and *swipe file*.

risk reduction the attempt by the consumer to minimize the perceived dangers associated with a wrong choice of product or other marketplace decision; the presence of high perceived risk is likely to result in extensive problem solving by the consumer, while a low perceived risk typically results in limited or routine problem solving. See also *risk-taking, extensive problem solving, limited problem solving,* and *routine problem solving.* Also see *high-involvement decision making* and *low-involvement decision making.*

risk-taking encountering the hazards and uncertainties that are an integral part of marketing, from both the marketer's and the consumer's side; e.g., a consumer purchase may involve one or several risks, such as performance risk, financial risk, physical risk, social risk, or time-loss risk, or an intermediary faces risk by making a buying commitment in advance of a selling season. See also *performance risk, financial risk, physical risk, social risk,* and *time-loss risk.* Also see *risk reduction.*

roadblocking in television advertising, a media scheduling technique that calls for placing the same commercial on all networks at the exact same time so they are broadcast simultaneously; or placing the same commercial at the exact same time on several stations within a single market area. Those individuals watching television at that time likely will be exposed to the same commercial simultaneously.

Robinson-Patman Act a federal law, passed in 1936 to supplement the *Clayton Antitrust Act,* prohibiting undue price discrimination and also regulating and controlling promotional allowances given by manufacturers to retailers; all such allowances must be made available to the trade on "proportionally equal terms." Banned offering different prices to different buyers of the same commodity when the effect would be to lessen competition or create a monopoly. Hoped to protect small independent retailers from chain-store competition (sometimes referred to as the "Anti-Chain-Store Act"). See also *Clayton Antitrust Act.*

roles of intermediaries see *middleman functions.*

roll-out a process of expanding advertising or other promotion activity into additional geographic or market areas over time; in the same way, also refers to a product's introduction into new areas. Geographic expansion may proceed from a single or limited number of test markets to a regional and then a national market over a period of time. Typically, the strategy employed during the *commercialization stage,* and final stage, of the *new-product development process.*

rolling billboard an advertising sign, billboard, or other display mounted or painted on a truck, van, or other vehicle that moves from one location to another, e.g., from one event to another or one city to another; also refers to auto racing cars with the painted signs and decals of a race team's sponsors displayed all over the vehicle, not to mention the huge van that transports the race cars from one speedway to another all over the country, with the main sponsor's name painted on the sides of the van. Also called a *mobile billboard* or a *traveling display.* See also *bus wrap* and *car wrap.*

rolling stock generally refers to a company vehicle or delivery truck with the name of the company painted on the sides; the vehicle is used to carry out the normal day's work, such as delivery or repairs, going from job to job, as opposed to a *rolling billboard,* which is strictly for promotional purposes. See also *rolling billboard.*

Rolodex agency an advertising agency that consists of just a small number of people, instead hiring specialists such as copywriters, art directors, media planners, and marketing strategists on a project-by-project basis; similar to a group of *freelance* advertising people. See also *freelance.*

romance copy alluring and enticing advertising copy, heavy on imagery, designed to attract the target audience through connection with their feelings and emotions; very much a soft-sell approach. See also *soft-sell advertising.*

RoperASW   a leading consumer marketing and advertising research firm; see also *Starch Readership Reports.*

roster   the list of advertising agencies used by a particular company; see also *agency of record.*

roster recall   in advertising research, a method in which respondents are shown a list of television or radio programs and then asked to identify those they remember seeing or hearing.

rotary   see *rotary bulletin.*

rotary bulletin   in *outdoor advertising,* one of two standard-size billboards at 14′ high × 48′ wide; the bulletin is moved periodically to different locations in the same market at fixed intervals, e.g., every 30, 60, or 90 days, to achieve balanced *reach* in the market area without having a large number of billboards. Also called a *rotary* or a *rotating bulletin.* See also *permanent bulletin* and *spectacular.*

rotary plan   see *rotary bulletin.*

rotation   in television and radio, a method of advertising scheduling in which several commercials that comprise a set are run in a regular sequence continuously from first to last, over and over; can also be used to mean an advertiser's strategy of scheduling television commercials by rotating them among several different programs or time periods (i.e., an *orbit*). The term may refer to the outdoor advertising practice of periodically moving billboards to different locations within a market. See also *rotary bulletin* and *orbit.*

rotational signage   at any given fixed location at a sports arena, stadium, or other venue, sponsors' signage that changes or rotates through various advertiser/sponsor names at predetermined intervals of time.

rotogravure   in print production, a process in which the printing surface is etched into a printing plate, rather than flat (as in *offset lithography* printing) or raised (as in *letterpress* printing); excellent for reproducing pictures, and particularly prevalent in printing newspaper supplements and inserts as well as mail-order catalogs. See also *offset lithography* and *letterpress.*

rough   any of a number of different forms of a less-than-finished advertisement or commercial; a proposed execution.

rough layout   a sketch or drawing in actual size, done in pencil or via computer, that shows a proposed advertisement's layout, with the arrangement of all the elements such as headline, illustrations, and *copy;* comes after the *thumbnail* in the layout development process. Very often used by the advertising agency in its initial presentation to the client. The term *rough* can also refer to an unfinished television commercial, such as an *animatic, photomatic,* or *ripomatic.* Also known as a *pencil drawing* or a *thumbnail sketch.* See also *layout development process, thumbnail, comprehensive,* and *mechanical.*

routine problem solving   consumer decision making characterized by little or no search for new information, with the consumer having and relying on considerable previous experience; typically involves repeat choices or habitual buying. Often involves low-involvement purchases or those the consumer does not regard as especially important. See also *extensive problem solving* and *limited problem solving.* Also see *high-involvement decision making* and *low-involvement decision making.*

run-of-book (ROB)   in magazine advertising, an advertising position anywhere within the publication, as opposed to a *preferred position* specified by the advertiser; position is selected by the publisher. Regular rate applies. See also *preferred position.*

run-of-network   see *run-of-schedule (ROS).*

run-of-paper (ROP)   see *run-of-press (ROP).*

run-of-press (ROP)   in newspaper or magazine advertising, an advertising position anywhere, any page, or any location on a page, within the publication at the convenience and judgment of the newspaper, as opposed to a *preferred position* specified by the advertiser; advertiser may request a particular section of the newspaper or magazine, but the publisher selects the position, usually trying to accommodate the advertiser's request. Regular rate applies. Sometimes called *run-of-paper (ROP).* See also *preferred position.*

run-of-schedule (ROS)   in television or radio advertising, an advertising position that can be anytime during the broadcast day at the station's choosing, as opposed to a *preferred position;* generally, an advertiser will request a particular time period, say, daytime or nighttime, leaving exact placement of the commercial to the discretion of the network or station. Regular rate applies. Sometimes called *run-of-station* or *floating time.* See also *preferred position* and *best-time-available.*

run-of-site in Internet advertising, an advertisement that is placed to rotate on all nonfeatured advertising spaces on a Web site.

run-of-station see *run-of-schedule (ROS).*

rushes see *dailies.*

S

SAU   see *Standard Advertising Unit.*

SFX   see *sound effects.*

SIC   see *Standard Industrial Classification.*

SMRB   see *Simmons Market Research Bureau.*

SMSA   see *Standard Metropolitan Statistical Area.*

SRDS   see *Standard Rate and Data Service.*

S-shaped response curve   a model of the relationship between advertising expenditures and sales, in which initial advertising outlays have little effect on sales but, with increased expenditures, there are incremental increases in sales—up to a point where continued increases in advertising dollars have diminishing effects; the initial period of flat sales, followed by a period of increased sales, and then a leveling off produces an "S"-shaped response function when plotted on a grid with advertising expenditures on the "x" axis and sales on the "y" axis. See also *concave response curve.*

safety risk   see *physical risk.*

sale   a promotional offer of a temporary reduction in a product's retail price.

sale advertising   retail advertising that focuses on merchandise that is being offered at reduced prices; an attempt to get a fast response to generate store traffic and move certain products. Sometimes referred to as *direct-action advertising.*

sales aids   collateral promotional materials designed to help the personal selling effort achieve greater effectiveness; e.g., sales literature, demonstration kits, audiovisual materials. Can also refer to merchandising activities at the retail level.

sales analysis   the use of sales figures to measure and evaluate marketing and promotion performance; accomplished with a detailed investigation of the company's sales records.

sales area test   see *test marketing.*

sales audit   measurement and examination of a product's movement through retail stores.

sales contest   a trade sales promotion tool used as an incentive for an organization's sales force or for the dealers; specific objectives and criteria vary, but generally involve factors such as sales volume, profit, new accounts or customers, or other considerations important to the company (and to the participants).

sales control   all efforts directed at measuring and evaluating sales performance on a regular periodic basis for the purpose of monitoring progress toward sales objectives, and taking action as required to keep results on track.

sales decline stage   see *decline stage.*

sales effect of advertising   the extent to which advertising results in increased sales of a product or service; see also *communications effect of advertising, sales response function,* and *advertising response curve.*

sales effectiveness test   a measurement and analysis of advertising and promotion activities and programs relative to the sales levels achieved.

sales force   all individuals directly involved with an organization's personal sales efforts and interacting with potential buyers, including those who are engaged in actual selling as well as nonselling activities such as missionary and customer servicing efforts.

sales force composite   see *composite of sales force opinion.*

sales forecast   an estimate of expected future sales from a specific marketing plan for a specified period of time; e.g., a one-year sales projection that becomes a goal for the marketing and promotion effort. Several different methods are used, often in combination. See also *composite of sales force opinion, expert opinion, jury of executive opinion, survey of buying intention, test marketing, market potential,* and *sales potential.*

sales growth price objective setting price at a level that allows the company to achieve a specified dollar or unit sales level; see also *target return, profit maximization, market share,* and *meeting competition price objectives.*

sales incentive any of a variety of means used by an organization to stimulate the efforts of the sales force; e.g., a contest, premium, gift, travel, or other inducement aimed at generating greater productivity by the sales force. A short-term inducement, over and above the compensation plan and the other regular incentives.

sales letter in direct mail, a missive whose purpose is to do the selling job for the advertiser by generating acceptance of an idea, prompting an inquiry, or stimulating an order; the most common type of *direct mail.*

sales management the planning, organizing, implementing, evaluating, and controlling of the sales effort, including activities such as recruiting, supervising, motivating, and compensating the sales force in a way that fosters achievement of goals.

sales manager the governor and chief administrator of an organization's sales department and the sales force's personal selling program.

sales objectives goals and targets for the sales effort, stated in terms of volume, profit, market share, or other basis; also refers to advertising or promotion objectives that are stated in terms of a particular level of sales to be achieved in a certain period of time, say, a specific campaign.

sales potential an estimate of a particular firm's portion of the market potential; see also *market potential* and *sales forecast.*

sales presentation a sales representative's persuasive delivery of an offering to prospective buyers.

sales promotion promotional marketing activities and programs (other than advertising, direct marketing, public relations) involving a wide range of limited-time inducements designed to stimulate relatively quick consumer action and dealer or sales force support and effectiveness, as well as to add value to the firm's offering; aim is typically for immediate or short-term results. See also *consumer sales promotion* and *trade sales promotion.*

sales promotion agency a firm that specializes in handling the sales promotion activities and programs of organizations.

sales promotion fallacy that a marketer must always provide some sort of a deal to attract and keep customers.

sales promotion trap a situation resulting from many competitors making extensive use of a continuous stream of sales promotion activities, thereby forcing any one competitor to offer similar inducements just to keep up.

sales quota see *quota.*

sales representative the individual who, via face-to-face contact, attempts to inform, persuade, or assist the target audience to take a particular action that has commercial significance to the seller; in advertising media sales, the person acting on behalf of a *media vehicle* to sell advertising time or space to advertisers on a national basis or in cities other than where the media vehicle is located. See also *media rep* and *rep firm.*

sales response function the pattern and level of sales that result from different levels of advertising or promotional activity; see also *advertising response curve* and *sales effect of advertising.*

sales support nonselling activities designed to promote sales; e.g., service personnel who assist with the installation of equipment or customer service personnel who provide instructions on use of equipment or after-sale maintenance service.

sales territory the geographic boundaries of a sales representative's duties and responsibilities.

sales test a method of measuring the success or effectiveness of an advertising campaign or individual advertisements comprising the campaign.

salient beliefs the relatively few beliefs held by an individual that are the most important determinants of his or her attitudes and that greatly influence product purchase behavior.

salting regarding a list used for direct-marketing purposes, a technique for tracking a list buyer's or user's use of the list to make sure the list-use agreement is not violated; involves placing a *decoy* or dummy name on the list to be able to track it for possible violation of the agreement between list provider and list user. Also called *seeding.*

sample   in marketing and advertising research, a representative portion of a target population used by researchers in their activities, such as determining the effectiveness of a particular *copy* approach or *execution format* for planning advertising; in sales promotion, refers to a free trial size (or actual size) of a product. See also *sampling program* and *census.*

sample book   a collection of representative examples of the work of an advertising agency or an individual, such as a copywriter or a layout specialist; if used by an individual in the job-search process, may contain actual as well as speculative work. Sometimes referred to as a *portfolio.*

sample frame   in survey research, the population from which potential individuals or households are selected for inclusion in the survey; see also *sample unit.*

sample package   in direct marketing, a replica of a direct-mail package that is to be mailed to a particular list; submitted by the list user to the list owner for approval prior to commitment for one-time use of the list. See also *list owner, list user,* and *one-time use.*

sample size   in survey research, the number of individuals or households selected for inclusion in the research; must be of a size appropriate to allow accurate judgments to be made about the larger population.

sample unit   in marketing and advertising research, the specific individual or household selected to be a part of the study; see also *sample frame.*

sampling   the process of selecting and then obtaining information from a comparatively small number of people who are representative of the larger population, so that information collected can be used to make judgments about the total population represented by the chosen respondents.

sampling error   in survey research, the discrepancy between the results obtained in a survey and the results that would have been obtained had a complete study of the entire population been undertaken; see also *nonresponse error.*

sampling plan   in marketing and advertising research, the entire set of instructions governing the selection of respondents for a research project; see also *research design* and *research methodology.*

sampling program   a sales promotion activity of distributing free trial sizes (or actual sizes) of a product to the target audience, with the underlying notion that "the best advertising for the product is the product itself"; main purpose is to gain consumer trial of the product. Used in new-product introductions, as well as to rejuvenate sales of existing products or to tap a new market segment. Samples can be distributed directly to the household via mail or other delivery or it can be done as an in-store promotion.

sandwich board   an advertising sign consisting of two boards suspended over an individual's shoulders by means of straps, with one board hanging in front, the other in back; the person walks a route carrying the advertising.

sans serif   in print advertising, type that has no small lines that appear at the ends of the main strokes in a type font, as appear in a *serif* typeface; see also *serif.*

satellite   see *communications satellite.*

satellite station   in broadcasting, a station located in a fringe reception area that serves to boost the range of the main station's signal; smaller-market stations that carry the same programming as a larger nearby station, thereby extending geographical coverage. Often used to form a "network" of stations to give a large region the opportunity to hear the broadcast of a baseball team's games; e.g., radio broadcasts of the Boston Red Sox throughout New England, although the flagship station itself reaches only a limited area. See also *parent station.*

satellite television   see *direct broadcast satellite (DBS).*

saturation   a media scheduling pattern that combines extensive *reach* and high *frequency* in an attempt to gain maximum coverage and impact over a given period of time; i.e., *advertising weight* far heavier and beyond the normal scheduling intensity of an advertiser. See also *advertising weight.*

saturation plan   see *total audience plan (TAP).*

saturation showing   in outdoor or transit advertising, a *showing* of maximum intensity that, with repeat exposures taken into consideration, achieves even greater exposure than a *100 showing* indicates; see also *100 showing.*

scanner an electronic device that reads the universal product code (UPC) on product packages at the checkout counter at retail stores.

scanner data data recorded for all transactions in a store, including product name, price, size, flavor, and particular variety; also includes information relative to advertising and promotion activity for the product at the time of purchase, such as *point-of-purchase displays.* See also *single-source data.*

SCANTRACK an industry standard for scanner-based marketing and sales information on product movement and merchandising, in which comprehensive data are gathered weekly from an enormous sample of retail stores in major markets throughout the United States; provides basic tracking information at multiple levels ranging from category-level total U.S. sales volume to single-item performance in one specific market. Monitors performance trends and evaluates price and promotion effectiveness by tracking and forecasting nonpromoted as well as promotional product movement. A *single-source data* system. A product of *A.C. Nielsen.* See also *A.C. Nielsen* and *single-source data.*

Scarborough data see *Scarborough Research.*

Scarborough Research a provider of syndicated local-market consumer data, covering most of the major *DMAs* in the United States; compiles comprehensive data on local-market consumer shopping behavior, product use and consumption, media usage, psychographics (lifestyles), and demographics.

scatter market in broadcast television, the collection of unsold advertising dates, times, and programs available for purchase after the *up-front,* or preseason, buying period; see also *up-front market.*

scatter plan in television or radio advertising, the placement of commercials during a wide range of dates and times on several different programs over a given period of time; essentially, the notion of scheduling commercials on a random basis.

schedule a list of the media and media vehicles to be used in an advertising campaign and the manner in which the advertising is programmed over time,

including the specific dates, times, issues, pages, and other particulars; see also *media flowchart* and *media schedule.*

scheduling the process of determining a *media schedule;* see also *continuous scheduling, flighting, pulsing,* and *media scheduling.*

scrambled merchandising a retailer's practice of carrying an extremely wide range of different and unrelated product lines.

scratch track in the television commercial creation process, a musical score that uses only a piano and substitute vocalist (even prerecorded) to give a rough approximation of what the sound may be like in the finished commercial; may be used in an *animatic, photomatic,* or other rough version of the commercial.

screamer in print advertising, a large-type boldface headline.

screener see *gatekeeper.*

script a detailed written description of the video and/or audio content of a television or radio commercial.

search the investigation of electronic databases; see also *search engine.*

search consultant see *agency search consultant.*

search engine on the Internet, a computer system software tool that permits Internet users to find links to Web sites and information of interest to them, by typing a keyword to start the search; a means used to find Web sites of interest to the Internet user. Examples: Google, Yahoo!, Lycos, AltaVista, HotBot, Webcrawler, Excite. See also *keyword.*

seasonal discount a price reduction offered to consumers; an incentive to purchase or make a commitment to purchase a product or service outside its normal or busiest season.

second cover (2C) the inside front cover of a magazine, for which a premium advertising rate is paid.

secondary audience in print media, individuals who read a particular publication, but who are not subscribers or purchasers of the publication; i.e., *pass-along readership.*

secondary data existing data that have been collected for a purpose other than the specific research effort presently being undertaken; includes both *internal secondary data* and *external secondary data.* See also *primary data, internal secondary data,* and *external secondary data.*

secondary demand see *selective demand.*

secondary demand advertising see *selective demand advertising.*

secondary group a group characterized by relatively infrequent interpersonal contact; generally less influential than a primary group in shaping an individual's behavior. Example: a professional association. See also *primary group, formal group, informal group,* and *reference group.*

secondary listening area the outlying or fringe area in which a television's or radio's transmission signal fades out or has static; see also *primary listening area.*

secondary market see *secondary target market.*

secondary readership the number of individuals who read a given issue of a particular publication in addition to the publication's subscribers and news-stand buyers; also called *pass-along readership.*

secondary target market individuals, households, or market segment that a marketer considers worthy of its attention as an attractive opportunity for sales and profit, but not at the level of another more attractive opportunity; while the emphasis is on the primary target market, some part of the marketing and promotion program is intended to extend and be appealing to another consumer group. For example, a marketer of cameras may see avid amateur photographers as its primary target market for a particular campaign, but may design the campaign in a way that it hopes will attract the occasional photographer, perhaps by media selection, slightly altered appeals, a different model of camera, or other means. See also *target market, target marketing,* and *primary target market.*

sectional magazine a publication whose distribution (i.e., total circulation) covers only a particular geographical region of the United States, rather than the entire country; not the same as a *regional edition.* Also called a *regional magazine.* See also *regional edition.*

seeding see *salting.*

segment see *market segment.*

segment sponsorship see *partial sponsorship.*

segmentation see *market segmentation.*

selective attention the phenomenon by which individuals screen out certain stimuli and focus on others; the processing of just a few ads among the many encountered. Something of a defense mechanism, since people are exposed to a large amount of stimuli in their daily lives. Strongly suggests why the advertiser must be clever in finding approaches to increase the likelihood of its message getting noticed. See also *selective comprehension, selective distortion, selective exposure, selective retention,* and *selective perception.*

selective binding a publishing process that allows any issue of a magazine to be custom-designed for small groups of potential customers, with editorial content and advertising matching the interests of the specific target audience.

selective comprehension the way in which the consumer interprets the advertiser's message; based on a variety of factors, such as the individual's attitudes, motives, or previous experience. A particular interpretation of the information in an advertiser's message often supports the individual's existing beliefs. See also *selective attention, selective distortion, selective exposure, selective retention,* and *selective perception.*

selective demand the demand for a specific brand within a product category; e.g., the demand for Sony digital cameras, GE microwave ovens, or Benjamin Moore house paint. Also called *secondary demand.* See also *primary demand.*

selective demand advertising an advertising message aimed at promoting and stimulating demand for a specific brand in a product category, e.g., stimulating demand for Black & Decker power tools, Tropicana orange juice, or Panasonic video tape recorders; also called *secondary demand advertising.* See also *primary demand advertising.*

selective distortion the phenomenon in which individuals tend to interpret information in a manner that will support their preexisting views; helps to explain why some messages are not received in the way or with the meaning intended by the advertiser or marketer. See also *perception, selective attention, selective comprehension, selective exposure, selective retention,* and *selective perception.*

selective distribution a distribution intensity approach in which the advertiser uses a limited number of retail outlets for its product, fewer than would be used for *intensive distribution* (all available outlets) and more than for *exclusive distribution* (one or extremely few outlets); only those retailers that are most compatible with the advertiser, its philosophy, and its approach to marketing, advertising, and promotion are used. See also *intensive distribution* and *exclusive distribution.*

selective exposure   the process whereby an individual chooses whether or not to be exposed to a stimulus such as an advertiser's message; for example, changing the television channel during a commercial break or rapidly turning a magazine page containing an advertisement. See also *perception, selective attention, selective comprehension, selective distortion, selective retention,* and *selective perception.*

selective magazine   see *special-interest magazine.*

selective marketing   see *differentiated marketing.*

selective perception   essentially, an individual's defense mechanism, whereby he or she filters the large number of marketing stimuli competing for attention; the filtering process determines what stimuli are received and how they are interpreted. A process by which individuals screen out some ideas, information, and messages, but take in or retain others, which they then interpret according to their personal experience, self-concept, attitudes, beliefs, and other factors. A process by which individuals give greater awareness to stimuli (e.g., advertising, a point-of-purchase display, a coupon, an infomercial) that are relevant to their needs and interests. See also *perception, selective attention, selective comprehension, selective distortion, selective exposure,* and *selective retention.*

selective retention   the idea that consumers do not remember all the information they receive from an advertiser, even though they may have noticed and absorbed that information; the phenomenon in which individuals tend to retain information that is consistent with and supports their existing beliefs and attitudes. See also *perception, selective attention, selective comprehension, selective distortion, selective exposure,* and *selective perception.*

selectivity   an advertising medium's ability to reach a specific target audience.

self-concept   see *self-image.*

self-image   the way people perceive themselves, in terms of who they are and who they want to be; see also *ideal self.*

self-expressive benefits   the emotional gain consumers perceive will be theirs by purchasing and using a product or brand they believe will enhance their standing or image with other people or groups they consider important, such as a *reference group.*

self-liquidating premium   a sales promotion technique in which a *premium* is offered to consumers for a fee that simply covers the premium plus handling costs; the advertiser breaks even, making no profit on the offer.

self-mailer   in direct mail, promotional material that is delivered without an envelope; e.g., a brochure or sales literature that is folded and stapled or taped.

self-regulation   the practice by which members of the advertising industry supervise, govern, and control their own members, programs, and activities so as to avoid outside interference such as government; voluntary self-governance by members of the advertising industry (including advertisers, advertising agencies, the media, trade associations), and businesses. See also *federal regulation, state regulation, local regulation,* and *in-house regulation.* Also see *Better Business Bureau (BBB), Council of Better Business Bureaus (CBBB), National Advertising Division (NAD),* and *Children's Advertising Review Unit (CARU),* plus various industry trade associations and organizations.

sell-in   the process of getting the advertiser's product through the distribution channel to the retailer in advance of a particular promotion campaign; making sure the product is available in sufficient quantities for a forthcoming campaign.

selling agent   an agent *middleman* (does not take title to the goods) that assumes the entire marketing job for the manufacturer, not just selling; has considerable flexibility and latitude in virtually every phase of the marketing program. See also *manufacturers' representative.*

selling premise   the rationale underlying a particular advertising message; see also *copy platform.*

selling samples   small versions of a product or, sometimes, the regular product, given by the sales force to the trade to acquaint them with a new product that is soon to be distributed; also refers to the sample given to the trade as part of the selling process in the attempt to land a new account.

selling up   the practice of convincing the consumer to purchase a more expensive product than the one that first captured his or her interest.

sell-off   selling advertising time or space that previously had been sold but will not be used by the buyer; also refers to the last-minute sale of still-available time or space.

sell-off period   in sales promotion, the beginning-to-end duration of a special deal or any other sales promotion effort; the time period during which a product is sold as a special deal.

sell-through   a promotional effort aimed at increasing the rate at which an advertiser's product is sold at the retail level; not to be confused with a *sell-in,* or getting the product to the retailer in advance of a campaign. See also *sell-in.*

sell-through quantity   the quantity of merchandise needed for the entire duration of a particular sales promotion program, such as a consumer deal, *coupon* program, *premium* offer, or *point-of-purchase display.*

semantic differential scale   a research technique using a scale that lists several sets of bipolar adjectives (or opposites), and on which a respondent rates a particular object, such as a company, a specific product, or a firm's advertising, along a continuum between the bipolar adjectives; a rating scale with polar adjectives or phrases on each end of the scale, providing seven interval spaces, for example, for a respondent to rate a particular object or topic. An overall company, product, or promotion profile can be generated from results. Example: research asking respondents to rate a particular company's advertising on several bases, shown on a scale with polar opposites such as effective-ineffective, lively-dull, believable-not believable, likable-not likable, and informative-not informative. Also called an *Osgood Scale.*

sender   the originator of an advertising or promotional message; see also *encoding.*

sentence completion test   in qualitative advertising research, a projective technique in which the respondent is given incomplete sentences and asked to complete the thought for each one; e.g., "People who buy season tickets to professional football games are . . . ," "Going on a cruise is . . . ," "Membership in a country club is . . . ," "Taking pictures with a digital camera is . . . ," "People who buy a Lexus are . . ." See *word association test, story completion test, cartoon method, third-person method,* and *picture response test,* as well as *qualitative research* and *projective research techniques.*

separation   in television and radio advertising, the time period between the airing of commercials of competitors; a station's promise to an advertiser that no competitor's product will be advertised within a particular time period of the advertiser's commercial. Sometimes applies to print advertising and the amount of space (i.e., number of pages) between competitors' advertisements. Often called *product protection, competitive separation, or commercial protection.*

sequence   the particular order in which an individual reads or views the several elements as they are arranged in an advertisement; e.g., eye movement in looking over an advertisement, going from headline, to graphic, to body copy, to tagline.

serif   in print advertising, the small lines that appear at the ends of the main strokes in a type font, as opposed to a *sans serif* typeface; see also *sans serif.*

server   on the Internet, the software program that makes it possible for a user's computer to "talk" with it and exchange information with it.

services   intangible benefit-producing activities that are offered for sale to consumers, but that do not provide the consumer with ownership; e.g., banking, travel, movie theaters, home repair, health care. Also refers to the benefits accompanying a physical product, such as a repair contract for a home appliance or computer.

service mark   the same as a *trademark,* except that it identifies and distinguishes the source of a service rather than a product; a name or a symbol for a service, as opposed to a tangible good; see also *trademark, certification mark,* and *Lanham Act.*

services advertising   advertising messages promoting services, as opposed to products; see also *nonproduct advertising* and *product advertising.*

services marketing   all the activities and processes relating to the marketing of services or something intangible, as opposed to a physical object or tangible good; see also *services, product marketing,* and *product.*

service wholesaler a merchant wholesaler (takes title to the goods) that provides all the functions normally associated with wholesaling; also called *full-function wholesaler* and *full-service wholesaler.* See also *middleman functions* and *limited-function wholesaler.*

session fee compensation paid by an advertiser to performers for a television or radio commercial shooting session; see also *residual* and *talent cost.*

setback in outdoor billboard advertising, the distance between the line of travel and the center of the poster, i.e., the distance from the area where the traffic flows to the advertising structure.

set shoot in television commercial production, filming the commercial at a studio or other site specifically designed and constructed to be the setting for the commercial; see also *location shoot* and *production stage.*

sets-in-use technically, the number of television sets or radios that are turned on, or in use, at any given time; popular usage, though, refers to the percentage of households that have a television set or radio turned on at any given time. See also *households using radio (HUR)* and *households using television (HUT).*

set-tuning meter an electronic device used to measure how television programs perform in specific markets throughout the United States, i.e., local television markets; located in 55 of the largest television markets in the country, these approximately 18,000 meters provide the tuning status of household television sets (set on/set off, channel, time). Results attained from these meters provide the basis for *overnight ratings.* Tuning status data are supplemented by diary information collected from separate samples of homes in these markets. Especially important during the *sweeps* months of November, February, May, and July. Not to be confused with the *People Meter,* which measures audiences of programs that reach the entire nation. See also *diary method, metered markets, overnight ratings, People Meter, telephone coincidental,* and *sweeps.*

17.65 percent see *production add-on* and *markup charge.*

75 showing in outdoor advertising, an expression indicating that 75 percent of a given market's population

will be reached by (i.e., will have the opportunity to see) a particular advertising message by virtue of the number and placement of an advertiser's billboard panels in the market, in a 30-day period; see also *outdoor advertising, showing, 25 showing, 50 showing,* and *100 showing.*

shadow shopping see *mystery shopper studies.*

share the percentage of those television sets or radios in use that are tuned to a given program during a specified time period; also called *program share.* Example: in a given geographic market and at a particular time of the day, if 400,000 television households have their television sets turned on and 88,000 of those households with their sets on at that time are watching a specific program, that program is said to have a 22 share. See also *program share, rating,* and *sets-in-use.*

share of audience see *share.*

share of market a given brand's percentage of total sales in a product category.

share of mind the percentage of a particular population or audience who indicate awareness of or preference for a specific brand within a product category; the extent to which a particular brand is thought of within the context of a specific product category. Also referred to as *brand association.*

share of space the percentage of the retail space taken up by each brand carried by a store.

share of voice a brand's share of the total advertising expenditures for a product category; calculated by dividing brand spending by total category spending. May be the percentage of all promotion, not just advertising, in a specific product category that is spent by a particular brand.

share point a share of the audience or the market, with each share equal to one percent of the total; see also *rating point.*

shared identification in television, a station's identification (ID) during a commercial, with the call letters superimposed on the television screen; also called a *shared ID.*

shared mailing see *cooperative mailing.*

shelf card a display card on a retail store shelf.

shelf display the arrangement of goods on a retail shelf.

shelf talker   on a retail store shelf, a sign with an advertising message that hangs over the shelf's edge.

shelter magazine   a periodical whose editorial content focuses on the home, including decorating, maintenance, improvement ideas, and a variety of other domestic matters; e.g., *Better Homes & Gardens.*

Sherman Antitrust Act   an 1890 act designed to prohibit monopolies and to assure free competition, in opposition to the concentration of economic power in large corporations; see also *Clayton Antitrust Act.*

shipper display   a specially designed shipping carton that, when opened, is formed into a display unit for the product, complete with signage.

shock-effect advertising   intentionally controversial advertising; also called simply *shock advertising.*

shoehorning   inserting or cramming additional *copy* into an existing advertisement or commercial where, at first glance, there is little or no room for it; often a last-minute move and always one that must be done very carefully.

shoot   in the production of television advertising, the actual filming of the commercial; see also *location shoot, set shoot,* and *production stage.*

shop   see *advertising agency.*

shopper   see *shopping newspaper.*

shoppers network/programs   in television, cable networks and individual programs that feature sales presentations, demonstrations, and product offerings available for immediate purchase from home via direct response such as telephoning an order.

shopping products   products for which consumers typically make comparisons among different brands or versions before buying in the belief the end result will be worth the effort; comparison criteria include product features, brand image, price, service, warranty, store reputation, and other factors the consumer thinks relevant in making the right buying decision. See also *homogeneous shopping products, heterogeneous shopping products, consumer products classification system, convenience products, specialty products,* and *unsought products.*

shopping newspaper   a free publication, usually a weekly, containing mostly advertising and distributed to households or available to shoppers at the *point-of-purchase;* may contain a small amount of editorial matter. Also called a *shopper.*

short list   the finalists in an advertiser's search for a new advertising agency.

short rate   an advertising rate charged by a media vehicle to an advertiser that does not use the entire amount of space or time it contracted for over a given period of time; the rate is determined by the difference between the standard rate for the actual amount of space or time used and the discounted or lower contract rate negotiated at the start. The difference between the earned rate and the contract rate. Essentially a penalty fee paid by the advertiser for not fulfilling the space or time requirements set forth in the contract. See also *contract rate* and *earned rate.*

show producer   see *trade show producer.*

showing   in outdoor advertising, the total number of *panels* in a buy; most commonly, specified in terms of a #100 showing, #75 showing, #50 showing, or #25 showing, with the numbers relating directly to the percentage of a market's population. For example, in a market whose population is 800,000 people, a #50 showing will deliver 400,000 daily *exposures* (i.e., 50 percent of the market's population). The showing *size* (e.g., 100, 75) does not indicate the number of poster panels used. In *transit advertising,* the term refers to the collection of *car cards* in the vehicles of a transit line system, with a rating based on the percentage of the transit line's vehicles having a car card. See also *outdoor advertising, 25 showing, 50 showing, 75 showing, 100 showing,* as well as *full showing, half run, half showing,* and *riding the showing.* Also see *gross rating point (GRP)* and *target rating point (TRP).*

side position   in *transit advertising,* placement of a *car card* above the windows on a vehicle's sides; also, placement of advertising posters on the exterior sides of a bus or other transit vehicle.

sign   any structure used to display information about a product, service, or whatever the client is promoting; see also *out-of-home advertising, outdoor advertising, bulletin, point-of-purchase advertising,* and *poster.*

signage   in sponsorship marketing, the banners, billboards, electronic messages, and other fixed-position messages identifying sponsors that are displayed on the site of the sponsored property.

signature the name of the advertiser, usually appearing at the end of a commercial or the bottom of an advertisement; often used together with the advertiser's *logo.*

signature cut see *logo.*

Silver Anvil Awards annual awards given by the Public Relations Society of America in recognition of public relations programs that meet the highest standards of performance by incorporating sound research, planning, execution, and measures of appraisal.

Simmons data see *Simmons Market Research Bureau (SMRB).*

Simmons Market Research Bureau (SMRB) a multimedia research company with an enormous database of more than 8,000 brands in over 400 product categories, statistics on all media, and extremely detailed data on consumer lifestyles, demographics, product purchasing habits, use and consumption, media use, and other aspects of shopping behavior; provides both syndicated and custom research.

simple random sample in survey research for marketing and advertising, a type of probability sample that employs a method of choosing respondents in which each individual in a given population has an equal chance of being selected; see also *probability sample, stratified random sample, cluster sample, non-probability sample,* and *survey method.*

simulated test market in marketing and advertising research, an experiment in which selected participants are observed or questioned about their attitudes, opinions, and thoughts toward the product or advertising or whatever is being tested; also called a *laboratory test* or *test market simulation.* See also *field test* and *experiment method.*

simulcast a simultaneous broadcast of one radio or television station's program by another station.

single target market approach after identifying and evaluating market segments, selecting one as the target segment and then designing a *marketing mix* for that specific market; see also *multiple target market approach.*

single-rate card a media rate card containing one rate for all advertisers, on a per-insertion basis, with no rate differences according to time, position, or volume of advertising.

single-source data data collected on the product purchase behavior and media habits of a single household or family or an individual; data accumulated by monitoring a specific consumer group's (such as a family or household) exposure to advertising and promotion efforts and then tracking the group's decision making and purchase behavior over time (e.g., professional women 35–44 with a household of 3+ and a household income of $80,000 or more). A technique that has come about with increasingly sophisticated research methods and advances in information technology such as *scanners.* See also *tracking, BehaviorScan, InfoScan,* and *SCANTRACK.*

single-source tracking measures through the use of devices that record television viewing habits, along with grocery store scanning technology, individual consumers are monitored as to the brands they purchase, their exposure to advertising, and their use of sales promotion offers such as coupons; an approach to *posttesting* advertising messages.

single-source tracking services research firms that collect and analyze individual consumers' data on brands purchased and media exposure, in addition to complete demographic data; see also *single-source data, BehaviorScan, InfoScan,* and *SCANTRACK.*

situational determinants factors associated with the setting in which a product or service is to be used that influence a consumer's product and brand choice.

situation analysis in the promotion planning process, the investigation and evaluation of the factors that influence the development of a promotion strategy; includes exploration and analysis of internal and external capabilities and resources, previous promotion programs, the product's relative strengths and weaknesses, threats and opportunities, buyer behavior, competition, and the environment. See also *internal analysis* and *external analysis.*

:60 designation for a 60-second television or radio commercial.

sizzle the pleasure, stimulation, and excitement generated by advertising or other marketing activity.

skewing in allocating advertising effort, putting extra weight or activity toward a particular market segment; see also *geographical weighting.*

skimming price policy in new-product pricing, when the marketer sets a high initial price, expecting to capitalize on the inelastic demand for the product, i.e., where the consumer is not price-sensitive in buying the product; future price cuts are aimed at the more price-sensitive segments of the market. Often an effective way to segment the market based on price-sensitivity. See also *penetration price policy, introductory price dealing, elastic demand,* and *inelastic demand.*

skyscraper ad   in Internet advertising, a vertical ad shape with 120×600 dimensions (width × height, in pixels); a *wide skyscraper ad* = 160×600 dimensions. See also *pixels, banner ad, rectangle ad,* and *square pop-up ad.*

skywriting   an advertising message delivered in the sky by a specially equipped small airplane that discharges smoke to form the message; see also *aerial advertising.*

slice-of-life format   in advertising, a creative *execution format* that presents a realistic enactment of a common, everyday-life situation featuring typical people, often appearing as a "mini-drama" when combined with a *problem-solution format;* e.g., a commercial in which a person observes new siding being installed on the house next door and engages in conversation with the homeowner, or two people enjoying a homemade sandwich and chatting about food storage bags while watching a kids' baseball game. See also *straightforward factual, news, demonstration, problem-solution, dramatization, symbolic association, fantasy, animation, still-life, humor, spokesperson, testimonial,* and *comparison formats.*

slick   a print advertisement proof made on glossy paper and suitable for reproduction; e.g., a *camera-ready advertisement* supplied by a manufacturer to a retailer in a *cooperative advertising program.* Also may refer to a *slick magazine.*

slick magazine   a magazine printed on glossy paper stock; sometime referred to as a *slick publication.*

sliding commission   see *sliding rate (scale).*

sliding rate (scale)   for time or space in a *media vehicle,* an advertising rate that decreases as the amount of time or space used by an advertiser in that vehicle increases within a specified period of time; may also refer to the advertising agency's compensation plan that calls for the agency commission to decrease with an increase in the amount of time or space bought on behalf of an advertiser. See also *negotiated commission.*

Also see *agency compensation method, agency commission, fee method, commission method, combination method,* and *performance-based method.*

slogan   an advertiser's statement, phrase, or theme presented in memorable words to provide continuity or linkage between the different advertisements and commercials in an advertising or promotion campaign; i.e., something of a *positioning* statement. Conveys the image, identity, and position of a brand or organization. Gets people to remember and associate. Comes from the Gaelic "*slugh gairm,*" meaning "battle cry." Also called a *tag line* or a *theme line.*

slotting allowance   a fee charged by retailers to manufacturers for the shelf space, or slot, occupied by a new product; the fee can be paid as a direct cash payment or in free merchandise. Considered part of *trade sales promotion.* Also called a *slotting fee* or a *stocking allowance.*

sneak-in   in television and radio advertising, bringing music in at a low volume, gradually increasing it to the desired level; done for effect and to prevent the audience from being distracted from the commercial's message.

snipe   an adhesive *patch* or vinyl sheet that is affixed to an outdoor poster subsequent to the poster going up; e.g., a sheet bearing the local advertiser's name, address, and telephone number (e.g., a dealer imprint), or, more commonly, a patch that is pasted over an existing portion of a poster to make a correction in the copy or to change information such as price or to announce the final days of an offer. Sometimes referred to as an *overlay.* See also *dealer imprint.*

social class   a person's standing in the social hierarchy; e.g., upper class, middle class, or lower class. Reasonably similar groupings of people based on shared lifestyles, values, interests, behaviors, and other characteristics. One of the variables used in *market segmentation.*

social influences   in consumer behavior, the interpersonal elements and relationships that affect an individual's buying process; i.e., the way in which an individual interacts with other people, such as family, friends, *opinion leaders, reference groups,* and others. See also *psychological influences.*

social marketing   marketing communications programs aimed at creating and maintaining positive attitudes toward significant social issues, such as conservation of natural resources, responsible drinking, a drug-free environment, or recycling.

social responsibility for a marketer or advertiser, the obligation to operate and act in the public interest as determined by what society believes is right, and generally improve the well-being of people.

social risk in consumer decision making, the chance the product purchased will not meet with the approval of friends or relatives; see also *risk-taking, performance risk, financial risk, physical risk,* and *time-loss risk.*

soft goods see *nondurable goods.*

soft-sell advertising an advertising style in which the message uses a low-key approach to communicating, as opposed to being bold, direct, fast-paced, aggressive, and, often, intimidating; see also *hard-sell advertising.*

sole sponsor when a company is the exclusive, i.e., the only, sponsor of a property.

sound effects (SFX) in television and radio advertising, the audio that accompanies the picture and/or spoken words in a commercial to add a particular feeling to the advertising; e.g., the sound of a crowd at a ballgame, the roar of an automobile engine, the howling wind, or the sound of a golf ball falling into the cup. A type of special effects, which actually encompasses a broader range of activity. See also *special effects.*

source the originator of a promotional message who creates the message and sends it through a channel to the receiver; e.g., an advertiser. See also *encoding.*

source credibility the extent to which an audience believes an advertiser's message, an occurrence governed by the audience's perception of the sender's expertise, trustworthiness, accuracy, and objectivity.

source effect the impact a message has by virtue of the power, attractiveness, and credibility of the sender of the message.

space in print media, that part of a publication or surface (in outdoor or transit advertising) that is available for advertising; on the Internet, the location on a Web page in which an advertisement can be placed.

space bank in print advertising, a media buying service's inventory of space available for sale to advertisers and agencies; see also *time bank.*

space buyer an individual at an advertising agency or a media buying organization who is responsible for purchasing advertising space in print media for clients; the space equivalent of a *time buyer.* See also *time buyer* and *media buyer.*

space charge the cost of advertising space in a given print media vehicle.

space contract a formal agreement between an advertiser and a print media vehicle, in which the vehicle guarantees the advertiser a particular rate for a given period of time, based on the amount of space the advertiser expects to use; see also *short rate.*

space discount a reduction in the cost of a print media vehicle's advertising space offered to the advertiser, based on the amount of space purchased in a specified period of time.

space order in print advertising, an advertiser's formal agreement or commitment to use advertising space in a particular publication such as a specific issue of a magazine; also called an *insertion order.* See also *insertion order.*

space position value (SPV) in outdoor advertising, a measure of the suitability or effectiveness of a poster panel location; typically based on factors such as length of approach with visibility, travel speed, panel angle to the road, and adjacency to other panels. See also *rated structure.*

space schedule a listing of all the print advertising space to be used in a campaign, including the media vehicle, the name of the advertisement, and the date, size, position, and cost of each ad.

spec advertising see *speculative presentation.*

special effects in television or radio advertising, visual and/or audio effects that are beyond the normal or the usual; see also *sound effects (SFX).*

special event a particular occasion that is noteworthy or distinctive by its specific purpose or cause, and that provides a venue for an advertiser to deliver its message to a focused and targeted audience; e.g., a music festival, a 10K foot race for a specific charitable cause, or a Little League baseball game to benefit local police and firefighters. See also *sponsorship.*

special-interest magazine a publication whose editorial content focuses on a particular activity or subject and is aimed toward devotees of that activity or interest: e.g., *Runner's World, Skiing, Car and Driver, Golf Digest, Popular Photography.* Also called an *enthusiast publication, niche magazine,* or *custom magazine.*

special-interest marketing   see *diversity marketing.*

specialty advertising   a sales promotion tool in which useful items such as caps, pens, and coffee mugs are imprinted with an advertiser's name, logo, message, slogan, or other promotional words and given away as goodwill and a reminder of the advertiser's name; commonly referred to as *promotional products marketing.* See also *advertising promotional products.*

Specialty Advertising Association International the trade association representing the interests of specialty advertising practitioners; dedicated to promoting the highest standards of excellence and integrity in the specialty advertising industry, and promoting the use of specialty advertising as an integral part of promotion programs.

specialty products   products, especially a particular brand, that the consumer feels compelled to have and is habitually willing to make a special effort to locate and buy; the consumer insists on having the product for its unique or distinctive attributes. See also *consumer products classification system, convenience products, shopping products,* and *unsought products.*

specifications   formal guidelines, instructions, rules, and requirements that must be met in dealing with a particular organization or party; e.g., a magazine advertisement submitted to a particular media vehicle is subject to certain requirements as to the precise form in which it is handed over to the publication, or a billboard advertisement must meet certain dimensional requirements.

spectacular   a very large, elaborate, built-to-order outdoor advertising sign with *embellishments* such as lights, brilliant color, movement, action, and other special mechanical and electrical devices and effects; placed in prime high-traffic areas, it has the highest unit cost of all outdoor signs. Larger than the standard *bulletin,* which is 14′ × 48′. See also *bulletin, permanent bulletin,* and *rotary bulletin.*

speculative pitch   see *speculative presentation.*

speculative presentation   presentation of advertising and promotion ideas or even an entire marketing communications campaign plan to a prospective client, without the client sharing in the costs associated with the preparation and presentation of the campaign's elements and executions; sometimes involves elaborate plans and high costs to the agency. A high-risk attempt to win an account. Also called a *speculative pitch.*

specs   see *specifications.*

spiffs   see *push money (PM).*

spill-in   when a television signal from outside the area penetrates a local market area; within a given market, the viewership of television stations that originates outside that market and is expressed as a percentage of the total viewing within the market that is receiving signals.

spill-out   when a television signal goes beyond its own market area to another station's market; the portion of a television station's total audience that falls outside the originating station's market. Generally expressed as a percentage.

spillover media   see *spill-in* and *spill-out.*

spin   a public relations phenomenon in which there is an attempt to shape certain news in the media so it receives extensive coverage; also refers to a situation where an advertising campaign is so notable that it generates considerable follow-on publicity in the media. Also called *top-spin* or *over-spin.*

SPINdex   an index score of the extent of editorial coverage of issues, topics, products, and other marketing-related matters by major media outlets in five categories—network television, daily newspapers, newsweekly magazines, trade magazines, and wire services. A service of *Medialink Research.*

splash page   in Internet advertising, a preliminary page that precedes the regular homepage of a Web site, usually promoting a particular site feature or providing advertising. Also referred to as an *interstitial.*

split commercial   see *piggyback.*

split run   placing two or more versions of an advertisement in alternate copies of the same newspaper or magazine issue, or, in the case of geographical editions, the different versions of the advertisement may be placed in different regional or metro editions, depending on the various editions offered by the publisher; can be achieved using a *geographic split* or a *demographic split.* Also, there can be a *subscription/ newsstand sales split* or an every-other-copy split, called an *A/B split.* See also *split-run test, demographic split run, geographic split run, subscription/newsstand split run,* and *A/B split.*

split :30   a 30-second (:30) television commercial in which the same advertiser promotes two different products with two different messages; e.g., the :30 is broken into two :15s, or a :20 and a :10.

split-cable testing   in advertising research, a technique in which two or more groups or separate samples of subscriber households in a cable television system are exposed to different commercials; by monitoring the purchases of the different receivers of the commercials, the advertiser can make a judgment as to the effectiveness of each commercial. Can also determine best commercials as to recall and persuasion effects via a follow-up telephone survey, e.g., *day-after-recall* method. See also *BehaviorScan* and *day-after-recall.*

split-list experiment   in direct marketing, a type of effectiveness-testing in which two or more versions of a direct-mail piece or package are sent to different individuals on a mailing list; segment A gets ad or package A and segment B gets ad or package B. Used to determine which version generates the best response. The direct-mail version of *split run* and *split-cable testing.*

split-run test   for purposes of measuring the effectiveness of advertisements, placement of two or more different versions of an ad in alternate copies of the same publication (newspaper or magazine) on the same day or in the same edition; record is kept of coupon returns, inquiries, trial orders, or whatever *direct response* action is requested in the ads. See *split run, demographic split run, geographic split run, subscription/newsstand split run,* and *A/B split.*

spokesperson format   in advertising, a creative *execution format* featuring an individual who speaks on behalf of an advertiser or its product; the person may be a celebrity, expert, authority figure, created character, or a typical consumer. If the spokesperson is a user of the product and is speaking from actual experience, he or she is providing a *testimonial.* All testimonials come from spokespersons, but not all spokespersons provide testimonials. All spokespersons are used to

provide endorsements. For example, a commercial featuring a garage mechanic recommending Fram oil filters, an advertisement with a veterinarian recommending a certain Alpo product for older dogs, a commercial with Reba McIntire speaking on the importance of finishing high school, or a commercial in which Dale Earnhardt, Jr. pushes Goodyear tires. See also *straightforward factual, news, demonstration, problem-solution, slice-of-life, dramatization, symbolic association, fantasy, animation, still-life, humor, testimonial,* and *comparison formats.* Also see *endorsement.*

sponsor   an entity such as a company that pays a *property* (e.g., a cultural event, an entertainment tour, a festival, a sporting event or series, or a sports team) for the right to advertise and promote itself in association with the property; also refers to an advertiser who pays for commercial time on television or radio. See also *title sponsor, primary sponsor, associate sponsor, presenting sponsor, naming rights, right-of-first-refusal, sponsorship,* and *property.*

sponsor identification   the brief mention of the advertisers on a particular television or radio program, prior to and/or after the program segment in which the particular sponsor's commercial appears.

sponsored imagery   see *virtual placement process.*

Sponsors Report   comprehensive documentation of sponsor exposure during nationally televised sports and special events, by means of electronically monitoring and tabulating in-focus exposure time; contains data on each individual sponsor. In evaluating sponsorship impact, a value is derived by combining the exact visual time and sponsor mentions during a telecast and comparing it to the broadcaster's nondiscounted rate per :30 commercial, i.e., what the combined in-focus exposure time and sponsor mentions would have cost the sponsor to purchase commercial time on the telecast. A service of Joyce Julius & Associates. See also *in-focus exposure time, NTIV Analysis,* and *Joyce Julius & Associates.*

sponsorship   the practice whereby a company or a product (i.e., *sponsor*) pays a *property* (e.g., a cultural event, an entertainment tour, a festival, a sporting event or series or a sports team) for the right to advertise and promote itself in association with the property; in television or radio advertising, when an advertiser takes over the entire responsibility for producing a program and is the sole exclusive advertiser on that show; may also refer to when one advertiser purchases only a part of a television or radio program, and another advertiser also purchases a part. Often a big part of a company's efforts at *relationship marketing*. See also *cosponsorship* and *relationship marketing.*

sponsorship fee   payment made by a company to a *property* for some level of sponsorship rights; usually refers to actual cash payment, though may refer to products or services given in lieu of cash. See also *in-kind sponsorship deal.*

sponsorship marketing   all the activities and processes that go into a marketer's sponsorship program; see also *sponsorship* and *relationship marketing.*

sponsorship property   see *property.*

sports marketing   the practice by which a company links itself to or sponsors a sports team, league, or competition.

spot   a television or radio time slot designated for a commercial; the television or radio advertising time that is purchased directly from a local station (i.e., on a market-by-market basis), as opposed to a national *network*. When a national advertiser buys time on a local station, it is a *national spot,* though usually referred to as simply a *spot.* When a local advertiser buys time on a local station, it is a *local spot,* though usually referred to as *local radio* or *local television.*

spot advertising   television or radio advertising done by national or local advertisers on individual stations in which the commercial time is purchased directly from each local station; see also *local spot* and *national spot.*

spot announcement   an advertiser's commercial message that runs between television or radio programs; time is purchased directly from individual stations, and placement ranges from national to local. Also, popular usage makes reference to any advertising in which the commercial time is bought from a local station and, therefore, the commercial itself becomes a spot announcement or *spot.*

spot radio   radio time purchased by national advertisers from individual local stations for airing commercials.

spot schedule   a listing of all spot television or spot radio advertising time to be used in a campaign, including the individual station, program, name of the commercial, and the date, *daypart, position,* length, and cost of each commercial in the schedule.

spot television   broadcast or cable television time purchased by national advertisers from individual local stations for airing commercials; see also *local spot* and *national spot.*

spotted map   in out-of-home advertising, a map of a specific market that shows, by means of dots drawn in or pinned on, the location of advertising structures available and/or already bought; i.e., the locations of the outdoor units comprising an outdoor advertising campaign. Also called a *location map.*

spread   in print advertising, an advertisement that is printed across two facing pages of a publication; also called a *double truck, two-page spread,* or *double spread.* See also *double truck* and *two-page spread.* Also see *two pages facing.*

SQAD (Service Quality Analytics Data)   an industry leader in providing, via its *Media Market Guide,* comprehensive media data for advertisers, agencies, media buying services, TV and radio stations, TV program syndicators, magazines, newspapers, out-of-home organizations, and others; information includes *cost-per-point (CPP)* and *cost-per-thousand (CPM)* data for network and spot television and radio, broken down by :30 and :60 spots on a market-by-market *(DMA)* and *daypart*-specific basis, all updated monthly, plus key data on other major media.

square pop-up ad   in Internet advertising, an ad shape with 250×250 dimensions (width $\times$ height, in pixels); see also *pixels, banner ad, skyscraper ad, rectangle ad,* and *pop-up advertising.*

SRDS Business Publication Advertising Source a directory that provides comprehensive information on trade publications, including advertising rates, closing dates, production specifications, contact information, and links to online *media kits;* see also *Standard Rate and Data Service (SRDS).*

SRDS Canadian Advertising Rates & Data   a directory that provides comprehensive information on a broad range of Canadian media, demographics, and advertising rates; see also *Standard Rate and Data Service (SRDS).*

SRDS Community Publication Advertising Source a directory that provides comprehensive information on local weeklies and shoppers, including advertising rates, closing dates, production specifications, and contact information; see also *Standard Rate and Data Service (SRDS).*

SRDS Consumer Magazine Advertising Source a directory that provides comprehensive information on domestic and international consumer magazines, including advertising rates, closing dates, production specifications, contact information, and links to online *media kits;* also identifies links to magazine Web sites and audit statements on readership for each magazine. See also *Standard Rate and Data Service (SRDS).*

SRDS Direct Marketing List Source a directory that provides comprehensive information on mailing list rentals, including list sources, selections, and costs; see also *Standard Rate and Data Service (SRDS).*

SRDS Hispanic Media and Market Source a directory that provides comprehensive information on the demographics of the Hispanic market and how to reach it; see also *Standard Rate and Data Service (SRDS).*

SRDS Interactive Advertising Source a directory that provides comprehensive information on online advertising vehicles, including advertising rates, contact information, usage, audience profiles, and links to Web sites and audit statements for each site; see also *Standard Rate and Data Service (SRDS).*

SRDS International Media Guides a directory that provides comprehensive information on newspapers, consumer magazines, and business publications in more than 200 countries, including advertising rates, contact information, and production specifications; see also *Standard Rate and Data Service (SRDS).*

SRDS Mexican Audiovisual Rates & Data a directory that provides comprehensive information on Mexican television and radio stations; see also *Standard Rate and Data Service (SRDS).*

SRDS Mexican Print Media Rates & Data a directory that provides comprehensive information on Mexican consumer and business magazines and newspapers, as well as outdoor and transit media; see also *Standard Rate and Data Service (SRDS).*

SRDS Newspaper Advertising Source a directory that provides comprehensive information on daily newspapers, newspaper groups, ethnic newspapers, college newspapers, comics, and newspaper-distributed magazines, including advertising rates, closing dates, production specifications, and contact information; also includes links to online *media kits* and newspaper Web sites that give additional readership information. See also *Standard Rate and Data Service (SRDS).*

SRDS Out-of-Home Advertising Source a directory that provides comprehensive information on a vast range of out-of-home media (21 media categories, including outdoor, stadium, hotel, bus shelter, transit, shopping mall, airport, college campus, event, and others), including advertising rates, closing dates, production specifications, contact information, and links to Web sites; see also *Standard Rate and Data Service (SRDS).*

SRDS Print Media Production Source a directory that provides comprehensive information on production specifications and deadlines for consumer as well as business magazines and newspapers; see also *Standard Rate and Data Service (SRDS).*

SRDS Radio Advertising Source a directory that provides comprehensive information on AM and FM commercial radio stations, including format, demographics, and contact information; see also *Standard Rate and Data Service (SRDS).*

SRDS Technology Media Source a directory that provides comprehensive information on media targeted to the high-tech industry, including advertising rates, closing dates, production specifications, and contact information; see also *Standard Rate and Data Service (SRDS).*

SRDS TV & Cable Source a directory that provides comprehensive information on broadcast, cable, and syndicated television stations and networks throughout the entire country; see also *Standard Rate and Data Service (SRDS).*

stacked panels in out-of-home advertising, structures with *facings* built on top of each other; also called *deck panels.* See also *premiere square.*

stadium signage billboards or other displays at a sports venue; may be referred to as *arena signage.*

staggered schedule several advertisements scheduled in two or more periodicals in an alternating pattern; e.g., four different ads scheduled in four separate periodicals, with each ad appearing in each periodical once every four weeks on a set schedule over a period of time.

stakeholders the different groups of people in whom a company or organization has a special interest by virtue of the relationship each group has with the firm; e.g., customers, employees, suppliers, public interest groups, government agencies, stockholders, financial institutions, and the media. Also referred to as *publics.*

Standard Advertising Unit (SAU) an industry-wide system for standardizing newspaper advertising sizes and page dimensions, so that advertisements will be sized in *columns* and *inches* (rather than *agate lines*) and one *mechanical* will be accepted by all newspapers; *broadsheet* newspapers can take 56 different sizes of ads and *tabloid* newspapers can take 33. Designed by the American Newspaper Publishers Association (ANPA). See also *broadsheet, column inch, agate line, mechanical,* and *tabloid.*

standard art see *stock art.*

standard deviation a statistical measure denoting the extent of variation within a sample.

Standard Directory of Advertisers an advertising industry guide with a comprehensive database containing detailed profiles of approximately 24,000 U.S. and international advertisers, each of which spends more than $200,000 annually on advertising; each listing includes advertising expenditures by specific medium, the advertiser's current agency, annual sales, brand-name information, number of employees, addresses and telephone numbers, Web site, key personnel, contact information, and other important data. One of the *Red Books.*

Standard Directory of Advertising Agencies an advertising industry guide with a comprehensive database containing approximately 13,500 U.S. and international advertising agencies, each of which has detailed information on the accounts currently being served, fields of specialization, breakdown of billings by medium, number of employees, addresses and telephone numbers, Web site, key personnel, contact information, and other important information. One of the *Red Books.*

Standard Directory of International Advertisers & Agencies an advertising industry guide with a comprehensive database on international advertisers and agencies; see also *Standard Directory of Advertisers* and *Standard Directory of Advertising Agencies.* One of the *Red Books.*

Standard Industrial Classification (SIC) until replaced by the *North American Industry Classification System (NAICS),* for many years, the coding system, using numbers, to classify business establishments according to the primary end product manufactured or service provided; developed by the U.S. Bureau of the Budget. See also *North American Industry Classification System (NAICS).*

standard magazine typically measures approximately 10½ inches deep by 8 inches wide, although there are several variations.

Standard Metropolitan Statistical Area (SMSA) no longer used; see also *Metropolitan Area (MA), Metropolitan Statistical Area (MSA), Consolidated Metropolitan Statistical Area (CMSA),* and *Primary Metropolitan Statistical Area (PMSA).*

Standard Rate and Data Service (SRDS) a service that publishes a wide range of data, such as circulation figures, advertising rates, advertising specifications, and contact information, for virtually all media that accept advertising; e.g., consumer magazines, radio, TV & cable, newspapers, business publications, interactive, direct marketing, out-of-home, and others. Service includes volumes for international media and market-specific media (e.g., Hispanic media and markets). See individual listings under *SRDS.*

standardized structure in outdoor advertising, a structure such as a *panel* or a *bulletin* that is built to the specifications of the *Outdoor Advertising Association of America (OAAA).* Also called a *standardized unit.*

standardized unit see *standardized structure.*

Standards of Practice a comprehensive set of fundamental principles advanced by the *American Association of Advertising Agencies (AAAA)* and designed to serve as a model for the highest level of ethical conduct of advertising agencies; a code of conduct that governs the responsibilities and obligations of advertising agencies to their clients, the public, the media, and to their counterparts in the advertising world. See also *American Association of Advertising Agencies (AAAA), Creative Code,* and *Guidelines for Comparative Advertising.*

standard-size newspaper see *broadsheet.*

stand-by space magazine advertising space purchased by an advertiser at a discount, with the agreement that the magazine will run the advertisement at a time and in a position of its choosing, i.e., when the magazine has space its wants to fill in a particular issue; not all magazines do this.

standing ad   an advertisement that runs in several consecutive issues of a publication or on several consecutive episodes of a program; refers to the same advertisement or commercial rather than a different one.

standing-room-only (SRO)   see *last-chance method.*

staples   the basic products that consumers buy frequently and with little thought or effort; the routinely purchased necessities.

Starch   the leading print advertising research organization; part of *RoperASW.*

Starch Readership Studies   in print advertising research and testing, a measurement of the performance of individual magazine advertisements among readers, i.e., the extent to which advertisements are seen and read; respondents who claim readership of the particular magazine issued being tested are placed in a "Noted," "Associated," "Read Some," or "Read Most" category. *Noted* = the percentage of the readers of a specific issue of a magazine who remember having previously seen, i.e., recognized, a particular advertisement at the time of reading the magazine; *Associated* = the percentage of readers of a specific issue of a magazine who not only *noted* a particular advertisement but also saw or read some part of it that clearly indicated the brand or the advertiser; *Read Some* = the percentage of readers of a specific issue of a magazine who read any part of a particular advertisement's copy; *Read Most* = the percentage of readers of a specific issue of a magazine who read one-half or more of the written material in a particular advertisement's copy.

Starch scores   see *Starch Readership Studies.*

state edition   an edition of a national magazine that is only distributed to a particular state in the United States, e.g., *Sports Illustrated* has an edition for every state in the country; an advertiser can buy space in the state edition without having to purchase a larger circulation. A type of *partial-run edition.* See also *demographic edition, metro edition,* and *regional edition.*

statement stuffer   an advertisement or other promotional material enclosed with a monthly statement

or invoice that is mailed to customers by banks, department stores, utility companies, oil companies, and others; also called a *hitchhiker* and a *ride-along,* as well as a *bill enclosure.*

state regulation   legislation, consumer protection measures, and other efforts at the state level designed to monitor and control marketing activities such as advertising; individual states vary in their approach to governing unfair and deceptive marketing practices, but every state has the power to investigate and prosecute cases, and each is a valuable extension of the federal regulatory mechanisms aimed at consumer protection and the preservation of competition. See also *federal regulation, local regulation, in-house regulation,* and *self-regulation.*

static ad placement   in Internet advertising, inserting a "permanent" advertisement into a particular space on a Web site's page; unlike *dynamic ad placement,* the same ad is seen by all visitors to the page on which the ad is located. See also *dynamic ad placement.*

station   in television and radio, a specific free-standing broadcasting facility; in out-of-home advertising, a transit station or terminal.

station break   in television or radio, the time between programs or within a program between individual segments, to permit a station to identify itself by channel number, call letters, or location, as well as to run spot announcements or commercials; specific time is designated by program originator.

station compensation   in broadcast media, payment by a network to an affiliated station for carrying the network's programming; also called *network compensation.*

station domination   in transit advertising, when one advertiser buys all or most of the message spaces in one confined site or terminal, such as a bus, train, or subway station; greatly enhances chance to catch the eyes of on-the-go commuters and passersby.

station identification (ID)   in television or radio, the announcement of the station's channel number, call letters, or location during a station break; see also *station break* and *network identification.*

station lineup   in television and radio, the list of affiliated stations that carry a particular network program.

station log   in television and radio, the official record of a station's programming and commercials during the entire broadcast day.

station option time   see *station time.*

station poster   see *terminal poster.*

station promo   in television or radio, a promotional announcement by a station on its own behalf, or for an advertiser or other entity such as a not-for-profit cause or event at no cost.

station rep   an individual who serves as a sales representative for several different television and/or radio stations in dealings with national advertisers.

station time   in television or radio, broadcast time for which an individual station has the option of selling advertising time (rather than the networks having the option); also called *station option time.* See also *network time.*

status-quo marketing   see *defensive marketing.*

stealomatic   see *ripomatic.*

stereotype   see *mat.*

stickiness   in Web marketing, the extent to which people return to an advertiser's site on a regular basis, as well as the amount of time people spend on the site during any given visit.

still production   in television advertising production, a technique of filming and editing a series of photographs to give the appearance of movement and action in the finished commercial.

still-life format   in advertising, a creative *execution format* in which the product stands alone, with virtually no *copy;* e.g., a full-page magazine advertisement featuring a Coca-Cola soft-drink bottle or an Absolut vodka bottle with no copy, a Nike advertisement showing just a single running shoe with no copy on the page, or a Lexus advertisement consisting of a picture of the automobile with only a single word of copy, "Luxury." See also *straightforward factual, news, demonstration, problem-solution, slice-of-life, dramatization, symbolic association, fantasy, animation, humor, spokesperson, testimonial,* and *comparison formats.*

stimulus   a factor that directly influences the activity of an individual and serves as the impetus for a particular behavior.

stimulus-response theory   the theory that says a stimulus results in a consumer's need or desire to respond to it; e.g., an advertisement featuring an attractive offer results in the consumer taking action to accept the offer. Also called *conditioning theory.*

stock art   ready-made images, designs, and other artwork for advertisers to purchase and use in advertising; also called *standard art* or *library art.*

stock footage   existing film containing a wide variety of shots, scenes, actions, and special effects, available for purchase and use by an advertiser in a television or radio commercial; e.g., a crowd at a baseball game rising and cheering for a ball walloped out of the park.

stock formats   in direct-mail marketing, templates that have preprinted illustrations or headings and subheadings, ready for an advertiser to add its own copy.

stock music   existing, recorded music of all varieties available for purchase and use by an advertiser in a television or radio commercial.

stock photos   existing photographs of all kinds available for purchase and use by an advertiser in an advertisement.

stock posters   in outdoor advertising, existing, premade, and ready-to-go 30-sheet posters in a variety of designs and messages available for purchase and use by an advertiser who only has to add its name to the display via a dealer imprint; may refer to a standard design for a particular business category, available for use by a company or retailer in that category that simply adds its name using a dealer imprint. See also *dealer imprint.*

stock shot   see *stock footage.*

stocking allowance   see *slotting allowance.*

stockpiling   occurs when consumers buy multiple units or greater-than-normal amounts of a product to take advantage of a sales promotion deal.

stockturn rate   the number of times a retailer's or wholesaler's average inventory is sold during a specified period of time, usually one year; indicates how fast a company's or store's inventory is moving. Several ways to calculate the rate, one of which is: unit sales divided by average inventory in units.

stopping power the ability of a commercial or advertisement to arrest the audience's attention; the advertising's capacity to make people take notice.

Storage Instantaneous Audimeter (SIA) an electronic meter, introduced in 1973 by Nielsen, that was attached to the television set and automatically recorded minute-by-minute television viewing data on channel selection, time of day, and length of time the TV was tuned to a particular channel; the meter was connected to a central computer by a telephone line and all data were immediately fed to the central location. The SIA marked the beginning of daily national and local television ratings being available to advertisers and their agencies. See also *diary method, metered-market overnights, Nielsen Media Research, People Meter, set-tuning meter, overnight ratings, telephone coincidental,* and *sweeps.*

store audit a formal accounting and authentication of the product and brand movement at the retail level; in addition to sales numbers, may include other factors such as number of displays or other promotional activities.

store check an examination of a retail store's layout, merchandise display, general décor, selling capabilities, and other factors associated with the store's marketing efforts; a complete review of a store and its way of serving the customer.

store image the particular way in which a retailer is perceived or regarded relative to the competition, by customers as well as noncustomers.

store panel a limited number of representative retail stores that are used regularly by researchers over a period of time to collect data on product movement.

store-redeemable coupon a manufacturer-issued *coupon* that can be redeemed at any retail store carrying the particular product.

store-switching the extent to which consumers change stores to satisfy a particular product or service need; the store equivalent of *brand-switching* behavior.

story completion test in qualitative advertising research, a projective technique in which the respondent completes an already-started story in his or her own words; a variant of the sentence completion test. See also *word association test, sentence completion test, cartoon method, third-person method,* and *picture*

response test, as well as *qualitative research* and *projective research techniques.*

storyboard in the television commercial planning process, a series of drawings depicting a proposed commercial; usually on poster board (later reduced to an 8½″ × 11″ sheet of paper) containing six to twelve television screen frames, sketches are drawn or there is a photo sequence in each frame to show key scenes or action, with the audio part (*voice-over*) and *special effects (SFX)* described below each frame. Used at various stages in the development of a commercial, especially to present to the advertiser for approval. Once the commercial is finished and ready to run, a final storyboard is produced using freeze-frames of the actual commercial, along with the final copy and special effects written below each frame, and printed on coated paper, to serve as a permanent record for the advertising agency and the advertiser. Sometimes used in pretesting the television commercial. See also *pretesting, liveamatic, photomatic, ripomatic, storyboard,* and *rough.*

STP marketing an acronym for *segmentation, targeting, positioning,* or the core activities in designing a marketing communications program; see also *segmentation, targeting,* and *positioning.*

straight announcement a television commercial in which the advertiser's message is delivered by an announcer directly to the camera, or the announcer may be off-screen while a film or other graphic is showing; the oldest form of television commercial.

straight copy in radio advertising, a commercial consisting of words only, with no music or sound effects of any kind; read by the station's talk-show host, disk jockey, newscaster, sportscaster, or other individual on air at the time scheduled for the commercial.

straight-fee method a method of advertising agency compensation; see also *fee method.*

straightforward factual format in advertising, a creative *execution format* involving a basic presentation of information in an unadorned, matter-of-fact manner, essentially letting consumers make their own judgments based on the facts presented; e.g., an anti-drug abuse or antismoking advertisement that presents statistics about drug or tobacco abuse as well as known consequences of product usage, or an ad that focuses solely on the ingredients and nutrition value of a particular food product. See also *news, demonstration, problem-solution, slice-of-life, dramatization, symbolic association, fantasy, animation, still-life, humor, spokesperson, testimonial,* and *comparison formats.*

straight-line copy a print advertisement that uses a direct, no-frills approach to why a consumer will benefit from use of the product or service; typically, the *body copy* starts off immediately explaining the headline, often including a series of bullet points in a straightforward way of selling the product. Also called *straight-selling copy.*

straight-selling copy see *straight-line copy.*

stratified random sample in survey research for marketing and advertising, a type of probability sample using a method of choosing respondents in which the population is broken into mutually exclusive groups (age groups, gender groups, education groups) and a random sample is drawn from each group; see also *probability sample, simple random sample, cluster sample, nonprobability sample,* and *survey method.*

street furniture in out-of-home advertising, a general term for displays located at close proximity to foot traffic or vehicular traffic; e.g., transit shelters, kiosks, shopping mall and convenience store panels, newspaper stands.

street money cash offered to distributors by manufacturers for reaching performance goals or meeting certain conditions asked for by the distributor; essentially the same as *push money.* See also *push money (PM).*

strip ad in newspaper advertising, an elongated or shallow advertisement that runs across the entire bottom of a newspaper page; e.g., an advertisement measuring 3″ deep × 6 columns wide. See also *broadsheet* and *tabloid.*

strip programming a particular television or radio program that airs (different episodes) at the same time of day on consecutive days of the week, e.g., Monday through Friday at 10:00 A.M., or any *daypart* other than *prime time;* as opposed to *checkerboard programming,* which is the standard for prime time. Also refers to a commercial that is scheduled the same way. Also called *stripping* and *across-the-board.* See also *checkerboard programming, strip scheduling, daypart,* and *prime time.*

strip scheduling in television or radio advertising, an advertiser's commercial that is run at the same time on consecutive days of the week, e.g., Monday through Friday at 3:00 P.M.; also called *across-the-board.* See also *strip scheduling.*

stripping see *strip programming.*

structured questions see *closed-end questions.*

stuffer an advertising enclosure that is put in vehicles such as a newspaper, invoice mailing, mailed packages containing purchased merchandise, and the like; see also *envelope stuffer, newspaper insert,* and *package insert.*

stunting in television or radio advertising, frills (stunts) that occur on a station during the *sweeps* months when viewership or listenership is closely monitored for ratings purposes; "sensationalism" designed to get increased ratings during a sweeps period. For example, a television station's week-long or month-long exposé of alleged corruption in a local public service department. See also *sweeps.*

style a manner of expression or presentation; see also *fad* and *fashion.*

subculture in a society, a group of individuals who are distinct in that the members share common characteristics and beliefs, as well as common life experiences.

subhead a secondary headline that is generally smaller than the main headline but larger than the *body copy,* and that often serves as transition from the headline to the body copy of an advertisement; can be above or below the main headline. Contains information that is not in the headline. Also may refer to a heading that sets off blocks of copy in the text part of the advertisement. See also *main head* and *headline.*

subject to nonrenewal advertising time or space that becomes available for purchase if the current advertiser in that time or space does not renew or continue its contract with a *media vehicle.*

subliminal advertising an advertising message that tries to reach the consumer by using a stimulus that is below the conscious awareness or perception of the individual (on a subconscious level); extremely controversial as to whether or not it can be achieved. See also *subliminal perception.*

subliminal perception a process whereby an individual notices a stimulus, such as a "hidden" visual in an advertisement, even though it is below the threshold of conscious awareness; see also *subliminal advertising.*

subscriber an individual who, via a formal purchase agreement, consents to receive a particular medium or media vehicle; e.g., a magazine or cable television service.

subscriber study a research study of the demographic, psychographic, and behavioral characteristics of a periodical's subscribers; typically commissioned to an independent research organization by the publisher, with results summarized and highlighted in the vehicle's *media kit* to attract advertisers.

subscription television (STV) a pay-television service that broadcasts programs using a scrambled signal, with only those homes having a special signal decoder able to receive a clear signal; a monthly fee is charged. See also *pay-per-view (PPV).*

subscription/newsstand sales split run placement of one advertisement in the copies of a publication that are sent to subscribers and a different advertisement in the copies of the same publication that are distributed to newsstands; often used to test and compare the effectiveness of alternate advertisements. See also *split run, split-run test, demographic split run, geographic split run, subscription/newsstand split run,* and *A/B split.*

substantiation of claims see *advertising substantiation.*

substitute products products or services that can be used in place of each other; the price of one product and the demand for the other change in the same direction; e.g., when the price of one product rises, the demand for the substitute also increases. Examples: Rawlings and Spalding basketballs, beef and chicken, butter and oleomargarine, compact disks and audiocassettes. See also *complementary products* and *independent products.*

Sunday supplement a preprinted magazine included as a separate publication, inserted into the Sunday newspaper; may be a *local supplement* (e.g., *The Boston Globe Magazine*), or one that is typically prepared internally by the newspaper and that features local editorial content and advertising, or it may be a *national supplement* (e.g., *Parade Magazine*), or one that is published by an outside organization and is distributed with newspapers throughout the country.

super in a television commercial, *copy* or words superimposed on the screen while the announcer talks or the film is run; e.g., product name, package, slogan, or key benefit placed in front of another picture on the screen. Short for *superimposition.*

superagency an extremely large, full-service advertising agency capable of providing a comprehensive integrated marketing communications program on a worldwide basis.

Superbrands an annual special issue of *Brandweek* magazine that provides data and information on the top 2,000 brands in the United States, covering 25 product categories; information includes rank in the category, identity of the advertising agency, sales figures, advertising expenditures, and a brand equity score. See also *Brandweek.*

superimposition see *super.*

supermarket a large, self-service retail store featuring a wide assortment of food and nonfood items.

superstation an independent television station whose signal is transmitted to cable systems across the country via satellite for greatly expanded coverage and viewership; e.g., WTBS (Atlanta), WGN (Chicago), WWOR (New York).

superstore a retail store that carries a seemingly unlimited assortment of products to meet consumers' far-ranging needs and wants; also called a *supercenter* or *hypermarket.*

supplement see *Sunday supplement.*

suppliers organizations and individuals who provide a wide range of specialized services that assist advertisers and agencies in the creation and execution of advertising and promotional material, such as printing, photography, production, specialty items, and other activities.

supplies products required for the conduct of business that are not part of the finished product.

supply the amount of a product or service available for purchase or use by the consumer; the various amounts of a product or service a producer is able and willing to make and offer for sale at different prices. See also *demand*.

supply chain the entire collection of firms, facilities, and logistics involved in getting products to the market, from raw materials to delivery of the finished product to the final customer; the entire network of producers, suppliers, and distributors involved in the complete set of activities and processes required to get a product into the hands of the customer. Also called *value-delivery network*.

support media the so-called "nontraditional media" used by advertisers; e.g., shopping carts, parking meters, park benches, elevators. Typically used to supplement and reinforce the traditional broadcast and print media used in campaigns. Can also be used to mean any medium that plays a secondary role to another medium that is primary and carries the greatest share of the load. Often referred to as *nontraditional media, alternative media,* or *unmeasured media*. See also *unmeasured media*.

support salespeople individuals whose assistance and efforts are instrumental to the order-getting salespeople, but who do not attempt to get orders themselves; see also *sales support* and *technical specialist*.

surface arteries for outdoor advertising purposes, the major and easily accessible streets in cities and towns that carry a heavy flow of vehicular traffic.

surfing see *channel grazing*.

survey in marketing and advertising research, a basic method of collecting data from people and/or organizations; data may be collected via personal interviews, mail, telephone, or over the Internet.

survey of buyer intention a sales forecasting method that involves directly asking individuals about their buying plans for a specified future period; purchase intention data are obtained via mail surveys, personal interviews, telephone surveys, or any other research technique. See also *sales forecast, composite of sales force opinion, expert opinion, jury of executive opinion, test marketing, market potential,* and *sales potential*.

Survey of Buying Power an annual special issue of *Sales and Marketing Management* magazine, serving as a comprehensive reference guide for marketers, advertisers, media planners, researchers, and others

involved in the broad range of business activities; contains up-to-date statistics on U.S. population, effective buying income, and retail sales by regions, metropolitan areas, and *DMAs*. Known for its *Buying Power Index (BPI)*. See also *Buying Power Index (BPI)*.

survey method a research technique that involves gathering data from respondents by use of a questionnaire administered by mail, personal interview, telephone, or the Internet; see also *experimental method* and *observation method*.

survey research see *survey method*.

suspect an individual or organization thought to be a possible legitimate potential buyer, but lacking at least one of the characteristics required to be classified as a prospect, i.e., having a need for the particular product or service being offered, the ability to pay for it, and the authority and willingness to consummate the deal; see also *prospect*.

sustaining advertising in an advertising campaign, a period during which advertising intensity is reduced to levels below normal for the campaign, to simply keep the product name in front of the audience as a reminder and to maintain demand; i.e., advertising used to remind vs. persuade. Very often happens after a period of heavy persuasive advertising. See also *pulsing*.

sustaining period see *sustaining advertising*.

sustaining program in television or radio, a particular program that is supported entirely by an individual station or a network, without any advertiser participation or sponsorship; typically involves public interest programs.

sweeps in television advertising, a means of surveying all U.S. markets—advertising rates are set according to audience delivered; the four-times-a-year rating periods during which *Nielsen Media Research* uses *diary-method* measurement for each of its 210 television markets (*DMAs*) in the country, to measure the audiences for local television. Local stations use the rating numbers gathered during these periods to help set television advertising rates. Rating periods are November, February, May, and July, with the diaries being mailed to the participating households in advance of the rating periods. See also *Nielsen Media Research, Nielsen Station Index (NSI), Nielsen Television Index (NTI), Designated Market Area*

(DMA), diary method, metered markets, People Meter, overnight ratings, set-tuning meter, telephone coincidental, and *ratings.*

sweeps report   a formal account of the results of the surveys to determine television audience size; see also *sweeps.*

sweepstakes   a consumer sales promotion activity in which prizewinners are determined on the basis of a random chance drawing alone; there is no requirement for the entrant to purchase the product, i.e., individuals need only submit their names to qualify.

swipe file   material amassed over time from a variety of sources, such as previous advertising or magazine-picture cutouts, for use in *roughs* for print and television advertising; see also *ripomatic.*

switchers   see *brand switchers* and *brand switching.*

SWOT analysis   an acronym for the review and evaluation of the *strengths, weaknesses, opportunities,* and *threats* associated with a particular brand or company; an important part of developing marketing and promotion plans.

symbol   a physical representation or image intended to convey a particular impression on an individual by virtue of its emotional or suggestive meaning.

symbolic association format   in advertising, a creative *execution format* that links the advertiser's product to a person or situation that has a very pleasant aura or feel; e.g., a Lenox fine china advertisement or commercial featuring the elegant entertaining possibilities using the advertiser's product, a jewelry store commercial in which a man is seen giving his wife a pearl necklace as an anniversary gift in a romantic setting, a Hallmark commercial showing a person receiving a friendship card from a special person, or an HMO commercial featuring a family's reaction to good news about the health of a loved one. See also *straightforward factual, news, demonstration, problem-solution, slice-of-life, dramatization, fantasy, animation, still-life, humor, spokesperson, testimonial,* and *comparison formats.*

symbolic value   the emotional or suggestive meaning a product has for an individual; highly individualistic in nature.

symmetric balance   see *formal balance.*

syndicated data   data collected by organizations specializing in research and data collection, and sold to several subscribers or any advertiser willing to pay for the data; as opposed to proprietary research done for a single client and that is not available to others, except at the will of the client. See also *syndicated research service.*

syndicated music   for purposes of local broadcast advertising production, music services that provide recordings to local radio and television stations on a subscription basis for the stations to make available to local advertisers.

syndicated program   see *syndication program.*

syndicated research service   a research organization that regularly monitors certain activities, collects data, and periodically publishes the results and other information of interest to subscribers, such as advertisers, with each of the different published reports generally following a standardized format; e.g., data on television viewership, radio listenership, advertising spending, retail-store product movement, and the like. Results are sold to subscribers who have contracted for the service. Examples of such services are *A.C. Nielsen, Mediamark Research, Inc. (MRI), Information Resources, Inc. (IRI), Scarborough Research Corp.,* and *Simmons Market Research Bureau (SMRB).* See also *syndicated data.*

syndication   in television, the market-by-market sale of "nonnetwork" or off-network programs by a *syndicator,* or owner of the programs, to individual television stations in more than 200 markets; see also *barter syndication, cash syndication, cash-barter syndication, first-run syndication, off-network syndication,* and *syndicator.*

syndication program   in television, "nonnetwork" or off-network programs sold or distributed to local stations on a market-by-market basis by independent organizations outside the national network structure; also called *syndicated program.* See also *syndication, first-run syndication,* and *off-network syndication.* Concept also applies to radio.

syndicator   a company that produces and sells a packaged program series; the owner of the television program that is sold in the syndication market. Also called a *packager.* See also *syndication.*

synergistic effect the result achieved when the combination of elements in a marketing communications program provide greater impact than the sum total of each individual element of the program; i.e., the whole is greater than the sum of its parts. For example, when planned, executed, and coordinated effectively, advertising and sales promotion, working together, can provide greater impact than the sum of each activity used alone. See also *integrated marketing communications.*

T

TAB   see *Traffic Audit Bureau of Media Measurement.*

TAT   see *Thematic Apperception Test.*

TAP   see *total audience plan.*

TNS   see *Taylor Nelson Sofres.*

TOMA   see *top-of-mind awareness.*

TRPs   see *target rating points.*

TSA   see *total survey area.*

TVB   see *Television Advertising Bureau.*

TVHH   see *television households.*

tab   see *tabloid newspaper.*

table display allowance   in trade promotion, a payment by a manufacturer to a retailer to display or highlight a product on a separate auxiliary table.

tabloid newspaper   a less-than-standard-size newspaper, measuring approximately 14″ deep × 10½″ wide, with five columns; as opposed to a standard-size (broadsheet) newspaper, which measures about 22″ deep × 13½″ wide, with six columns. For advertising purposes, a full page measures 70 column inches (14 × 5). See also *broadsheet.*

tachistoscope   in marketing and advertising research, a device that regulates a respondent's exposure time to a particular stimulus, such as the amount of time an individual sees a television commercial or a billboard; used to help study learning, attention, and perceptual processes.

tactics   the very specific actions a marketer or advertiser employs in the short term to achieve goals.

tag   in television or radio advertising, a local retailer's message at the end of an advertiser's commercial; generally to indicate where the advertised product can be bought. The broadcast equivalent of a *dealer imprint* or *dealer tie-in* for print advertising. See also *dealer imprint* and *dealer tie-in.*

tag line   see *slogan.*

taillight poster   an advertising sign mounted below the rear window on the outside of a bus or rapid transit vehicle; measures approximately 21″ high × 72″ wide. Also called a *rear-end display* or taillight display. See also *exterior bus, headlight poster, queen-size poster,* and *king-size poster.*

take-one   a mail reply card, coupon, or other promotional literature attached to an advertisement, or as a free-standing unit; often a request for further information. Also called a *tear-off.*

talent   the people or cast who perform in a television commercial; also includes news anchors, reporters, sports people, weather forecasters, as well as musicians and off-camera announcers.

talent cost   the expenditure for the people or cast who perform in a television commercial, including residuals. See also *residual* and *session fee.*

talent payment   see *residual, talent cost,* and *session fee.*

target audience   see *target market.*

target cost-per-thousand (target CPM)   see *cost-per-thousand—target audience (CPM-TA).*

target market   the specific individuals, market segment, or customer group that is the focus or objective of an advertiser's promotion plan and campaign efforts; the individuals the company or organization has decided to go after and who are the object of the advertiser's message or other promotional effort. A result of evaluating each market segment's attractiveness in terms of factors such as sales volume, profitability, accessibility, and the ability of the company to implement a marketing program for a given market.

target marketing the process of planning, designing, and implementing a *marketing mix* that is tailored to the needs of a specific customer group or market segment, rather than the entire market; evaluating the attractiveness of each market segment and then selecting one or more to enter with a specific and customized marketing program(s).

target rating points (TRPs) the number of individuals in the advertiser's primary target audience the media or media vehicle will reach and the number of times; essentially the same as *gross rating point (GRP),* provided the audience demographics are stated; i.e., represents an adjustment of a media vehicle's rating to take into account only those individuals who match the target audience sought by the advertiser. See also *gross rating points (GRPs).*

target return price objective setting price at a level to achieve a specific profit plateau; see also *profit maximization, sales growth, market share,* and *meeting competition price objectives.*

target segment the particular group of individuals that is the focus of an advertiser's attention; i.e., the prime prospects for a particular campaign. A subgroup of a larger segment, e.g., women 35–54 who play golf at least twice a week. See also *target audience* and *target market.*

targetcasting see *narrowcasting.*

targeting identifying, evaluating, prioritizing, and selecting the specific audience(s) that will be the focus of the marketer's communications program.

task method see *objective-and-task method.*

taste a general term referring to consumer preferences.

taxi-top a two-sided advertising sign mounted on a taxicab's roof, or a single-sided sign attached to the rear or side of the taxicab; also referred to as a *taxi-display.*

Taylor Nelson Sofres a leading worldwide provider of an enormous range and depth of marketing and advertising information, based on continuous and custom research programs, and market analysis; parent of *Competitive Media Reporting (CMR).*

team selling two or more sales representatives who combine efforts and work together to sell a particular account.

tear pad the pad of coupons or literature sheets from which the consumer can tear off one for him-or herself, i.e., the pad containing a *take-one.* See also *take-one.*

tear-off see *take-one.*

tearsheet the entire page of a publication on which an advertisement appeared, torn from the newspaper, for example, and sent to the advertising agency and advertiser as proof that the advertisement appeared as scheduled and in the exact detail as expected; a proof of performance. The print equivalent of TV's *affidavit of performance.* Also called *advertiser's copy* or *checking copy.*

teaser campaign advertising, promotion, or publicity done in advance of a campaign or event, to arouse curiosity among the target audience; typically done without showing the product.

technical specialist an individual who assists an order-getting sales representative by providing specialized technical expertise during the selling process; see also *sales support* and *support salespeople.*

telecommunications the transmission of information, such as voice, image, graphics, video, and data, between or among different locations; service is offered by a *telecommunications carrier* directly to the public for a fee.

Telecommunications Act a law passed in 1996 that brought major changes to the laws pertaining to cable TV, the Internet, and *telecommunications;* the basic intent was to promote competition by industry deregulation. The *Federal Communications Commission (FCC)* is responsible for determining the rules and policies and for enforcing the law.

telecommunications carrier any provider of *telecommunications* services; e.g., a cable TV network, a local telephone company, or an Internet Web site.

telemarketing a direct-marketing activity that involves using the telephone to market and sell products and services directly to customers; includes both initiating calls and receiving orders from buyers. See also *inbound telemarketing* and *outbound telemarketing.*

telephone coincidental a research technique used to determine viewership of television programs by making telephone calls while programs are in progress; usually used to determine viewership of a particular program. A method employed by *Nielsen Media Research,* along with its *People Meter, set-tuning meter,* and TV diary. See also *Nielsen Media Research, diary method, metered markets, overnight ratings, People Meter, set-tuning meter,* and *sweeps.*

telephone interview   a *survey method* of *data collection* using the telephone to contact and then question respondents.

television   an advertising *medium* combining visual images and accompanying sounds that are transmitted from a location by electromagnetic waves, and ultimately received by a television set.

Television Bureau of Advertising (TVB)   a trade association of the broadcast television industry.

television dayparts   see *dayparts.*

television households (TVHH)   the number of households with one or more television sets; may pertain to the entire United States or to *DMAs* on a market-by-market basis.

television network   see *network.*

television syndication   see *syndication program.*

tell-all copy   in trade magazines, advertising copy that provides every bit of information the reader needs to make a buying decision.

temporary display   a display such as a *point-of-purchase display* designed for short-term use, usually two months or less; also called an *in-out display.*

:10   designation for a 10-second television or radio commercial announcement.

tent card   a small display card carrying an advertising message, folded and set up so the message is visible on both sides of the "tent"; e.g., an 8½″ × 11″ heavy stock card, so when folded and placed upright, each side is 4″ high × 11″ wide, with the advertiser's message visible from both sides. Often placed on a counter.

terminal poster   any of a variety of posters (one-sheet and two-sheet), signs, or displays, including floor displays, electronic signs, island displays or showcases, dioramas, and *commuter clocks* that carry advertisers' messages in bus, subway, train, and airline terminals; see also *one-sheet poster, two-sheet poster, commuter clock, diorama,* and *island display.*

testimonial format   in advertising, a creative *execution format* (a type of endorsement) in which a spokesperson (sometimes a celebrity) in an advertising message makes a statement about a product based on personal use of and experience with the product; must be based on actual use of the product, as opposed to an *endorsement,* which may or may not be based on actual use. Examples: a magazine advertisement in which the chief mechanic for a professional auto racing team explains why his racing automobiles get only Quaker State motor oil, a commercial featuring a local sports star telling why a particular bank is the one he uses, a commercial showing Annika Sorenstam and why she uses only Callaway golf clubs, or a Weight Watchers advertisement showing a satisfied user. See also *straightforward factual, news, demonstration, problem-solution, slice-of-life, dramatization, symbolic association, fantasy, animation, still-life, humor, spokesperson,* and *comparison formats.* Also see *endorsement.*

test market   a specific city or geographic marketing area that serves as the region in which a market test is done; see also *test marketing.*

test market spot   in television advertising research, a *spot* commercial used only in a particular test market(s) for purposes of determining its effectiveness; i.e., *test marketing* a television commercial.

test marketing   conducting an advertising, sales promotion, or other promotion test in a limited geographical area (i.e., a select number of representative markets), and measuring results; or placing a new product into a similarly limited geographical area, and measuring performance to determine the likely success in the larger scale or national market—all under a proposed marketing plan, including the marketing communications portion of that plan. Testing a product's and a marketing program's performance in a small-scale reproduction of the large-scale market. Can be used to help develop a *sales forecast,* especially for new products, or an established product entering a new territory, or one using a new distribution channel. Also, the seventh stage of the new-product development process. Often called a *sales area test.* See also *new-product development process, idea generation, idea screening, concept testing, market evaluation, product development, marketing plan,* and *commercialization.*

test market simulation   see *simulated test market.*

test store   a retail store used to collect data on product movement, store buying procedures, consumer buying habits, advertising, promotion, merchandising practices, and other data; generally, several stores considered representative are used for such measurements.

text   the words used to tell an advertisement's or a commercial's story; does not include headlines, illustrations, or any element other than the basic copy. See also *body copy.*

text matter   see *editorial matter.*

theater advertising   an advertiser-sponsored commercial message delivered on the screen of a movie theater.

theater test   in advertising research, a method of pretesting television commercials; respondents view the commercials in a theater or other location set up to resemble a theater and indicate their approval or disapproval of the commercials shown, sometimes by using electronic devices. Usually, respondents are invited to preview a pilot television program, complete with commercials, and then are subjected to questions about the program and the advertising. See also *pretesting.*

Thematic Apperception Test (TAT)   see *cartoon method* and *picture response test.*

theme   the major selling idea that is the central premise of a marketing communications campaign.

theme line   see *slogan.*

theory of cognitive dissonance   see *cognitive dissonance.*

third cover (3C)   the inside back cover of a magazine, for which a premium advertising rate is paid.

third-party endorsement   a reputable source's blessing for a product, service, idea, or company where the source has no personal interest in the success or failure of the object of the promotional effort; e.g., the *Good Housekeeping* magazine seal of approval for a household cleaning product or the American Dental Association backing an electric toothbrush.

third-person method   in qualitative advertising research, a projective technique in which the respondent is asked to comment about someone else, such as a neighbor or friend, as to why the other person might, for example, go on a cruise, buy a luxury automobile, enroll children in an exclusive private school, join a health and fitness club, or engage in another behavior or action; a respondent may be shown a shopping list and asked to describe the person who goes shopping with that list. Designed to elicit attitudes and opinions the respondent may hold, but would not admit to as one's own. See also *word association test, sentence completion test, story completion test,* and *picture response test,* as well as *qualitative research* and *projective research techniques.*

:30   designation for a 30-second television or radio commercial.

30-sheet poster   an outdoor advertising sign measuring 12′ high × 25′ wide, with a 10′5″ × 22′8″ live copy area; the most basic outdoor advertising sign, it is printed on the paper and then mounted on the structure by hand. About half the size of a traditional permanent bulletin. See also *outdoor bulletin, out-of-home media, outdoor poster, 8-sheet poster, 24-sheet poster, permanent bulletin,* and *poster panel.*

thought listing   in advertising research, having consumers articulate whatever thoughts come to mind upon seeing an advertisement or commercial.

three-hit theory   a theory on optimum advertising frequency put forth by researcher Herbert Krugman, suggesting that three exposures are needed to make an effective impression on a consumer, i.e., to induce learning. Subject to considerable debate among advertising researchers and practitioners.

three-point layout   in print advertising, an advertisement with three featured elements that dominate the ad; e.g., a headline, a logo, and an illustration.

through-the-book method   in print media research, a method of determining an individual's magazine readership by examining his or her reading of various articles in a particular magazine; an aided recognition research technique to determine a particular magazine's audience—respondents are allowed to view a test issue of the publication and then are asked which articles or items they found most interesting—and those who indicate previous exposure and interest are counted as part of that magazine's audience.

throwback ads   see *retro ads.*

thumbnail (sketch)   the first draft of an advertising layout, in the creative phase of the advertising design process, i.e., a very rough drawing or sketch of the advertisement without attention to detail; usually done in a much smaller size than the actual advertisement and represents the first step in turning an idea into an advertisement. See also *layout development process, rough layout, comprehensive,* and *mechanical.*

tie-in see *tie-in promotion.*

tie-in advertising an advertisement promoting more than one product or brand, sometimes involving more than one advertiser; also refers to a manufacturer's advertisement that mentions local dealers (not to be confused with *cooperative advertising*). Can also refer to an advertisement that makes reference to another advertisement in the same publication. See also *dealer tie-in* and *tie-in promotion.*

tie-in promotion a cooperative or joint promotion of two or more different advertisers' products under a common theme; usually, consumers are given an incentive to purchase both products. In contrast to a promotion featuring two or more brands of the same advertiser, i.e., a *group promotion.* Example: Toro and Scotts joining together for a "Get Ready for Summer" promotion, featuring Toro-brand lawnmowers and Scotts-brand fertilizers. Also called a *joint promotion, partnership promotion,* or *cross-promotion.* See also *group promotion.*

till forbid (TF) an instruction from an advertiser to a newspaper to continue running a particular advertisement until further notice to stop.

time in broadcast media, that part of a program that is available for advertising.

time bank in television advertising, a media buying service's inventory of time available for sale to advertisers and agencies; see also *space bank.*

time buyer an individual at an advertising agency or a media buying organization who is responsible for purchasing advertising time in television or radio for clients; the broadcast equivalent of a *space buyer.* See also *space buyer* and *media buyer.*

time charge the cost of advertising time on a given television or radio network or station.

time contract a formal agreement between an advertiser and a television or radio network or station, in which the advertiser is guaranteed a particular rate for a given period, based on the amount of time the advertiser expects to use; see also *short rate.*

time discount a reduction in the cost of a network's or a station's advertising time given to the advertiser, based on the amount of television or radio time purchased during a specified period.

time schedule a listing of all the television and radio time to be used in a campaign; includes the station, network, program, the name of the commercial, and the date, *daypart, position,* length, and cost of each commercial.

time sheet a form used to detail advertising agency personnel's use of their time in servicing an account; may sometimes refer to a form detailing with all aspects of a broadcast *media buy.*

time slot a specific time period available for a television or radio commercial.

time utility the benefits to a consumer from the marketer making a product or service available when the consumer wants it; see also *utility, possession utility, form utility,* and *place utility.*

time-loss risk in consumer decision making, the chance the product will require significant time for maintenance; see also *risk-taking, performance risk, financial risk, physical risk,* and *social risk.*

time-period rating in television or radio, the rating for a particular time interval, such as every 15 minutes during the broadcast of a feature-length movie or a football game; as opposed to the rating for a full program. See also *program rating.*

time-sensitive ad a broadcast commercial or print advertisement that must be run on or by a particular date, and that essentially has an expiration date; e.g., commercials or advertisements focusing on a particular holiday, a special store sale, Opening Day at the ballpark, a golf championship event, the New York Marathon, or other such event.

time-spent-listening in radio audience research, an estimate of the number of quarter-hours the average person spends listening to the radio or a particular station during a specified time period; see also *average quarter-hour audience, average quarter-hour rating,* and *average quarter-hour share.*

time-spent-viewing in television audience research, an estimate of the number of quarter-hours the average person spends watching television or a particular station during a specified time period; see also *average* *quarter-hour audience, average quarter-hour rating,* and *average quarter-hour share.*

tip-in   an advertiser's preprinted advertisement submitted to a magazine to be glued into the binding of the publication; usually a response device and printed on heavier stock.

tip-on   an advertiser's preprinted card that is inserted into a magazine by means of gluing one edge of the card onto an advertisement; usually a response device. See also *tip-in.*

title sponsor   the sponsor that has its name incorporated into the name of the sponsored property; e.g., the Jiffy Lube 300, Pepsi 400, Goody's Headache Powder 500, or Coca-Cola 600—all of which are on the NASCAR auto racing schedule. Not to be confused with *sole sponsor.* See also *primary sponsor, associate sponsor, presenting sponsor, naming rights, right-of-first-refusal, sponsor,* and *property.*

TiVo   see *digital video recorder (DVR).*

tombstone advertisement   a small advertisement containing only the most basic, straightforward facts about a product or store, with no selling copy; often used to announce a stock offering to meet legal requirements.

tone   the look, feel, and character of a commercial or advertisement, as reflected in its mood, style, or personality; e.g., energetic, serious, bold, sophisticated, romantic, happy, old-fashioned, warm, and so forth.

top-down approach to budgeting   a procedure for establishing the marketing communications or individual promotion element budget, such as for advertising; a dollar amount is established at the executive level and given to the individual departments, such as advertising, sales promotion, direct marketing, or public relations. See also *affordable method, arbitrary method, competitive parity method, percentage-of-sales method,* and *build-up approach to budgeting.*

top-end display   in transit advertising, a *car card* advertisement over the door, on the inside of the vehicle; also called an *over-door display.*

top-of-mind awareness (TOMA)   the advertiser, brand, or campaign that a respondent mentions as coming to mind first, when questioned in an advertising research study on awareness; see also *share of mind.*

topper   a small, permanent advertising piece placed on top of a cash register at a retail checkout area; may also refer to a *taxi-top* advertising sign. See also *taxi-top.*

top-spin   see *spin.*

total audience   generally, the total number of unduplicated readers; in television, the total number of homes reached by a particular program, as determined by the number of homes viewing any 5-minute portion of that program.

total audience plan (TAP)   in radio and television advertising, a package of *spot* commercials giving the advertiser a set number of spots in each of the station's *dayparts* or time classifications; such a schedule allows the advertiser to reach all of the station's listeners or viewers in the particular time periods chosen for the plan. Also referred to as an *impact plan* or a *saturation plan.*

total bus   in transit advertising, the purchase by a single advertiser of all the exterior advertising space on a bus or other transit vehicle; i.e., exclusive use of the advertising space on the outside of a bus or other transit vehicle. See also *exterior bus.*

total circulation   the number of copies of a publication that are distributed via subscriber sales, newsstand purchases, and as free copies.

total cost   the sum total of fixed costs and total variable costs; see also *fixed costs* and *variable costs.*

total impression   the overall mark or effect left on the audience by an advertisement or commercial; used in determining misleading or deceptive advertising.

total impressions   see *gross impressions.*

total listenership   the radio version of total audience; see also *total audience.*

total net paid   see *net paid.*

total readership   the sum of a publication's circulation and its pass-along readership.

total survey area (TSA)   in measuring television and radio audiences, the geographic area consisting of a metro area and additional counties in which a significant amount of viewing or listening is to stations that originate in the metro area; often, the outlying areas are part of an adjacent *metro area* or *Designated Market Area (DMA).*

total viewership   see *total audience.*

total weight   the sum of all target audience exposures to the media vehicles in a media plan, including duplications; see also *gross impressions.*

tracking   popular method of monitoring the performance of an advertising campaign over time by means of periodic surveys (called *waves*) among the target audience; a study is generally done prior to the advertising campaign to serve as a benchmark or comparison basis for how well the campaign is meeting its objectives. Permits measurement of the effectiveness of an advertising campaign as reflected by changes over time in awareness, attitudes, sales, or other dimensions. Also permits analysis and reassessment of *copy* and media strategies, as well as midcampaign corrections. See also *benchmark study* and *wave.*

trade   see *trade market.*

trade advertising   advertising directed to intermediaries (e.g., wholesalers, distributors, retailers) that buy or handle an advertiser's products for resale to customers; purpose is to stimulate intermediaries' buying for inventory and then sale to the ultimate customer.

trade allowance   a price reduction or other promotional incentive offered by an advertiser to a retailer or dealer for support given to the advertiser's product or promotion campaign such as displaying merchandise, featuring the brand in advertising, or some other extra push for the product; see also *trade deal* and *allowances.*

trade area   the geographical region in which a particular advertiser's product is sold.

trade association   an organization representing the firms in a particular industry, acting on their behalf on important matters, doing industry research, disseminating newsletters, periodicals, and other items of current interest to the members, organizing meetings, trade shows, and a variety of other activities for the betterment of the industry and its members; see also *Encyclopedia of Associations.*

trade book   see *trade publication.*

trade channel   the distribution network and organizations a producer uses to get its product or service to the ultimate consumer or user; see also *marketing channel.*

trade character   a representation of a person, animal, or other being that is personified and used to identify a company or its product; exclusive use is guaranteed only if registered as a *trademark.*

trade contest   a sales promotion tool used by a marketer to encourage performance by members of the *distribution channel;* participants compete for prizes or money, with entries judged on the basis of performance, such as opening new accounts or achieving the highest level of sales during the contest period.

trade customers   see *organizational buyers.*

trade deal   any of a variety of sales promotion inducements offered to encourage dealers to stock and merchandise the manufacturer's products; e.g., special discounts, free merchandise, cash. See also *trade allowance* and *consumer deal.*

trade discount   a price reduction offered to a retailer or other intermediary for the functions performed in the movement of goods from manufacturer to consumer or user; also called a *functional discount.*

trade incentives   a general term referring to a wide range of incentives given to retailers and/or their salespeople to perform certain tasks and provide extra *push* for an advertiser's product; see also *trade allowance* and *trade deal.*

trade journal   see *trade publication.*

trade magazine   see *trade publication.*

trade market   the distributors, wholesalers, retailers, or other manufacturers or organizations in the advertiser's marketing efforts; as opposed to the *consumer market.* Also referred to as the *business market* or *organizational market.* See also *business market, consumer market,* and *organizational market.*

trade name   the legal name under which an organization does business; not the name of a specific product.

trade paper   see *trade publication.*

trade promotion   see *trade sales promotion.*

trade publication   a specialized business print publication aimed at retailers, wholesalers, distributors, and other intermediaries who buy and sell for resale, and other individuals who in some way are involved with the movement of goods through *distribution channels;* editorial matter (and advertising) is directed toward a specific industry, profession, or occupation. Also referred to as a *business publication, business* or *trade book, business* or *trade journal, business* or *trade magazine,* and *business* or *trade paper.* See also *horizontal publication* and *vertical publication.*

Trade Regulation Rules (TRRs) industry-by-industry rules established by the *Federal Trade Commission (FTC)* that provide definitions of what advertising practices are considered unfair; see also *Industry Guides* and *Trade Regulation Rules.*

trade sales promotion sales promotion activities and techniques directed to intermediaries, such as wholesalers and retailers; aimed at stimulating the dealers to carry an advertiser's product, improve the reseller's merchandising program, get resellers to market the advertiser's products more effectively, and otherwise gain support and participation in the advertiser's promotional efforts. Part of a *push strategy.* See also *consumer sales promotion, push strategy,* and *sales promotion.*

trade show an industry-specific exhibition at which manufacturers, dealers, existing and potential buyers, industry members, media representatives, and other interested parties assemble for displays, demonstrations, dialogue, checking out state-of-the-art developments, making contacts, engaging in sales transactions, and conducting other business; especially important in business-to-business marketing. Considered a *trade sales promotion* activity. See also *trade sales promotion.*

trade show producer an organization that organizes and manages trade shows.

trademark a legally protected *brand name, brand mark,* or *trade character* (or some combination), registered with the government and reserved for exclusive use by its owner; i.e., words, names, initials, symbols, or designs that identify a product as being from a specific firm and that firm only. Legal definition: "Any word, name, symbol, device or any combination thereof adopted by a manufacturer or merchant to identify his goods and distinguish them from those manufactured or sold by others" (*Lanham Act*). See also *Lanham Act, Trademark Law Revision Act, Federal Trademark Dilution Act, service mark,* and *certification mark.*

Trademark Law Revision Act a federal act, passed in 1988, that permits civil action against an advertiser who "misrepresents the nature, characteristics, qualities, or geographical origin of his or her or another person's goods, services, or commercial activities"; i.e., prohibits false claims an advertiser makes about its product, as well as false claims made about another's product, with civil action allowed in either case. See also *Lanham Act* and *Federal Trademark Dilution Act.*

trademark protection see *trademark, Trademark Law Revision Act, Lanham Act,* and *Federal Trademark Dilution Act.*

trading area a geographical region in which the residents make the majority of their purchases; usually one or more counties surrounding a central metropolitan market.

traditional marketing system see *conventional marketing system.*

traditional media the advertising media that have been used over the longest period of time; the commonly used broadcast, print, and out-of-home media (such as billboard or transit) that typically account for the bulk of the media budget. See also *alternative media, nontraditional media, support media,* and *unmeasured media.*

traffic a measure of the volume of individual visits (i.e., "hits") to a Web site. See also *hit.*

traffic audit in out-of-home advertising, an independent third-party verification of the circulation in a particular market.

Traffic Audit Bureau for Media Measurement (TAB) a trade association of the outdoor advertising industry, serving outdoor advertising locations and media owners, advertisers, and advertising agencies; performs independent standardized measurements of outdoor audience size via traffic counts according to national procedures approved by the buyers and sellers of outdoor advertising. Also provides demographic data.

traffic count in out-of-home advertising, the total number of vehicles and pedestrians passing a particular poster location or any out-of-home advertising unit during a specified period of time; volume and direction of traffic going past an outdoor location at various times of the day. May refer to the number of potential customers or people who pass by a particular store display during a specified time period. See also *Daily*

Effective Circulation (DEC), hand count, official count, and *counting station.*

traffic department the section of an advertising agency that schedules and coordinates all phases in the creation and production of advertising, ensuring that all tasks and projects keep on schedule from beginning to end.

traffic flow map a map for a particular market area that indicates the volume and direction of traffic on the streets in that market, by different times and days, over a specified period of time; used to help determine outdoor advertising locations.

traffic manager an individual in an advertising agency responsible for directing the traffic department activities involved in scheduling and tracking advertising as it is being produced; the agency person who controls the flow of work throughout the production process. See also *traffic department.*

traffic-builder any of a wide variety of promotional activities designed to attract and increase the number of individuals visiting a retail store.

trailer a promotional announcement immediately following a television or radio program, promoting a forthcoming program on that same station; a commercial added at the end of a program or another commercial. A filmed commercial shown before the feature movie in a theater (generally longer and more elaborate than a television commercial). See also *tag.*

trailer test in advertising research, consumer awareness, preference, and attitude studies that are conducted in mobile trailers that are moved from one location to another during the course of the research study; typically set up for business in shopping center parking lots, with shoppers screened and invited into the trailer to view television commercials and answer questions.

transient rate a basic, one-time advertising rate with no discounts; applies to all media. See also *open rate.*

transit advertising out-of-home advertising messages placed on the inside or outside of public transportation vehicles such as buses, trains, subways, taxis, and airplanes; also includes advertising posters placed at station, terminal, platform, and shelter locations. May refer to mobile advertising signage such as those on trucks.

transit poster in transit advertising, a poster attached to the exterior of a bus or commuter train; also refers to posters at stations.

transit shelter advertising see *transit advertising.*

transit spectacular in transit advertising, a single advertiser purchasing all space on one or both sides of a public transit vehicle's interior or exterior; see also *total bus.*

transition time see *fringe.*

transportation the physical movement of products from one party or place to another through the *distribution channel.*

transportation advertising see *transit advertising.*

traveling display a promotional display that moves from one location to another; also refers to the advertising on the exterior of buses and other transit vehicles. See also *mobile billboard* and *rolling billboard.*

tray pack a cardboard carton that, when its top is removed, becomes a display unit that fits conveniently on a store shelf.

trial first-time use of a product by a consumer, especially that resulting from a sales promotion tool such as *sampling* or a *coupon;* often the main objective of a consumer sales promotion program.

trial offer a sales promotion technique in which a product is made available to a consumer for use on a trial basis, in the hope it will lead to purchase; often used for expensive items where there is significant financial or other type of risk, e.g., golf clubs or a riding lawn mower.

trial size a smaller-than-regular-size package of a product, often given away free in a *sampling program* to introduce a product to a consumer.

trial stage the fourth stage of the adoption process, in which the consumer actually buys and/or uses the product to help form a judgment on whether to adopt or reject it; see also *adoption process, awareness stage, interest stage, evaluation stage,* and *adoption stage.*

trivision board in outdoor advertising, a "motorized" billboard sign that uses moving slatted panels to rotate its surface and that has three different advertising messages, each appearing at about 8-second or 10-second intervals before rotating to the next execution; can be programmed to rotate at virtually any interval and in any order. May be one advertiser with three different products and executions or three different advertisers, each with its own message. Sometimes called a *post-turn*.

truckside advertising   an advertising sign placed on the side of an over-the-road truck; a "billboard-style" advertising medium. See also *mobile billboard*.

trustworthiness   a combination of the honesty, credibility, reliability, and integrity of the communications source; an essential component for effective communications.

turnover   in radio or television advertising, the frequency with which a particular program's audience changes over a period of time; see also *audience turnover* and *audience flow*.

TV market   the geographical area over which a particular television station's signal carries; the number and description of households that receive a particular television station's programming.

TV usage   total television viewership; see also *households using television (HUT)* and *persons using television (PUT)*.

:20   designation for a 20-second television or radio commercial.

25 showing   in outdoor advertising, an expression indicating that 25 percent of a given market's population will be reached by (i.e., will have the opportunity to see) a particular advertising message by virtue of the number and placement of an advertiser's billboard panels in the market, in a 30-day period; see also *outdoor advertising, showing, 50 showing, 75 showing,* and *100 showing*.

24-sheet poster   in outdoor advertising, a standard billboard unit, with a copy area 8′8″ high × 19′6″ wide; see also *outdoor bulletin, out-of-home media, outdoor poster, 8-sheet poster, 30-sheet poster, permanent bulletin,* and *poster panel*.

twin pack   in consumer sales promotion, a specially designed unit, containing two packages of the same product, sold at a special price below what the two units would cost if purchased separately; see also *bonus pack*.

two pages facing   in print advertising, anytime there are two pages of advertising opposite each other with no printing or editorial matter between them in the *gutter position;* each page has an advertisement for a different product or contains different executions for the same product. Not to be confused with *two-page spread*. See also *two-page spread*.

two-page spread   in print advertising, a single advertisement that is spread out horizontally across two facing pages in a publication; not to be confused with a *center spread,* which occupies two facing pages at the exact middle in a publication. Also called *double-page spread, double spread,* and *double truck*. See also *center spread*. Also see *two pages facing*.

two-sheet poster   an advertising poster or sign, measuring approximately 46″ high × 60″ wide, especially common in rapid-transit train and subway station platforms in downtown business and shopping districts; see also *one-sheet poster* and *terminal poster*.

two-sided message   an advertising, sales, or other promotion message that presents both favorable and unfavorable aspects of an advertiser's product, citing advantages as well as limitations; see also *one-sided message*.

Type I error   in survey research, the occurrence of a survey revealing a statistically significant result, when in fact it is not so; a situation that grows out of the fact that a survey does not include all individuals or objects in the population of interest to the researcher. See also *Type II error*.

Type II error   in survey research, the occurrence of a survey revealing a result that is not statistically significant, when in fact it is; a situation that grows out of the fact that a survey does not include all individuals or objects in the population of interest to the researcher. See also *Type I error*.

type family   a group of related type styles and designs (i.e., typefaces), with variations in width, boldness, and other properties; also called a *type group*.

type font   a complete assortment of any one specific size and style of a particular typeface; the entire array of lowercase letters, capital letters, numbers, and punctuation marks in any one typeface, which is unique in design from all others. For example, Arial, Bookman Old Style, or Times New Roman. See also *typeface*.

type group   see *type family*.

type style   see *typeface*.

typeface the basic design and style of a letter of type; includes classes such as roman, text, italic, gothic, and script.

typography the process and art of determining the best typefaces for a given advertising or promotion message, and arranging the letters and words for maximum effectiveness and impact; involves the style, arrangement, and appearance of the advertising copy. A major design element, carefully selected for aesthetics and readability, and setting the tone for the advertising message.

U

UPC   see *Universal Product Code.*

URL   see *Uniform Resource Locator.*

USP   see *Unique Selling Proposition.*

ultra high frequency (UHF)   in television, channels 14–83; generally, the signal of such a channel has a more limited range or coverage area than a *very high frequency (VHF)* channel. Assigned by the *Federal Communications Commission (FCC).* See also *very high frequency (VHF).*

unaided recall   in measuring and evaluating advertising and other promotion elements, a research technique in which the respondent is questioned about what he or she remembers about something, with no verbal or visual clues provided by the interviewer to aid the respondent in his or her recollection of the facts; for example, in determining an individual's recall of a particular television commercial, no information that would help the respondent remember the specific commercial is provided by the interviewer (that is, no information beyond what it takes to ascertain whether the person watched the program on which the commercial appeared). Researcher might ask: "What advertising do you recall seeing on TV last night?" See also *aided recall.*

unbundling   the practice by which a client takes media planning/buying away from the brand agencies that handle creative and gives it to a third party devoted exclusively to media planning/buying. Consolidation of the entire media responsibility for a company's products in one firm, separate and apart from the company's advertising agency(s) that handles creative for the products.

uncontrollables   those elements and factors affecting the marketing program over which the marketing manager has little or no command or control, and to which the *marketing mix* must adapt and adjust; e.g., social, psychological, cultural, economic, governmental, and competitive factors. Although the marketer may attempt to influence the factors with a particular marketing strategy, they are a "given" at the time the marketing mix is designed. See also *controllables* and *marketing mix.*

under-delivery   when a *media vehicle* delivers fewer than the promised number of *impressions* in a particular campaign or time period; see also *make-good.*

under-the-radar marketing   promotion techniques in which a marketer hires an individual(s) who then is strategically placed among people as they are going about their usual activities, for the sole purpose of spreading the word about a product or service in the attempt to get the people talking or at least thinking about it; may involve two company "agents" engaged in conversation about a product within earshot of a group of people, or placing an appliance carton, a shoebox, or a digital camera box with the company logo in clear view in the lobby of an apartment or office building (paying the attendant to make sure it stays there for a period of time). Similar to *lean-over marketing,* but involves techniques beyond conversation. A questionable practice from an ethical viewpoint. See also *lean-over marketing, viral marketing,* and *word-of-mouth advertising.*

undifferentiated marketing   a marketing strategy whereby a firm or organization pursues the whole market with one product and one marketing program, choosing not to recognize different market segments; also called *mass marketing.* See also *concentrated marketing* and *differentiated marketing.*

unduplicated audience   the total number of different individuals exposed to the media carrying an advertiser's message; may refer to a particular medium, media vehicle, or entire campaign. See also *reach* and *cumulative audience.*

unearned discount that part of an advertising rate discount an advertiser fails to qualify for by not using the amount of space or time contracted for over a specified period of time; it is charged back to the advertiser. See also *short rate.*

unfair advertising legally defined as "acts or practices that cause or are likely to cause substantial injury to consumers, which is not reasonably avoidable by consumers themselves and not outweighed by the countervailing benefits to consumers or competition" (*Federal Trade Commission*).

Unfair Trade Practices Act a federal law protecting consumers and businesses from a wide range of false, misleading, and deceptive practices; most states have adopted the law or have their own similar laws. Banned practices include any misrepresentation of goods or services such as claiming to have the approval or endorsement of a group when they do not, claiming certain ingredients, characteristics, or benefits that are nonexistent, advertising that disparages the competition, and a host of other unfair practices that create confusion and misunderstanding.

unforced-rating scale in marketing and advertising research, a scale on which a neutral or "no opinion" choice is allowed; see also *forced-rating scale.*

Uniform Product Code (UPC) the set of lines appearing on all packaged consumer goods, to specifically identify the product and to facilitate checkout pricing, inventory, and other marketing procedures.

Uniform Resource Locator (URL) the Internet address and access description for a Web site; the actual link to a Web site, fully written out, as in *http:// www. babsonbaseball.com.* Essentially the same as *domain name,* except that the domain name is simply the *babson-baseball.com portion of the URL. See also domain name.*

unilluminated panel see *nonilluminated panel.*

unipole see *monopole.*

unique audience on the Internet, the number of different individuals visiting a Web site or viewing a banner or other type of advertisement, often cited on a per-day basis; identification of visitors relies on user registration, tracking technology, or other recognition system. Also called *unique visitors* or *unique users* or just *visitors* or *users.*

unique selling proposition (USP) a promise in an advertising message that the particular product being advertised will provide a specific, relevant, distinctive ("unique") benefit to the consumer; a term coined by advertising legend Rosser Reeves.

unique user see *unique audience.*

unique visitor see *unique audience.*

unit a single advertisement or commercial; e.g., a full-page ad or a two-page spread, a :30 or a :60 commercial, or a single poster panel or painted bulletin or any out-of-home advertising display.

U.S. Department of Commerce the cabinet-level executive department of the federal government dealing with all aspects of business, economics, and trade; its work and jurisdiction encompass many bureaus and agencies including, among others, the Census Bureau, Patent and Trademark Office, Bureau of Economic Analysis, Economics and Statistics Administration, Economic Development Administration, Bureau of Industry and Security, International Trade Association, National Telecommunications & Information Administration, and the National Institute of Standards & Technology.

U.S. Patent and Trademark Office the federal agency, under the U.S. Department of Commerce, that has jurisdiction over all patents, trademarks, brand marks, and service marks; supervises and controls the application, registration, and protective standards and guidelines for all of the above, including the way they may be used by marketers and advertisers.

U.S. Postal Service the federal authority that regulates and controls advertising and promotional practices, messages, and communications that use the postal system.

unit-of-sales method in advertising budgeting, allocating a specific dollar amount of advertising for each unit of product expected to be sold during the budget period; a *top-down approach to budgeting;* see also *affordable method, arbitrary method, competitive parity method, objective-and-task method,* and *percentage-of-sales method.* See also *build-up approach to budgeting* and *top-down approach to budgeting.*

unit pricing putting a product's price-per-ounce (or other meaningful quantity) next to or on the item itself; a legal requirement for every item in a store in some states.

unity in advertising design and layout, the principle that all components and elements of an advertising execution should be uniform or related to one another to achieve full impact, or *synergistic effect;* see also *balance, contrast, emphasis, flow, gaze motion,* and *harmony.*

universal coupon   a single *coupon* redeemable on the consumer's choice of the particular manufacturer's brands; e.g., a coupon issued by a cereal manufacturer and redeemable on any one of the manufacturer's brands featured on the coupon.

universe   in marketing and advertising research, the entire population of individuals or organizations that make up the target for a particular research project; the entire group being studied. Also referred to as the research *population.*

unload   to sell merchandise extremely quickly by offering any of several incentive-laden promotional inducements to consumers; i.e., to move products off retail shelves at a fast pace in a short time.

unmeasured media   refers to advertising expenditures in media that are not regularly and formally monitored, but for which estimates are made as to advertising spending; includes direct mail, sales promotion, cooperative advertising, couponing, catalogs, business and farm publications, special events, and other *support media* for advertising. Expenditures are published annually by *Advertising Age* in its *100 Leading National Advertisers* issue, as well as at periodic intervals throughout the year. Sometimes referred to as *alternative media* or *nontraditional media.* See also *measured media* and *support media.*

unpaid distribution   in the *Audit Bureau of Circulations (ABC)* reports for print advertising, the circulation or distribution of copies for trade shows and conventions, as well those used as checking copies and promotion copies for advertisers and agencies; see also *checking copy* and *promotion copy.*

unsought products   consumer products for which the potential customer does not yet have a need or want, or knowledge they even exist; see also *new unsought products, regularly unsought products, consumer products classification system, convenience products, shopping products,* and *specialty products.*

unstructured questions   see *open-end questions.*

untapped market   a particular market segment with an existing but as yet unfulfilled need, either because the product does not exist or because current products do not fully satisfy the need; represents a marketing opportunity. A market waiting for a product to come along.

unusable diaries   diaries, when returned to *Aribitron* or *Nielsen,* that are judged to be unusable according to the established criteria; see also *diary* and *diary method.*

unwired network   see *wireless communications.*

up-front buying   the purchase of network television program advertising time at the initial offering by the networks or when the season schedule is first announced, usually several months in advance of the programs on which the advertising time will be used by the advertiser; e.g., buying advertising time in the spring for programs that will begin airing in the fall season. Also applies to the purchase of cable television and syndicated television time. See also *up-front market.*

up-front market   the buying period for network television advertising time that occurs well in advance of an upcoming television season, when advertisers and networks make commitments for large blocks of commercial time; also applies to cable television and syndicated television time. See also *up-front buying.*

upmarket   that portion of the market for premium and luxury products and brands; e.g., very high-end automobiles, apparel, jewelry, or china.

upscale   a descriptive term for an individual or group located at the higher end of the socioeconomic ranking; see also *downscale.*

up-selling   in the inbound telemarketing process, an attempt by the person handling the transaction to sell additional merchandise to the caller; see also *inbound telemarketing.*

urban panel   in out-of-home advertising, an above-ground panel located at the entrance to a subway station; see also *panel.*

urban wallscape   see *wallscape.*

usage data   facts that describe consumer purchasing habits and consumption patterns for a particular product or brand; see also *usage rate* and *user profile.*

usage rate   the extent to which consumers use or consume a particular product; typically categorized as heavy, medium, light, and nonusage. A common market segmentation variable. See also *behavioristic segmentation* and *market segmentation.*

usage-and-attitude studies   research that aims to describe users, as well as nonusers, of a product, along with their attitudes toward the product.

use positioning   see *positioning by use.*

user   the individual or organization that actually uses or consumes the product; in Internet advertising, an individual who visits a particular Web site.

user positioning   see *positioning by user.*

user profile   a description of the buying habits and the *demographic, geographic, psychographic,* and *behavioral* characteristics of individuals who use a particular product or brand; see also *consumer profile.*

user status   a behavioristic segmentation variable that breaks consumers into categories such as non-users, ex-users, potential users, first-time users, or regular users; see also *behavioristic segmentation.*

utility   the need-satisfying power of a product or service; the satisfaction and pleasure an individual gets from having or using the product or service. See also *utility, form utility, possession utility, place utility,* and *time utility.*

V

VALS   see *Values and Lifestyles System.*

VMS   see *vertical marketing system.*

VNR   see *video news release.*

VNU   see *VNU Media Measurement & Information Group.*

VO   see *voice-over.*

VPVH   see *viewers per viewing household.*

VSP   see *vendor support program.*

validity   in marketing, advertising, and promotion research, the ability of a measurement instrument to actually measure what it is intended to measure; e.g., the ability of a given questionnaire to accurately measure a target audience's awareness of an advertiser's brand before and after a particular advertising campaign. See also *reliability.*

value   see *customer value.*

value pricing   a strategy of offering competitive-quality products at relatively low prices in the hope of attracting high customer volume; not to be confused with *value-based pricing.*

value proposition   a formal statement of the benefits a brand delivers to consumers in the target market; generally, the entire set of qualities of a product or service that makes it capable of providing need-satisfying benefits to the consumer or user. The essence of the advertising and promotion backing the product or service.

value-added   the market value of a firm's output minus the value of the inputs the firm has purchased from others to produce its final product; e.g., what the wholesaler adds to a product by virtue of buying it from a manufacturer and then reselling it to a retailer.

value-added reseller   an intermediary, such as a retailer, who performs some activity or operation on a product to increase its value between receipt from the manufacturer or distributor and sale to the consumer; e.g., an intermediary who assembles lawnmowers before they are sold.

value-based pricing   setting a product's or service's price on the basis of the consumer's perception of value, as opposed to the marketer's cost of the product or service; not to be confused with *value pricing.*

value-delivery network   see *supply chain.*

values   the various expressions of words and actions that define what an individual considers important; guidelines by which people choose to live their lives.

Values and Lifestyles System (VALS)   a classification scheme for segmenting consumer markets into groups based on psychographics, i.e., values, attitudes, and lifestyles; defines eight segments of adult consumers who have different attitudes and exhibit distinctive behavior and decision-making patterns. Segments include: Actualizers, Fulfilleds, Believers, Achievers, Strivers, Experiencers, Makers, and Strugglers. Used to help predict consumer behavior regarding media and products. Developed at Stanford Research Institute. See also *psychographic segmentation.*

variable commission   see *sliding rate (scale).*

variable costs   costs that vary according to the quantity produced or sold; see also *fixed costs.*

variable message sign   an electronic mobile *billboard* whose message changes at periodic intervals; e.g., a roadside sign alerting drivers to the latest road conditions, with an advertising message promoting a local radio station appearing at regular intervals, such as every 20 minutes. Use is regulated by individual states and municipalities.

variable rate   see *sliding rate (scale).*

varied media mix a strategy of spreading an advertiser's media budget over a wide range of media, as opposed to putting all dollars into just one or very few media classes; see also *concentrated media mix.*

variety seekers see *brand switchers.*

variety seeking see *brand switching.*

vehicle the particular means within a *media class* or *media subclass* by which the advertiser's message is delivered to the target audience, i.e., a specific magazine, newspaper, or television program; e.g., *Good Housekeeping, The Washington Post,* or *60 Minutes.* See also *media vehicle.*

vehicle option source effect in comparing one advertising medium against another or one advertising media vehicle against another vehicle, the difference of one option vs. another in terms of the impact on the same individual; the ability of one media option to have a greater impact on a person than another media option.

vendor an organization that provides products or services to another organization.

vendor analysis a formal performance appraisal of a marketer's suppliers.

vendor support program (VSP) an advertising and promotion program initiated by a retailer and offered by the retailer to a manufacturer (i.e., vendor) to get it to participate in the campaign and to pay a portion of the media cost; retailer and local media generally cooperate by jointly planning and designing the campaign proposal. In contrast to *cooperative advertising,* which is initiated by the manufacturer. See also *cooperative advertising.*

venue the specific site at which an event takes place and the location at which the advertiser engages in its sponsorship or other marketing and promotion activities associated with the event; see also *venue marketing.*

venue marketing an advertising and promotion strategy in which a sponsor establishes a link to a physical site, such as a stadium, arena, amusement park, auditorium, or other such site; involves signage, displays, exhibits, and other means of exposing a company and its products at the site.

venue survey see *event survey.*

verified data data that are guaranteed accurate and truthful by an information or auditing service, such as the *Audit Bureau of Circulations (ABC);* for example, see *guaranteed rate base* and *non-guaranteed rate base.* Also see *Audit Bureau of Circulations (ABC).*

vertical rectangle ad see *rectangle ad.*

vertical audit see *functional audit.*

vertical buy buying advertising time or space in several different vehicles in the same media class, such as buying space in several magazines or buying time on several radio stations; in contrast to a *horizontal buy,* or buying advertising time or space in several different media classes (e.g., television, radio, magazines, and outdoor) to achieve maximum *reach* or exposure. See also *horizontal buy.*

vertical cooperative advertising a joint advertising effort between a manufacturer and a retailer or distributor, in which the advertising cost is shared, usually on a 50–50 basis, when the dealer features the manufacturer's brand in the advertising; the manufacturer usually provides the finished advertisement or commercial, with the retailer inserting its name and location. See also *cooperative advertising* and *horizontal cooperative advertising.* Also see *cooperative advertising kit.*

vertical cume in television or radio, the total number of different people tuned to successive broadcast programs on a particular station or network; see also *horizontal cume* and *cumulative audience.*

vertical half-page in print advertising, an advertisement that occupies one-half the width and the entire height of a page in a periodical; see also *horizontal half-page.*

vertical marketing system (VMS) a distribution channel arrangement in which all parties, i.e., manufacturers, wholesalers, and retailers, operate as a unified and coordinated network or system; parties may be bound together by one channel member owning all the others, by contractual agreement, or by virtue of one channel member having such compelling size and power as to get agreement from all others to cooperate. See also *corporate VMS, contractual VMS, administered VMS, conventional marketing system, horizontal marketing system,* and *hybrid marketing system.*

vertical publication a trade magazine or paper editorially designed for individuals who perform a variety of functions in a specific industry; covers virtually every aspect and topic of interest and importance to those in that industry, e.g., *Supermarket News, Modern Tire Dealer, Candy Industry, Beverage Industry, Sporting Goods Business.* See also *horizontal publication.*

vertical saturation (rotation) in television or radio advertising, scheduling multiple commercials throughout a single day, on the same or different channels or stations, and usually in several *dayparts;* designed to reach a maximum number of individuals or households in a short time span, often in conjunction with an event or a special sale. See also *horizontal saturation* and *dayparts.*

very high frequency (VHF) in television, channels 2–13; generally, the signal of such a channel has a greater range or coverage area than an *ultra high frequency (UHF)* channel. Assigned by the *Federal Communications Commission (FCC).* See also *ultra high frequency (UHF).*

video the visual or picture portion of a television commercial or program; i.e., the action, on-screen copy, and visual effects. See also *audio.*

video advertising an advertising message that is part of a videotape, such as a movie rental, sports highlights, or free demo tape for home fitness equipment.

video billboard a large-scale video display, especially those seen at both outdoor and indoor sports and entertainment venues.

video news release (VNR) a videotape produced by an advertiser to deliver a public relations message such as a news item or feature story, and sent to television stations for airing; the television equivalent of a *press release* sent to print publications.

view in Internet advertising, when an advertisement is downloaded by the user; also called an *ad impression* or *ad view.*

viewer an individual watching television.

viewer profile the demographic and psychographic characteristics of a television station's audience.

viewers per viewing household (VPVH) the number of persons viewing television at a particular time in households where the television set is on; typically reported on a "per 1000 viewing households" basis.

viewing area in television, the geographical area receiving a particular station's signal.

vignette commercial a television commercial that consists of a sequence of separate brief scenes, incidents, and situations, as opposed to a smooth, coherent, seamless narrative; e.g., one scene showing a mother on a telephone with her child, whereupon the scene abruptly shifts to the mother cheering for her child playing softball, and finally, the two of them at an ice cream shop on the way home—all within 30 seconds.

vinyl wrap see *bus wrap.*

viral marketing in Internet advertising, another name for word-of-mouth advertising, whereby consumers are encouraged to communicate with one another about the merits of a particular product or a particular issue, especially via e-mail or redirecting information to another party; goal is to expand the *reach* of the message. See also *word-of-mouth advertising.* Also see *lean-over marketing* and *under-the-radar marketing.*

virtual advertising see *virtual placement process* and *virtual signage.*

virtual mall on the Internet, a group of several *storefronts,* allowing the user to click on any one to gain access to a particular site on the "mall"; the gateway to retail stores on the Internet.

virtual placement process digital placement or insertion of products, brand names, logos, and other advertising images in scenes of television programs; e.g., a Coke machine in a police station, a Maxwell House coffee can on the counter of a staff lunchroom at a hospital, a Valvoline motor oil can on the infield of a motorsports speedway, or a Sony brand name on the backstop behind home plate during a game telecast. A nontraditional way to reach consumers. Payment is separate from what advertisers pay to run *spots* during commercial breaks. Also called *digital insertion system, live-video insertion system,* and *sponsored imagery.* Sometimes referred to as *product placement,* although the virtual placement process involves putting a product or image into a scene by digital technology (i.e., inserting a product, logo, or image onto the television screen where no actual product is at the scene). Also called *virtual advertising.*

virtual signage in event marketing, electronic insertion of an advertiser's name, logo, or very brief message during a television broadcast, even though the sign cannot be seen at the event (because it is not actually there); e.g., a sign on the backstop behind home plate during a baseball game telecast or a sign at the scorer's table of a basketball game, electronically inserted into the picture. Part of the broader virtual placement process. Also referred to as *virtual advertising*. See also *virtual placement process* and *rotational signage*.

visit on the Internet, when a *user* calls up a particular Web site; see also *unique audience*.

visitor survey see *event survey*.

visualization in the creation of advertising, the process of putting together all elements of the advertising in one's mind to form a concept or picture of what the advertising should say and how it should appear; also called *conceptualization*.

visuals all the pictures and nonverbal elements of an advertisement.

VNU Media Measurement & Information Group a premier provider of information for a broad range of marketing organizations involved in the media and entertainment industries, including television and radio broadcasters, advertisers, agencies, media planners, music companies, publishers, motion picture studios, distributors and exhibitors, and the Internet industry; the parent of *Nielsen Media Research*. See also *Nielsen Media Research*.

voice see *share of voice*.

voice-of-the-customer the collective thoughts and actions of consumers, as expressed by their making known a position on a particular issue or by specific purchase or marketplace behavior.

voice-of-the-customer research seeking the attitudes and opinions of consumers, whether by formal or informal market research techniques.

voice-over (VO) refers to an individual's voice being heard in a television commercial without the person being seen on camera; also known as an *off-screen announcer* or *off-camera*. Considerably less expensive than if the *talent* appears on camera.

voice-pitch analysis (VOPAN) in advertising research, a physiological method of pretesting in which a respondent's comments about an advertisement or commercial are subjected to computer analysis to detect changes in voice pitch as the respondent describes his or her reaction to different parts of the execution; different voice pitches reflect different emotional levels experienced by the consumer and, hence, the ability of the execution to have impact. See also *physiological testing measures*.

Voice Trak an advertising research service that provides comprehensive data on local-market advertising media spending activity throughout the United States; especially useful for media planning, budget allocation, and evaluating advertising results.

volume discount a discount offered by a *media vehicle* to an advertiser, based on the amount of space or time purchased by the advertiser during a specified period of time; see also *space discount* and *time discount*.

volume merchandising allowance a merchandising allowance (e.g., free merchandise or direct payment) whose magnitude is based on the extent or number of displays, in-store promotions, or other activities provided by the dealer on behalf of the advertiser; the greater the activity, the more the allowance. See also *merchandising allowance*.

voluntary regulation see *self-regulation*.

WWW see *World Wide Web.*

wait order in newspaper advertising, an advertisement (already in possession of the publisher) that is ready to run, upon notice from the advertiser as to the exact date for insertion; an order or request to hold an advertisement until a later date before running it.

wallscape in outdoor advertising, advertising located on the exterior wall or surface of a building; the advertising display is painted on or is self-adhesive vinyl. Sometimes referred to as a *wall mural* or *urban wallscape.*

wants consumer needs that are formed by an individual's personality, culture, and the surrounding environment in which he or she lives; the specific way in which a consumer satisfies needs. See also *need.*

warmth monitor in advertising research, a testing technique used to measure the consumer's emotional reactions to advertising, ranging from a complete absence of warmth or emotion to a truly emotional response; accomplished by the respondent manipulating a computer joystick to track emotions during the viewing of a television commercial, listening to a radio commercial, or, less frequently, reading of a print advertisement, as well as by having the respondent use a pencil to mark on a sheet of paper his or her emotions along a horizontal plane with variations according to the vertical scale of emotions from top to bottom (similar to a polygraph needle or an EKG reading).

Warranty Act see *Magnusson-Moss Warranty Act.*

waste audience that portion of a television or radio audience who are not legitimate prospects or in the target market for an advertiser's product; also refers to the station's signal going to areas where the advertiser's product is not available. See also *waste circulation.*

waste coverage see *waste audience* and *waste circulation.*

waste circulation that portion of a publication's audience who are not legitimate prospects or in the target market for an advertiser's product; also refers to a publication's distribution into areas where the advertiser's product is not available. See also *waste audience.*

wave in tracking or ongoing research studies, each separate survey; also may refer to each period of advertising in a *flighting* pattern of *media scheduling.* See also *tracking* and *flighting.*

wave posting in out-of-home advertising, a series of posters in a succession of areas within a particular market; often done to call attention to an advertiser's special promotions in that market.

wave scheduling see *flighting.*

wearout the amount of time or the point at which an advertising message or a particular promotional activity or program loses its effectiveness; e.g., excessive repetition or overexposure causes annoyance, negative reaction, indifference, or nonattention on the part of the target audience. The decline in advertising's or promotion's power to positively influence purchase or other behavior. The diminished effectiveness of advertising over time.

Web see *World Wide Web.*

Web content all the text, information, and graphics on a Web site.

Web design firm a company that specializes in planning, developing, and executing Web sites for organizations and individuals desiring a presence on the Internet.

Web marketing see *online marketing.*

Web page on a Web site, a single document (i.e., file) that may take up several screens, requiring scrolling to view the entire page; sometimes refers to the content that appears on a single screen.

Web site   a specific location, i.e., address, on the World Wide Web; often used interchangeably with *homepage* and *Web page.*

Webcasting   broadcasting information on a Web site, e.g., radio programming or nearly instantaneous play-by-play accounts of a baseball or football game.

Webmaster   the designer or manager of a Web site who is responsible for the content, functionality, and maintenance of the site.

Weber's Law   a principle that seeks to explain the relationship between the size of a stimulus and the amount by which the stimulus must be increased or decreased for an individual to "just notice a difference"; a psychological law that attempts to quantify the minimum amount of change in a stimulus needed to produce a "just noticeable difference" in a person's mind. Much depends, of course, on the size of the stimulus in its initial state (e.g., the price level prior to a change). Can be expressed mathematically. Helps to shed light on questions related to how much a product's price must be lowered (or raised) for the consumer to just notice the price change, or how many brands must a retailer add (or subtract) for the consumer to just notice there has been an increase (or decrease) in the store's assortment. In essence, whether it is a price change, a change in product attributes, or some other change, there is a threshold below which consumers do not recognize a difference and above which they do, and that threshold is dependent upon the starting point and the magnitude of the change relative to that starting point. Named after E.H. Weber, a 19th-century experimental psychologist

weekly   a magazine or newspaper published once a week, as opposed to a *daily, monthly, bi-weekly,* or *bi-monthly* publishing schedule.

weight   see *advertising weight.*

weighted cost-per-thousand   see *cost-per-thousand—target audience.*

Wheeler-Lea Amendment   passed in 1938 as an amendment to Section 5 of the *Federal Trade Commission Act;* amendment says: "Unfair methods of competition in commerce and unfair or deceptive acts or practices in commerce are hereby declared unlawful." Made deceptive and misleading advertising illegal. The amendment gives the *Federal Trade Commission (FTC)* the power to act whenever there is evidence of injury to the public, whether or not there is injury to a competitor. Among other things, the amendment also gave the *FTC* power to issue cease-and-desist orders and levy fines on violators of the law. See also *Federal Trade Commission (FTC), Federal Trade Commission Act,* and *cease-and-desist order.*

white space   the space in a print advertisement that does not contain any text, illustrations, or graphics; the blank space in and around the individual elements of an advertisement. An important advertising design factor.

wholesaling   all the activities involved in selling and marketing to retailers and users (e.g., industrial, institutional, or commercial) other than final consumers.

wholesaler   a *middleman* who buys, handles, or otherwise facilitates the flow of manufacturers' goods to retailers and other dealers for resale or to organizational users; does not sell in any appreciable amount to final consumers. See also *middleman, service wholesaler, limited-function wholesaler,* and *retailer.*

wide skyscraper ad   see *skyscraper ad.*

width of assortment   see *product assortment width.*

widow   in print advertising, when the last line of a copy paragraph has only one or two words and the line is left standing conspicuously alone; generally speaking, something to be avoided, as the reader's eye may be distracted by it.

window advertising   advertising attached to a store window.

window display   in retail merchandising, a display placed in a store's window to attract the attention of passersby in hopes they will be sufficiently interested to enter the store.

window streamer   see *window advertising.*

wipe   an optical technique for making a transition between scenes in a television commercial; one picture disappears on the screen as another takes its place. The transition can be done in a horizontal, vertical, or rotating (clockwise or counterclockwise) motion.

wireless communications   communications over airwaves, e.g., satellites, cellular technology, as opposed to cables or telephone lines; such communication transmissions include voice, video, data, and images.

within-vehicle duplication a particular audience's exposure to the same advertisement or commercial in the same *media vehicle,* usually at different times, although the duplication may be the same execution repeated during the same program or even in the same publication; e.g., the same commercial aired in the first quarter of a college football game, again just before halftime, and maybe yet again during the fourth quarter of the game. See also *across-vehicle duplication.*

word association test in qualitative advertising research, a projective technique in which a person responds with a word or phrase that immediately pops into his or her mind upon seeing or hearing a particular word or list of words, a brand name, logo, or slogan; e.g., the word or phrase that first occurs to the respondent upon seeing the McDonald's logo or the "Diamonds are forever" slogan. See also *sentence completion test, story completion test, cartoon method, third-person method,* and *picture response test,* as well as *qualitative research* and *projective research techniques.*

word-of-mouth advertising informal communications about an advertiser's product or service between one individual and another, e.g., friends, family, co-workers; as opposed to communications between an advertiser and an individual or target audience. Sometimes referred to as *viral marketing,* although such usage is usually limited to the Internet version.

work flowchart a diagram charting the sequence of key activities in a project, such as an advertising or promotion campaign; for example, in scheduling a direct-mail program, another promotional program, or an advertising research project, taking the launch date, broadcast date, event kickoff date, mailing date, or other key deadline date, and working backward to determine when each project activity must be completed to make sure of meeting the final deadline. The result is a work flowchart identifying the stages of the

process. Also called a *reverse timetable* or *reverse work flowchart.* See also *campaign flowchart* and *media flowchart.*

work print the first version of a television commercial filmed and assembled with no special effects, titles, music, or the like, permitting any changes to be made; essentially a *rough* of a television commercial. See also *rushes* and *rough.*

work sample library a collection of the advertising and other promotion work created by an agency, especially for the purpose of showing prospective clients the capabilities of the agency; agency search consultants maintain a library for use in assisting clients in the selection of a new advertising agency. See also *agency search consultant.*

working the territory coined by advertising legend Paul Harper, a term to describe the notion that effective advertising depends on the creators acquiring a thorough knowledge of the target customers and the conditions of use for the product; prerequisites for advertising messages that truly connect with the audience include talking with the product users, observation, asking questions, and listening, i.e., doing the homework and the preparation.

World Wide Web (WWW) a system or service that allows an individual with a personal computer and a modem to navigate the Internet; a global system comprising the entire collection of Internet sites and pages that can be read and interacted with by computer. See also *Internet.*

wraparound commercial in television or radio advertising, a commercial sandwiched between non-commercial material, such as a sports trivia question and the answer; e.g., Question: What is the given name of Atlanta Braves player "Chipper" Jones? Question might be followed by a :30 for AFLAC insurance, and then the answer: Larry Wayne Jones.

YPPA see *Yellow Pages Publishers Association.*

Yellow Pages advertising an advertiser's message that appears in the yellow pages or special editions of telephone directories.

Yellow Pages Publishers Association (YPPA) the trade association representing the publishers of the Yellow Pages directory, and dedicated to the promotion and advancement of the Yellow Pages as an effective advertising medium.

Z

zapping changing television channels via the remote control device, especially to avoid commercials; also refers to erasing commercials entirely from videotaped television programs.

zip code analysis in direct-mail marketing, the evaluation of responses according to postal zip codes to determine purchasing patterns and obtain a measure of which areas are the most receptive to direct-mail marketing efforts.

zipping on television programs that have been videotaped with a VCR, using the remote control to fast-forward through the commercials to avoid them.

zone pricing geographical pricing whereby the marketer establishes a series of zones and assesses the same freight charge to all customers within a particular zone, with each zone having a different price.

zoned edition a newspaper's practice of printing special editions covering only a portion of the total geographical market served by the newspaper, usually by means of a special weekly section that is devoted to editorial matter of interest to the people in that particular area; advertisers may purchase ads in the copies of the newspaper that go to that area, that are specifically targeted to that population. For example, the *West Weekly* special section of the *Boston Sunday Globe* that goes to 32 communities in the west suburbs of Boston, with editorial matter geared to those communities and an opportunity for advertisers to target their messages.

zoom in television advertising, to move the camera in on a scene or away from it; done by "zooming in" or "zooming out" with the camera lens in shooting the commercial.

Resources

Books & Directories

Aaker, D. A., Kumar, V., & Day, G. S. (2001). *Marketing Research* (7th ed.). New York: Wiley.

American Association of Advertising Agencies. (n.d.). *Guide to Media Research.* New York: Author.

Arens, W. F. (2002). *Contemporary Advertising* (8th ed.). Burr Ridge, IL: McGraw-Hill Irwin.

Baker, M. J. (1998). *Macmillan Dictionary of Marketing and Advertising* (3rd ed.). London: Macmillan.

Barban, A. M., Jugenheimer, D. W., & Turk, P. B. (1989). *Advertising Media Sourcebook* (3rd ed.). Lincolnwood, IL: NTC Business Books.

Belch, G. E., & Belch, M. A. (2004). *Advertising and Promotion* (6th ed.). Burr Ridge, IL: McGraw-Hill Irwin.

Bennett, P. D. (1995). *Dictionary of Marketing Terms* (2nd ed.). Lincolnwood, IL: NTC Business Books.

Book, A. C., & Schick, C. D. (1990). *Fundamentals of Copy & Layout* (2nd ed.). Lincolnwood, IL: NTC Business Books.

Boone, L. E., & Kurtz, D. L. (2004). *Contemporary Marketing* (11th ed.). Mason, OH: South-Western.

Bovee, C. L., Thill, J. V., Dovel, G. V., & Wood, M. B. (1995). *Advertising Excellence.* New York: McGraw-Hill.

Burns, A. C., & Bush, R. F. (2000). *Marketing Research* (3rd ed.). Upper Saddle River, NJ: Prentice Hall.

Burton, P. W. (1999). *Advertising Copywriting* (7th ed.). Lincolnwood, IL: NTC Business Books.

Busko, D. (Ed.). (1997). *Dartnell's Advertising Manager's Handbook.* Chicago: Dartnell.

Churchill, G. A., Jr. (2001). *Basic Marketing Research* (4th ed.). Fort Worth, TX: Dryden.

Clemente, M. N. (1992). *The Marketing Glossary.* New York: American Management Association.

Clow, K. E., & Baack, D. (2002). *Integrated Advertising, Promotion, and Marketing Communications.* Upper Saddle River, NJ: Prentice Hall.

Davis, J. J. (1997). *Advertising Research: Theory and Practice.* Upper Saddle River, NJ: Prentice Hall.

Duncan, T. (2002). *IMC: Using Advertising & Promotion to Build Brands.* Burr Ridge, IL: McGraw-Hill Irwin.

Hawkins, D., Best, R., & Coney, K. (1995). *Consumer Behavior* (6th ed.). Chicago: Irwin.

Ingram, T. N., LaForge, R. W., & Schwepker, C. H., Jr. (1997). *Sales Management* (3rd ed.). Forth Worth, TX: Dryden.

Keller, K. L. (1998). *Strategic Brand Management.* Upper Saddle River, NJ: Prentice Hall.

Kinnear, T. C., & Taylor, J. R. (1996). *Marketing Research* (5th ed.). New York: McGraw-Hill.

Kotler, P. (2003). *Marketing Management* (11th ed.). Upper Saddle River, NJ: Prentice Hall.

Kotler, P., & Armstrong, G. (2004). *Principles of Marketing* (10th ed.). Upper Saddle River, NJ: Prentice Hall.

Lamb, C. W., Hair, J. F., & McDaniel, C. (2004). *Marketing* (7th ed.). Mason, OH: South-Western.

Lehmann, D. R., Gupta, S., & Steckel, J. H. (1998). *Marketing Research.* Reading, MA: Addison-Wesley.

McConnell, C. R., & Brue, S. L. (1999). *Economics: Principles, Problems, and Policies* (14th ed.). Burr Ridge, IL: McGraw-Hill Irwin.

O'Guinn, T. C., Allen, C. T., & Semenik, R. J. (2003). *Advertising and Integrated Brand Promotion* (3rd ed.). Mason, OH: South-Western.

Perreault, W. D., Jr., & McCarthy, E. J. (2002). *Basic Marketing* (14th ed.). Burr Ridge, IL: McGraw-Hill Irwin.

Russell, J. T., & Lane, W. R. (1999). *Kleppner's Advertising Procedure* (14th ed.). Upper Saddle River, NJ: Prentice Hall.

Schultz, D. E., & Barnes, B. E. (1999). *Strategic Brand Communication Campaigns* (5th ed.). Lincolnwood, IL: NTC Business Books.

Schultz, D. E., Robinson, W. A., & Petrison, L. A. (1993). *Sales Promotion Essentials* (2nd ed.). Lincolnwood, IL: NTC Business Books.

Semenik, R. J. (2002). *Promotion and Integrated Marketing Communications.* Cincinnati, OH: South-Western.

Shimp, T. A. (2003). *Advertising, Promotion, and Supplemental Aspects of Integrated Marketing Communications* (6th ed.). Mason, OH: South-Western.

Sissors, J. Z., & Bumba, L. (1993). *Advertising Media Planning* (4th ed.). Lincolnwood, IL: NTC Business Books.

Solomon, M. R. (2002). *Consumer Behavior* (5th ed.). Upper Saddle River, NJ: Prentice Hall.

Standard Rate and Data Service. (2003). *Business Publication Advertising Source.* Des Plaines, IL: Author.

Standard Rate and Data Service. (2003). *Circulation.* Des Plaines, IL: Author.

Standard Rate and Data Service. (2003). *Community Publication Advertising Source.* Des Plaines, IL: Author.

Standard Rate and Data Service. (2003). *Consumer Magazine Advertising Source.* Des Plaines, IL: Author.

Standard Rate and Data Service. (2003). *Direct Marketing List Source.* Des Plaines, IL: Author.

Standard Rate and Data Service. (2003). *DirectNet.* Des Plaines, IL: Author.

Standard Rate and Data Service. (2003). *Hispanic Media & Market Source.* Des Plaines, IL: Author.

Standard Rate and Data Service. (2003). *Interactive Advertising Source.* Des Plaines, IL: Author.

Standard Rate and Data Service. (2003). *International Media Guides.* Des Plaines, IL: Author.

Standard Rate and Data Service. (2003). *The Lifestyle Market Analyst.* Des Plaines, IL: Author.

Standard Rate and Data Service. (2003). *Media Planning System.* Des Plaines, IL: Author.

Standard Rate and Data Service. (2003). *Newspaper Advertising Source.* Des Plaines, IL: Author.

Standard Rate and Data Service. (2003). *Out-of-Home Advertising Source.* Des Plaines, IL: Author.

Standard Rate and Data Service. (2003). *Print Media Production Source.* Des Plaines, IL: Author.

Standard Rate and Data Service. (2003). *Radio Advertising Source.* Des Plaines, IL: Author.

Standard Rate and Data Service. (2003). *Technology Media Source.* Des Plaines, IL: Author.

Standard Rate and Data Service. (2003). *TV & Cable Source.* Des Plaines, IL: Author.

Stone, B. (1994). *Successful Direct Marketing Methods* (7th ed.). Lincolnwood, IL: NTC Business Books.

Surmanek, J. (1993). *Introduction to Advertising Media.* Lincolnwood, IL: NTC Business Books.

Tellis, G. J. (1998). *Advertising and Sales Promotion Strategy.* Reading, MA: Addison-Wesley.

Toffler, B., & Imber, J. (1994). *Dictionary of Marketing Terms* (2nd ed.). Hauppauge, NY: Barron's Educational Series.

VNU. (2003). *Marketer's Guide to Media.* New York: VNU Business Media.

Weiner, R. (1996). *Webster's New World Dictionary of Media and Communications* (Rev. ed.) New York: Simon & Schuster Macmillan.

Wells, W., Burnett, J., & Moriarty, S. (1998). *Advertising: Principles & Practice* (4th ed.). Upper Saddle River, NJ: Prentice Hall.

Wiechmann, J. G. (1993). *Dictionary of Advertising* (2nd ed.). Lincolnwood, IL: NTC Business Books.

Zikmund, W. G. (2003). *Exploring Marketing Research* (8th ed.). Mason, OH: South-Western.

Journals

Advertising Age. Detroit: Crain Communications.

AdWeek. New York: VNU Business Publications.

B to B. Chicago: Crain Communications.

BrandWeek. New York: VNU Business Publications.

Broadcasting & Cable. New York: Reed Business Information.

Electronic Media (Renamed *Television Week*). Chicago: Crain Communications.

MediaWeek. New York: VNU Business Publications.

PROMO. New York: Primedia Business Magazines and Media.

SportsBusiness Journal. Charlotte, NC: American City Business Journals.

Web Sites

http://www.marketers-reference.com
http://www.nielsenmedia.com
http://www.acnielsen.com
http://www.smrb.com
http://www.mediamark.com
http://www.arbitron.com
http://www.aaaa.org
http://www.netlingo.com
http://adres.internet.com
http://www.glossarist.com
http://www.smartbiz.com
http://www.iab.net
http://www.whatis.com
http://www.learnpr.com
http://www.aboutpr.com
http://marketing.about.com
http://www.the-dma.org
http://www.rab.com
http://www.tvb.org
http://www.interactivejargonguide.org
http://www.zenithmedia.com
http://www.doubleclick.com
http://www.partnerslevit.com
http://www.buseco.monash.edu.au
http://www.amlist.com
http://www.pt3.org
http://www.marketingterms.com
http://www.tutor2u.net
http://www.scarborough.com
http://www.horizonmedia.com
http://www.5metacom.com
http://www.targetonline.com
http://www.matisse.net
http://www.americanbusinesspress.com
http://www.marcommwise.com
http://www.marketingmonthly.com
http://www.sponsorship.com
http://www.magazine.org

http://www.internetnews.com
http://advertising.utexas.edu
http://www.catalogsuccess.com
http://www.billfryer.com
http://www.dmlr.com
http://www.econworld.com

http://www.iab.net
http://www.matrixnetsystems.com
http://www.justsell.com
http://www.exhibitornet.com
http://www.audiencedialogue.org

About the Author

Norman A. Govoni is Professor of Marketing at Babson College, and served as Division Chair for fifteen years (1975–1990). He is the coauthor of several textbooks including *Promotional Management, Fundamentals of Modern Marketing, Sales Management,* and *Cases in Marketing.* Among his honors are the Carpenter Prize for Outstanding Contributions to Babson College, Professor of the Year, and The Staake Award for Contributions to Athletics. Since 1992, Dr. Govoni has served as assistant coach of the Babson College baseball team. In September 2002, ceremonies were held to dedicate the Babson baseball field as "Govoni Field," in recognition of the contributions of Norm and his wife, Terry, to athletics at Babson College.